Librarianship and
Information Work Worldwide
2000

This is the last edition (see Foreword)

Librarianship and
Information Work Worldwide
2000

General Editor
Maurice Line

Editors
Graham Mackenzie
Paul Sturges

BOWKER
SAUR

London • Melbourne • Munich • New Providence, N.J.

British Library Cataloguing in Publication Data
A catalogue record for this title is available from the British Library

Library of Congress Cataloging-in-Publication Data
A catalog record for this book is available from the Library of Congress

Published by Bowker-Saur, part of Reed Business Information Limited
Windsor Court, East Grinstead House,
East Grinstead, West Sussex RH19 1XA, UK
Tel: +44 (0) 1342 26972 Fax: +44 (0) 1342 336197
E-mail: lis@bowker-saur.co.uk
Internet Website: http://www.bowker-saur.co.uk

ISBN 1-85739-263-9

Cover design by John Cole
Typeset by The Castlefield Press, Kettering, Northants
Printed on acid-free paper
Printed and bound in Great Britain by Antony Rowe Ltd, Chippenham

Contents

About the editors

Maurice B. Line is a consultant specializing in strategic planning, staff development and the management of change. He retired in 1988 as Director-General, Science Technology and Industry, of the British Library. Before that he worked in five university libraries. He is a Professor Associate at Sheffield University. He has honorary doctorates from Heriot-Watt and Southampton Universities, and a fellowship from Birmingham Polytechnic. He was President of the UK Library Association in 1990, and was awarded the IFLA Medal in the same year. He has travelled widely on professional work. He edits *Alexandria* and has written 14 books and 370 articles and papers, covering a wide variety of topics from bibliometrics to library management; translations have appeared in 20 languages.

Graham Mackenzie read Classics at Glasgow. He was the founding Librarian at the University of Lancaster in 1963, establishing its Library Research Unit in 1967, and he was Librarian of the University of St Andrews from 1976 until he retired in 1989. A member of the Editorial Board of the *Journal of Documentation* since 1965, he has published widely, and retains a long-standing interest in consultancy work.

Paul Sturges is Reader in Libraries in Social Development at the Department of Information Science, Loughborough University, and was Associate Dean (Research) in the School of Education and Humanities (1993–1996). He is Chair of the Library Association's International Group (IGLA) and has held various other offices in the Library Association, Institute of Information Scientists and IFLA. He has lectured and spoken at conferences in many countries, and researched and written across the field of information and library studies. His recent published work includes articles on Africa, on the history of the British public libraries, and on legal and ethical issues in information work. He is joint editor (with John Feather) of the *International encyclopedia of information and library science*.

About the contributors

Tatjana Aparac is an Associate Professor in the Department of Information Sciences, Faculty of Philosophy, University of Zagreb, where she has taught at undergraduate level since 1984 and at postgraduate level since 1993. She has a PhD in Information Sciences. She has published over 60 professional and research articles and edits a series of professional books on LIS theory and practice. Currently she is organizing a series of educational courses in Dubrovnik and is in charge of a research project concerned with organizing and digitizing the Croatian written heritage. She is a member of IFLA's Standing Committee on Education and Training and of the Croatian Council on Libraries. She is a member of the editorial boards of several professional journals.

Janette Burke has worked in academic libraries for the last 17 years. She has a BA (Library Studies) from the University of South Australia and a MCom (Business Information Systems) from the University of Wollongong. She worked as a Faculty Librarian at the University of Central Queensland and at the University of Wollongong before being promoted to Systems Librarian. She was instrumental in the introduction of ARIEL and the automation of interlibrary loan processes at the University of Wollongong. This interest continued with her work at the University of Ballarat and Monash University, where she introduced the automation of many interlibrary loan processes. She now works on a casual basis at the University of Wollongong, where she will be further improving document delivery packages.

Rev. **Graham Cornish** is the Copyright Officer for the British Library and has worked in copyright law since 1983. He has written and lectured extensively on the subject throughout the world, and his book *Copyright: interpreting the law for libraries, archives and information services* is a standard text in the field. He is a Fellow of both the Institute of Information Scientists and the Library Association, and is currently (2000) President of the latter. He manages the IFLA Core Programme for Universal Availability of Publications. His research interests include library cooperation, document supply, national libraries and changing professional roles.

Michael v. Cotta-Schønberg has a Bachelier en Philosophie degree from the University in Louvain, and a Mag. Art. (Psychology) from the University of Copenhagen. He went to the Royal Library in Copenhagen in 1973 as an Academic Librarian, and became Head of the Public Relations Department at the same library in 1978, with administrative duties in the National Librarian's Office from 1981. He was appointed Director of the Library of the Copenhagen Business School in 1985. He was President of the European Business Librarians' Group 1994–96.

Michael Koenig is Dean and Professor at the Palmer School of Library and Information Science at Long Island University. He is a past President of the International Society for Scientometrics and Informetrics. His academic background includes an MA in Library and Information Science and an MBA from the University of Chicago, and a PhD in Information Science from Drexel University. His corporate background includes management positions at Pfizer, the Institute for Scientific Information, Swets and Zeitlinger, and Tradenet. Research interests include the relationship between information services and the information environment versus organizational productivity.

Brigitte M.R. Kühne is Director of the University Library in Växjö, Sweden, and is also Coordinator of the EU-funded project DERAL (Distance Education in Rural Areas via Libraries). She previously worked in public libraries, and between 1997 and 1998 she was an Associate Professor at the University of Lund, where she taught library and information science. Her first career was as a school psychologist and her doctoral thesis considered the integration of school libraries in the curriculum of the elementary and secondary school system in Sweden. She has written a number of articles, primarily about school libraries, but also on the DERAL project and the Swedish library system.

Edward Lim is currently University Librarian and Adjunct Professor, School of Information Management and Systems, Faculty of Information Technology, Monash University, Australia. He has been a member of the Executive Committee of the Victorian Division of Australian Council of Library and Information Services, and has chaired its Research Subcommittee. He is currently a Branch Councillor with the Victorian Branch of the Australian Library and Information Association. He has served as a consultant on a number of occasions for UNESCO and the International Development Research Centre, and is on the editorial boards of several professional journals. He has more than 50 publications to his credit, including two books.

Ann Matheson was educated at the Universities of St Andrews and Edinburgh. She has had experience in private industry and in teaching overseas. She has worked in the National Library of Scotland in a variety of posts, and as Keeper responsible for the printed and new media collections since 1983. She is involved with a number of UK and European committees, and has recently chaired the UK Copyright Libraries Shared Cataloguing Committee and the NEWSPLAN Panel. She is General Secretary of the Ligue des Bibliothèques Européennes de Recherche (LIBER). She was awarded the OBE in 1998 and a Hon. DLitt from St Andrews University in 1999.

Philip Payne has been Head of Learning Support Services at Leeds Metropolitan University since 1997. He previously worked at Hatfield Polytechnic, Lancaster University, and the City of London Polytechnic before being appointed as Senior Librarian at Leeds Polytechnic in 1990. He is Chair of the Library and Information Research Group and has published papers on the library needs of adult learners, user empowerment in academic libraries, and research methods.

Donald E. Riggs has served as Vice President for Information Services and University Librarian at Nova Southeastern University at Fort Lauderdale, Florida since 1997. Prior to his current position, Riggs served as Dean of Libraries and Senior Professor at the University of Michigan for 6 years and for 12 years as Dean of Libraries at Arizona State University. He has authored or edited 8 books and written 76 journal articles and 41 book chapters. He has served as founding editor of *Library Administration and Management* and editor of *Library Hi Tech*, and currently edits *College and Research Libraries*. He has held several leadership positions in the American Library Association, including President of the Library Administration and Management Association. In 1991, he received ALA's prestigious Hugh C. Atkinson Memorial Award for his leadership and innovation in library technology.

Guiseppe Vitiello is in charge of the Digital content, Books and Archives Project of the Council of Europe. He also holds positions as Visiting Professor at the Information Schools of Stuttgart and Visiting Fellow at Loughborough University Department of Information Science. Earlier he was a Lecturer in Italian and Linguistics at the Universities of Toulouse and Orléans and Assistant to the Director of the Biblioteca Nazionale Centrale in Florence. Between 1989 and 1991 he was seconded to the European Commission as a national expert. He has been consultant for various private firms and for the Portuguese Government, and he has written various works on the history of culture and translation and in the library and information field.

Elizabeth Waller has worked since 1990 in the Learning Centre at Leeds Metropolitan University, where she currently holds a Senior Learning Advisor post and is working on the development of information literacy skills for students and IT skills for Learning Centre staff. She was previously employed at Thames Valley University and Bradford and Ilkley Community College.

Editorial advisory board

Foreword

This is the ninth volume of *LIWW* to appear. Alas, it is also the last.

LIWW has had consistently excellent reviews since the first volume. We have also been fortunate in obtaining the services of good authors – several of whom have commented that writing chapters was much harder than they expected, but that they had learned a great deal in the process. Sales, which were for the first few years disappointing, have increased substantially as the work became better known. So why is it ceasing publication?

There are two reasons. One is that it was becoming increasingly hard to find good authors as the workload of nearly everyone has grown relentlessly. The other is that I, as general editor, was planning to pass the work over to someone else after nine years. At the same time, Graham Mackenzie, who has been with *LIWW* from the beginning, was also planning to retire as one of the editors; and Paul Sturges, the other editor, was finding it very hard to fit the work into his busy schedule. We have searched hard for potential successors, but no one has been found who is prepared to take the jobs on.

It may be that such works as *LIWW* are about to give way to online services, though at present there is no sign of anything resembling it on the Web. Many have told me personally how useful they have found it and, if they are lecturers, how their students too have used it. It is a great pity that it has to come to an end now. The consolation is that the publishers are looking for some kind of alternative that might serve similar purposes.

I would like to thank all the many authors who have contributed to *LIWW*, and also the editors: Ray Prytherch, John Feather, Paul Sturges and, most of all in view of his long service, Graham Mackenzie. I must express appreciation too to the persons who have served unpaid on our Editorial Advisory Board over the years, giving help as requested to the authors who have contacted them.

Indexes are generally mentioned in reviews only when they are inadequate. It is therefore gratifying that the indexes to *LIWW* have been singled out by several reviewers for complimentary comments. They were all done by my wife, Joyce Line, who has had long experience as a professional indexer.

Maurice B. Line
November 1999

Note on alphabetization in References and Index

Dutch prefixes

Names beginning with such as 'van', 'te' or 'ter' (e.g. van der Hoogen, te Bockhorst) are filed under the prefix 'van' etc. We are aware that Dutch practice is to file such names under the main part; but native English-speaking authors with Dutch names are known under the prefix. We decided on the above practice because readers will not always know whether authors are Dutch (or Flemish or South African). We do not always know ourselves, since Dutch authors often write in English. We hope that Dutch-speaking readers will not be offended by this policy.

European vowels

The following practices are used for the filing of vowels in some European languages. We are aware that the practices of some of the languages are different, but most of *LIWW*'s readers are English-speaking.

	filed as
å (Danish, Norwegian, Swedish)	**aa**
æ (Danish, Icelandic, Norwegian) and ä (Finnish, German, Swedish)	**ae**
ø (Danish, Norwegian), ö (Finnish, German, Hungarian, Icelandic, Swedish) and ő (Hungarian)	**oe**
ü (German, Hungarian) and ű (Hungarian)	**ue**

Scottish and Irish surnames

Mac, Mc and M' are all filed as **Mac**

Library and information work in context

1

Donald E. Riggs

Introduction

Change and ambiguity

Never before in the history of librarianship and information work have there been the high rapidity of change and the growing magnitude of ambiguity as we are experiencing today. We can no longer rely on what worked in libraries in the past to be the best approach in the future. Theobald (1987) was one of the earlier prognosticators to alert us to this oncoming torrent of change. He predicted that the familiar would vanish and we would be swept downstream by the white water so fast that we would not notice the speed of change. Unquestionably, technology is the primary engine driving the change. It has played a greater role in creating and implementing change in libraries than in just about any other dimension of our volatile culture. Technology has vastly improved the effectiveness of libraries. As a result of sophisticated technology, users can now access intellectual resources held in various libraries throughout the world. In the digital age, libraries are performing a key educational role. They provide meaningful content for the Internet, reinforcing the role of the library as an essential link between knowledge and democracy (Cole and Jenkins, 1999).

Changes occurring today in librarianship and information are not only happening with more rapidity, but they are discontinuous. They no longer follow a pattern. This characteristic makes it more difficult to plan for, manage, and execute change. Ambiguity is certainly a result of discontinuous change. Librarians must now have a greater tolerance of uncertainty. We must acknowledge that technology will bring forth more ambiguity. Morgan (1993) believes we are leaving the age of organized organizations and moving into an era where the ability to understand, facilitate, and encourage the process of self-organization will become a key competence. Notwithstanding the discomfort, anxiety, and stress brought forth by greater ambiguity, libraries are expected to continue refinement and improvement (Riggs, 1996). Radical changes and ambiguity in libraries are becoming more the norm than the uncommon.

Global Information Infrastructure

Common components and concerns

Broadly speaking, the global information infrastructure (GII) consists of four parts: hardware, software, supporting physical and human resources, and data/information/knowledge (Horton, 1987). Infrastructure refers to the underlying foundation or basic framework of an organization or system. In the information age, we are increasingly substituting 'machine intelligence' for 'human intelligence'. A common concern throughout the world centres on how the worldwide informational resources can be best shared. In short, how and when will we develop the global library? As expected, there are many barriers to implementing the global library. National policies are tightly controlled, and they discourage and prohibit transnational data flows. Because of the lack of a global library vision, there is a lack of interest on the part of some information professionals. The lack of common standards for both manual and machine-readable cataloguing, interchange codes, protocols, and character sets is a major barrier to the realization of the global library. However, it is encouraging to note the progress that has been made in Europe towards reducing these barriers by the CoBRA project (Lehman, 1996; Dale, 1999). The limited availability and cost of telecommunications have to be overcome. The issue of different languages has to be addressed and accommodated by modern technology. And differences in library policies and practices is hindering the development of the global library (Chen, 1994).

Convergence of visions

The right for everyone to have access to a global library is widely recognized across the world. Even though this concept remains a common dream, its value in improving the human condition is possibly misunderstood and unappreciated in some parts of the world. Wireless technologies can technically connect people with people around the globe. In many countries telephone companies are skipping the wire lines for wireless telecommunications. For example, Motorola is well known for its efforts in developing a wireless phone system in China. The cyberspace era has brought forth many new challenges for librarians. For example, Siddiqui (1997) observed that in Saudi Arabia there is a vast difference in the availability and use of information technology in university libraries. And the interconnectivity with libraries outside Saudi Arabia reflects even more inequity. In a research project involving two Israeli universities, Shoham (1998) discovered that patterns for obtaining information remain conservative and resist transformation. Journals remain the most important tools for obtaining professional information and monographs still play a major role. Eden (1997) conducted two extensive studies on preservation policies in nearly all types of library in the UK. He discovered that librarians and archivists may have different attitudes to preservation, but they face similar problems regardless of profession. Digitization can offer researchers distant access to surrogates of important materials via networked systems as part of the global library. There is a need, however, for a coherent and comprehensive UK national preservation strategy.

Oh and Meadows (1998) investigated the use of electronic communications in a stratified sample of South Korean universities. They discovered that, though infrastructural limitations are important, optimal deployment of communication technologies will require organizational changes within the university system. Turning from academic libraries to public libraries, Ormes (1998) conducted an extensive study of three public libraries in Denmark. She found that the three public libraries have a strong vision of what their role will be in the information society. They enjoy a management culture that encourages staff to have more control over their work and to look on change as a challenge rather than a threat, and the ability to be flexible and look for funding from outside normal sources. Denmark is a country with strong egalitarian beliefs and is willing to fund these beliefs through high taxation. Consequently, public libraries operate in a supportive political context that usually recognizes the importance of their role in society and the value of being informed. Denmark is a good example of a country well poised to participate in the global library.

Some countries have established models of Internet control. For example, the model of Internet control used by the Singapore government has been influential among authoritarian states in Asia. Other Asian countries, including Vietnam and China, are exploring the model used by Singapore (Rodan, 1998). Time will reveal the impact these models have on the global library.

Responsibilities

Cyberspace ignores the territorial boundaries and categories that usually serve as the reference points for the apportionment of responsibilities among those who take part in electronic communication. This makes it all the more necessary to clarify the consequences, from the standpoint of the law or other established norms, of the generalization of an open electronic environment that is extending its operations regardless of the national territories which constitute the traditional frame of reference for defining the different responsibilities (Trudel, 1997). In the construct of the GII, users dissatisfied with the services they are receiving (e.g. from the Internet) are generally free to connect up elsewhere. Thus, the sovereignty of the user does exist. Digital information and proliferation of networks for its delivery are accelerating the development of the global library (a crucial component of the GII). Its technical development and widespread use have, however, outpaced consideration for security, privacy, and the ethics of the production and the dissemination of content. The creation of the universal library where the whole of human knowledge would be accumulated has long been a dream of librarians and scholars (Kruk, 1999). Saksida (1997) noted that the prospects offered today by both the multimedia traffic and the million of users accessing and transmitting digital information have also prompted the creation of large multinational conglomerates and agreements to exploit the resulting market potential. In addition to the foregoing responsibilities, confidentiality of information, security, ethics, and respect for international laws are very important components of the responsibilities associated with the creation and implementation of the GII.

Rights, laws, and legislation

Copyright

Both houses of the US Congress passed the Copyright Extension Act on 7 October, 1998, lengthening the current life plus 50-year copyright term by twenty years. President Clinton signed the bill on 27 October, 1998, along with the Digital Millennium Copyright Act (Flagg, 1998b). These two acts are of great significance to libraries in the USA and throughout the world. Until 1995, European nations also protected works for the life of the artist plus 50 years (Reid, 1998). Library and consumer groups opposed the legislation for the new US copyright extension, but major corporations like Disney and Time Warner lobbied extensively for its passage. There are many issues associated with the copyright law. Some people believe its passage was driven by organizations that had the most to lose in terms of money. The entire issue of copyright law has been profoundly compounded by multimedia and its worldwide distribution and use. Several notable questions linger in the minds of librarians about the copyright extension legislation. One obvious question is whether libraries will be able to provide a range of content that justifies the enthusiasm for universal access. What impact will copyright have on the creation of the global library? Another question, no less pressing, is how much the copyright extension will disallow users to create and use various online resources (Nunberg, 1998). The copyright extension has had a profound impact on various industries: (for example, restaurants getting permission via the 'fair use' provision to play free background music; online record stores allowing shoppers a twenty-second sample before they buy (Avalon, 1999)).

The intricacies of the copyright law require librarians to be fully aware of what they can or cannot do legally. The copyright law applies to pictorial works, film, video, broadcast recordings, music, distance learning, and computer software. A pictorial work may or may not be protected by the same copyright, or absence of copyright, as the work in which it is contained. Thus, permission to copy a written work does not necessarily apply to pictures contained within the work (Hoon, 1998). Multimedia integrate text, audio, graphic, still image, and moving pictures into a single, computer-controlled product. This variety of sources requires the producer to understand a wide variety of legal constraints. Transmission and downloading, implementation guidelines, distribution, retention, storage procedures, and computer authoring systems are complexities and concerns that students, faculty, and other library users must better understand (Arn *et al.*, 1998). Moreover, the vagaries of software licence agreements can vary widely in type and extent of use allowed. Copyright licensing is further complicated by the absence of a single clearance agency that provides information for obtaining rights to use a specific work. Some privately owned agencies are available to assist in identifying the owner of a pre-existing work and negotiating a licence. A US Multimedia Clearinghouse has been proposed to assist in the licensing process.

On 4 March, 1909, the US Congress passed the Copyright Law. The law was designed to give copyright owners exclusive rights to print, reprint, publish, copy, and vend the copyrighted work. It went on to describe a process by which the courts would help define a doctrine of 'fair use' that could be used to help decide cases involving copyright infringement. What is fair use? Today, 90 years after Congress passed the Copyright Law, the courts are still wrestling with the fair use issue. The Internet has only further muddied an already opaque doctrine (Griffith, 1998). For example, today the Internet makes copyright infringement easier than at any other time in history. The Internet is a perfect source for locating reliable copyright information, but the number of sites one could select is enormous. For example, Yahoo! lists seven categories and 456 copyright sites, HotBot gives 38,717 title pages, and Infoseek provides 80,137 documents (Ardito and Eiblum, 1999).

The copyright reform bill passed in October 1998 codified the World Intellectual Property Organization's (WIPO) treaty, signed in December 1997, which updates the Berne Convention to protect intellectual property among the different countries. The Berne Convention's original intent to honour copyright laws among various countries has not been effective in recent years. Codification is abundantly evident in the digital age. US copyright now provides more flexibility regarding liability provision, which was out of kilter when applied to an online environment. The application of strict liability to online library services made little sense from an operational, economic, or First Amendment perspective. The Digital Millennium Copyright Act (DMCA) has provided the necessary framework for intellectual property protection in the digital age. The DMCA makes the needed changes to US law to implement the WIPO copyright treaties. The treaties are designed to update the copyright law for the digital age and balance the concerns of copyright owners with those of information technology manufacturers, consumers, libraries, and others.

Filtering

Public use of the Internet has raised awareness of the legal issues surrounding its use. First Amendment rights have been debated over the use of filtering software in schools and public libraries (Bales, 1998). Schools and public libraries in the US have encountered a major issue evolving from the use of the Internet. Pornography, sadism, and bestiality available on the Internet have caused some schools and public libraries to install filters on some of their public access terminals. The primary focus is on protecting children from the undesirable content (especially pornography) on the Internet. Filters, however, do not block all questionable sites, and they often make many good and useful sites inaccessible.

Some libraries have employed the practice of filtering some computers and not others. Libraries have been sued for using filters and for not using them. Librarians have long supported the familiar principles of free access. The American Library Association has developed a strong stance against libraries' use of filtering software. This stance, however, has been criticized forcefully in some open hearings. The National Commission on Libraries and Information Science (NCLIS) believes that governing boards of schools and public libraries should establish, approve, and review a written acceptable use policy statement on Internet access (Rogers and Oder, 1999). Should the filtering issue be a local matter? NCLIS argues that it should be handled locally.

Hagloch (1999) indicates that most libraries in the state of Ohio rely on the 'tap on the shoulder' policy (in which library staff members tell users to leave an Internet site they consider inappropriate), rather than filtering the Internet access, and that few have received complaints as a result of unfettered access to the Internet. In Ohio and other states filters are used most frequently in the larger public libraries. At smaller libraries, the clientele may be more likely to be personally known to the staff and therefore more self-conscious about accessing questionable sites. Also, the use of filters is more common in politically conservative communities. It will be interesting to see how other countries handle the filtering issue.

E-rate

A digital divide has been created by the educational and library components of the Internet. Serious concern arose in the USA regarding some schools and public libraries not being able to pay the telecommunications costs associated with the Internet. Passed by the US Congress in 1996, the e-rate (a reduced rate for school and public libraries) came under attack in 1998 from several lawmakers and from long-distance companies required to pay into its discount fund (Margolis and Glick, 1998).

On 23 November, 1998, Vice President Al Gore announced that over the next two months up to 7,000 libraries and 40,000 schools across the USA would receive $1.275 billion in federal subsidies for Internet connections (Flagg, 1999). The e-rate provides large savings for most schools and public libraries. The new rate allows more access to the Internet and other electronic information services. However, during hearings on the e-rate there was a surprising amount of criticism on the topic from some members of Congress; they expressed concerns about the e-rate not being necessary or that it should be administered as state block grants (Flagg, 1998a). Fierce congressional criticism has also been directed toward the Federal Communications Commission regarding its proposed method of managing the programme. The criticism is widespread including the claim that long-distance carriers may have cut their rates to assist the e-rate programme, but the proclaimed savings by these companies are difficult to find (Saunders, 1998). It is assumed by some members of Congress that schools and libraries subscribing to the e-rate programmes will be responsible for providing a front-line protection policy for children who utilize the libraries' computers to access the Internet. However, there has to be assurance that decisions on how best to achieve safe, responsible, and appropriate Internet use by children be made at the local level, not by federal mandate. Despite all of the criticism of the management of e-rate, no one can argue with the benefits of this programme; it is certainly a step forward in realizing universal service and reducing the gap between the information 'haves' and the information 'have nots.' The lessons learned from the e-rate experience in the USA will be valuable to other countries as they create and implement policies allowing reduced telecommunications costs for school and public libraries.

Notable advances

Virtual collections

Building and managing the collection remains a vital concern for all types of libraries. While the global output of new book titles continues to increase annually, the acquisitions budgets for many libraries do not increase enough each year to offset inflation and to acquire a larger number of books and journals. The growing Internet and emerging network technologies have been revolutionizing society by making information available to people in new ways. There is an obvious growing dependence on electronic resources. Zhang (1998) defines Internet-based electronic resources as those available from the Internet and used as alternatives/ additions to traditional means of scholarly communication. Electronic resources include e-mail correspondence, messages posted to mailing lists and newsgroups, publications available via Web or file transfer protocol (which could be self-publications, articles in electronic journals, newsletters or other electronic serials, working documents, technical reports, preprints, conference papers, and books), and commercial electronic resources such as Lexis-Nexis. The ongoing expansion of electronic publication and dissemination of federal government information in Canada prompted a study of readiness of depository libraries to adopt the new technologies (Vaughan, 1999).

Online full-text books remain the exception rather than the rule. Prognosticators and experts in publishing both feel we are several years from having a significant number of books online. However, we are witnessing more and more reference books coming available online. Several digital initiatives offer encouragement to those who prefer electronic access to contents of books. The Library of Congress, via its National Digital Library, plans to digitize five million items. The theme of the items (no longer protected by copyright) to be digitized is 'The Making of America' (Carter, 1997). Even if librarians desired more electronic books, Muir (1998) found in her research that there is still some degree of conflict between publishers and librarians who wish to use new technology to deliver services. The thought of reading an entire book from a fuzzy computer screen can conjure up many reasons for not doing so, including eye strain. Computer screens are designed for watching, not reading; they are descendants of television sets, not books.

As expected, the electronic journal is evolving much easier and faster than the electronic book. There are various definitions of electronic journal. Tomney and Burton (1998) offer a realistic definition of the present state of electronic dissemination of information in journal form by describing an electronic journal as 'the concept of storing articles on, and enabling user access over, a computer network, or of distribution of articles over a network to subscribers'. Will this description change in the new future? Probably not. A significant change will require closer collaboration among publishers, technologists, and librarians. The acquisition, storage, and use of journals in the future will depend on the new telecommunications, information technologies, and people (Barker, 1998). There are many challenges facing the conversion to electronic formats. To a larger or lesser extent, information technology is being used and records (including journals) in digital form are being created. The capacity and ability of archivists to deal with this relatively new medium, however, reflect the huge disparities between developed and developing countries pertaining to the spread and usage of information technologies (Mazikana, 1997). Much work needs to be done toward creating archival standards for electronic journals that could be followed throughout the world.

The 22-campus California State University envisions a digital library that would provide direct access, via the World Wide Web, to the electronic texts of millions of scholarly articles with one simple, yet all-encompassing search. Their strategy is to lay out a plan describing exactly what they want, and to entice database companies and publishers to compete for its business. Instead of negotiating individual deals that offer electronic access to fixed sets of journals, the university wants to pay someone to build a customized database for all its campuses; a database that would offer full-text access to more than 1,250 journals (Guernsey, 1999a). The approach by California State turns the tables on conventional modes of paying for electronic journals, and it has caused librarians and publishing companies to sit up and take notice.

A new initiative by the University of Pittsburgh enables scholars in the USA to receive copies of journal articles from more than 10,000 Chinese academic journals housed in libraries throughout mainland China, Hong Kong, and Taiwan. Scholars in the six Chinese participating universities have access to journals in the USA via the University of Pittsburgh Library using the WWW and the Ariel interlibrary loan delivery system (Guernsey, 1999b). We will be witnessing more global library cooperative programmes like the one between the University of Pittsburgh and China/Hong Kong/Taiwan as the technology advances and barriers in the global information infrastructure are removed.

SPARC

Journal subscriptions, especially scientific titles, continue to be much higher in price than academic libraries can readily afford. As a consequence, the Scholarly Publishing and Academic Resources Coalition (SPARC) (1998) began as an initiative of the Association of Research Libraries (ARL). SPARC's aim is to reduce the cost of scientific journals by fostering competition. Membership in SPARC is now open beyond the ranks of ARL. The SPARC membership plan invites international support from academic and research institutions that share an interest in creating a more diverse marketplace for scholarly communication by encouraging the development of high quality, economical journals. SPARC will influence the marketplace positively by encouraging publishers to enter markets where the prices are the highest and competition is needed most, primarily in the science, technical, and medical areas. SPARC's membership continues to grow; the Royal Society of Chemistry, based in the UK, and SPARC (1999) have agreed to collaborate on a series of new high quality, peer-reviewed electronic journals that will be offered at far below the prices of competing commercially published journals. SPARC (New journal, 1999) has also agreed to endorse a University of Arizona biology professor (Michael Rosenzweig) who has launched a new low-cost ecology journal as a protest against subscription prices set by commercial publishers. He is abandoning a similar journal, *Evolutionary Ecology*, which he founded in 1987. Rosenzweig claims the publisher has made the journal so expensive that many libraries and colleagues can no longer afford it. His new journal, *Evolutionary Ecology Research*, will be one-third the cost of the other journal. Will this type of action become a trend? Only time will tell; nevertheless, publishers will certainly be more conscious of their high prices and, hopefully, will do better in making their prices affordable by libraries.

Distance library services

Institutions of higher education throughout the world are engaged in offering distance education. Time and space barriers are being eliminated via new technology delivery systems. In the USA, it is well known that about 90% of the universities with 10,000 or more students offer distance education courses. Distance learning is an emerging educational market of compelling interest to higher education. Driven by economics and enabled by innovations in educational technology, this new market presents significant marketing challenges to academic libraries. However, the role of the public library in independent learning online should not be forgotten (McCormick, 1999). According to Wolpert (1998), libraries should approach support to distance education as a new business opportunity, utilizing techniques of market evaluation and analysis. The distance learner has to be perceived in the same value structure as the on-campus learner. If this is not the case, then distance education could be viewed as second rate. Riggs (1998) believes that distance education students should expect comparable library services to those received by on-campus students. Students at distant sites must have some means of getting the proper documents to support their research and class assignments. The main campus library may deliver the documents, or it may contract with an agency, e.g. UnCover and UMI's Dissertation Express, for document delivery. It is of importance to have a document delivery system that is very efficient. Not having immediate access to a library collection, distance education students must receive their requested information in a timely manner. The number of students enrolled in distance education will increase tremendously in the near future. We should expect to find an increasing number of older people engaged in lifelong learning via distance education classes. Libraries must provide effective and efficient services for distance education students, regardless of their geographical location. Technology is the engine driving many distance education initiatives. Libraries should use the enabling technology to the hilt while providing services for distance education programs.

School libraries

For too long, school libraries have been treated like a forgotten species. For example, the school library situation in California went from bad to worse during the 1990s. California ranks last among all 50 states for the number of school library media specialists per pupil, only one for every 6,334 students. The national student school librarian is one librarian per 885 students (Goldberg, 1999). However, the newly installed governor of California, Gary Davis, has placed public education (including school libraries) as a top agenda item. Now the challenge is to find enough librarians: Goldberg (1999) noted that as of January 1999 there were over 400 openings for school librarians in Los Angeles. School library media centres can be lively, exciting, and a central learning environment, owing to the new technology. Kaiser (1998) reported that 85% of US schools were hooked on the Internet in the 1997–98 school year, but almost one-fourth of the wired schools said none of their teachers was using the Internet in teaching. This unfortunate circumstance poses a great challenge for school librarians to provide technology training for the teachers and integrate the new technology and electronic resources in the curriculum. School librarians have four major components in the role they play in developing a school library programme. They act as instructional leaders; they work in partnership with classroom teachers to develop curriculum; they champion the cause of school libraries through various advocacy programmes; and they manage a budget, a support staff, and the learning resources under their purview (Doiron, 1999).

In our information society, it is necessary to introduce children to books, journals, CD-ROMs, and the various online databases as early as possible. All countries are encouraged to develop and support effective school libraries. Many countries are advancing school libraries. Mustafa (1998) describes the recent turnaround of emphasis on school libraries via the Gulf Co-operation Council comprised of six oil rich countries (Saudi Arabia; United Arab Emirates; Kuwait; Sultanate of Oman; Qatar; Bahrain). For many years school libraries had been ignored in these six countries. Thus, they are primarily book-based, and CD-ROMs and online services are almost non-existent. Computer skills are being introduced in the elementary schools; new libraries are being established in the Sultante of Oman; new funds are being invested in technology; and greater attention is being given to school libraries in all six countries. It is encouraging to see the growing attention and improved funding being given to school libraries in various countries. Denmark gives a high priority to school libraries. After years of neglect, the UK is now giving much better treatment to school libraries. Even though the library profession has never given much emphasis to school libraries, they are very important in the formation of the young minds of our world. And if these minds can comprehend the marvels held by libraries at an early age, perhaps they will use and appreciate libraries throughout their lives.

Growing cooperative library endeavours

Library consortia in the world

There has been incredible growth in library consortia in the USA during the past few years. These consortia have enabled libraries to do collectively what they could not achieve through individual efforts. Consortia permit libraries to continue pursuing their respective individual missions while reaping many benefits from additional products and services and the interdependency provided by the consortia. Due to the tremendous growth in library consortia in the USA, one could conclude that library consortia are a phenomenon peculiar to that country. This is far from true. Consortia are alive and well on every continent except Antarctica. Library consortia did not spread from the USA, but appeared spontaneously in large numbers across the globe (Helmer, 1999).

The Gauteng and Environs Library Consortium (GAELIC) is the largest academic library consortium in South Africa. GAELIC was formed in 1996 primarily in recognition of the need to foster better library cooperation and to make its member libraries more cost effective. Notwithstanding the legitimate claim of many accomplishments in the higher education sector of South Africa, it is still characterized by teaching and research policies that favour academic insularity, with little response to the needs of South African society and the challenges and problems of Africa in a broader context (South Africa Department of Education, 1996). GAELIC strives to better utilize and develop library and information resources of the region for the purpose of promoting education, research, and lifelong learning among its clients, as a contribution to the development of South Africa. GAELIC maintains close connectivity and cooperation with the other library consortia in Africa.

In 1996 the libraries of the eight state-funded universities of Catalonia (Spain) and the Biblioteca de Catalunya formed a consortium to act as a channel for library cooperation. The Consortium of Academic Libraries of Catalonia was initially established to develop a collective catalogue, but it is now focusing on the joint purchase of equipment, training, benchmarking, and the creation of a digital library (Anglada, 1999).

Costello (1999) describes the Council of Australian University Librarians (CAUL) as a dynamic organization promoting collaboration and cooperation among Australia's university libraries. It coordinates national research projects, lobbies government on legal and regulatory reform in areas such as copyright and telecommunications, acts as a broker for consortium purchasing of electronic information resources, and serves as a conduit for information exchange among members. CAUL continues to evolve and annually assumes more responsibilities (e.g. representing the universities in negotiating terms and conditions for electronic databases).

The above library consortia have, as expected, similarities and differences. Regardless of their home country, consortia normally need to overcome political issues, funding challenges, vendor negotiations, and the egos of individuals and institutions. As library consortia grow and expand, we will witness more consortia working together to glean greater benefits for the individual library's users. The recent renaissance in library consortia brings with it the necessity to be more objective in assessing their expectations and results. The International Coalition of Library Consortia (ICOLC) fosters cooperation among the world's library consortia. Exchange of information among the members of ICOLC should certainly result in improving efficiency and effectiveness in the daily operations and annual planning of each consortium.

Joint use libraries

Todaro (1999) informs us that the concept of librarians from a variety of library settings working together to better serve patrons is not new. Nevertheless, the current momentum in the development of joint use library partnerships is unprecedented. The partnerships range from joint public and school libraries to joint private university and public libraries. Most of these joint use libraries are found in the USA. The trend, however, is spreading throughout the world (e.g. the University of Cologne/Germany Library serving both the university community and the city).

The joint library facility between the city of San Jose (California) and San Jose State University received much attention in 1999. Estimated to cost $171 million, the joint project will provide a building that neither the city nor the university could afford to build alone (Rockman, 1999).

Nova Southeastern University and Broward County Public Library (Florida) are jointly constructing a library that will serve both the local public and the university. This new facility will include 290,000 sq ft of space distributed over five floors (Davis, 1999). It is designed with heavy emphasis on technology. The public will have full access to the facility. As part of the partnership, the university and county will also build a $15 million parking garage. This joint use library will bring forth a classic case of synergy where $1 + 1 = 3$ (i.e. the joint use library will result in improved and expanded user benefits that could not be realized by individual library efforts).

Leadership

This chapter concludes with some observations on library leadership or the lack thereof. Unlike many other professions, leadership is not understood, cherished, or encouraged in librarianship. Such an observation may border on being an overstatement, but it contains much truth. Very few, if any, schools of information and library science teach a leadership course, while schools of business have been teaching leadership courses for the past two decades. Many of the ills of librarianship are directly tied to the lack of leadership. Based on the vast ambiguity and difficulty associated with leading change in the library profession today, one could surmise that librarianship is suffering from a leadership crisis.

We are seeing more journal articles appearing on leadership in librarianship, but very few definitive pieces can be identified. Mech and McCabe (1998) recently edited *Leadership and academic librarians*; this work is one of the better books on academic library leadership. Burns (1978) is credited with writing the most definitive book (*Leadership*) on the topic. The following definition of leadership comes from Burns:

> Leadership over human beings is exercised when persons with certain motives and purposes mobilize, in competition or conflict with others, institutional, political, psychological, and other resources to arouse, engage, and satisfy the motives of followers.

Followership is a critical component of leadership. For followers, leaders offer inspiration, direction, a sense of purpose, confidence, and renewal. Followers and leaders must work together in questioning the status quo, revisiting the library's assumptions, and clarifying and refreshing the library's values.

There are unlimited opportunities for leadership in librarianship. Evolving technology offers unprecedented opportunities for creativity, innovation, and entrepreneurship. It is easy to confuse management with leadership. They are both important for any library, but they are two separate hemispheres. Library managers tend to work within defined bounds of known quantities, using well-established techniques to accomplish predetermined ends; the manager tends to stress means and neglect ends. The library leader's task is to hold before the entire library staff a vision of what the library's mission is and how it can be reached more effectively. Leadership involves looking forward, as well as inward. If librarianship is going to survive and thrive in the new millennium, then it must have more visionary, creative, and transformational leadership. Bennis (1973) distinguishes leadership from administration/management:

> If a leader is not careful, one will be sucked into spending all one's time in the important but stifling and inevitably mundane tasks of organizational maintenance. Leadership is the capacity to infuse new values and goals into the organization, to provide perspective on events and environments which, if unnoticed, can impose constraints on the institution. Leadership involves planning, auditing, communicating, relating to outside constituents, insisting on the highest quality of performance and people, keeping an eye out for forces which may lead to or disable important reforms. Administration is managing given resources efficiently for a given mission. Leaders question the mission. Once the leader gets sucked into the incredibly strong undertow of routine work, one is no longer leading, one is following, which one is not paid to do.

It is encouraging to see more articles and books being written on library leadership. Are we in a library leadership crisis? Not yet! Should we devote more time to discussing, researching, and writing about library leadership? Absolutely! In the new millennium we need more transformational leaders who can formulate a compelling vision of the library's future and make it happen.

References

Anglada, L. (1999) Working together, learning together: the consortium of academic libraries of Catalonia. *Information Technology and Libraries*, **18**(3), 139–144.

Ardito, S.C. and Eiblum, P. (1999) Copyright web sites. *Online*, **23**(l), 83–87.

Arn, J. V. *et al.* (1998) Multimedia copyright laws and guidelines: take the test. *Business Communication Quarterly*, **61**(4), 32–39.

Avalon, M. (1999) Entertainment law conference. *Keyboard*, **25**(3), 58–63.

Bales, J. (1998) Copyright in the digital era. *Computers in Libraries*, **18**(6), 38–40.

Barker, P. (1998) Collection development: access in the virtual library. *Electronic Library*, **16**(6), 401–402.

Bennis, W. (1973) *The leaning ivory tower*. San Francisco: Jossey-Bass, pp. 83–84.

Burns, J.M. (1978) *Leadership*. New York: Harper and Row, p. 1.

Carter, K. (1997) National digital library under construction. *Technology and Learning*, **17**(7), 54–55.

Chen, C. (1994) Information superhighway and the digital global library: realities and challenges. *Microcomputers for Information Management*, **11**(3), 143–155.

Cole, J. and Jenkins, J. (1999) Celebrate with the Library of Congress in 2000. *American Libraries*, **30**(l), 106–107.

Costello, D. (1999) More, better, cheaper: the impossible dream? *Information Technology and Libraries*, **18**(3), 154–157.

Dale, P.W. (1999) CoBRA+: a review, with a look to the future. *Alexandria*, **11**(3), 161–166.

Davis, M. (1999) University and public library to build research center in Florida, *College & Research Libraries News*, **60**(8), 609.

Doiron, R. (1999) Partnerships in support of school libraries. *Teacher Librarian*, **26**(3), 918.

Eden, P. (1997) Concern for the future: preservation management in libraries and archives. *Journal of Librarianship and Information Science*, **29**(3), 121–129.

Flagg, G. (1998a) House joint hearings focuses on e-rate. *American Libraries*, **29**(10), 16.

Flagg, G. (1998b) President signs copyright extension act. *American Libraries*, **29**(11), 13.

Flagg, G. (1999) First round of e-rate subsidies finally awarded. *American Libraries*, **30**(l), 13–14.

Goldberg, B. (1999) Study ranks California last in student-librarian ratio. *American Libraries*, **30**(2), 8–9.

Griffith, C. (1998) Fair use and free speech on the Web. *Information Today*, **15**(7), 18–24.

Guernsey, L. (1999a) California State University tries to create a new way to buy online journals. *Chronicle of Higher Education*, **45**(20), A18.

Guernsey, L. (1999b) University of Pittsburgh library opens research gateway to Chinese journal articles. *Chronicle of Higher Education*, **45**(22), A29.

Haglock, S.B. (1999) To filter or not: internet access in Ohio. *Library Journal*, **124**(2), 5051.

Helmer, J. (1999) Epidemiology of the consortial spore. *Information Technology and Libraries*, **18**(3), 119–120.

Hoon, P. (1998) *Guidelines for educational use of copyrighted materials.* Pullman, WA: Washington State University Press.

Horton, F. (1987) Viewpoint: a business format for the national information infrastructure. *Information Management Review,* **3**(l), 71–79.

Kaiser, J. (1998) Wired schools remain unconnected. *Science,* **282**(5389), 587–588.

Kruk, M. (1999) The internet and the revival of the myth of the universal library, *The Australian Library Journal,* **48**(2), 137–147.

Lehmann, K.-D. (1996) European national libraries and the CoBRA Forum of the EU Libraries Programme. *Alexandria,* **8**(3), 155–166.

McCormick, A. (1999) Independent learning online, *Scottish Libraries,* **13**(1), 14–17.

Mazikana, P. (1997) The challenges of archiving digital information. *International Information and Library Review.* **29**(4), 307–317.

Margolis, R. and Glick, A. (1998) Feds say the e-rate is coming at last. *School Library Journal,* **44**(12), 16.

Mech, T. and McCabe, G. (1998) (eds) *Leadership and academic librarians.* Westport, CT: Greenwood Press.

Morgan, G. (1993) *Imaginization: the art of creative management.* Newbury Park, CA: Sage.

Muir, A. (1998) Publishers' views of electronic short-loan collections and copyright clearance issues. *Journal of Information Science,* **24**(4), 215–229.

Mustafa, A.S. (1998) School libraries in the Gulf cooperation – what next? *Online and CD ROM Review,* **22**(5), 339–340.

New journal (1999) protests prices. *American Libraries,* **30**(l), 27.

Nunberg, G. (1998) Will libraries survive? *American Prospect,* **41**(8), 16–23.

Oh, K. and Meadows, J. (1998) Use of communication technologies in South Korean universities. *Journal of Information Science,* **24**(l), 33–38.

Ormes, S. (1998) Danish public libraries. *Journal of Librarianship and Information Science,* **30**(2), 123–132.

Reid, C. (1998) Congress extends copyright 20 years. *Publishers Weekly,* **245**(42), 14.

Riggs, D. (1996) Creating and managing change: some controversy, some level-headedness. *College and Research Libraries,* **57**(5), 402–404.

Riggs, D. (1998) Library services for distance education. In: *Proceedings of the international conference on new missions of academic libraries in the 21st century.* Beijing: Peking University Press, pp. 587–589.

Rockman, I. (1999) Joint use facilities: the view from San Jose. *Library Administration and Management,* **13**(2), 64–67.

Rodan, G. (1998) The internet and political control in Singapore. *Political Science Quarterly,* **113**(l), 63–89.

Rogers, M. and Oder, N. (1999) Senator McCain expected to reintroduce filtering bill. *Library Journal,* **124**(2), 14.

Saksida, M. (1997) The information society in the 21st century: converting from analogue to digital. *International Information and Library Review,* **29**(3), 261–267.

Saunders, S. (1998) Irate over e-rate. *Data Communications,* **27**(17), 4–7.

Shoham, S. (1998) Scholarly communication: a study of Israeli academic researchers. *Journal of Librarianship and Information Science,* **30**(2), 113–119.

Siddiqui, M. (1997) The use of information technology in academic libraries in Saudi Arabia. *Journal of Librarianship and Information Science,* **30**(4), 195–203.

South Africa Department of Education. (1996) *Green paper on higher education transformation*, Pretoria, South Africa: Department of Education, p. 4.

SPARC (1998) seeks an expanded membership for electronic journal initiative. *Information Intelligence, Online Libraries, and Microcomputers,* **16**(11), 4–6.

SPARC (1999) announces European publishing partnership. *Computers in Libraries,* **19**(1), 45–46.

Theobald, R. (1987) *The rapids of change: social entrepreneurship in turbulent times.* Indianapolis, IN: Knowledge Systems.

Todaro, J. (1999) A vision of the past for the future. *Library Administration and Management,* **13**(2), 78–80.

Tomney, H. and Burton, P.E. (1998) Electronic journals: a study of usage and attitudes among academics. *Journal of Information Science,* **24**(6), 419–429.

Trudel, P. (1997) Responsibilities in the context of the global information infrastructure. *International Information and Library Review,* **29**(1), 479–482.

Vaughan, L. (1998) Transition to electronic access of government information: are the depository libraries prepared? *Canadian Journal of Information and Library Science,* **23**(4), 62–67.

Wolpert, A. (1998) Services to remote users: marketing the library's role. *Library Trends,* **47**(1), 21–41.

Zhang, Y. (1998) The impact of internet-based electronic resources on formal scholarly communication in the area of library and information science: a citation analysis. *Journal of Information Science,* **24**(4), 241–254.

National libraries

Tatjana Aparac

Introduction

This chapter covers, rather subjectively, many trends and important issues that characterize the development and performance of national libraries in the year 1998. Bearing in mind that in the 1990s several national libraries have played an active role in assuring the importance of LIS activities in the digital era, it looks at recent developments and activities of national libraries in different parts of the world, drawing on published material and reports from important conferences and meetings, as well as on personal experience gained at international conferences. These activities will be related to the circumstances that have developed as a result of new methods of communication, the impact of information technology on everyday life, and recent demands for making the services of national libraries more open and accessible to the general public.

In previous chapters of *LIWW* devoted to national libraries, as well as in regular literature reviews in professional journals (e.g. *Alexandria*, *LIBER Bulletin*), emphasis has been placed on the 'rapid onslaught of technology', which was characterized by the decision of the leading national libraries to 'travel into cyberspace' (Cornish, 1998; Beer, 1999; McCormick and Scott, 1999). This suggests that national libraries in developing countries are less fortunate. However, they have been some way behind the leading ones in other areas, and there are other reasons for their slower development. Among these are a low awareness among policymakers of the importance of LIS services for countries that are moving towards democratization and economic development (and, thus, for progress and culture in general); a low rate of investment in education; the absence of strategic plans and programmes in the educational, cultural and informational sector; and the lack of an educational structure for LIS personnel. One of the main problems of national libraries in developing countries – a lack of financial support even for basic services – is the result of constant financial constraints.

Struggling against numerous obstacles, these national libraries look at information technology as a two-sided coin. On one side it offers an opportunity to overcome a number of difficulties, especially in relation to better connections with other libraries, networks and colleagues, and a possibility of improving access to much-needed literature and information sources; on the other side, these new possibilities are also seen as a source of frustration because of inadequate technical and intellectual support for the new ways of communicating. Computer illiteracy is another cause for worry. The computer market in most developing countries is 'highly fragmented, riddled by ridiculously high costs as well as being controlled by risk-averse, profit-driven vendors or investors who crowd the scene with usually outdated computer hardwares and softwares' (Duru, 1997).

However, when looking at the future of national libraries around the world, one clearly observes the phenomenal increase in electronic media and the way in which these will, sooner or later, produce changes in the organizational, staffing and service patterns of national libraries in the next millennium. To illustrate this statement, account will be taken of various issues that are increasingly influenced by the new technology, and especially by services available on the Internet. The impact of IT can be seen at the level of planning national library services: national libraries have a growing responsibility for national LIS development as well as for designing national information policy. In almost every developed country, as well as in some of the developing countries, the national library is a leader or an active participant in the planning of digital libraries. Also taken into account will be the problems of collection building in general, and more specifically of issues relating to legal deposit and electronic publications.

There are two additional topics that attract much attention in national libraries around the world: ideas and programmes relating to bibliographic control – the production of national bibliographies in a digital age and their coverage, the coordination of bibliographic activities, standardization, and the theory and practice of conservation and preservation.

The chapter will then look at the space requirements of national libraries, and at new buildings and extensions, the needs of their growing collections, user demands, and the impact of new technology on their internal organization and administration. Finally, cooperative initiatives from around the world will be considered.

Planning national library services

Most national libraries in the western world are regarded as important national institutions, but at the same time they often seem to the ordinary citizen like museums with restricted access. A number of authors (Nilsen, 1998; Line, 1999) write about the need to open up the services of the national library in order to change the image they present to the public, and to make people realize that the national library is not an institution that exists merely to keep 'dusty old books' for eternity. Another feature common to all national libraries, as well as to museums, archives, theatres and other cultural institutions, is the effort they make to attract financial resources; these are now more important then ever. Since commercial values have come to be part of daily life, taxpayers and governments are questioning the contribution made by national libraries to the individual and to society as a whole (Line, 1999).

Almost every national library in developed countries has prepared a 'vision' paper, along with a strategic plan and a methodology for performance evaluation. These documents have been extensively presented and commented on in previous years. However, new issues are now being considered by planners: the new role national libraries are expected to play in approaching 'ordinary' people, the role they will have to play in promoting national culture and heritage, and their willingness to play an even greater part in exploiting the digital environment.

Two questions must to be addressed. The first is what priorities the national library sets in order to improve the visibility of its collections and services, and to promote them. The second is how the new technological opportunities can be used to make it more visible within its national culture (Lidman, 1998b; Nilsen, 1998; Line, 1999). It is obvious that as newly created opportunities arise in the global information environment, the national library's opportunities for performing a wider range of cultural functions also increase. Plans for new approaches to its performance take into account the global situation and the specifics of each state and nation. Differences can be observed, however, since financing and the level of performance of national libraries vary in developing as well as in developed countries.

National libraries in the Russian Federation serve as centres for preparing and implementing information models of the national culture (Kuznetsova, 1997). This model comprises four basic elements: a national bibliography, a national system of machine-readable union catalogues, a restructured system of regional bibliographies and operational information, and a communications framework for the development of the specific national culture. Although the model has not been completely worked out, Russian professionals are aware of the importance of national libraries in promoting the national culture.

Nasjonalbiblioteket, the Norwegian National Library, is trying to improve its visibility and promote its collections by the use of new technology. Nilsen (1998) stresses that the newly created opportunities offered by separation from Oslo University Library and the renewal of the library's building are a good base for the introduction of a wider range of cultural aspects of the library's performance. Strategic planning in the National and University Library in Croatia is in its infancy, but the Library Law of 1997 provoked a discussion about internal reorganization. Skender (1998) gives an overview of the impact of this law on the library's constitution and its future plans. In Nigeria, emerging trends and plans for the future of the National Library, which recently celebrated its thirtieth birthday, are presented by Enyia (1998). In Hungary, a long-range programme was elaborated in the National Information Strategy. This dealt with the evolution of the information society; the goals set for 1997–98 included the introduction of shared cataloguing, the creation of a joint recording system and a new computer system for the National Széchényi Library, coordination of the digitization of cultural treasures, and accommodation of a national multimedia collection (Ronai and Skaliczki, 1997).

In transitional countries new laws can bring a certain amount of confusion. Hogh (1998) discusses problems caused in Slovakia by the 1997 Law on Matica Slovenska. As a result of this the Narodna Knjiznica Slovenska in Martin became an independent institution, but on the other side, the Minister of Culture decided to reallocate the functions of the central national library of the Slovak Republic to the University Library in Bratislava. These regulations and decisions require a reformulation of the role and tasks of the library in Martin.

Despite a wide range of efforts, national libraries worldwide are faced with severe funding constraints, which have a considerable impact upon their ability to introduce new initiatives and programmes, or to perform known tasks at the current level of service. Thus, it is not surprising that even in the wealthy USA the Librarian of Congress had to ask for an increased budget for 1999 of $369.3 million in net appropriations and $27.7 million in authority to use receipts from the Copyright Office and the Cataloging Distribution Service – a net increase of 6.5% over 1998. The major components of this requested increase are funding for mandatory pay rises and other unavoidable increases (House, 1998). Other key items in the request include the replacement of outdated PCs, security improvements, off-site storage, realization of a plan for the Congressional Research Service, and 'talking books' for blind and physically handicapped users (Library, 1998; Ohnemus, 1998). On a general level, strategic planning issues at the Library of Congress are discussed by Bryant (1998).

The British Library (BL) was asked to plan for three years (1998–2000 to 2001–02) on the basis of no increase on the 1998–99 cash settlement, despite the growth of legal deposit intake and user demand and trends in book and serial price inflation. It had already been estimated that about £8 million extra would be needed merely to maintain the library's existing programmes and to meet deficits carried over from 1997–98. The likely outcome would have been reductions in overtime budgets and on expenditure for acquisitions and conservation (Stoker, 1998). Fortunately, the government later relented and provided more money.

Data analysed by Smethurst (1998) show that in several other countries (e.g. Germany, Hungary, the Netherlands, Romania, Russia, Slovenia, Spain) severe staff cuts have been made. Some countries have introduced an annual user's fee to finance temporary staff or to support conservation efforts.

Because of difficult economic circumstances Helsinki University Library (HUL) began several reform processes to strengthen the leadership abilities of middle managers and improve both decision-making and service efficiency. Järvenpää

(1998) describes the results of this action, and mentions also the responsibility given to HUL in 1998 by the new University Law for the allocation of all salaries within an overall budget, a task previously carried out by the university's central administration.

In Denmark, Det Kongelige Bibliotek, the Royal Library, signed a fresh performance contract with the Ministry of Culture for the period 1998 to 2001, in order to be able to carry out medium-term development. The contract specified conditions for the library's operations and services when the new building opened in 1999. The overall aim was to improve access to the collections by increasing opening hours, making larger reference collections directly accessible to the public, digitization, etc. (Larsen, 1998). A similar contract was signed by the State and University Library in Aarhus.

Strategic management has been of considerable interest to the national library community, including IFLA's Section on National Libraries, for many years. Following the agreement that the Section should continue to explore those aspects of strategic management that were identified in a 1996–97 survey as being of high priority, the section at the 64th IFLA General Conference in Amsterdam discussed three of these areas: core competencies of library staff; client needs in the 21st century; and the use of performance indicators. As Scott (1998) reports, as part of its action plan based on the strategic planning session in February 1996, the National Library of Canada (NLC) decided to hold several brainstorming meetings to forecast its position in the year 2001; one of the key issues was the development of staff expertise. The National Library of Scotland specified its general aims and objectives in a corporate plan, as well as specific objectives for the plan's first year, and income and expenditure flow (with bids for additional expenditure), and defined key performance targets and performance indicators (McGowan, 1998).

Lor (1998) discusses the role of library services in developing countries at a national level, their relationship with the state, and the autonomy and authority of the national library or other relevant agencies. He suggests that the status and powers of such institutions should find a proper place in national legislation, and describes desirable components of such a legislation.

Marketing of library and information services is another topic of interest. Hendrikz (1998), for example, describes a pilot marketing effort for the supply of products and services of the State Library in Pretoria, which found that the market was not confined to libraries, and outlines the library's marketing strategy and plans for promoting its services in future.

Automation and digitization projects

National libraries worldwide are improving existing IT, hardware and software, to facilitate internal as well as external network services. In 1998 the National

Széchényi Library of Hungary and the National Library of Australia both chose the library management system AMICUS for the implementation of their automation and network services (New, 1998; News, 1998). In doing so, they joined the National Library of Canada, which has been using the system since 1995, and the British Library (British, 1998a), which planned for the new system to be fully operational from early 1999. The National Széchényi Library expects the new system to support its original cataloguing, while making transfers of data from other sources also possible (Horváth, 1998). Jeremiah (1998) describes a procurement process for a new system for processing non-print materials at the National Library of Wales.

Kungliga Biblioteket, the Swedish Royal Library, signed a contract for the installation of Aleph 500 as its integrated local library system; during 1998 Web OPAC, interlibrary loan, and circulation (including special management of reading rooms, loans and automated requests for material from the closed stacks) were offered to users (Lidman, 1998b, 1998c). As discussed by Jakac-Bizjak (1998b), the National and University Library in Ljubljana has been expanding its IT facilities as well as building a new laboratory equipped for teaching purposes.

In Swaziland, a country which in common with most African countries faces numerous socioeconomic challenges, the allocation of financial, material and human resources is lagging behind expectations. IT is seen by professionals as a welcome opportunity to improve existing services and to introduce new ones, but the government has indicated that the provision of computers to libraries is not an immediate priority (Menou, 1998; Muswazi, 1998). In Zambia, Namibia, Ghana and Nigeria, as well as in Swaziland, non-governmental and aid organizations have been the sole driving force for Internet connectivity and development. Although the Internet circuit in Nigeria seems to be 'grossly underutilized because of the seeming high cost of services', libraries are expected to create networks for cataloguing and acquisitions, as well as for interlending, document delivery and resource-sharing networks. In this respect the National Information and Documentation Centre of the National Library of Nigeria has been extremely useful (Duru, 1997).

It is generally accepted that the Internet is an important yet chaotic environment. National libraries are directing their interest not only to bringing structure to it, but also to the presentation of its potential for national information strategies. Websites can contribute to the dissemination of important decisions, changes and new services of the library, as well as acting as tools providing access to a country's cultural heritage (de Niet, 1998a).

The recommendations resulting from the workshop organized by the Conference of European National Librarians (CENL) at the Biblioteka Narodowa (National Library of Poland) in 1997 were submitted to CENL (International, 1998b). It was accepted that Web services have become central to the strategy of European national libraries, and that their maintenance and development should be appropriately managed and supported. It was also believed that CENL members should cooperate in this area, and that the set of elements defining the core content of Web services should be defined, as well as guidelines on appropriate tools for running, maintaining and providing access to Web services.

Gabriel, which can be considered to be the only existing pan-European library service (*Gabriel*), had 38 members in 1998, 29 of them having their own Internet services (de Niet, 1998a). Browsing through Web pages makes it obvious that there are differences between member libraries of CENL. Some of them cannot cope with the technical equipment and connections of others, and some are not able to keep up to date. Financial support for the digital library projects also varies greatly.

One of the main objectives of the BL is to provide simple, fast access to its collections and digitized materials for users from all over the world through computer networks, particularly the Internet (Carpenter *et al.*, 1998). The library has been involved in several projects and is searching for the necessary digital infrastructure. Following the end of the Digital Library PFI (Private Financial Initiative) project in December 1998 the library started to explore alternative solutions for its digital library requirements (British Library, 1998c).

The digitization of collections in the National Library of Norway has high priority, but it has to be done in accordance with a project plan for the renewal of the old building. Among projects in progress is a critical edition of Ibsen's work, planned together with the Centre for Ibsen Studies at the University of Oslo (Christensen *et al.*, 1998). All the relevant manuscripts in the National Libraries in Norway and Denmark will be digitized, the Music Collection will carry out research into the music used for Ibsen's works, the Theatre Collection will contribute with posters, programmes, etc.

At the end of 1997 the Finnish Ministry of Education launched a new library programme, 'The National Electronic Library', and responsibility for its implementation was given to the national library (Helsinki University Library). Simultaneously, the library started a process of upgrading the present automation systems software in the country's university libraries. The question of data format, whether to maintain a national format or to change to USMARC, has also been raised. The results of the conversion process show that about 95% of all HUL's catalogues are accessible online, and conversion of the national bibliography has been completed. Within the framework of the Finnish Government Information Society Programme, HUL is leading or taking part in a number of library programmes and initiatives, such as ELEKTRA, MUISTI, EVA, FINELIB. In addition to these projects, it participates in a number of new projects within the EU Telematics Programme (Häkli, 1998a).

In Austria the union catalogue was supported in 1998 by a new system, ALEPH 500. An additional service – ordering books via e-mail – has also been started as a pilot project. A future high-priority project for the Österreichische Nationalbibliothek (Austrian National Library) will be the setting up of an electronic system for the archival storage of over a million picture documents in its collections of portraits and photographs. In addition to scanning the basic bibliographic information in a card catalogue of 1.3 million records, there is also a need to set up a digital picture catalogue to avoid the need to consult the originals. Depending on the budget available, the project under consideration will involve holdings amounting to between one and three thousand digital pictures (L. Lang, 1998; Marte, 1998).

In Denmark the Ministry of Culture, the Ministry of Research and the Ministry of Education have taken an initiative to establish an 'Electronic Research Library of Denmark' for the purpose of accelerating and coordinating development within the library sector. The initiative involves cooperative effort of twelve major research libraries to create a digital library; the costs may amount to $29 million for the basic scenario, $30 million for the extended scenario and more than $40 million for the advanced scenario (*Electronic*, 1997; Kvaenderup and Thorhauge, 1998). The Royal Library is constructing a national image database, which in 1998 held more than 50,000 scanned engravings, pictures and photographs. Digitization of 100,000 Danish portraits is planned from 1998 to 2000. Some special collections have also been digitized, like Müller's Pinakoteque 1500–1795, Denmark during the German Occupation, and Portraits of H. C. Andersen (Fischer Jonge, 1998).

In France, one of the initial concepts of the Bibliothèque nationale de France (BnF) was the creation of a digital library with 300,000 images and 50,000 books. In 1998 some 100,000 reference books and periodicals and 300,000 pictorial sources were digitized in black and white images, 40% of them directly from the source documents and the remainder from photographs or microforms (Renoult, 1998). At the Vienna Conference (Age, 1998), Schaer stated that in future Gallica collection material should concentrate on holdings in the special collections, so that emphasis could be placed on unique items and documents that cannot easily be found elsewhere. The first multimedia work station was opened, along with reading rooms for academic research, in October 1998, thereby enabling consultation and hypertextual consultation of documents.

The National and University Library of Iceland believes that digitization will be of great importance in the preservation of, and access to, vital parts of its collections, especially manuscripts and graphic material. The library is also determined to preserve cultural values in digital form, with priority given to cataloguing of rare and damaged works (Sigurðsson, 1998a, 1998b). The Ministry of Culture has established a working group to investigate and make proposals for a new library system based on international standards like Z39.50, and for flexible gateways.

In Italy, one of the functions of the Servizio Bibliotecario Nazionale is to network national libraries and interconnect universities with local and municipal libraries, in order to supply integrated services to users. Thus, the SBN was recognized as a focal point for the planning and coordination of digitization efforts. An investigation carried out by the Ufficio Centrale per i Beni Librari, le Istituzioni Culturali e l'Editoria showed that there were 41 projects aimed either at full digital reproduction of printed documents and manuscripts or at digitization of their important parts (Sicco, 1998). The Biblioteca de Catalunya in Barcelona designed a digitization programme for old and rare documents, with the dual objectives of preservation and dissemination. It is considered very important to make the first written sources in the Catalan language available on the Internet (Planet, 1998).

Access to research material in the digital era is a high priority topic on the agenda of the Koninklijke Bibliotheek (KB, the National Library of the Netherlands), Dutch universities, the Netherlands Organization for Scientific Research and the Royal Netherlands Academy of Arts and Sciences. Within the programme for Innovation in the Provision of Scientific Information, a study named 'The Library that Expands Horizons' has the goal of exploring the future, and of coordinating national and local efforts towards the creation of digital services and the establishment of the 'virtual scientific library'. In January 1998 the IBM Digital Library System for storing and handling electronic journals became operational at the KB (Steenbakkers, 1998). During 1998 additional functionality was added to the KB's Networked Information Service, including such features as the use of customized user profiles and a mechanism for authorization, authentication and accounting in order to offer charged services and to be able to differentiate between services restricted access and free public services (Noordermeer *et al.*, 1998). A pilot project of the KB known as Advanced Information Workstation led to the development of a multimedia workstation with special attention to needs of researchers in the humanities (de Niet, 1998b).

In the Czech Republic the CASLIN project is strengthened by the new ALEPH system, with Czech and Slovak versions. In addition, the RETROCON project of the Czech National Library may be seen as a supplementary part of the whole CASLIN project, as it contributes both to adding data to the union catalogue and providing libraries everywhere with bibliographic records (Balik, 1998a). The digitization of old and rare books in the Czech National Library, which is a part of UNESCO's Memory of the World programme, is seen by Knoll (1998) as a complex task.

In Germany a Global Info Programme was developed in 1997, to run for six years until 2003. The role of Die Deutsche Bibliothek (DB) is planned according to activity no. 5 (archiving) of the programme (Schmiede, 1998). On 1 July 1998 the DB started its collection of networked digital publications, consisting initially of dissertations (Deutsche Bibliothek, 1998). Regarding retrospective digitization of library holdings as one of the major sources of content for the digital library of the future, the Deutsche Forschungsgemeinschaft (DFG) decided to set up two centres for digitization, in Göttingen University Library and the Bayerische Staatsbibliothek, and was later involved in the installation of a new LAN (Bunzel, 1998a, 1998b; Hefele, 1998).

In 1997 the Biblioteca National of Portugal defined a new organic structure, from which emerged a new 'Innovation and Development Service'. Its main goal is to define strategy and to promote and coordinate new initiatives for a 'national digital library'. Meanwhile several projects have been started, such as a virtual library of Portuguese authors, a digital library of Portuguese science and technology and a digital library of high school newspapers. Since it is also involved in the MALVINE project, the library has been working on PORBASE, the national catalogue compiled through the collaborative effort of more than 200 Portuguese libraries. Among these, the Biblioteca Nacional is responsible for maintaining the bibliographic service (Borbinha, 1998).

In the USA, 50 staff are working on a major digitization project, American Memory Programs, directed by the Library of Congress (Fischer, 1998). Following the plans, the National Digital Program, which is already widely accepted as the library's major gift to the nation (Billington, 1998), will enable LC to distribute important items online in local communities throughout America by the year 2000, when the library will celebrate its bicentenary (200, 1998).

In December 1998 the National Library of Australia issued an information paper on the Digital Services Project to provide potential suppliers of products and services with guidance on the new requirements, and to obtain the industry's comment on the issue. The Digital Services Project is expected to be built on the outcomes of the library's Kinetica Project (*Digital*, 1998). The aim of another Australian digitization project, the Cooperative Digitization Project, is to create a unique research infrastructure in Australian studies through the digital conversion of Australian serials and fiction of the seminal period 1840–45 (Ferguson, 1998).

The digital library projects in Japan are expected to be fully operational when the Kansai-kan building opens in 2002. In March 1998 a proposal was submitted to the Committee for Promotion of the Electronic Library, which was the basis for the preparation of drafting the National Diet Library's digitization plan. It is agreed that the project will proceed in four directions. These matters are explained in detail by Ogata (1998).

One of the recent trends in LIS today is the deployment of metadata, using the Dublin Core Metadata Element Set in libraries' web pages. Thornely (1998) describes the State Library of Queensland Metadata Project, which is also seen as an initial attempt to set standards for metadata deployment in other state libraries' Web pages.

Collections and access

Some national libraries are changing their collection policies to cope with the increasing amount of printed material and the wide range of media. Several national libraries have attempted cooperative acquisition programmes, but as Line (1998) points out, these initiatives rarely succeed, for logistic and other reasons. Other libraries, like the National Library of Australia, have taken 'a realistic approach' to their collection policy.

In building its collections the Biblioteca de Catalunya is concentrating on coordination of its purchasing activities with other Catalan university libraries, to avoid unnecessary duplication. Gaps in its collections have been filled from the acquisitions budget by means of auctions and direct purchase (Planet, 1998).

The collections of the Bibliothèque nationale du Québec are described in detail by Sauvageau (1998). Documents of all types, including microforms and software, are collected by legal deposit, purchase or exchange. Majerova (1998) writes about the rich special collections of the National Library of Slovakia, pointing that they have two main functions: to be useful to future users, and to serve as a record of Slovakian history.

Smirnova (1997) comments on the role of newly created national libraries in the Russian Federation and their interrelationship; she describes collections and information resources in national libraries of Turkmenistan, Belarus, the Ukraine, Kazakhstan and Kyrgyzstan, and methods of information and document exchange among them. Peic (1998) reports on the destruction of the National and University Library of Bosnia and Hercegovina in Sarajevo. The salvaged 10% of its collection was moved to temporary premises, and one of the main tasks of the library is to rebuild its collection.

The Biblioteca Nacional de Venezuela, which acts as a centre for collecting Latin American government publications and music manuscripts, contributes to the European Register of Microform Masters by providing microfilms of Latin American holdings from libraries in Venezuela and from national libraries in Chile, Peru, Columbia, Costa Rica and Brazil, as well as from the Biblioteca Hispanica in Spain and the Interamerican University in Panama (National Library of Venezuela, 1998).

In building collections of electronic publications, national libraries focus primarily on materials that are easy to handle such as standard media types (CD-ROM, CD-I) and machine-readable formats (ASCII, PostScript), but they are gradually expanding their policies to include other formats, often supported by experimental projects.

The National Library of Australia decided to take a selective approach and develop a set of practices concerning a few selected Australian online publications (Layland, 1998a). The NLA continues to develop its RAAM project (Register of Australian Archives and Manuscripts), and has been also planning similar projects for different types of documentary heritage.

National libraries in developing countries have been faced with insufficient funding for collection development; thus they have been relying on cooperative projects and ILL systems such as the Southern African Interlending Scheme, SAILS (Muswazi, 1998).

The number of libraries using interlending services is growing. The BL Document Supply Centre, one of the world's largest storehouses of published documents, reports regularly on demand and service issues. In answering users' demands (86% of them are using automated request facilities), the library succeeds in responding to 100% within two hours (Demand, 1998). As M. Smith reports (1998), it is expected that the adoption of the ISO ILL protocol will provide a common gateway for document requests, and thus save even more of users' time.

Legal deposit

As one of the most important features of a national library, the future of legal deposit is the subject of lively discussion. A number of libraries, particularly in transitional countries, continue to report that arrangements for legal deposit do not seem to be working effectively. One of the major reasons is the gradual growth of a non-centralized publishing market, as well as an ineffective penalty system for those who fail to make deposits. Evidence for this statement is given in the report by Smethurst (1998). In Russia less than half of published works are collected by the legal deposit arrangements (Tolèinskaya, 1998). In Croatia some 40% of items published are not even registered (*Kulturna*, 1998). There have been criticisms of Poland's Legal Deposit Law of 1996, which covers a broad spectrum of publications including non-book materials. These concern mainly important omissions and gaps, such as unclear information goals of legal deposit in the area of bibliographic control, inconsistencies and lack of proper definitions of basic principles, and the increased number of libraries receiving legal deposit material (Ramlau-Klekowska, 1998).

Fullerton (1998) discusses issues related to collecting electronic material and offers 14 recommendations for future collaborative action. The National Library of Australia opened a website for further discussions (National Library of Australia, 1999).

Leading national libraries such as the British Library, the Deutsche Bibliothek and the Library of Congress are concerned with the comprehensiveness of those legal deposit collections that consist of a full range of media, including digital records, as well as with the authenticity of digital legal records and future possibilities of retrieving them. Peters (1998) discusses provisions of the present US Copyright Law, the practical experience of the Office of Copyright, and other issues such as definitions of publication, the concept of the copyright work and its editions, exemptions and the future availability and use of all items collected in the Library of Congress.

A number of leading academic and professional publishers are cooperating with the British Library in a voluntary pilot scheme for electronic deposit (Davies, 1998). Many of the problems connected with the legal deposit of electronic documents are presented in the findings of a Working Group of the Conference of Directors of National Libraries (CDNL). Nevertheless, a year later, at the Workshop of the Section in Amsterdam, B. Lang (1998) pointed out that the changes were not so rapid as had been expected two years before.

Meanwhile, libraries and publishers have started working together (Bourne, 1998), for example through the CDNL, CoBRA (Lehmann, 1996; Dale, 1999), and NEDLIB projects (NEDLIB). There is no doubt that the production of electronic documents has brought about a major change in thinking among policymakers, publishers and national libraries about the importance of securing the national written heritage and of including digital issues in collection policies. National libraries are aware that, in order to maintain comprehensive collections of national publications for present and future generations of users, it will be necessary to deal with an increasing amount of material in forms other than printed paper.

Legal issues

Although legal deposit legislation evolved throughout the 20th century, the most significant changes came about in the 1990s, leading to discussions about the conceptual and practical issues of legal deposit collections. Countries currently without legal deposit legislation are being urged to introduce it, and others, where necessary, to revise existing legislation. Few countries have identical legal deposit rules; it is also clear that even the most comprehensive law cannot guarantee that the obligation to send designated items will be observed in practice.

Generally, legislation enables designated repositories to receive physical objects such as printed publications, audiovisual material and CD-ROMs, but not electronic publications. New deposit laws, or regulations pursuant to such laws, not only state the objectives of legal deposit but also attempt to ensure that all existing types of media are included. Nevertheless, as Line (1998) states, 'even if the legal deposit law is all-inclusive, as in Norway, the problems of enforcing it are almost insuperable, and the burden of collecting is insupportable'.

In Austria since 1981 the law has provided for obligatory deposit copies of conventional material. In order to avoid gaps in the archival storage of the national cultural heritage before appropriate legislation encompassing new media comes through, the National Library has asked all producers of offline media for voluntary deposit copies of their products. The library's initiative was supported by the VIW, the Austrian association for private enterprises in the field of information, and has been successful. It also offers valuable steps towards a legal solution. The library has started to store online publications and is confronted with familiar problems such as changing software, updating databases, questions of copyright and so on (Age, 1998).

Copyright deposit in Monaco, briefly described by Garrod (1998), dates from 1925, when it was made obligatory to submit copies of all published matter to the Department of the Interior. Since the department does not regularly forward these copies to the Bibliothèque Notary, the library is unable to prepare a complete listing of Monegasque publications. Thus, a modification of the law to ensure that the library receives all publications directly is under consideration.

In Finland a revision of the Legal Deposit Law of 1980 was started in September 1997. A working group suggested that there should be only two comprehensive collections of printed and electronic material; the first one would be in Helsinki University Library, while the second one should be split so that the printed material was in Turku University Library, but the collection of electronic material was in Jyväskylä University Library. It is also proposed that the law should allow the library to reformat and copy publications to ensure their permanent survival. The revised Legal Deposit Act should be operational at the beginning of the year 2000 (Häkli, 1998b; 1998c).

Following the Danish Act on Copyright Deposit of Published Works (10 June 1997), which came into force on 1 January 1998, two copies of any work published in Denmark, regardless of the medium used for production, must be deposited with a copyright deposit institution. In the case of works that can be made accessible only by the use of technical equipment, the producer must provide appropriate instructions with the deposited copies. Where digital publications and publications make use of non-standard equipment, the act requires that, if the copyright deposit institution requests, the publisher must deposit any technical documentation necessary to use the work as soon as the required technical equipment is no longer on the general market. When works are published in the form of databases, the law requires the copyright holder to inform the deposit institution of the fact of publication, and simultaneously submit passwords and any other information necessary for the institution to gain access to the works (Denmark, 1997).

In Iceland, a committee was appointed in August 1997 by the Minister of Education and Culture to revise the Legal Deposit Act of 1977, and a draft version was prepared (Sigurðsson, 1998b). The National Library of the Netherlands has begun discussions with the Dutch Publishers Association in an attempt to reach a general agreement on the deposit and preservation of electronic documents. Agreements have been made with a number of publishers concerning electronic research journals (Noordermeer *et al.*, 1998). Special attention has been given to criteria for selecting material for deposit: geographic origin, the pattern of distribution, the size of the edition, etc.

The National and University Library in Slovenia does not archive any online documents, believing that it is necessary to resolve a number of questions relating to the identification, collection, cataloguing, preservation and usage of such materials before proposing new rules in the legal deposit scheme. A special brochure was published to inform publishers and other libraries about these concerns and the necessary procedures for the collecting of electronic documents (Jakac-Bizjak, 1998b).

In Japan the National Diet Library (NDL) acts as the sole deposit library. The legal deposit system applies not only to books and serials but also to other types of publications, including a growing number of electronic publications. However, there has been a good deal of discussion on how to apply the system to electronic publications in order to assure their receipt and preservation without obstacles. An Electronic Publications Committee submitted in March 1998 a report (Ogata, 1998) which defines 'packaged electronic publications' as electronic publications fixed on physical media, such as CD-ROMs, and 'networked electronic publications' as electronic publications transmitted and received over a communications network. The committee recommended that 'packaged electronic publications' should be included in the legal deposit system, and that for the time being the legal deposit system will not apply to 'networked electronic publications'; issues of compensation and of lease contracts were left to a newly established Committee on Legislation, which reported at the end of 1998.

The Swedish strategy is designed to acquire digital copies of all Swedish electronic publications, including Web pages. The Kungliga Biblioteket uses an archival robot to harvest material from the Web (Arvidson and Lettenström, 1998). The current emphasis is on capture, because of difficult legal questions about access, and because a sense of urgency is felt about acquiring copies of electronic publications before they vanish.

The National Library of Australia is faced with the fact that electronic material is not yet covered by the legal deposit provisions of the Copyright Act, though a voluntary scheme was started in 1995. Up to 1998 about 60 publishers responded positively by lodging their material; where publishers have not agreed, the library has decided to purchase material instead (Layland, 1998a). The Australians are pursuing a strategy based on responsibility distributed between the National Library, for electronic publications of national significance, and state and local authorities, for significant publications within their regions. This also means starting to demarcate areas of responsibility for preservation, which will allow other institutions to turn their attention to neglected issues.

Die Deutsche Bibliothek cooperates with the Association of German Booksellers, more precisely with its Publishers Committee, in order to establish procedures for voluntary submission of free copies of networked publications. After an experimental period of three to five years such cooperation could produce a basis for rules related to archiving, long-term preservation measures, cataloguing and availability of materials for use in the library's reading rooms without charge (Lehmann, 1998a, 1998b, 1998c).

In the UK, following the publication in early 1997 of a consultative document on legal deposit (British Library, 1998b), a government working group was established under Sir Anthony Kenny to study the problem and to consider how a voluntary scheme of deposit for non-book material might operate (Prochaska, 1998).

Access

Among discussions about access to the collections of national libraries, increasingly common issues include the commercial and copyright interests of publishers and authors worldwide. Libraries have been cooperating to work out suitable arrangements with publishers to assure conditional access to commercially published electronic documents as well as to outputs from them such as CD-ROMs. A European library declaration (1998) calls upon the European Commission and governments within the European Union to 'utilize the full range of lawful possibilities offered by the WIPO Copyright Treaty to formulate well-balanced copyright regulations that will cover the needs of education, information and research, ensuring equal access to electronic and the traditional printed material'.

The British Library has direct agreements with 20 publishers which allow the electronic storage of material. Also, the library has reached agreement with nine publishers of scientific, technical and medical journal literature to improve its availability to researchers and students. The agreement allows the library to deliver copies of journal articles by facsimile and other controlled methods of electronic transmission, as well as by conventional document delivery. Some of the publishers involved have also agreed in principle to the provision of electronic bibliographic data and access to full text in electronic format. As part of its policy of improved services to its remote users the library is developing its Inside service – an integrated current awareness, document ordering and document delivery service based on the collections at the BL Document Supply Centre (British, 1998b; British Library, 1998b).

Bélaval (1998) explains that a framework contract was drawn up with the French Publishers' Association permitting two-year use of electronic texts in the library's reading rooms. The Selection Committee on On-line Australian Publications (SCOAP) has developed a set of selection guidelines. Pandora (1998) currently provides access to more than 1,000 Australian electronic journals, magazines, and ephemeral digital items.

In order to increase network resources available to Finnish research libraries, Helsinki University Library started negotiating national licences for electronic journals, the first one being signed with the Academic Press (Häkli, 1998a). KOPIOSTO, the Finnish Joint Copyright Organization, planned and negotiated an open and flexible model for copyright owners to grant permission for use of their works in the Electra project. While in its early stage, the project accepted several principles applying to copyright transfer, thus enabling HUL to digitize articles from the journals involved in the project and download them onto the Electra database (Salonharju, 1998).

Worldwide it can be seen that national libraries are struggling both for the right to copy publications for preservation purposes (archival copy), and the right to provide access to the publications (on-site consultation).

Cataloguing and bibliographic control

Before the globalization of bibliographic record supply, cataloguers were central to the effective use and exploitation of a library's collection, as Oddy (1999) reminds us. Nowadays, that is obviously not the case – even to cataloguers – she argues, but this might be true only in a developed library environment. Less developed countries still struggle for a sound national programme of shared bibliographic action, especially when it comes to the bibliographic control of their own published and electronic material. Muswazi (1998) explains why the idea of the Swaziland Union Catalogue failed. Among the main reasons for failure, which led to the decision to continue to deposit bibliographic records in the State Library of South Africa in Pretoria, were the uneven distribution of expertise and the limited supply of professional skills. Shared cataloguing and bibliographic work are often made difficult, or at worst impossible, by the absence of proper technical equipment and connections, or by the need to use obsolete software; in consequence, joint arrangements to share bibliographic records are spreading. Also, experienced bibliographic networks offer assistance in retrospective conversion and/or downloading of records.

The National Library of Taiwan, for example, has been using Bibliofile and OCLC CatCD Database Search for cataloguing foreign publications (Cataloging, 1997). In 1998 OCLC's WorldCat continued to attract new members and load records of several national collections. In February 1998 more than 60,000 book records from the National Library of Australia were loaded through Batchload software; now loading of records obtained from the Library of Congress is done on a monthly basis (Kozsely, 1998). LC is also involved in promoting cooperation in cataloguing in developing countries (Fineberg, 1998).

The National Széchényi Library in Budapest makes it possible for its records to be downloaded by other libraries. The library's OPAC allows users to search simultaneously its own catalogue and the catalogues of other libraries that are suitably equipped (Horváth, 1998).

Conversion of the existing catalogues of national libraries has been going on for almost 20 years. National libraries are still confronted with two main problems: file size and data structure do not always allow the use of conventional methods. In the UK, the BL's OPAC 97 now provides free access via the Web to more than 8.5 million records in seven catalogues, covering its major collections in London and Boston Spa, with dates of publication ranging from 1450 to the present day (Ashton, 1998).

The implementation of the Z39.50 protocol in Canada, the USA, Australia and Europe was promoted by the availability of public domain software and a demonstration client system. Some national libraries are preparing for full implementation; others, like the National Library of Canada, are investigating the compatibility of Z39.50 with the Interlibrary Loan Protocol Standard in order to use it for requests, holdings and circulation information. It is planned that the

Canadian virtual catalogue should complement the existing union catalogue at the NLC by providing access to all types of information resources held by libraries. The library purchased more than eight million bibliographic records from 46 Canadian libraries; this represents a valuable contribution to the virtual Canadian union catalogue. The records for electronic publications are included in *Canadiana* (National, 1998). Following the decision on new levels of cataloguing for *Canadiana*, the NLC succeeded in reducing backlogs and improving the availability of records to other libraries (McKeen, 1998).

Discussing the future of the *British National Bibliography*, the UK Library and Information Commission (LIC) prepared a response paper to the British Library stating its policy. LIC recommended that the BL should retain responsibility for the production of *BNB*; processes should be put in place to improve coverage and content, and output and access routes should be prioritized to take into account the electronic environment within which the UK information society operates. Plans for the future of *BNB* should also include a strategy for continuous product enhancement so that it has the flexibility to be a genuinely inclusive bibliography for the UK (Library and Information Commission, 1998).

Bell (1998) presents results of her investigation on the state of the art and development of national bibliographies in the Commonwealth of Independent States. She describes the scope, coverage, arrangement, classification scheme and indexes in the current national bibliography within each state of the CIS.

Kovács (1997) describes the current state of the Hungarian programme for a national bibliographic network, and Berke (1998) gives an overview of the Hungarian retrospective bibliography, describing especially failed plans and problems that have still to be solved. A decision has to be made whether a computerized retrospective national bibliography or a computerized retrospective online catalogue is to be prepared. She also makes detailed proposals for complete retroconversion. Van den Berg (1998) writes about the state of the art and trends in bibliographic control in the Netherlands.

The main problems and issues of bibliographic control were discussed at an International Conference on National Bibliographic Services held in Copenhagen (International, 1998b). The conference endorsed the concept of Universal Bibliographic Control (UBC) as a worldwide system for the control and exchange of bibliographic information. The need was again emphasized to strengthen national bibliographic control, as a prerequisite for universal control. Although it is widely accepted that national libraries and national bibliographic agencies may work cooperatively with other agencies, it is felt that the overall responsibility for coordination and implementation of standards should rest with the national bibliographic agency. The inclusion of bibliographic records for electronic publications in the same catalogue as other materials is advisable for the convenience of readers. It is important, however, that these publications can be identified in such a way that listings may be produced for preservation and other purposes. The Copenhagen conference reaffirmed the value of legal deposit as a means of ensuring that the cultural and intellectual heritage and linguistic diversity of each state is preserved and made accessible for current and future users.

Issues related to national bibliographic records in the digital environment with special attention to metadata, links and standards are discussed by Day *et al.* (1999). There is no doubt among the profession that the creation of records for electronic publications should be based on standardized cataloguing rules. However, as the legal deposit of electronic publications is a new area which is still developing, obviously national libraries are not yet able to provide records for the majority of electronic publications. Thus, the inclusion of this material in the national bibliography need not depend on their availability through the deposit system, and additional sources of records should be sought.

Preservation and conservation

In the age of global communications digital preservation is a global problem. Several reports emphasize the need to prepare national preservation strategies as well as to develop and adopt international standards while carrying out long-term digital preservation programmes (e.g. Björdal, 1998; Stephan, 1998; Tsagouria, 1998; Whiffin and Havermans, 1998).

Lyall (1998) reports on a survey carried out in early 1997. A questionnaire designed to collect information on national preservation programmes was distributed to the 123 national libraries registered with the IFLA Section on National Libraries. Only 50 responses were received, 26 of which indicated that their country did not have such a national plan. Lyall highlights some focal points to be considered in developing a national preservation programme.

In 1998 a worldwide survey of digitized collections in major cultural institutions – an IFLA PAC/UAP Joint Project – began with the distribution of questionnaires to national libraries to gather information on their digitization programmes. Information is also being collected on preservation issues relating to digitized material (Worldwide, 1999).

Some existing national strategies are described in the literature. In the UK the National Preservation Office at the British Library is developing a national strategy for digital preservation which includes 'assembling best practices; developing scaleable and costed models for converting, accessing, and preserving digital information; identifying areas needing research and evaluation; coordinating UK initiatives in these areas; exploring funding models; and mobilizing resources' (British Library, 1998a).

In Sweden, the Royal Library is leading work on standards for metadata and digital preservation strategies for electronic publications. As Lidman (1998b) reports, 'Kulturar W3', the Swedish Web Archiving Project, was initially financed by a government grant of SKr3 million to test methods of collecting, preserving and providing access to Swedish electronic documents; it is using robots to identify and download all Swedish Web pages.

In Australia, distributed responsibilities in the preservation and access field are commonly accepted. The National Library's Pandora Project is capturing, archiving and providing long-term access to significant Australian online publications. Like the policies being adopted for preservation of official electronic records, the Australian national strategy for long-term access to electronic publications assumes cooperative arrangements among creators, publishers, libraries and archives. The development of standards, the use of metadata, the establishment of criteria and priorities, and the distribution of responsibility for preservation are all matters of great concern. Only about 10% of electronic publications identified by the National Library of Australia as having potential research value have so far been selected for preservation; of about 180 titles among them only 30 are used to test business principles and technical capability through a 'proof-of-concept' archive (Layland, 1998b; W. Smith, 1998).

Perminova (1998) writes about preservation in Russian libraries and the role of the Russian State Library as a centre for preservation. An investigation in which 170 libraries and museums participated shows that a great number of documents – 735,000 – needed to be preserved.

Deacidification treatment is another important protection issue. The Library of Congress Mass Deacidification Program, which has strong support from the US Congress, provides leadership in the development and evaluation of deacidification processes on a mass scale, and in their application to increasingly large numbers of books and other paper-based items, so as to achieve economies of scale. Within four years, the library intends to deacidify up to 275,000 books. This treatment is reserved for books, manuscripts and archival material that are at risk of loss; the fact that 'Americana' are to be selected for early treatment indicates the stress placed on rescuing endangered volumes from collections that are central to the library's mission (Dizard, 1998; Harris, 1998; Library, 1998).

A number of national libraries are using microfilming as a method of protecting their national cultural heritage. In the Staatsbibliothek zu Berlin, Preussischer Kulturbesitz, some 80% of the J.S. Bach's autographs are stored in microform. Most of them are threatened with disintegration through corrosion caused by Bach's use of iron gall ink, which changes over time from black to a dull brown. When the project Musikhandschriften der Staatsbibliothek zu Berlin was conceived, it was clear that in addition to preserving and restoring the originals it would also be necessary to create a security (or master) copy, particularly valuable sources on film (Penzold, 1997).

The goals and recent achievements of UNESCO's Memory of the World programme are presented by Abid (1998) with special attention to its pilot projects, while IFLA's PAC Core Programme is overviewed by Varlamoff (1998), who specifies activities in regional centres as well as the plans for the new regional centre in Moscow.

Buildings

In attempting to focus on questions related to spatial problems of national libraries, one should not exclude two problems which are influencing the 'era of new national library buildings'. The first is a consequence of the ever-increasing use of IT in libraries in general, the other arises from the need for national libraries to provide accessible services to the general public. Some of the new buildings are good examples of such services in at least two ways: by allowing the public to use restricted services, such as open reading rooms (e.g. in the Bibliothèque nationale de France), and by digitizing the most wanted materials such as newspapers.

The concepts behind new national library buildings, the projects themselves, and the phases of their building are described and discussed in professional journals and newsletters, as well as on Web pages all over the world. Italians have translated Melot's article (1998) and contributed with their views on the relevant issues (*Biblioteca*, 1998; Bruni, 1998; Lùperi, 1998; Solimine, 1998). Whole issues of two major architecture journals, one English and the other French, were devoted to major library buildings (*Architectural Review*, 1998; *Techniques et Architecture*, 1998). Among national libraries described were those in London, Stockholm, Frankfurt a/M and Paris. Fritz (1998) reviewed a LIBER – Architecture Group Seminar in London in April 1998, where 130 participants from 20 European countries contributed to a discussion on the concept of the multifunctional library. The aim of an international conference on construction issues of national libraries, held in Riga in August 1998, was to analyse both the basic social and professional ideas that had led to changes in the con-ceptualization of European national library buildings, and practical experiences in their construction (International, 1998a).

Last but not least, there are a comprehensive book on the design and construction of the new British Library building in London by its architect (Wilson, 1998), and a lengthy article which discusses the ideas, political implications, planning process and first results of the BnF (Davies and Johnson, 1998).

Jakac-Bizjak (1998a) examines the acute working and storage problems of the National and University Library in Ljubljana. The library was forced to hire additional depositories, scattered around Ljubljana and its surroundings, as well as to convert former reading rooms into working and storage areas. In accordance with the decision of the Slovenian government, the projects of the new library for the National and University Library (NUL) and the Ljubljana University Library were together named Ljubljana University Library (LUL) Project. The new building is meant to house both libraries, but the title of the project creates confusion and a misunderstanding in the public mind that only a university library is being built. The problems related to the perception of the role of the Czech National Library within the county's cultural context, and the implications for the planning of its projected new building, are elaborated by Balik (1998b).

In cooperation with the Directorate of Public Construction and Property, the National Library of Norway has planned how to improve and reconstruct the old building in Oslo while keeping its exterior and parts of its interior untouched. Since it was expected that from January 1999 the situation of the library would change, as the Oslo Division separated from the University of Oslo Library, parliament decided that the old main building of Oslo University Library in the centre of Oslo, which dates from 1913, should be transferred to the National Library in 1999. It was planned to transfer parts of the collections to the new University of Oslo Library, and to keep the Norwegian and Nordic collections, as well as the special collections, in the Oslo Division of the National Library (Nilsen, 1998).

Helsinki University Library's Fabiania building, next to the main library building, opened on 1 June 1998. This old institute building has been restored and equipped with modern facilities for use as a library. The final goal, for all services of the library to be under one roof, will be achieved when the restored rotunda in the main building is opened in autumn 1999 and the underground stacks in 2000 (Linnovaara, 1998). In Canada a new facility was announced, to be located in Montreal; this will combine the holdings of the Bibliothèque municipale de Montréal and the Bibliothèque nationale du Québec (Sauvageau, 1998).

The National Library of Australia has built a new warehouse for about 850,000 volumes (15% of its holdings). This is, as Welbourn (1998) reports, the world's only major library using mechanical stock-pickers for getting volumes from unusually high shelves. The renovation of the research reading room in the Deutsche Bücherei in Leipzig is examined by Neumann (1998).

The British Library and the Bibliothèque nationale de France attracted much public attention both in their respective countries and abroad, in newspapers and on TV as well as in the professional literature. There are numerous articles about their new buildings, strategic plans, new services, expectations and the experiences of users and colleagues, etc. (Davies and Johnson, 1998; Day, 1998a; 1998b; Foot, 1998; James, 1998; Jouguelet, 1998; B. Smith, 1998). They cannot be covered in detail in this chapter, but are worthy of mentioning as a source of comments and opinions.

In special issues of *LIBER Quarterly* dedicated to map librarianship spatial problems of map departments are dealt with (Bäärnhielm, 1998; Höhener, 1998; Pelletier and Dumoulin, 1998).

International cooperation

A number of Europe-wide projects have been supported by the European Union's Library and Telematics Programme. Some of the projects already have visible results in networked access to the catalogues of national libraries; others report regularly at conferences or on their respective Web pages.

Bourne (1998) describes trends and issues in bibliographic cooperation among European national libraries, focusing on COBRA (Lehmann, 1996) and COBRA+ (Dale, 1999), BIBLINK (BIBLINK), DELICAT (DELICAT) and NEDLIB (NEDLIB) activities. It is clear that European national libraries can and do work together, to their mutual benefit.

There have been notable international initiatives in authority control. The requirement for, and development of, the Anglo-American Authority File (AAAF) to underpin international cooperation has been recognized and executed through IFLA, the British Library, the Library of Congress and the American Library Association, as well as in the EC-funded project AUTHOR (Danskin, 1998).

Bunzel (1998a) reports on British–German cooperation in the realization of the DBV/OSI project. Several results of Z39.50 development in DBV/OSI have been transported to European level with the ONE project and its follow up ONE II. Gömpel (1998) describes the cooperative efforts of the national libraries of France, Germany, Switzerland and the UK in a project which started in 1998 and is aimed at developing a prototype for multilingual subject access, thus allowing interconnection between subject headings in English, French and German.

In July 1998 the European Commission and the German Libraries Institute (DBI) signed a contract for a project called EXPLOIT; this is a Pan-European project on Exploitation of the Results of the Libraries Programme, which is part of the EU Telematics Applications Programme (*EXPLOIT*). The other main partners in the project are the British Council and UKOLN at the University of Bath.

The Biblioteca Nacional of Spain, in addition to sending bibliographic data to the Research Libraries Group (RLG), has continued to build bridges with libraries in South America. The library works closely with ABINIA (Asociación de Bibliotecas Nationales de Iberoamérica), as does the Biblioteca Nacional of Portugal. For the Novum Regestrum (union catalogue of rare books) an agreement was signed with the Biblioteca Nacional of Argentina to exchange bibliographic records, to update the database and to exchange staff under an internal scheme (Planet, 1998).

Cooperation in the Nordic countries has changed, as Lidman (1998a) reports: NORDINFO now concentrates on supporting specialized IT projects. The national libraries in Scandinavian countries are cooperating more and more closely, and are finding common solutions in various problem areas. Meanwhile, constructive regional cooperation between the libraries in the Baltic region flourishes, with notable involvement of the national libraries of Estonia, Lithuania and Latvia.

The cooperative activities of the National Diet Library, and their results, were reported regularly in *NDL News* in 1988. The mutual visit programme is described, with particular attention to questioning the functions of national libraries in the digital age. Other 'traditional' issues which have been raised at previous visits, such as staff exchange, cooperation in the development and use of bibliographic databases, and cooperation in document supply, are also covered. In connection with a planned Asian Resource Information Centre in the new Kansai-kan building, the contribution of the National Library of China, and of other important national libraries in the region, in obtaining Chinese material was discussed at various meetings, e.g. with representatives of the Korean National Library (Exchange, 1998).

On the international stage an important role is played by IFLA's Section on National Libraries. In 1998, at the General Conference in Amsterdam, a new Medium Term Programme (1998–2001) for the section was set out (IFLA, 1998). The action plan for 1998–99 encompassed ten tasks, ranging from the development and implementation of strategic and business plans for national libraries, development of guidelines for exploitation and preservation of the national imprint (which calls for the revision of the *Guidelines for Legal Deposit*), to the further fostering of international and regional cooperation and examination of the tasks of the national library as a bibliographic agency.

Conclusion

The values and mission of national libraries in the digital era are challenged in both new and old ways. National libraries continue to concentrate on their traditional symbolic functions, as well as developing new public services. They also continue to report on historical themes and ongoing projects related to the study of book and library history (e.g. Cobabus, 1997; Frolova, 1998). But they are aware that new challenges have to be met with new ideas, clear vision and professional competence. Simultaneously they are looking for new partners to make their services available as widely as possible, not only to researchers but to the general public.

Coordination is also an essential element in an environment where digital materials are distributed and responsibility is shared. A number of examples illustrate how coordination might be accomplished, nationally and internationally, between sectors based on the Global Information Infrastructure. There should, for example, be linkages between higher education and discipline-based information centres, and across the different spheres of libraries, archives, and museums. Although efforts to achieve higher levels of coordination at an international level often become too unwieldy or too distant from many of the actors and stakeholders, there are examples of sound cooperative projects and of the exchange of ideas, knowledge and experience. There is still plenty of research and development to be done internationally in the areas of standards, software and systems development. The contribution of national libraries in all these areas is significant.

Acknowledgements

The author would like to thank colleagues from the Royal School of Library and Information Science's Library in Copenhagen, the National Széchényi Library in Budapest and the National and University Library in Ljubljana for their kindness and help.

References

200 (1998) years: new projects celebrate Library's bicentennial. *Library of Congress Bulletin*, **57**(11), 264.

Abid, A. (1998) *Memoire du monde: preserver notre patrimoine documentaire*. [Paper presented at the 64th IFLA Conference, Amsterdam. (Booklet 0. 099-69-F, 82–94).]

Age (1998) of Information and National Libraries. [Conference held at the Österreichische Nationalbibliothek, 3–4 April, 1998.] *Presentations*.
   http://www.onb.ac.at/newsev/sympo1/sy1fr.htm

Architectural Review (1998) June.

Arvidson, A. and Lettenström, F. (1998) The Kulturarw Project: the Swedish Royal Web Archive. *Electronic Library*, **16**(2), 105–108.

Ashton, J. (1998) Development of the British Library's OPAC 97: the value of a user-centred approach. *Program*, **32**(1), 1–24.

Bäärnhielm, G. (1998) Rebuilding of the Royal Library, Stockholm. *LIBER Bulletin*, **8**(2), 194–202.

Balik, V. (1998a). The National Electronic Library: the situation in the Czech Republic. *LIBER Quarterly*, **8**(1), 7–14.

Balik, V. (1998b) *A new building for the Czech National Library?* [Paper presented at the Conference 'Construction of new national libraries', Riga, Latvia, 24–26 August 1998.]
   http://vip.latnet.lv/lnb/KONF/balik.htm

Beer, J. de (1999) National libraries around the world, 1996–97: a review of the literature. *Alexandria*, **10**(1), 3–37.

Bélaval, P. (1998) The Bibliothèque nationale de France: an update. *Alexandria*, **10**(1), 85–86.

Bell, B.L. (1998) Current national bibliographies in the Commonwealth of Independent States and the Baltic states. *Alexandria*, **10**(3), 171–177.

Berke, B.A (1998) Magyar Nemzeti Bibliográfia retrospectiv adatbázisa. [The retrospective database of the Hungarian National Bibliography.] *Könyvtári Figyelö*, **44**(2), 229–238.

BIBLINK. http://hosted.ukoln.ac.uk/biblink/

Biblioteca (1998) *tra spazio e progetto*. Milano: Editrice Bibliografica.

Billington, J.H. (1998) Libraries, the Library of Congress, and the information age. In: S.R. Graubard and P. LeClerc. (eds) *Books, bricks & bytes: libraries in the twenty-first century*. New Brunswick, NJ: Transaction Publishers, pp. 35–54.

Björdal, L. (1998) A national preservation plan for Swedish libraries.
   http://www.kb.se/ENG/Bjor-pa.htm (accessed 15.05.2000).

Borbinha, J.L. (1998) Digital libraries: a perspective from Portugal. *LIBER Quarterly*, **8**(1), 81–85.

Bourne, R. (1998) Towards bibliographic cooperation amongst European national libraries. *LIBER Quarterly*, **8**(1), 106–109.

British (1998a) Library selects AMICUS software. *Program*, **32**(1), 67–68.

British (1998b) Library signs right agreements with publishers. *Program*, **32**(1), 69–70.

British Library (1998a) *Digital remit*.
http://minos.bl.uk/services/preservation/digital.htm (accessed 15.05.2000).

British Library (1998b) *Legal deposit of publications: a consultation paper*.
http://www.bl.uk/information/legal-deposit (accessed 15.05.2000).

British Library (1998c) *Toward the digital library*.
http://www.bl.uk/services/ric/diglib/digilib.html (accessed 11.05.2000).

Bruni, R. (1998) Da tognèt a Sir Anthony. *Biblioteche Oggi*, **16**(2), 10–15.

Bryant, T. (1998) Strategic planning at the Library of Congress. *LIBER Quarterly*, **8**(4), 370–372.

Bunzel, J. (1998a) Building the digital library in Germany: an overview. *LIBER Quarterly*, **8**(1), 23–37.

Bunzel, J. (1998b) The Digital Library Programme of the Deutsche Forschungsgemeinschaft. *ABI-Technik*, **18**(2), 132–137.

Carpenter, L. *et al.* (1998) (eds) *Towards the digital library: the Initiatives for Access Programme*. London: British Library.

Cataloging (1997) foreign publications at the NCL. *National Central Library* [of Taiwan] *Newsletter*, **29**(2), 5–6.

Christensen, K. *et al.* (1998) Electronic libraries in Norway. *LIBER Quarterly*, **8**(1), 334–341.

Cobabus, N. (1997) Ein doppelter Grund zum Feiern: Deutsche Bibliothek, Frankfurt am Main. *Laurentius: von Menschen, Büchern und Bibliotheken*, **14**(2), 71–75.

Cornish, G.P. (1998) National libraries. In: M.B. Line (ed.) *Librarianship and Information Work Worldwide 1998*. East Grinstead: Bowker Saur, pp. 19–40.

Dale, P. (1999) CoBRA+: a review, with a look to the future. *Alexandria*, **11**(3), 161–166.

Danskin, A. (1998) International initiatives in authority control. *Library Review*, **47**(4), 200–205.

Davies, J. (1998) Safe deposit: a UK publishing view. *Alexandria*, **10**(2), 159–166.

Davies, S. and Johnson, I.M. (1998) The Mitterrand Library in context: the Bibliothèque nationale de France and library provision in France. *Libri*, **48**(4), 187–211.

Day, A. (1998a) I was there. *Library Review*, **47**(3/4), 179–182.

Day, A. (1998b) *Inside the British Library*. London: Library Association Publishing.

Day, M. *et al.* (1999) National bibliographic records in the digital information environment: metadata, links and standards. *Journal of Documentation*, **55**(1), 16–32.

DELICAT Project [Data Enhancement of Library Catalogues.]
http://www.bl.uk/gabriel/en/projects/delicat.html (accessed 11.05.2000)

Demand (1998) 1997/98. *British Library Document Supply News*, (58), 1.

de Niet, M. (1998a) Europe's national libraries in line: a report of the Gabriel workshop 1997. *Program*, **32**(3), 303–311.

de Niet, M. (1998b) A single access point to information resources: the advanced information workstation of the National Library of the Netherlands. *Resource Sharing and Information Networks*, **13**(2), 29–37.

Denmark (1997) *Act on Copyright Deposit of Published Works.*
  http://www.sb.aau.dk/english/legal_deposit.html#act (accessed 15.05.2000).
Deutsche Bibliothek (1998) Erste Schritte zur nationalen digitalen Bibliothek. *BuB-Journal,*
  50(12), 684.
Digital (1998) *Services Project.* http://www.nla.gov.au/dsp
Dizard, R. (1998) Safe and sound: protecting the collections at the Library of Congress.
  Library of Congress Information Bulletin, **57**(6), 144–145.
Duru, E.C. (1997) Internet connectivity in libraries and information centres in Nigeria.
  Information Services and Use, **17**(1), 61–68.
Electronic (1997) *Research Library of Denmark. Summary.* H.M. Kvaenderup (ed.)
  Copenhagen: National Library Authority.
Enyia, C.O. (1998) National Library of Nigeria at 30: its history and prospects. *Journal of
  Government Information,* **25**(2), 149–159.
European (1998) library declaration on behalf of European national, academic and research
  libraries. *LIBER Quarterly,* **8**(1), 491–494.
Exchange (1998) Programme of NDL. *NDL Newsletter,* (106), 1–8.
EXPLOIT: a project designed to support the distribution and exploitation of EU research results.
  http://www.di-berlin.de/exploit.htm
Ferguson (1998) *Project.* http://www.nla.gov.au/ferg (accessed 15.05.2000).
Fineberg, G. (1998) Cooperative cataloguing: LC promotes cooperation at Asian Materials
  Seminar. *Library of Congress Information Bulletin,* **57**(5), 120–121.
Fischer, A. (1998) The year in review: milestones and achievement mark 1997. *Library of
  Congress Information Bulletin,* **57**(3) 58–61, 63.
Fischer Jonge, I. (1998). The National Museum of Photography at the Royal Library,
  Copenhagen. *Art Libraries Journal,* **23**(1), 8–12.
Foot, R. (1998) Automating the British Library – a case study in project implementation.
  New Library World, **99**(1140), 69–71.
Fritz, G. (1998) The multifunctional library: Das LIBER-Architecture-Group Seminar in
  London. *ABI-Technik,* **18**(3), 266–271.
Frolova, I.I. (1998) The study of the history of the Russian book at the Russian National
  Library. *Solanus,* (12), 5–11.
Fullerton, J. (1998) Developing national collections of electronic publications: issues to
  be considered and recommendations for future collaborative actions. *Newsletter of the
  IFLA Section on National Libraries,* (December), 45–50.
Gabriel: gateway to Europe's national libraries. http://www.bl.uk/gabriel
Garrod, J. (1998) Libraries in the Principality of Monaco. *Focus on International Librarianship,*
  29(1), 3–7.
Gömpel, R. (1998) Das war 1997. *Dialog mit Bibliotheken,* **10**(1), 5–8.
Häkli, E. (1998a) Developing strategies for electronic libraries. *Helsinki University Library
  Bulletin,* 3–5. http://renki.lib.helsinki.fi/
Häkli, E. (1998b) The development of a national electronic library in Finland. *LIBER
  Quarterly,* **8**(1), 342–350.
Häkli, E. (1998c) Towards a new legal deposit act. *Helsinki University Library Bulletin,* 14–15.
  http://renki.lib.helsinki.fi/
Harris, K.E. (1998) Library of Congress Mass Deacidification Program. *ARL: a Bimonthly
  Newsletter of Research Library Issues and Actions,* (119).
  http://www.arl.org/newsltr/199/harris.html

Hefele, B. (1998) Das neue Netzwerk (LAN) der Bayerischen Staatsbibliothek. *ABI-Technik*, **18**(3), 234–242.

Hendrikz, F. (1998) Marketing a national library: practical experiences from the State Library of South Africa. *Alexandria*, **10**(3), 179–190.

Höhener, H.-P. (1998) The problem of the map department within the construction of a new library: the case of the Zentralbibliothek Zürich. *LIBER Bulletin*, **8**(2), 203–211.

Hogh, H. (1998) Slovenská národná knjižnica v Matici Slovenskej v roku 1998. *Knižnice a informácie*, **30**(1), 1–4.

Horváth, Á. (1998) Rendeszervaltas az OSZK-ban, a kozremukodo szemevel [Changing systems in the National Széchényi Library.] *Könyvtári Figyelö*, **44**(2), 219–228.

House (1998) hears LC budget request: Librarian requests 6.5% increase for FY 1999. *Library of Congress Information Bulletin*, **57**(3), 43, 65–67.

IFLA. (1998) National Libraries Section. Medium Term Programme/1998–2001/. *Newsletter of IFLA's Section on National Libraries*, (December), 5.

International (1998a) Conference. Construction of new national libraries: a phenomenon of the end of 20th century Europe. Riga, Latvia, 24–26 August [*Proceedings*]. http://vip.latnet.lv/lnb/KONF/conf2.htm

International (1998b) Conference on National Bibliographic Services. *Final recommendations*. http://www.ifla.org/VI/3/icnbs/fina.htm

Jakac-Bizjak, V. (1998a) The National and University Library in Ljubljana: the reasons for a new building. *Zeitschrift für Bibliothekswesen und Bibliographie*, (70) 59–63 [special issue].

Jakac-Bizjak, V. (1998b) Planning the national electronic library in Slovenia. *LIBER Quarterly*, **8**(1) 285–297.

James, S. (1998) Moving the British Library. *Library Review*, **47**(3), 183–186.

Järvenpää, M. (1998) Less money, more management. *Helsinki University Library Bulletin*, 22–24. http://renki.lib.helsinki.fi/

Jeremiah, D. (1998) Procurements of a system to process non-print materials at the National Library of Wales. *Program*, **32**(1), 49–54.

Jouguelet, S. (1998) Various applications of the Dewey Decimal Classification at the Bibliothèque nationale de France. *Library Review*, **47**(4), 206–210.

Knoll, A. (1998) Digitisation of old documents in the National Library of the Czech Republic: a complex solution. *VINE*, (107), 44–50.

Kovács, I. (1997) Az OSZK hungarika bibliográfiai programjanak helyzete és fejlesztési tervei. [The state of the Hungarica Bibliography Programme and plans for further development]. *Könyv, könyvtár, konyvtáros*, (October), 31–36.

Kozsely, M. (1998) National bibliographies from libraries around the world enrich WorldCat. *OCLC Newsletter*, (May/June), 41.

Kulturna (1998) *politika Republike Hrvatske: nacionalni izvještaj* [Cultural policy of the Republic of Croatia: a national report]. Zagreb: Ministarstvo kulture Republike Hrvatske (European programme for the evaluation of national cultural policies).

Kuznetsova, T.J. (1997) Nacional'nye biblioteki Respublik Rossii kak centry informacionnogo modelirovanija nacional'nyh kul'tur. *Bibliotekovedenie*, (3), 3–17.

Kvaenderup, H.M. and Thorhauge, J. (1998) Denmark's Electronic Research Library. *LIBER Quarterly*, **8**(1), 15–22.

Lang, B. (1998) Legal deposit of electronic materials. [Summary.] *Newsletter of the IFLA Section on National Libraries*, (December), 25.

Lang, L. (1998). 4. GKD-Redaktion an der Österreichischen Nationalbibliothek in Wien. *Mitteilungen der Vereiningung Österreichischer Bibliothekarinnen und Bibliothekare*, **51**(3/4), 79–80.

Larsen, S. (1998) Contract management in research libraries: the Danish case: the contract of the State and University Library and the Royal Library with the Ministry of Culture. *LIBER Quarterly*, **8**(3), 351–363.

Layland, P. (1998a) Electronic dilemma. *National Library of Australia News*, **8**(1), 13–15.

Layland, P. (1998b) The Register of Australian Archives and Manuscripts (RAM). *National Library of Australia News*, **8**(4), 8–9.

Lehmann, K.-D. (1996). European national libraries and the CoBRA Forum of the EU Libraries Programme. *Alexandria*, **8**(3), 155–166.

Lehmann, K.-D. (1998a) Die Deutsche Bibliothek as a European digital deposit library. *LIBER Quarterly*, **8**(3), 319–333.

Lehmann, K.-D. (1998b) La Deutsche Bibliothek: son rôle dans création d'une bibliothèque numérique pour l'Europe. *Bulletin des Bibliothèques de France*, **43**(4), 28–35.

Lehmann, K.-D. (1998c) Das elektonische Plichtexemplar: die Role der Nationalbibliothek. [Paper presented at the 4th European Bielefeld Kolloquium, Bielefeld, 10–12 February, 1998.]

Library and Information Commission [UK] (1998) *Consultation paper on the future of the national bibliography*. http://www.bl.uk/services/bsds/nbs/bnbcons.html

Library (1998) of Congress initiates massive library automation effort. *Information Retrieval and Library Automation*, **34**(1), 4–5.

Lidman, T. (1998a) National libraries as a resource for the future provision of information. [Paper presented at the 4th European Bielefeld Kolloquium, Bielefeld, 10–12 February, 1998.]

Lidman, T. (1998b) The problems with web-archiving: experiences from the Cultural Heritage Project in Sweden. *Newsletter of the IFLA Section on National Libraries*, (December), 31–38.

Lidman, T. (1998c) Towards the National Electronic Library: Sweden. *LIBER Quarterly*, **8**(1), 86–89.

Line, M.B. (1998) What do national libraries do in the age of the Internet? *Ariadne*, (13), 6–7. http://www.ariadne.ac.uk/issues13/main/intro.html (accessed 15.05.2000).

Line, M.B. (1999) National libraries and service to the general public [editorial]. *Alexandria*, **11**(1), 1–2.

Linnovaara, K. (1998) Fabiania – new building, better services. *Helsinki University Library Bulletin*, 16–18. http://renki.lib.helsinki.fi/

Lor, P. (1998) Legislation for national library services in developing countries. *Alexandria*, **10**(2), 93–103.

Lùperi, P. (1998) The British Library: progetti di ieri e di oggi. *Biblioteche Oggi*, **16**(9), 22–25.

Lyall, J. (1998) National preservation programmes: 'such stuff as dreams are made on'. *IFLA Journal*, **24**(1), 42–47.

McCormick, P. and Scott, M. (1999) National libraries. In: M.B. Line (ed.) *Librarianship and Information Work Worldwide 1999*. East Grinstead: Bowker Saur, pp. 15–44.

McGowan, I. (1998) Measuring results of programmes. *Newsletter of the IFLA Section on National Libraries*, (December), 22–23.

McKeen, L. (1998) Canadiana levels of cataloguing. *National Library* [of Canada] *News*, **30**(1), 9–11.

Majerova, J. (1998) Fondy Slovenskej národnej knjižnice: kultúrno-informaèný fenomén a pamät národa. *Knjižnice a Informácie*, **30**(8/9), 304–307.

Marte, H. (1998) Gabriel: gateway to Europe's national libraries. *Mitteilungen der Vereiningung Österreichischer Bibliothekarinnen und Bibliothekare*, **51**(3/4), 84–87.

Melot, M. (1998) Le nuove biblioteche nazionali. *Biblioteche Oggi*, **16**(9), 10–17.

Menou, M. (1998) Networking in the French-speaking countries and current trends in international assistance. *Bulletin of the American Society for Information Science*, **24**(5), 22–24.

Muswazi, P. (1998) The practicality of the Swaziland Union Catalogue: a retrospective study. *Libri*, **48**(2), 124–130.

National (1998) library purchases file from A-G Canada Ltd. *National Library News*, **30**(3/4), 1–2.

National Library of Australia (1999) *PADI: Preserving Access to Digital Information*. http://www.nla.gov.au/padi

National Library of Venezuela (1998) contributes Latin American records to EROMM. *Preservation and Access Newsletter*, (3), 3.

NEDLIB: Networked European Deposit Library. http://www.kb.nl/coop/nedlib/

Neumann, H.G. (1998) Restaurierung und Sanierung der Deutschen Bücherei Leipzig. *Dialog mit Bibliotheken*, **10**(1), 12–15.

New (1998) national system: AMICUS comes in first. *Library Times International*, **14**(4), 41.

News (1998) from ELiAS. *Program*, **32**(3), 313–315.

Nilsen, S. (1998) *Modern national libraries – new opportunities for promoting culture. A case study from Norway*. [Paper presented at the International Conference: Construction of New National Libraries, Riga, Latvia, 24–26 August, 1998.] http://vip.latnet.lv/lnb/KONF/sisele.htm

Noordermeer, T. *et al.* (1998) Electronic library developments in the Netherlands. *LIBER Quarterly*, **8**(1), 57–80.

Oddy, P. (1999) The case for international cooperation in cataloguing: from copy cataloguing to multilingual subject access: experience within the British Library. *Program*, **33**(1), 29–39.

Ogata, S.-I. (1998) The National Diet Library of Japan and its plans for the 21st century. *Alexandria*, **10**(3), 203–215.

Ohnemus, E. (1998) House hears LC budget request. *Library of Congress Information Bulletin*, **57**(3), 43, 65–67.

Pandora (1998) http://www.nla.gov.au/pandora (accessed 15.05.2000).

Peic, S. (1998) The destruction of a nation's heritage: libraries in Bosnia and Hercegovina, with special reference to the National and University Library. *Alexandria*, **10**(1), 77–84.

Pelletier, M. and Dumoulin, M.-F. (1998) De nouveaux chantiers pour le Départment des Cartes et Plans de la Bibliothèque nationale de France. *LIBER Quarterly*, **8**(2), 172–177.

Penzold, L. (1997) Microfilming of the Bach manuscripts in the Staatsbibliothek Berlin. *Microfilming and Imaging Review*, **27**(2), 50–53.

Perminova, O.I. (1998) Problemii sohrannosti biblioteèniih fondov. [Storage problems of library material]. *Bibliotekovedenie*, (1), 82–91.

Peters, M. (1998) Deposit of electronic works under US copyright law: requirements, issues and practical experience. *Newsletter of the IFLA Section on National Libraries*, (December), 26–30.

Planet, A. (1998) The Biblioteca de Catalunya: towards the next millennium. *Alexandria*, 10(3), 191–202.

Prochaska, A. (1998) The British Library and its digital future as a research library. *Library Review*, 47(5/6), 311–316.

Ramlau-Klekowska, K. (1998) Nowa ustawa o egzemplarzu obowiazkowym na cenzurowanym. [New legal deposit law on scrutiny]. *Przglad Biblioteczny*, (1), 39–52.

Renoult, D. (1998) Innovation for arts and sciences: new technology in the French National Library. *Art Libraries Journal*, 23(3), 20–21.

Ronai, I. and Skaliczki, J. (1997) A könyvtárak és közgyûjtemények szerepe az informaciós társa dalomban [The role of libraries and other public collections in the information society]. *Könyv, Könyvtár, Könyvtáros*, (September), 39–45.

Salonharju, I. (1998) Electra – network access to scientific journal articles. *Helsinki University Library Bulletin*, 10–11. http://renki.lib.helsinki.fi/

Sauvageau, P. (1998) La Bibliothèque nationale du Québec. *Alexandria*, 10(2), 105–129.

Schmiede, R. (1998) GLOBAL INFO - The German Digital Library Project: development and perspective. *ABI-Technik*, 18(2), 147–153.

Scott, M. (1998) Core competencies. *Newsletter of the IFLA Section on National Libraries*, (December), 17–21.

Sicco, M. (1998) Guidelines for digitizing collections in Italian libraries. *LIBER Quarterly*, 8(1), 49–56.

Sigurðsson, E. (1998a) The National and University Library of Iceland. *Alexandria*, 10(2), 143–157.

Sigurðsson, E. (1998b) The national electronic library: Iceland. *LIBER Quarterly*, 8(1), 38–48.

Skender, D. (1998) National and University Library – library for the future – Zagreb, Croatia. *Zeitschrift für Bibliothekswesen und Bibliographie*, (70), 55–58 [special issue].

Smethurst, J.M. (1998) European national libraries: a review of the year's activities. *LIBER Quarterly*, 8(3), 235–284.

Smirnova, J.P. (1997) Informacionnoe vzaimodejstvie nacional'nykh bibliotek stran SNG. *Bibliotekovedenie*, (3), 3–10.

Smith, B. (1998) The new British Library: first anniversary. *New Library World*, 99(1145), 276–286.

Smith, M. (1998) Director's message. *Document Supply News*, (60), 1–3.

Smith, W. (1998) PANDORA: providing long-term access to Australia's online electronic publications. *Alexandria*, 10(1), 63–75.

Solimine, G. (1998) Grandi biblioteche a confronto. *Biblioteche Oggi*, 16(9), 18–21.

Steenbakkers, J. (1998) Handling electronic publications: practices and projects. *Newsletter of the IFLA Section on National Libraries*, (December), 38–45.

Stephan, W. (1998) *Die Deutsche Bibliothek: house of book and electronic archives*. http://www.kb.se/ENG/Steph_pa.htm (accessed 15.05.2000).

Stoker, D. (1998) Where does the British Library go from St. Pancras? *Journal of Librarianship and Information Science*, 30(3), 155–157.

Techniques et Architecture (1998), (436).

Thornely, J. (1998) The road to metadata: the implementation of Dublin Core metadata in the State Library of Queensland website. *Australian Library Journal*, 47(1), 74–82.

Tolèinskaja, L. (1998) Razvitie nacional'nogo fonda v novoj informacionnoj srede. *Biblioteka*, (6), 42–43.

Tsagouria, M.-L. (1998) *The preservation policy of the Bibliothèque nationale de France: its importance in preserving the cultural heritage of the French libraries.* http://www.kb.se/ENG/Tsagouri.htm (accessed 15.05.2000).

Van den Berg, K. (1998) Bibliographic control in the Netherlands. *International Cataloguing and Bibliographic Control,* **27**(2), 31–33.

Varlamoff, M-T. (1998) *PAC Core Programme: Preservation and Conservation.* [Paper presented at the 64th IFLA General Conference, Amsterdam (Booklet 0. 116-64-E, pp. 77–81).]

Welbourn, M. (1998) The library's new warehouse. *National Library of Australia News,* (February), 11–13.

Whiffin, J.I. and Havermans, J. (1998) (eds) *Library preservation and conservation in the '90s. Proceedings of the satellite meeting of the Section on Preservation and Conservation, Budapest, 15–17 August, 1995.* München: K.G. Saur (IFLA Publications 84).

Wilson, C. St John. (1998) *The design and construction of the British Library.* London: British Library.

Worldwide (1999) survey of digitized collections in major cultural institutions: an IFLA PAC/UAP joint project. *IFLA Journal,* **25**(2), 113.

Academic libraries 3

Philip Payne and
Elizabeth Waller

Introduction

As we enter the 21st century we are experiencing a tidal wave of change. This is sharply eroding the predominance of the printed word, transforming librarians' roles, sweeping away the library of the past, and altering the landscape of academic librarianship forever. It can be frightening, it can be threatening, but it is also one of the most exciting and exhilarating times to be working as an academic librarian.

The overwhelming preoccupation in the literature on academic libraries in 1998 is with the digital library, electronic services, global networking and communication, and their implications in every area of our work. Wilson (1998) talks of developments in academic libraries that are revolutionary in their impact and significance and Davies (1998) claims that 'uncertainty is the only certainty'. What role will academic libraries play in their institutions? How will technology change the processes of scholarly communication and what will this mean for libraries? How will academic libraries contribute to learning, teaching, and research? All of this is difficult to predict, especially as post-compulsory education, scholarly publishing, and the academic processes of learning, teaching, and research are evolving rapidly themselves. The changes that we are experiencing are more profound in their impact upon society, and more fundamental to today's world, than the invention of the printing press.

If the influences identified by Farley *et al.* (1998), Jordan (1998) and Edwards *et al.* (1998) are collated, the changes in higher education that are particularly affecting academic libraries are:

- *Mass higher education*: more students; greater diversity in the student population.
- *Consumerism*: higher expectations of students; increasing demand for 'any time, anywhere' education; more customer-oriented ethos among institutions.

- *Student finances*: students contributing more towards their education.
- *Course design*: trends towards a structure based on semesters and modules.
- *Teaching and learning methods*: growth of autonomous learning and resource-based learning, increased use of IT in learning, teaching and assessment.
- *Accountability of HE*: greater emphasis upon quality; new funding models to cope with mass higher education.
- *Funding*: demand for efficiency gains; pressures on library funding.

Three other interrelated drivers are having a particular effect on universities and upon their libraries:

- Growth of the information society.
- Developing communications and information technologies.
- Emphasis on lifelong learning.

The relationship between these drivers is complex but, collectively, they are having a fundamental effect on our lives. C.A. Lynch (1998a) states: 'We are in a time of great change; there are lots of cross-currents and opposing trends and forces surfacing as information technology begins to permeate our society and our institutions at all levels.'

Higher education and the information society

We are experiencing an explosion in the amount and diversity of information. Breivik (1998) reports the forecast of James Appleberry, the Executive Director of the American Association of State Schools and Colleges, that the sum of human knowledge will double every 73 days by 2020. There is also increased diversity of form, everything from the printed word to electronically delivered multimedia. The Internet offers a global infrastructure that fundamentally affects how people communicate and how information is accessed. This has led to a paradigm shift in the production, dissemination and utilization of information worldwide (Davies, 1998). People can now more readily share information, thoughts and ideas – through bulletin boards, newsgroups and their own Web sites. This has led to associated problems with information quality (Breivik, 1998; Dalton *et al.*, 1998; Haynes *et al.*, 1998; C.A. Lynch, 1998a) and the sheer amount of electronic information available, leading to information overload (Farley *et al.*, 1998; C.A. Lynch, 1998a; Walton and Edwards, 1998). Equally important, this paradigm shift is reinforcing old inequalities between developed and developing countries.

The lack of computing and communications infrastructures and the inability of researchers in the Third World fully to contribute to scientific communication mean that the gap between the 'information haves' and 'information have nots' is widening (Arunachalam, 1998). The imbalance in information access is exacerbated by the development of the global information industry, where the same electronic information products are increasingly being accessed worldwide, raising significant issues about creating an environment which sustains cultures, languages and diversity. Rosenberg (1998) concluded from a survey of nineteen university libraries in twelve countries in Africa that any library that shuns the introduction of IT threatens its own survival. Chisenga (1998) reports growing Internet connectivity in sub-Saharan Africa and that the setting up of websites allows university libraries to establish a presence on the Internet with the potential to contribute unique materials to the 'global digital library'. Younis (1998) highlights being connected to the Internet as a number one priority for Jordanian university libraries. Chuong (1998) stresses the importance of Internet access for enhancing the quality of the information resources and services available to Vietnam National University Library. Linking to the Internet is becoming as essential as being connected to water and electricity (Stein, 1998).

Governments are recognizing the growing significance and value of information in a wired-up world. There is widespread acceptance that healthy economic development depends upon the ability to compete in a global market (McLean, 1997). Certainly, the development of the information society is impacting significantly upon universities whose core business is the creation and utilization of knowledge. Hernández (1998) highlights the changes in communication within the international scientific community and the emergence of electronic scholarly journals. Tomney and Burton (1998) note that, although academics are not yet using e-journals extensively, they are becoming increasingly aware of the possibilities. However, there are concerns among academics about the quality and credibility of e-journals, which may affect use (Hamershlag, 1998; Picci, 1998; Pullinger, 1999; Tenner *et al.*, 1998). Tomney and Burton (1998) believe that the success or failure of e-journals rests with the academics themselves, as they contribute and read the articles. Valauskas (1998) observes that 'for many scholars, paper carries its own weight of authority, its very special solid aura that grants to each and every article a halo of acceptance and permanence; no electronic journal has this effect and none ever will'. Hamershlag concludes from a survey of academics at Tel Aviv University that they believe that career advancement may be threatened if they do not publish through traditional peer review processes. Nankivell (1999) highlights the concerns of senior academics at Birmingham University about the peer review process for e-journals. However, the substantive issue may be whether articles in electronic journals are given the same weight as those in print journals when the research productivity of academics is assessed (Tomney and Burton, 1998). Electronic journals are not new but the number of new titles is growing at a phenomenal rate. This is creating a critical mass which, as Tomney and Burton (1998) comment, need to be actively promoted and marketed by librarians, publishers, and professional associations.

Helfer (1998) describes the growing dissatisfaction among academics with the present publication system, especially the delay in publishing journal articles and with the surrender of intellectual property rights to publishers. Bentley (1998) believes that universities should take a more proactive role in the scholarly communication process. The economics of electronic publishing are not yet clear (McLean, 1997), but a senior executive with one major international scientific publisher believes that economics will lead to the transition from print to electronic journals irrespective of the views of academics (Hunter, 1998). Bot *et al.* (1998) describe a costing model for the *Electronic Journal of Comparative Law* (EJCL), a free-standing e-journal, which is jointly produced by Tilburg and Utrecht Universities in the Netherlands.

Beattie and McCallum (1998) report upon the Electronic Publishing Promotion Project in Canada. This project seeks to affirm the validity of the Internet as a publishing medium, to emphasize the cost saving of electronic publishing, and to declare the functionality and global accessibility of electronic formats. If this project fulfils its potential, and as other projects around the world come to fruition, we will see a radical change in the way publishing in the academic environment operates. Overall, Wilson (1998) believes that we are 'at the beginning of a very rapid revolution in scholarly communication, which has barely begun to impact upon many disciplines and which, yet, has had a readily discernible impact on others'. Hampson (1999) sees a greater emphasis upon print materials in arts and humanities, where serendipity may be important, and more electronic journals available in the sciences. Dalton *et al.* (1998) found that there is heavier dependence upon electronic information in business than in other disciplines. In most subjects there was an 80:20 split in favour of print, but the ratio was in favour of electronic information in business and only just in favour of print in physics (Nankivell, 1999). Bentley (1998) believes that print will predominate for some time because it is affordable, easy to use and familiar, and there is an in-built reluctance to change among scholars. Ray and Day (1998) report that most students do use electronic services but they still like to use electronic sources alongside print resources.

Most commentators feel that both print and electronic information sources will be important for the foreseeable future. Crawford (1998) of the US Research Libraries Group believes that electronic publishing and dissemination will grow in importance and that electronic publishing will displace print where it does the job better. Providing easy access to electronic information is as important to the academic library of the 21st century as building collections was to the academic library of the 20th century. Today's academic libraries are embracing technology as a way of delivering enhanced, cost-effective services to an increasingly diverse clientele, located both on and off the university campus. They are concerned with providing timely and appropriate access to information (Bentley, 1998) with many libraries adopting the 'just in time' rather than the 'just in case' philosophy of collection building (Davies, 1998; Oppenheim and Smithson, 1999). They are seeking to provide transparent, integrated, and seamless access to a range of print and electronic resources in what is increasingly being called the 'hybrid library' (Brophy and Fisher, 1998; Pinfield *et al.*, 1998; Rusbridge, 1998).

Higher education and information technologies

Developments in communications and information technologies are facilitating much of the change that we are all experiencing. These include greater interconnectivity and closer integration of IT systems, convergence of computer and communications technologies, the falling cost of PCs, greater portability of computing, and increased multimedia capabilities through the convergence of computing and media technologies. The creative use of these technologies acts as a driver for change as people identify new commercial and entrepreneurial opportunities in using the emerging technologies. The effect of these technological developments on our day-to-day lives and how we see the world is considerable. These technological developments enable the growth of global networking and communication. As C.A. Lynch (1998a) suggests, information technology and networking are leading to a fading of geography as an organizing principle – communities on the Internet can develop anywhere.

Developments in IT and telecommunications technologies are influencing and leading to changes in educational processes in higher education. Higher education institutions will evolve in a variety of ways to respond to an increasingly electronic environment (Edwards *et al.*, 1998). Technology offers new opportunities for the delivery of learning and potentially gives students greater choice of where, when, and how they study. Computerized services, such as bulletin boards, mailing lists and preprint servers are changing the face of scholarly communication and research (Day *et al.*, 1998). However, there are issues to be considered and resolved. McLean (1997) notes that there is a gap between the aspirations of HE institutions and national information infrastructures. The effectiveness of electronic learning materials is questioned by research reported by Garland *et al.* (1998), who found those using learning materials on an Intranet-based system performed less well than those who experienced more traditional teaching methods. Nankivell (1999) identifies serious concerns among senior university managers about the cost effectiveness and level of interaction provided by electronic teaching materials.

Technology offers new opportunities for the disabled community. McKenzie and Casey (1998) describe adaptive technology used in the USA to provide access for blind, partially sighted and dyslexic students, while Savenije (1998) mentions a workstation for the visually handicapped available through the Utrecht Electronic Library. Brophy and Fisher (1998), however, express concerns about the difficulties that users with disabilities may experience in using multimedia.

Higher education and lifelong learning

'Learning is the key to prosperity – for each of us as individuals, as well as for the nation as a whole' (*Learning*, 1998). Governments around the globe are placing increasing emphasis upon lifelong learning. This is viewed as the means of achieving and maintaining competitiveness in a global economy at a time when computing and other technologies are altering the way that we live and work. Brophy *et al.* (1998) note a broader agenda for lifelong learning associated with the democratization of education and elimination of inequality in education.

The growth of lifelong learning has profound implications for universities and poses some serious challenges. Hafner and Oblinger (1998) feel that higher education is under increasing scrutiny and businesses are increasingly turning to alternatives to higher education institutions for training because universities are not seen to be delivering. They argue that institutions are being pushed by customers taking charge, intensifying competition, and change becoming a constant. Universities have responded to the greater need for lifelong learning by offering improved opportunities to study, new course offerings, more post-experience courses, and a growth in opportunities to study without attending classes on campus. Technology opens up new possibilities for the delivery of distance learning on a worldwide level (Cronin, 1998; Kostopoulos, 1998). But, as both Cronin (1998) and MacDougall (1998) warn, the globalization of distance learning will lead to greater competitiveness between universities and between universities and other providers.

The information society brings a need for constant updating and upskilling and places a greater emphasis upon learning throughout life. This is leading to a requirement to have the skills to enable us to be effective learners. Quoting examples from Australia, South Africa and China, Breivik (1998) highlights the increasing recognition of educationalists and policymakers of the importance of information literacy to lifelong learning. Graduates who are not information literate could face 'drowning in a sea of information when making personal, business, and civic decisions'.

Supporting the learner

The growth in lifelong learning and the increasing number of students in post-compulsory education act as catalysts for new approaches to teaching and learning. Pressures to reduce costs, demands from students for greater flexibility in course delivery, and the availability of new possibilities for utilizing IT and media resources in learning are contributing to changing teaching methods. Institutions are reviewing their teaching, learning and assessment strategies and increasing emphasis is being placed on autonomous learning, resource based learning and group work. It is in this context that there has been a movement towards the integration of a range of library, IT and media facilities which students can access through a 'one-stop' shop (King, 1998; Line, 1998) accessible over long hours. Line describes this model not as a 'library' but as a 'learning and research centre'. The goal is to move from a library service to a learning support service where students can have seamless access and support in their use of a range of learning facilities. King stresses the increasing importance of facilities for groups of students in working together on projects and assignments. The emphasis in terms of support, however, is upon empowering users and furnishing them with skills to be effective learners.

Libraries often put in place unnecessarily complicated systems (Jordan, 1998) or badly designed systems (Ensor, 1998; Line, 1998) that require staff to explain them. As we move towards offering extended access through longer opening hours, and seek to deliver services with the same or fewer staff, we must demolish the obstacles that prevent autonomous learners from using the facilities and resources for themselves. Effective design of user interfaces to electronic systems and services, including expert systems, is essential to enable intuitive use which does not rely on human intermediaries (Heckart, 1998). Making services and systems easier to use will ultimately make our clientele less reliant on staff assistance, reduce the amount of instruction that they need, and enable them to become effective autonomous learners. However, Wilson (1998) warns that making access simpler can lead users to believe that they have better information skills than is the case.

Onwuegbuzie and Jiao (1998) and Chung (1998) investigate 'library anxiety' and draw out implications both for the learning environment and for library instruction. Jordan (1998) feels that the behaviour of library staff can contribute to this phenomenon. Indigenous students in Australia felt physically and psychologically intimidated by aspects of the library according to a study where students expressed their feelings about their learning environment through an experienced storyteller (Novak and Robinson, 1998). Kupersmith (1998a) describes the psychological state of 'technostress': this results in physical, cognitive, affective and behavioural symptoms, and arises where more and more information is available through remotely accessible systems. Part-time students and non-traditional students face particular difficulties in using libraries because of shortage of time and inadequate study skills (Brophy *et al.*, 1998).

Key skills

There has been much discussion about the key or transferable skills needed by students to prepare them for life in the 21st century. Corrall (1998a) suggests seven key skills: communication, learning and research, numeracy, problem solving, self-management, team working, and information (including IT). The importance of developing the information skills of students in a networked information environment, and for those skills to be integrated into the students' learning experience, is widely recognized by commentators (de Jager and

Nassimbeni, 1998; Dickstein, 1998; Jordan, 1998; Simpson, 1998). Breivik (1998) observes that 'in the next century, an "educated graduate" will no longer be defined as one who has absorbed a certain body of factual information, but as one who knows how to find, evaluate, and apply needed information'. Feo (1998) stresses the importance of students having the skills to find and handle information and describes a compulsory information methodology course at Paris University 8 – St. Denis.

The terms 'information literacy' and 'information competency' are used to embrace a wider range of skills than just the traditional bibliographic instruction (de Jager and Nassimbeni, 1998; Goetsch and Kaufman, 1998; Oberman *et al.*, 1998). The number of resources available and the speed of change preclude the covering of information skills in one or two sessions (Ensor, 1998). The emphasis is increasingly upon developing generic and transferable information skills, such as search strategies or critical skills, which underpin the use of information. There is general consensus that the development of critical and evaluative skills is essential (Basile, 1998; Goetsch and Kaufman, 1998; Jordan, 1998; Simpson, 1998; Whitmire, 1998). This takes on a particular importance in the context of the variable quality of Internet resources. Lappalainen-Happonen (1998) reports upon the use of group work at Joensuu University in Finland to develop students' information skills. Cooperative learning also enables students to develop a range of other personal and interpersonal skills. We see a convergence in the development of information skills and IT skills. Krissoff and Konrad (1998), for example, describe a training programme at the University of Wisconsin which covers the core competencies of operating systems, hardware basics and troubleshooting, software basics and troubleshooting, search concepts and techniques. However, we need to take account of existing competencies of new entrants to higher education. Smith and Phillips (1999) remind us that primary and secondary school pupils are increasingly using the Internet in their learning, while Ray and Day (1998) talk of a growing divide in the capabilities of students in using electronic services.

Discussion and partnership between LIS staff and academic colleagues are needed to identify the skills required by students, how and when these competencies are to be developed, and who will teach them (Ensor, 1998; Goetsch and Kaufman, 1998; Herrington, 1998; Jordan, 1998). In their article on developing information across the curriculum, Goetsch and Kaufman (1998) suggest that academic staff should deliver what they describe as the information competency requirements, which could release librarians to 'serve as coordinators, collaborative curriculum developers, and providers of supportive instructional services for faculty and students'. Breivik (1998) suggests that librarians might redirect efforts from library or bibliographic instruction to supporting the campus information strategy and to spend less time on direct teaching of students and more time on curriculum collaboration. However, faculty staff may have to be convinced of the importance of information literacy, believing that students either have skills already or will 'pick them up' (Breivik, 1998). This may be especially true for using Internet resources for, as Jacobs (1998) notes, the apparent ease of searching Internet-based resources may conceal the fact that self-tuition is probably not the best way to acquire these skills. There may also be fears among academic staff about librarians encroaching upon the curriculum: some of these concerns may result from their lacking the confidence and competencies to retrieve and manage information themselves (Breivik, 1998). This is a serious concern, because the attitude of academic staff to electronic resources is a crucial factor in determining whether students will use them (Day *et al.*, 1998; Parker and Jackson, 1998; Nankivell, 1999). Gerhard (1998) and Tomney and Burton (1998) emphasize the role of the librarian in the promotion of electronic services and resources. There is clearly a need to raise the awareness of academic staff and to work at encouraging them to 'buy in' to information literacy policies.

Help and enquiry services

The help and enquiry service plays a crucial role in educating students and assisting them to develop the skills that they need to be effective learners. Jordan (1998) talks of the 'teachable moment' – skills development through enquiry desk (or when assignments being prepared) when students have a clear need and motivation is high (Ensor, 1998). The importance of staff on the desk having good interpersonal skills is illustrated by a Chinese study that looked at the effect of the body language of reference librarians on student satisfaction (Hsieh, 1998).

The holistic approach of the library as a 'one-stop' shop for library and IT facilities has encouraged some institutions to bring together library enquiry and IT help desks into a single service. Clegg (1998) identifies a number of models for such integration. These range from the 'joint' enquiry/help desk where library and computing officers work alongside one another through to the 'converged' desk where multiskilled staff handle both library and IT enquiries. At the same time, the concept of the 'enquiry desk' is being challenged by the need to provide support to off-campus learners and the need to provide help/enquiry services to library users over longer opening hours. Libraries are increasingly looking at new ways of providing help and support services, including the increased use of self-instructional materials, virtual help and telephone/e-mail services. Milner (1999) even suggests the establishment of a centralized national call centre for enquiries from students.

Library buildings

There are many examples of new library buildings in the year's literature. The Adsetts Learning Centre at Sheffield Hallam University in the UK is typical of a building which brings together library, computing and media provision to support students' learning (Bulpitt, 1997; Line, 1998). There are also some interesting examples of conversions, including two from Germany: from a riding and gymnastics hall at Eichstätt University (Löffler, 1998) and from a municipal slaughterhouse at Konstanz (Haag, 1998). Some commentators feel that the design of library buildings is failing to keep up with the changing philosophy and practice of academic librarianship (Rettig, 1998; Wilson, 1998). The emphasis needs to be upon user-centred design and creating 'more of a workshop and less of a warehouse' (Rettig, 1998). Streatfield and Markless (1997) believe that either pressures on library space will decline as we create the 'virtual library', or library space will become more important to allow for a broader range of needs and the increased requirement for library-based group work. It is important that an environment conducive to study is created, as self-directed or autonomous learners will carry out a significant proportion of their learning in the library. Kuttler (1998) reports upon the new library at Weihenstephan Technical University which is 'flooded with light' through the creative use of glass and plants. Sadly, however, a recent extension to a major UK academic library is described by the architectural literature to be like a 'call centre rather than a learning environment' (Greenberg, 1998). King (1998) notes the following features in recent major US building projects:

- increased space, primarily to cater for IT needs;
- holistic 'one-stop shop' model with both library and IT facilities;
- built-in flexibility to allow for changes in utilization;
- adequate IT provision with the infrastructure to cater for increasing demand;
- space zoning to cater for different and possibly conflicting needs;
- group study facilities as well as individual study places.

Libraries are being designed for 24-hour operation and there is increasing need to consider security, including access control and CCTV (Bulpitt, 1997). Users also need to have a clear cognitive map of the building. Good design, clear signage and self-instructional orientation are essential parts of designing an environment where users can access the facilities over extended hours, without staff intervention and with confidence.

Off-campus learning

Academic libraries are increasingly seeking ways of delivering their services beyond their walls to meet the needs of those of who are studying off-campus. Even students at exclusively distance education institutions need access to library and information services (Sacchanand, 1998). Some countries have a long history of providing library provision to distance learners, for example, Australia, the

USA, and Canada (Brophy *et al.*, 1998). However, libraries are exploring new ways of delivering services, especially electronic services, to students who are studying off-campus. Thomas and Jones (1998) report on the Eighth Off-Campus Library Services Conference in Rhode Island where papers were presented on using IT, interactive television, conferencing, collaboration between institutions, teaching information skills, providing help and support, planning and promoting services, and evaluation of services.

However, provision for off-campus learners is variable. Bolton *et al.* (1998) identify four different approaches to providing information access to support distance courses from research in the UK and USA:

- Neglect: the institution takes no responsibility and no support is given.
- All reading material: packaging of information (e.g. 'course readers') which are sent to all students.
- Special services: e.g. telephone or e-mail reservations and renewals, telephone and e-mail enquiries, journal articles by post, postal loans, literature searches requested from a distance, help via interactive video, electronic services.
- Access to other libraries: which may be offered on a reciprocal or pay-as-you go basis.

Akeroyd (1998) identifies the potential of on-demand publishing for distance learners, where student fees could pay for rights clearances and students are able to get hold of core material.

The adequacy of information access to support distance courses is a significant quality issue. MacDougall (1998) highlights the development of a distance learning support service at Sheffield Hallam University, and Brophy *et al.* (1998) describe other similar services in the UK. This is not a new idea in North America and Australia but is a paradigm shift for UK libraries. However, as MacDougall notes, there is an acknowledgement for the first time that distance learners are entitled to equity in access to library services. Clarity is required, however, on respective responsibilities. Cajkler (1998) and Unwin *et al.* (1998) report upon differences in expectations between students, tutors and librarians.

There is a movement towards the delivery of services by electronic means. Sacchanand (1998) reports upon the use of modern information technologies and development of library networks to support Sukhothai Thammathirat Open University in Thailand. Students on courses franchised by the University of Central Lancashire are able to use the electronic services of VALNOW (Virtual Academic Library of the North West) and it is certain that the electronic library will be important to the emerging University of the Highlands and Islands (Brophy *et al.*, 1998). Electronic delivery is the simplest means by which instruction in information literacy skills can be delivered to off-campus learners (Basile, 1998). There is also an increasing use of technology to deliver 'virtual help'. Fishman (1998) describes such a service running at the University of Maryland as a logical progression to their usual in-house enquiry/help services. Heckart (1998) argues that the moves towards automated help and assistance mirror the notion of the digital library being underpinned by self-sufficiency. He points out that self-service facilities are available at any time, anywhere, as long as the user has access to a computer. In an increasingly networked environment, students will be seeking 24-hour access to network resources and the mobility to access these resources from home, work, and the university.

In their messages to the UK Mailbase newsgroup list, lis-link, West (1999) and Pelowski (1997) detail initiatives in the delivery of electronic enquiry services in the UK, USA and Germany. It would appear that many institutions are providing e-mail addresses for librarians/information specialists and some are extending this to a general enquiry service address. Heckart (1998) identifies the advantages of 'self-help' and notes that it empowers the clientele who can become self-reliant information seekers. However, the down side is that such systems can fail, sometimes catastrophically, leaving the user totally without any support. Staley (1998) describes an e-mail reference service at a US university and identifies good practice. However, we must not lose sight of the personal dimension. Cooper *et al.* (1998) found that remote users expressed a preference for, and an expectation of, personal contact.

Electronic services of this kind are increasingly not just limited to distance learners but enable a heterogeneous student population to access services and resources wherever they are located. These systems, although formulated with distance learners in mind, are also likely to be incorporated into the curriculum of resident students, and distinctions between distance learners and resident learners will blur (Heckart, 1998).

Digital library or hybrid library?

Chang and Hor (1998) view the digital library as the 'library without walls' to reflect the ability of digital libraries to deliver networked information services any time or anywhere. Oppenheim and Smithson (1999) define the digital library as one where all acquisition, storage, preservation, retrieval, access and display functions are delivered using digital technologies. The digital library has the features of integration, seamlessness and ease of use. Access to a distributed range of electronic services and support is delivered to the desktop through an intuitive, and possibly personalized, interface accessed through a single authentication system. Schirdewahn (1998), describing a project at Freiburg University in Germany, argues the benefits of access to scientific information from the desktop and the importance of having a friendly user interface. To help orientate the user, Kupersmith (1998b) suggests using virtual reality environments to design digital libraries around physical equivalents.

Brophy and Fisher (1998) see the truly digital library as being some way away yet. Too much has been invested and remains of value in 'legacy' print-based systems. Commentators are increasingly talking of the 'hybrid library' to describe the intermediate state between the conventional library and the digital library. Pinfield and McKenna (1998) explain that the hybrid library enables print and electronic resources to be accessed and used side by side in a more integrated way. They argue that most libraries are already hybrid libraries. Progress towards the digital library is gradual. Hampson (1999) concluded that many traditional library operations would exist for at least another five years. However, Chang and Hor (1998) argue that the electronic environment is leading to the boundaries between the functional areas of acquisition, organization and delivery being challenged. C.A. Lynch (1998b) suggests that the slow transition towards the digital library has helped LIS professionals to handle the change of the networked information environment. However, he goes on to warn that vast changes are imminent as the networked information environment reaches a critical mass and that 'once these changes begin, they will be surprisingly rapid and disruptive'.

One of the most obvious barriers to the digital library is the cost of developing new services (Hampson, 1999). This has implications particularly for the developing nations. Gupta (1998) catalogues a list of problems in India, including cost, lack of expertise, inappropriateness of foreign designed software and the need for regular upgrading of hardware and software, and lack of integrated systems. Both Younis (1998) and Chuong (1998) describe the problems of using foreign software products. Rosenberg (1998) highlights the lack of infrastructure in Africa. Even basic requirements, such as electricity supply, are not necessarily in place. Tuck and Grieves (1998), Tarvonen (1998) and Nankivell (1999) report problems of printing. Hampson (1999) reports wider infrastructure problems, while Nankivell (1999) cites lack of standardization of hardware and software across the university as a problem. Walton and Edwards (1998) point to the paradox in a digital revolution that provides access to a world of electronic information but where there are problems of reliability, cost and complexity of the systems which provide that access. There are also problems of slow network responses, viruses, costs of upgrading, passwords and authentication.

The hybrid library will provide access to a range of resources and services. Rusbridge (1998) uses the following classification of resources:

- *Legacy*: largely non-digital.
- *Transition*: materials which have been or are being digitized.
- *Future*: expressly created for the digital world.

The California Digital Library uses technology to enable 'discovering, sharing, accessing, manipulating and integrating scholarly content in all forms' (Ober, 1999). Kvist (1998) describes services available through electronic study libraries at Aalborg University in Denmark: WWW services and databases, electronic journals, selected links, news lists and library contacts. Hampson (1999) identifies the following services which could be usefully handled in an electronic environment: induction training, interlibrary loan, self-ordering of books, short loan collections and electronic journals.

Tarvonen (1998) and Sarvilinna (1998) report upon projects in Finland aimed at making available electronic textbooks. Ramsden *et al.* (1998) describe how an electronic collection of copyright and university documents was made available at De Montfort University in the UK. Many universities have sought to replace the traditional short loan collection with an electronic reserve. Successful projects exist in the UK, USA and Australia (Dugdale, 1998; Freiburger and Ralph, 1998; Gadd and Kingston, 1998). Electronic reserves improve the likelihood that students gain access to items which are recommended by lecturers or in heavy demand. Electronic reserves also have the potential advantages of 24-hour access, multiple access, security and remote access. They avoid some of the difficulties of short loan print collections: queues, taking stock out of general circulation, problems of access to journal articles, staff processing and circulation of stock, and theft and vandalism (Dugdale, 1998; Groenewegen, 1998; Muir, 1998). However, significant concerns are the need for copyright clearance and the lead time required in obtaining it (Muir, 1998). User response to electronic reserve is mixed. Nankivell (1999) felt that it was a useful way of making available key papers in demand by many students. Others felt that it just transferred the problem from access to information to obtaining access to a computer or printer. Crawford *et al.* (1998) suggest that resistance to electronic reserve may result from a lack of interest among students in IT applications and concerns about the costs of copying. However, some of these issues may be transient, as publishers and users become more familiar with the technologies themselves. Digitization may be applicable to rare and fragile materials, as well as documents in heavy demand. Mulder (1998) reports upon several projects at Utrecht University in the Netherlands where materials from special collections are digitized and consequently made more accessible.

The cataloguing of electronic resources will be of growing importance in the hybrid library. The user needs an effective means of identifying appropriate resources, and in the longer term the use of metadata could enable greater precision in the retrieval of relevant information. Chen (1998) describes the increasing importance of metadata in the creation and use of digital libraries with particular reference to the National Taiwan University. O'Daniel (1999) looks at issues associated with cataloguing Internet resources and examines three relevant projects: Dublin Core, OCLC Co-operative On-Line Resource Cataloguing Project, and the Coalition for Networked Information. However, Thomas and Griffin (1998) warn that standards for metadata will not be widely used by information creators unless there is a commercial benefit in generating and indexing reliable metadata.

The integration that is being sought through the hybrid library can be extended to cover seamless access to the full range of electronic services and systems used by students and staff. This might include course materials, help/support services, computer conferencing facilities and study skills support. Brown (1998) reports upon an initiative at the University of Derby to provide a 'single seamless system' to access information from a range of administrative and academic sources. Turunen (1998) describes bringing together curriculum materials with other electronic resources at Helsinki University, while Grobler (1998) gives an account of a joint initiative by the University of South Africa (UNISA) and Athabasca University in Canada to deliver an electronic masters programme using LotusNotes with associated electronic document delivery. When such initiatives are scaleable, they are sometimes called virtual universities or virtual campuses (Schlageter, 1998). Sandelands (1998) describes a virtual international university which delivers course materials via the Web, provides an online management library and an online bookshop, enables faculty and learners to hold online seminars, and offers course supervision. This moves us towards integration of the hybrid library into virtual learning environments and seeing the digital library as an integral part of the virtual university. However, such approaches require sound interfaces between academic and administrative computing systems, mechanisms for authentication of students, and the commitment of staff throughout the university.

Ober (1999) talks of the need to develop technologies to address 'known roadblocks' on the way to the digital library. These cover such areas as standards, customization of the user environment, new search processes and authentication. Kai (1998) sees copyright as a major area which needs to be addressed in the development of electronic libraries. Brown (1998) warns that the ability of non-authenticated users to access copyright material is a concern for the publishers. C. Lynch (1998) argues that access control needs to be a basic part of the infrastructure of networked information services. We need to be able to authenticate both on-campus users and remote users. Brown (1998), and Ramsden *et al.* (1998) describe technologies for handling the management of copyright. There is a consensus that archiving is essential to the electronic library; but that the issue has not as yet been adequately addressed (Day, 1998; De Gennaro, 1998; Guernsey, 1998; Guthrie, 1998; International, 1998; Tammaro, 1998). There are questions as to who should archive, how the economics should be handled, migration as new technology appears, and copyright/ownership issues.

Pinfield (1998) argues that one of the central elements of the hybrid library is the development and management of the 'glue technology' to achieve greater integration between different information resources including developing standards and testing emerging technologies. Brophy and Fisher (1998) also talk of the 'glue' which is required to achieve seamlessness and integration. The Web provides a ' "presentational layer" but much work needs to be done to enhance the interoperability between the systems in the underlying layers'.

Information selection for the hybrid library

Kai (1998) notes that the development of electronic libraries is blurring the distinction between information held internally and externally. There are complex issues for librarians around selection of material in the hybrid library. Both Gerhard (1998) and Ojiro (1998) feel that electronic resources tend to be an add-on rather than being integrated into existing collections. However, there are problems with funding electronic information sources while print resources are still wanted by the academic community (Rosenberg, 1998). Campbell (1998) writes about this increasing complexity, mentioning issues such as negotiating price, licensing, PC or networking requirements, changing commercial factors, data formats, standards, bibliographic access, training implications and user acceptance. Pricing models for e-journals can be very complex and sometimes print and electronic subscriptions are linked (Robnett, 1998). Librarians need to consider whether to purchase aggregations of e-journals or to pay for access to individual articles (McLean, 1997). Other players, intermediaries or aggregators, are increasingly offering packages of electronic publications from different publishers (Charton, 1998). There are problems about the composition of aggregations, especially as subject aggregations are more valuable than publisher aggregations (Walters *et al.*, 1998). Fishwick *et al.* (1998) argue that the optimal method of delivering journal articles in electronic form is a combination of payment by usage and subscription. Charging policies from publishers are a major concern (Guernsey, 1998). Even consortia risk putting in place charging regimes that could price smaller institutions out of the market (East *et al.*, 1998).

There is also sometimes a lack of clarity as to whether access is being purchased or leased. The International Coalition of Library Consortia argues that the provider should grant a perpetual licence when the consortium purchases the content, but there will be associated issues of archiving. Luther (1998) describes issues around site licensing while C.A. Lynch (1998a) is concerned about the possible restriction of user rights by licensing despite 'fair dealing' legislation. Nankivell (1999) points to the difficulties of budgeting for electronic information and the need for costing models. Christoffel *et al.* (1998) see a potential threat to the university library in that there will be an open market for document services on campus – the library will survive only if it is competitive. They describe the Unicats project at University of Karlsruhe in Germany, which uses systems to experiment with pricing models that are cost-transparent to the user while adding a competitive element. Schwartz (1998) argues that financial responsibility needs to be transferred to the most appropriate business unit – which implies departmental budgeting, or even each academic having a personal budget for information access.

Resource sharing

The growth of knowledge and the increasing cost of information resources have forced cash-starved libraries to consider greater cooperation through initiatives such as purchasing consortia (Allen and Hirshon, 1998) and the development of reciprocal access arrangements. But, as Dempsey *et al.* (1998) observe, there is a wider political agenda to encourage further collaboration between libraries, which is supported by a 'natural convergence of interests' with other information providers (e.g. museums and archives) and is facilitated by networking developments.

The networked information environment potentially alters our conceptual framework. Information resources, whether printed or electronic, can be seen as a distributed resource that can be identified and accessed from anywhere. There are significant issues about the ability of library management systems to 'inter-operate' which need to be addressed (Dempsey *et al.*, 1998). Rusbridge (1998) reports upon e-lib projects in the UK, in which libraries have collaborated upon large-scale resource discovery through CLUMPS. Phillips (1998) describes a similar collaboration in Ireland funded by the EU Telematics Programme. Both of these initiatives involve using Z39.50 protocols to provide a common search interface to allow users concurrently to search the catalogues of other libraries. Large-scale resource discovery of this kind clearly has implications for resource sharing, including reciprocal access (Pinfield, 1998). Nevertheless, the potential benefit to researchers could be enormous (Anderson, 1998) at a time when individual libraries can afford to purchase a declining proportion of the world's knowledge output (Bentley, 1998). Additionally, there are significant advantages in libraries working together to negotiate deals with information providers and rights owners (Guernsey, 1998).

There are many good examples of resource sharing and collaboration from around the world. A computer communication network has been established in India for linking libraries in university and research institutions to establish an infrastructure for sharing information resources (Gupta, 1998). Zongying *et al.* (1998) comment upon the close collaboration between Chinese academic libraries: book and catalogue information services, access to databases, interlibrary loans and library home pages are delivered through up-to-date telecommunication and computer technologies. Widenius (1998) describes cooperation between polytechnic and university libraries in Finland which includes access arrangements, establishment of purchasing consortia and collaborative training.

Lifelong learning adds a further dimension in that non-traditional students, and especially those learning at a distance, seek access to libraries closer to their home or work. Mulvaney and Lewis (1998) found that reciprocal borrowing arrangements were of more concern to distance students than extending the opening hours of the library. Unwin *et al.* (1998) found that postgraduate distance students had a greater preference for local access arrangements than for special services from their home institution. Collaboration and resource sharing need not be confined to the academic sector. Brophy *et al.* (1998) ask whether university libraries can work in tandem with public libraries to provide the network of resource centres which will enable lifelong learning to be a satisfying and fulfilling experience. Crawford (1998) advocates academic libraries making common cause with public libraries and learning from them. There are certainly examples of close cooperation between academic and public libraries (Eggink, 1998) and even initiatives to provide joint-use facilities between public and academic libraries: Hervey Bay Library in Australia (McPherson *et al.*, 1998) and Tasmania (Dunford, 1998). Such facilities provide a communal resource that facilitates close interaction between the community and the university and promotes lifelong learning. Benton (1998) too reports on higher education institutions in Australia sharing their facilities with public and school libraries. In the UK, the Library and Information Commission (1998) highlights how libraries of different host organizations could collaborate to deliver access to library and learning resources in a 'learning city'. Garnes (1998), however, suggests that additional funding is required by Norwegian university libraries if they are to continue to offer access to the general public.

Attitudes can be a significant barrier to cooperation. Bentley (1998) sees us merely paying 'lip service' to collaboration, with no expansion in this area. Kundu and Panda (1998) suggest resource sharing 'calls for the participating librarians to accept . . .a shift in perception from "my library resources" to "our library resources" and from "my users" to "our users" '. Phillips (1998) observes that the academic community's response to resource sharing is often to commend in principle and deplore in practice. He states that resource sharing is not likely to be accepted unless it is presented as part of a broader strategy which includes resource discovery, reciprocal access and document delivery.

The effective library: now and in the future

The goal of measuring library performance continues to focus the minds of commentators, but we still grapple with what constitutes a good library. Kao *et al.* (1998) note that the paramount goal of a library is to provide services to the university community, but warn that measuring the quality of service is 'rather difficult and disputable'. This may explain why Willemse (1998) discovered that many HE institutions do not have a written assessment policy for their libraries; just 29% of respondents to a worldwide IFLA survey had a written policy.

Winkworth (1998) reminds us that performance measurement is about influencing people and bringing about change. Different stakeholders (such as parent organizations, library managers, individual staff and teams, customers, and funders) have different needs and require different indicators. Winkworth argues that there are three golden rules:

- Tell a story – clear rationale.
- Use different language for different audiences
- Focus upon informing actual decisions.

Research by Crawford *et al.* (1998) identifies ten 'empirically viable' staff and student stakeholder groups in higher education institutions. The research identifies key performance issues related to all stakeholder groups, but there are significant differences in priorities between the various stakeholder groups, especially between librarians and user stakeholders.

University library evaluation can be reduced to just one line by funding bodies: spending per student (Winkworth, 1998). However, this single measure of inputs is of no value in comparing and benchmarking the performance of academic libraries. The interest in benchmarking is worldwide. Mano González (1998) proposes an evaluation system for Spanish university libraries to provide raw data on different aspects of university libraries and qualitative evaluation useful for well-grounded decision-making. Barton and Blagden (1998) propose a set of management statistics for UK academic libraries aimed at policymakers. Niemitalo (1998) describes the use of data envelopment analysis for measuring the relative efficiency of Finnish academic libraries. Santos (1998) looks at the use of benchmarking techniques at the Universidad de la Habana in Cuba. Kao *et al.* (1998) developed a set of criteria for ranking libraries in Taiwan based upon collections, personnel, expenditures, buildings and services. The CAVAL Working Party on Performance Measures for Reference Services in Australia has developed a set of indicators for benchmarking of enquiry desk services derived from data from user constituencies (Cotter *et al.*, 1998).

As students see themselves more as consumers of a service, higher education institutions have become more customer oriented and there is an increasing concern by libraries with gauging users' satisfaction with their services. University libraries employ a variety of different approaches to assess user satisfaction, including suggestion forms, questionnaire surveys (West, 1998) and focus groups (Hart *et al.*, 1998). Priority Search has developed a methodology which combines these methods and is now being widely used in UK academic libraries (Hayden, 1998; Horrocks, 1998). The approach is noteworthy because it places considerable emphasis upon ascertaining and ranking the priorities and concerns of the clientele.

The results of in-house studies of customer satisfaction are often not startling. Revill (1998) wryly comments that 'user complaints can be summarized roughly as: students want more books and study seats, academics want more PCs; seldom do they want more library staff'. Horrocks (1998) found that more books came out at the top of students' priorities in surveys at seven UK academic libraries. Yamada (1998) found that students at Jikei University Medical Library in Japan wanted more core textbooks and journals and, reflecting the times, more access to the Internet. Andaleeb and Simmonds (1998) conclude from their survey of a cross-section of users that academic libraries need to focus on two major elements: resources and the demeanour of library staff. However, they draw out the complexity of the resources issue by arguing that this is not just about the size of a library's collections, but about the way in which academic librarians work in partnership with the academic community in delivering the information access needed by students. Line (1998) teases out the differences between 'needs', 'wants', 'demands' and 'uses' and describes the relationship between them. Users often have 'wants' that are not based upon their 'needs'. Their 'demands' will be influenced by their expectations and they may not use everything that they demand. Horrocks (1998) queries whether students are in a position to judge their own learning requirements. Davies (1998) asks how vital it is for the user to receive a research paper within minutes or hours. Prior expectations, based upon internalized views of the world, clearly influence customer satisfaction. Stamatoplos and Mackoy (1998), for example, found that students' satisfaction with the library was influenced by how good they perceived their skills in using it to be. Nevertheless, satisfaction studies can provide ammunition for managers in arguing for resources, can facilitate discussion with stakeholders and demonstrate the library's commitment to the customer. The results can be used to guide management decision-making.

There is increasing interest in performance measurement in the electronic environment. The European-funded Equinox project (Equinox) has identified performance indicators which include market penetration of electronic services, number of log-ins, number and cost of electronic documents accessed, reference enquiries submitted electronically, use rate for workstations, waiting time to use workstations and system availability. Lancaster (1998) notes that evaluation becomes more difficult because users are remote and anonymous.

Revill (1998) contends that 'if libraries (and perhaps even computing services) ceased to be, the proportions of firsts, upper and lower seconds and thirds would barely change'. It is very difficult to measure the impact of a library or learning support service on a student's performance. However, there is interest in exploring how libraries contribute to the learning experience and how this contribution can be enhanced. Streatfield and Markless (1997), for example, present five models of an effective college library based upon their research.

Staffing and staff development

Walton and Edwards (1998) see this as an 'exciting time for LIS staff', presenting librarians with new challenges and new roles. They see the traditional 'subject specialist' as being under threat through budget cuts, multiskilling leading to more generalists, and more responsibility being devolved downwards with the advent of the paraprofessional. Oehling (1998) argues a contrary view, that the primary role of the academic librarian is as a subject specialist and Wefers (1998) also believes that this specialist workload will increase. Hampson (1999) sees librarians moving from being guardians to intermediaries, with the emphasis being placed on assuring the quality of electronic information sources and on training the end user. Oppenheim and Smithson (1999) point to a possible new pattern of staffing that will be required to support the hybrid library, with an emphasis upon cataloguing and resource selection of both print and electronic sources. Wilson (1998) sees a challenge for librarians in defining a role that justifies a continuing allocation of the institution's budget. Streatfield and Markless (1997) identify the role of the librarian as educator or teacher, not a new role but an important and vital one. McNamara and Core (1998) argue that higher education librarians need to develop the capacity to become effective educators of end-users if they are 'to fulfill their mandate to enhance end users' capacity to make effective use of networked information'.

Farley *et al.* (1998) suggest that the increasing use of paraprofessionals allows professional staff to concentrate upon meeting the new challenges brought by IT. Breivik (1998) argues that the need is not for more librarians but for more paraprofessional and technical support staff to relieve the pressure on librarians' time. There can be no doubt that paraprofessionals are taking on more of the front-line tasks. Harris and Marshall (1998) see librarians taking a 'giant step back from the front' as they leave behind 'what, for many, are the most significant roles in their work repertoire'.

Funding pressures continue and libraries are seeking imaginative ways to extend service delivery with fewer staff. Schibel (1998) argues the case for having regional subject specialists, since it is not possible for each library to employ specialists in every subject. Edwards (1998) describes the introduction of self-services at Sunderland University in the UK, including self-issue and self-return of loans and self-pickup of reserved items. Self-issue accounted for 20% of issues in 1995 but accounted in 1998 for 65% of circulation at each site. This frees up staff time to focus on the needs of independent lifelong learners. Di Marco and Van Dam (1998) report upon the experience of an extension in opening hours at Miami University Libraries until 2 am. Staffing concerns included the problem of recruitment, employee safety, security of the premises and facilities and unacceptable behaviour within the library.

Bénaud and Bordeianu (1998) examine outsourcing in academic libraries: this can be an important reengineering tool. Essential functions remain in-house while non-essential activities are outsourced. The outsourcing of technical functions, especially cataloguing, is common but there is virtually no outsourcing of public services. Jiang (1998) looks at the advantages of outsourcing cataloguing, but highlights the disadvantage of possibly sacrificing the quality of bibliographic records and the threat of job losses among technical staff. The loss of in-house expertise must also be considered.

Oppenheim and Smithson (1999) claim that the hybrid library can be seen as 'convergence in action', and will probably strengthen the argument for organizational convergence. Liang *et al.* (1998) describe the situation at Yuan Ze

University in Taiwan, where the need is to bring together separate delivery systems to create a more user-friendly environment. But is convergence a necessary prerequisite, or can the required close working be achieved through cross-departmental working? Hirshon (1998) concludes that institutions choose convergence for a variety of reasons, including bringing together information and technology, achieving better and more coordinated services, replacing weak service organizations, facilitating a new strategic vision or, just simply, as a result of an event such as a new building or a key administrator leaving. There is no consistent trend: some institutions choose convergence; others develop close working relationships between separate computing and library departments. There is no single model for convergence (Day *et al.*, 1998) and there may even be subsequent deconvergence (Stone, 1998). Hirshon (1998) reminds us that convergence is not an end in itself. B. Allen (1998) refers to cultural differences when staff from different backgrounds work together and the 'tensions and stresses' arising from new working relationships and practices following convergence. Organizational restructuring needs to be handled carefully. Farley *et al.* (1998) report that staff found an institutional merger particularly difficult. Jackson *et al.* (1998) describe difficulties in the reorganization of an information services department. Harris and Marshall (1998) argue that staff who have survived organizational downsizing must work harder and assume new tasks, often working in more than one department.

Greater emphasis is being placed upon team working and, especially, upon multidisciplinary team working. Tompkins *et al.* (1998) describe initiatives by the Coalition for Networked Information which bring together professionals from a variety of backgrounds. The IMPEL2 project at the University of Northumbria in the UK found that team working enables skills to be developed and shared. The team provides support for individuals, improves communication, and facilitates the sharing of responsibility. Jackson *et al.* (1998) note that team working is not without its problems: the roles and responsibilities of team members may be unclear and problems can arise through personality differences and competitiveness between teams.

Issues of equality and encouraging diversity must also be considered in LIS staffing. Recruitment strategies should support diversity related goals so that a broader range of cultural perspective informs library decision-making (Winston, 1998). There is a need in particular to tackle the under-representation of professionals from ethnic minorities. In a series of papers, looking at the situation of equal opportunity issues in selected US academic libraries, Fitzgerald and Jones (1997) question whether the academic environment is a welcoming one for minority librarians and argue that there is a need for the establishment of recruitment goals.

All of this has significant and profound implications for the development of LIS staff. But what skills and competencies will be required of library staff? The buzz word is 'multiskilling'. Oppenheim and Smithson (1999) suggest that the hybrid library needs 'hybrid skills' which lie between those of the traditional librarian and the traditional computer services officer. Clegg (1998) sought to create a multiskilled team to provide converged library/IT help, but some staff felt deskilled and highly qualified staff were dealing with low level work. Parker and Jackson (1998) present an extensive list of skills needed by librarians, including skills relating to teaching and learning.

The increasing need for staff to possess IT skills is frequently stressed. Younis (1998), Chisenga (1998) and Rosenberg (1998) all conclude that lack of skilled staff is a serious barrier to the implementation of new technologies in developing countries. Idowu (1998) concludes from a study of Nigerian librarians that previous IT experience and training promote a positive attitude towards the use of computers. However, staff are also facing the new pressures of 'technostress' arising from the assimilation of an increasing number of new electronic products and changing delivery platforms each year (Rose *et al.*, 1998). The task of keeping up to date with hardware and software installation and troubleshooting can be overwhelming, and the library community is rising to the problem in a variety of ways. Kirkpatrick (1998) reports on the widespread use of self-instruction, vendor manual and in-house training manuals to develop the IT competencies of staff. Idowu (1998) stresses the importance of staff having access to state-of-the art computer facilities in training. Grassian (1998) suggests a cascade approach where a group of staff develops expertise and trains others. Krissoff and Konrad (1998) describe staff IT training at the University of Wisconsin, where staff are encouraged to establish 'buddies', working together in developing and testing skills.

Training and development need to extend to all staff, especially as paraprofessionals take on more of the roles previously undertaken by professional librarians. The University of Lincolnshire and Humberside in the UK has developed a competency framework following the creation of a converged LIS department. The competencies for service advisers (ex-library assistants) are aligned with national frameworks covering behaviour, skill and knowledge in a range of areas (B. Allen, 1998).

Staff appraisal can provide a useful tool in developing staff to meet changing needs. However, Edwards and Williams (1998) give a review of literature in which they highlight that the appraisal process is often handled superficially and employees are often rated on the extent to which they conform to institutional philosophy. Performance appraisal can be used as an instrument of change and personal development, but this will not happen while appraisal is seen in terms of 'pro forma compliance'.

Management of change

Some commentators have questioned the future of academic libraries. As information services become easier to use, more learning is distributed and end users gain greater control of access to information, can the academic library survive? Wolpert (1998) suggests that the Web is seen by some as a 'reasonable competitor to the academic library': 'no facilities are needed and seating is unlimited'. The suggestion is made that funding pressures and development of technologies will squeeze the academic library's traditional role. It is a mistake to believe that there is no competitive substitute for libraries.

Farley *et al.* (1998) believe that the future of academic libraries depends upon their ability to adapt to a rapidly changing and turbulent environment. The way in which individual libraries adapt will depend on their particular role in the university. C.A. Lynch (1998b) sees an optimistic future for those libraries that can exploit new delivery and communication channels and make sense of an 'incoherent universe of information' on behalf of their host organizations. However, he goes on to observe that these libraries may be unrecognizable from today's libraries. Wolpert (1998) suggests that academic libraries will face the challenge of loss of 'brand identity' as they develop services to distance learners that are not based upon the library as a physical space. Libraries will need much more visibility and to think more carefully about marketing and promoting services in the future.

Crawford (1998) argues that libraries cannot lose the role of the 'information place' in the university because 'it's a role libraries have never really had'. Davies (1998) explains that users do not rely on documents and libraries for information: they draw upon colleagues, friends, specialists and bypass libraries. Corrall (1998b), however, sees a role for academic libraries in knowledge management within the university. Taking a more holistic view of knowledge which includes both academic (subject) knowledge and administrative (organizational) knowledge, she argues that librarians' expertise in information management can be used to exploit networked information resources to enhance organizational performance.

Wilson (1998) argues that there is a need for a fundamental reformulation and review of processes to take account of networked information, new methods of teaching and learning, and the interactions between teacher, learner and learning support in this new environment. Library strategic planning needs to be informed by campus-wide levels of analysis (Schwartz, 1998). Librarians clearly have an important role to play in conveying to their institutions the importance of networked information in learning, teaching and research (Pinfield and McKenna, 1998). However, Walton and Edwards (1998) warn that LIS departments often do not have the political influence or spending power, and that this inhibits their potential to influence strategies for IT provision and information provision. There is clearly an issue of the credibility of the academic library and its staff with influential players in universities and beyond. Dougherty and Montgomery (1997–98) point to a lack of shared vision on campus, faculty focused on its own work, and job security obviating the need for individual change by academics. This means that change in universities can be very slow.

Strategic library and information plans need to link with the university's institutional plans. However, change does not always result from overarching communications and information strategies (D. Allen, 1998). There may be a mismatch between institutional mission and strategies to achieve that mission (Day *et al.*, 1998). However, it is important that there is a shared 'vision' for the development for services and that this vision is supported by strategic alliances and partnerships within the university and outside. Many writers emphasize the importance of the relationship between the staff in library and computing departments. Lippincott (1998) argues that such relationships need to be based upon a shared vision, mutual respect between the heads of these units and senior administrators, and the creation of a climate where 'shared understandings' can be fostered.

Change strategies need to involve staff at all levels and demand skilled leadership. Farley *et al.* (1998) argue that change can be difficult, disturbing and risky, bringing with it uncertainty and the unknown, and the fear of change that people experience stems from this inherent unpredictability. Treadwell (1998) warns us that there are differences in the way in which individuals process the effects of change. There are many strategies for dealing with these fears and actively involving staff in the processes of change. Rettig (1998) suggests 'scenario planning'. Ambriz *et al.* (1998) describe the use of quality circles to effect a programme of continuous service improvement involving staff at the National Autonomous University of Mexico. Another approach is to seek funding for individual projects that can contribute to the realization of the overall vision and pilot innovations. Dougherty and Montgomery (1997–98) talk of multiple initiatives involving staff at all levels. Day *et al.* (1998) argue that getting staff to work together on short-term projects encourages flexibility and greater confidence at a time of change. Project management is growing in importance in academic libraries, although Chambers and Perrow (1998) found that UK academic library managers rarely use project management techniques. Projects can be important, but if they are to be of value beyond an individual library or even a small group of users, the projects must be 'scaleable' and, if they are to last over time, they must be 'sustainable' beyond the project phase (Brophy and Fisher, 1998). The outcomes, models or trial services may also need to be 'portable' to other libraries after the project phase (Goodman, 1998).

Dougherty and Montgomery (1997–98) argue that leadership in the future will be less concerned with building the largest collections or grandest buildings but with leading organizations through the 'permanent white-water' of change. It is necessary for managers to take informed risks and invest in change. Schwartz (1998) argues that many libraries have undertaken surveys of use; but why have so few reinvested in access services (and new titles)? Few have gone down the route of cancelling low-use, high-cost journals and investing instead in a heavily subsidized document delivery service so that users can get what they need even if it is not in the collection.

Conclusion

Academic libraries need to change fundamentally if they are to meet the needs of institutions which are themselves responding to the implications of the wired-up world. Cultural change is needed which will involve 'lasting structural and social changes' and 'lasting changes to the shared ways of thinking' (Oppenheim, 1998). It also requires a lot of learning by those who are in the business of learning. Fowler (1998) guides us with the concept of the 'learning organization'. Clearly, at a time of great change, we need to review, assess and learn from our own and others' successes and failures. Chang and Hor (1998) capture the flavour of the academic library as we enter the 21st century: 'As more changes will take place, more issues will surface; learning from the past, knowing the present; we shall be prepared for the future'.

References

Akeroyd, J. (1998) On demand publishing in higher education: the practicalities, benefits, and issues. *Program,* **32**(1), 25–35.

Allen, B. (1998) From library assistant to service supervisor: the role of competences in staff development at the University of Lincolnshire and Humberside. *SCONUL Newsletter*, (14), 27–29.

Allen, B.M. and Hirshon, A. (1998) Hanging together to avoid hanging separately: opportunities for academic libraries and consortia. *Information Technology and Libraries,* **17**(1), 36–43.

Allen, D. (1998) Information technology and transformational change in the HE sector. *Library and Information Research News,* **22**(71), 40–51.

Ambriz, G.S. *et al.* (1998) Círculos de calidad: una herramienta en al mejoramiento continuo de un sistema de información científica de la UNAM. *Revista AIBDA,* **19**(1), 75–101.

Andaleeb, S.S. and Simmonds, P.L. (1998) Explaining user satisfaction with academic libraries: strategic implications. *College and Research Libraries,* **59**(2), 156–167.

Anderson, M. (1998) Access to research collections in the UK: the Anderson Report updated. *Library Review,* **47**(5/6), 262–266.

Arunachalam, S. (1998) Information haves and have-nots: technology enhances inequalities in scientific research, too. *Educom Review,* **33**(6), 40–45. http://www.educause.edu/ir/library/html/erm9863.html

Barton, J. and Blagden, J. (1998) *Academic library effectiveness: a comparative approach.* London: British Library Research and Innovation Centre. [British Library Research and Innovation Reports, 120.]

Basile, A.J. (1998) Making the internet manageable for your users (and yourself). In: LaGuardia, C. (1998) (ed.), pp. 221–238.

Beattie, D. and McCallum, D. (1998) Electronic scholarly publishing initiatives at Industry Canada. In W. Jones (ed.), pp. 223–232.

Bénaud, C.-L. and Bordeianu, S. (1998) *Outsourcing library operations in academic libraries: an overview of issues and outcomes.* Englewood, NJ: Libraries Unlimited.

Bentley, S. (1998) New collections for old. In: C. LaGuardia (ed.), pp. 123–134.

Benton, L. (1998) University-TAFE libraries: a way to the future? A review of relevant literature. *Australian Library Journal*, **47**(1), 43–60.

Bolton, N. *et al.* (1998) The use of libraries by postgraduate distance learning students: whose responsibility? *Open Learning*, **13**(1), 3–8.

Bot, M. *et al.* (1998) The cost of publishing an electronic journal: a general model and case study. *D-Lib Magazine*, **4**(11). http://www.dlib.org/dlib/november98/11roes.html

Breivik, P.S. (1998) *Student learning in the information age.* Phoenix, AZ: Oryx Press. [American Council on Education Series on Higher Education.]

Brophy, P. and Fisher, S. (1998) The hybrid library. *New Review of Information and Library Research*, **4**, 3–15.

Brophy, P. *et al.* (1998) *The development of UK academic library services in the context of lifelong learning: a supporting study in the JISC Electronic Libraries (eLib) Programme.* Manchester: Manchester Metropolitan University, Centre for Research in Library and Information Management.

Brown, A. (1998) The electronic library at the University of Derby. *Managing Information*, **98**(5), 28–30.

Bulpitt, G. (1997) The Adsetts Learning Centre, Sheffield Hallam University. In: M.-F. Bisbrouk and M. Chauveinc (eds) *Intelligent library buildings. Proceedings of the tenth seminar of the IFLA Section on Library Buildings and Equipment, The Hague, August 1997.* http://www.ifla.org/VII/s20/rep/intlib.pdf

Cajkler, W. (1998) Distance learning: the tutor's experience. *Education Libraries Journal*, **41**(1), 13–20.

Campbell, J. (1998) Digital library = holistic library: collection decision making in the electronic environment. In: LaGuardia, C. and Mitchell, B.A. (1998) (eds), pp. 42–46.

Chambers, S. and Perrow, D. (1998) Introducing project management techniques to the Robinson Library, University of Newcastle. *Journal of Librarianship and Information Science*, **30**(4), 249–258.

Chang, H.-Y. and Hor, A. (1998) Is there life after paperless?: electronic information resources in the academic library. *Journal of Information, Communication and Library Science*, **4**(3), 9–21.

Charton, G. (1998) La presse scientifique électronique: analyse de l'offre des intermédiaires. *Bulletin des Bibliothèques de France*, **43**(3), 28–40.

Chen, H.-H. (1998) The role of metadata in National Taiwan University Digital Library/Museum Project [in Chinese]. *Journal of Library and Information Science*, **23**(2), 51–65.

Chisenga, J. (1998) A study of university libraries' home pages in sub-Saharan Africa. *Libri*, **48**(1), 49–57.

Christoffel, M. *et al.* (1998) Electronic market: the roadmap for university libraries and members to survive in the information jungle. *Sigmod Record*, **27**(4), 68–73.

Chung, T.-Y. (1998) The investigation of the library anxiety of the students of the National Chengchi University [in Chinese]. *Bulletin of Library and Information Science*, (25), 73–92.

Chuong, N.H. (1998) Automating Vietnam's academic libraries: the example of Vietnam National University. *Asian Libraries*, **7**(11), 333–338.

Clegg, S. (1998) Converged enquiry/help desks: rhetoric or reality? *Relay (LA UC&R Newsletter)*, (45), 7–10.

Cooper, R. *et al.* (1998) Remote library users – needs and expectations. *Library Trends,* **47**(1), 42–64.

Corrall, S. (1998a) Key skills for students in higher education. *SCONUL Newsletter,* (15), 25–28.

Corrall, S. (1998b) Knowledge management: are we in the knowledge management business? *Ariadne,* (18). http://www.ariadne.ac.uk/issue18/knowledge-mgt/

Cotter, R. *et al.* (1998) *CAVAL reference interest group: working party on performance measures for reference services: final report.* Victoria, Australia: Cooperative Action by Victorian Academic Libraries. http://www.caval.edu.au/wppmfirp.pdf

Crawford, J. *et al.* (1998) The stakeholder approach to the construction of performance measures. *Journal of Librarianship and Information Science,* **30**(2), 87–112.

Crawford, W. (1998) Uncommon knowledge: mythbreaking for the future. In: LaGuardia, C. and Mitchell, B.A. (1998) (eds), pp. 16–24.

Cronin, B. (1998) The electronic academy revisited. *Aslib Proceedings,* **50**(9), 241–254.

Dalton, P. *et al.* (1998) The hybrid library and university strategy: a consultation exercise with senior university managers. *New Review of Information and Library Research,* **4**, 43–52.

Davies, J.E. (1998) Strategic issues in managing information and document supply in academic libraries. *Library Management,* **19**(5), 318–326.

Day, J. *et al.* (1998) How do electronic libraries affect people? Insights from the IMPEL project. *New Review of Information and Library Research,* **4**, 53–66.

Day, M. (1998) Online serials: preservation issues. In: Jones, W. (1998) (ed.), pp. 199–221.

De Gennaro, R. (1998) JSTOR: building an internet accessible digital archive of retrospective journals. *INSPEL,* **32**(2), 88–92.

de Jager, K. and Nassimbeni, M. (1998) Roadmaps for the highway: the evaluation of an information literacy training programme for South African students. *Education for Information,* **16**(2), 131–143.

Dempsey, L. *et al.* (1998) Managing access to a distributed library resource: report from the fifth MODELS workshop. *Program,* **32**(3), 265–281.

Di Marco, S. and Van Dam, S. (1998) Late night in an academic library: issues, concerns, planning. *Library and Archival Security,* **14**(2), 7–23.

Dickstein, R. (1998) Listserv lemmings and fly-brarians on the wall. *College and Research Libraries,* **59**(1), 10–17.

Dougherty, R.M. and Montgomery, J.G. (1997–98) Inside Pandora's box: navigating permanent 'white-water' of organizational change. *Against the Grain,* **9**(6), 68–75.

Dugdale, C. (1998) Managing short loan collection in academic libraries: print and electronic alternatives for the new learning environment. *Journal of Librarianship and Information Science,* **30**(2), 133–140.

Dunford, H.M. (1998) Joint use libraries as services for remote areas: a Tasmanian case study. *Asian Libraries,* **7**(8), 177–183.

East, H. *et al.* (1998) Charging for access to university-wide networked database services in British academia. *Aslib Proceedings,* **50**(10), 297–307.

Edwards, C. *et al.* (1998) eLib's IMPel2 project: organisational structures and responses to change in academic libraries. *New Review of Academic Librarianship,* **4**, 53–70.

Edwards, R.G. and Williams, C.J. (1998) Performance appraisal in academic libraries: minor changes or major renovation. *Library Review,* **47**(1), 14–19.

Edwards, V. (1998) Self-services: transforming the role of library staff. *SCONUL Newsletter,* (14), 30–32.

Eggink, G. (1998) "We kunnen elkaars kwaliteit versterken": bibliotheek Enschede en Volksuniversiteit stevenen op verregaande samenweking af. *BibliotheekBlad*, **2**(14), 10–11.

Ensor, P. (1998) Virtual library instruction: training tomorrow's user today. In: LaGuardia, C. (1998) (ed.), pp. 221–238.

Equinox. http://equinox.dcu.ie/reports/pilist.html

Farley, T. *et al.* (1998) Academic libraries, people and change: a case study of the 1990s. *Library Management*, **19**(4), 238–251.

Feo, A. (1998) L'enseignement de méthodologie documentaire à l'Université Paris 8: un accompagnement bien tempéré. *Documentaliste*, **35**(3), 147–155.

Fishman, D.L. (1998) Managing the virtual reference desk: how to plan an effective reference e-mail system. *Medical Reference Services Quarterly*, **17**(1), 1–10.

Fishwick, F. *et al.* (1998) *Scholarly electronic journals: economic implications. A supporting study in the JISC Electronic Libraries (e-Lib) Programme.* London: Library Technology Centre.

Fitzgerald, A. and Jones, D. (eds) (1997) *ARL Partnerships Program: breaking down walls and building bridges.* Washington, DC: Association of Research Libraries. [SPEC Kit no. 225.]

Fowler, R.K. (1998) The university library as learning organization for innovation: an exploratory study. *College and Research Libraries*, **59**(3), 200–231.

Freiburger, G.A. and Ralph, L. (1998) Electronic reserves: the changing landscape of instructional support. *Bulletin of the Medical Library Association*, **86**(1) 17–25.

Gadd, E. and Kingston, P. (1998) The impact of an electronic short loan collection on academic staff. *Managing Information*, **5**(2), 37–40.

Garland, K.J. *et al.* (1998) The Intranet as a learning tool: a preliminary study. *Information Research*, **4**(1). http://www.shef.ac.uk/~is/publications/infres/paper51.html

Garnes, K. (1998) Universitetsbibliotekene: en Sareptas krukke for all; men hvem betaler for tjenestene? *Synposis*, **29**(3), 172–176.

Gerhard, K. (1998) Coordination and collaboration: a model for electronic resources management. In: Jones, W. (1998) (ed.), pp. 279–286.

Goetsch, L.A. and Kaufman, P.T. (1998) Readin'. writin', arithmatic, and information competency: adding a basic skills component to a university's curriculum. *Campus-wide Information Systems*, **15**(5), 158–163.

Goodman, R. (1998) Porting the ACORN (Access to Course Readings via Networks) model from Loughborough University to Leicester University. *Program*, **32**(2), 107–121.

Grassian, E. (1998) alt.help.I.can't.keep.up: support for the electronically challenged. In: LaGuardia, C. and Mitchell, B.A. (1998) (eds), pp. 136–139.

Greenberg, S. (1998) Reading between the lines. *RIBA Journal*, **105**(12), 46–53.

Groenewegen, H.W. (1998) Electronic reserves: key issues and innovations. *Australian Academic and Research Libraries*, **29**(1), 1–12.

Grobler, L. (1998) The 'electronic MBL': providing South African business students with remote access to information. *Mousaion*, **16**(1), 59–73.

Guernsey, L. (1998) Library groups, decrying 'Excessive pricing,' demand new policies on electronic journals. *Chronicle of Higher Education*, **44**(31), A33–A34.

Gupta, O.P. (1998) *Library and information services in university and college libraries in India.* New Delhi: Reliance Publishing House.

Guthrie, K.M (1998) JSTOR and the University of Michigan: an evolving collaboration. *Library Hi Tech*, **16**(1), 9–36.

Haag, C. (1998) 'Otto, lass die Sau raus!' oder Von heutigen Medien hinter gestrigen Mauern. Die neu Fachhochschul-Bibliothek in Konstanz am Bodensee. *Buch und Bibliothek*, **50**(5), 354–358.

Hafner, K.A. and Oblinger, D.G. (1998) Transforming the academy. In: D.A. Oblinger and S.C. Rush (eds) *The future compatible campus: planning, designing, and implementing information technology for the academy*. Boston, MA: Anker, pp. 2–23.

Hamershlag, G. (1998) Using electronic journals in medicine [in Hebrew]. *Information and Librarianship*, **23**(2), 5–16.

Hampson, A. (1999) *The impact of the hybrid library on information services staff*, vol. 1. Birmingham: University of Birmingham, Builder Project.
http://builder.bham.ac.uk/reports/html/focus.asp

Harris, R.M. and Marshall, V. (1998) Reorganizing Canadian libraries: a giant step back from the front. *Library Trends*, **46**(3), 564–580.

Hart, E. *et al.* (1998) The use of focus groups in the evaluation of services. In: *Proceedings* (1998), pp. 133–138.

Hayden, M. (1998) Satisfaction surveys using Libra software and focus groups. In D. Spiller (ed.) *Academic library surveys and statistics in practice: proceedings of a seminar held at Loughborough University, 2–3 June 1997*. Loughborough: Loughborough University Department of Information and Library Studies, Library and Information Statistics Unit, pp. 33–42.

Haynes, D. *et al.* (1998) Comparative evaluation of the subject based gateways approach to providing access to network resources – a report to JISC under the eLib supporting studies programme.
http://www.ukoln.ac.uk/services/elib/papers/tavistock/subject-gateway-access

Heckart, R.J. (1998) Machine help and human help in the emerging digital library. *College and Research Libraries*, **59**(3), 250–259.

Helfer, D.S. (1998) 'The fighting Varsity' – 'Hail, Purdue!!' and all you other libraries out there! *Searcher*, **6**(3), 53–55.

Hernández, A.L.R. (1998) Buscadores de revistas electrónicas. *El Professional de la Información*, **7**(4), 3–5.

Herrington, V.J. (1998) The way beyond BI: a look to the future. *Journal of Academic Librarianship*, **24**(5), 381–386.

Hirshon, A. (1998) Integrating computing and library services. [CAUSE Professional Paper #18.] http://www.educause.edu/asp/doclib/abstract.asp?ID=pub3018

Horrocks, A. (1998) What do students want?: using 'priority search' surveys to determine user satisfaction with library surveys. *SCONUL Newsletter*, (15), 21–24.

Hsieh, Y.-S. (1998) A study on the users' perception to the body language of reference librarians [in Chinese]. *Journal of Educational Media and Library Sciences*, **35**(3), 258–282.

Hunter, K. (1998) Electronic journal publishing: observations from inside. *D-Lib Magazine*, **4**(7/8). http://www.dlib.org/dlib/july98/07hunter.html

Idowu, A.O. (1998) Relationship between training/experience, knowledge of computer usage and attitudes of Nigerian librarians towards computers. *International Information and Library Review*, **30**(4), 303–309.

International (1998) Coalition of Library Consortia. Statement of current perspective and preferred practices for the selection and purchase of electronic information. *Information Technology and Libraries*, **17**(1), 45–49.

Jackson, M. *et al.* (1998) Changing UK library and information services: a case study at the University of Northumbria at Newcastle informed by the IMPEL2 project. *New Review of Academic Librarianship*, **4**, 71–85.

Jacobs, N. (1998) Academic researchers' use of the Internet, and their consequent support requirements. *Library and Information Research News*, **22**(70), 30–34.

Jiang, D. (1998) A feasibility study of the outsourcing of cataloguing in academic libraries. *Journal of Educational Media and Library Services*, **35**(4), 283–293.

Jones, W. (1998) (ed.) *E-serials: publishers, libraries, users, and standards*. New York: Haworth Press.

Jordan, P. (1998) *The academic library and its users*. Aldershot: Gower.

Kai, S. (1998) Floating electronic library on the network [in Japanese]. *Yakugaku Toshokan* [Pharmaceutical Library Bulletin], **43**(2), 112–119.

Kao, C. *et al.* (1998) Ranking university libraries: the Taiwan case. *Libri*, **48**(4), 212–223.

King, H.M. (1998) Academic library buildings for the next century: insights from the United States. *LASIE*, **29**(1), 21–31.

Kirkpatrick, T.E. (1998) The training of academic library staff on information technology within the libraries of the Minnesota State Colleges and Universities System. *College and Research Libraries*, **59** (1), 51–59.

Kostopoulos, G.K. (1998) Global delivery of education via the Internet. *Internet Research: Electronic Networking Applications and Policy*, **8**(3), 257–265.

Krissoff, A. and Konrad, L. (1998) Computer training for staff and patrons: a comprehensive academic model. *Computers in Libraries*, **18**(1), 28–32.

Kundu, A.K. and Panda, N.M. (1998) Inevitability of resource sharing among the university libraries in North-East India: a pragmatic approach. *Herald of Library Science*, **37**(1–2), 56–69.

Kupersmith, J. (1998a) Technostress in the bionic library. In: LaGuardia, C. (1998) (ed.), pp. 23–47.

Kupersmith, J. (1998b) You are here, but where is that?: architectural design metaphors in the electronic library. In: LaGuardia, C. and Mitchell, B.A. (1998) (eds), pp. 58–67.

Kuttler, C. (1998) 'Lichtdurchflutet' mit Durchblick studieren. Die Zentralbibliothek der Fachhochschüle Weihenstephan: von den Anfangen bis zum Neubau für ein modernes informationszentrum. *Bibliotheksforum Bayern*, **26**(2), 156–171.

Kvist, K.G. (1998) Aalborg Universitetsbibliotek som virtuelt bibliotek. *DF-Revy*, **22**(1), 3–6.

LaGuardia, C. (1998) (ed.) *Recreating the academic library: breaking virtual ground*. New York: Neal Schuman.

LaGuardia, C. and Mitchell, B.A. (1998) (eds) *Finding common ground: creating the library of the future without diminishing the library of the past*. New York: Neal-Schuman.

Lancaster, F.W. (1998) Evaluating the digital library. In: *Proceedings* (1998), pp. 47–57.

Lappalainen-Happonen, S.-L. (1998) Yhteistoiminnallisen oppimisem soveltamisesta tiedonhallintataitojen ja kirjastonkayton opetukseen. *Signum*, **31**(2), 26–29.

Learning (1998) *age. The*, London: Stationery Office [CM. 3790.]

Liang, C.C. *et al.* (1998) Reengineering university information services: Yuan Ze University's experience. *Cause/Effect*, **21**(4).
http://www.educause.edu/ir/library/html/cem9848.html

Library and Information Commission (1998) *Role of libraries in a learning society*. London: Library and Information Commission.

Line, M.B. (1998) Designing libraries round human beings. *Aslib Proceedings*, **50**(8), 221–229

Lippincott, J.K. (1998) Team-building, collaboration and the reengineering of library services: a two part discussion: part 1: Team-building, collaboration, and the reengineering of library services. In: LaGuardia, C. and Mitchell, B.A. (1998) (eds) pp. 434–439.

Löffler, M. (1998) Arbeiten, wo pferde trabten. . .Zum Um-und Teilneubau der Teilbibliothek 2 ('Aula') der Universitätsbibliothek Eichstätt. *Bibliotheksforum Bayern* **26**(1), 84–98.

Luther, J. (1998) Distance learning and the digital library. *Educom Review*, **33**(4), 22–26. http://www.educause.edu/ir/library/html/erm9842.html

Lynch, C. (1998) Access management for networked information resources. *Cause/Effect*, **21**(4). http://www.educause.edu/ir/library/html/cem9842.html

Lynch, C.A. (1998a) Finding common ground. In: LaGuardia, C. and Mitchell, B.A. (1998) (eds), pp. 1–15.

Lynch, C.A. (1998b) Recomputerizing the library: new roles for information technology in a time of networked information. In: LaGuardia, C. (1998) (ed.), pp. 3–22.

MacDougall, A. (1998) Supporting learners at a distance. *Ariadne*, (16). http://www.ariadne.ac.uk/issue16/main/

McKenzie, E.M. and Casey, K.E. (1998) Using adaptive technology to provide access to blind, low-vision, and dyslexic patrons. *Law Library Journal*, **90**(2), 157–182.

McLean, N. (1997) The global scholarly information infrastructure: the quest for sustainable solutions In: Mark Fresko Consultancy (ed.) *Beyond the beginning: the global digital library: an international conference organised by UKOLN on behalf of JISC, CNI, BLRIC, CAUSE, and CAUL, June 1997, London*. London: British Library Board. [British Library Research and Innovation Report 78.] http://www.ukoln.ac.uk/services/papers/bl/blri078/content/repor~10.htm

McNamara, D. and Core, J. (1998) (eds) *The EduLib Project: teaching for learning in libraries and information services: a series of educational development workshops*. Hull: University of Hull, EduLib.

McPherson, M. *et al.* (1998) Hervey Bay joint use library: lessons for tomorrow. *Australasian Public Libraries and Information Services*, **11**(2), 75–89.

Mano González, M. de la (1998) Propuesta de un sistema de evaluación para bibliotecas universitarias. *Revista Española de Documentación Científica*, **21**(2), 174–197.

Milner, E. (1999) Call centres: enhancing service delivery or 'dark satanic mills'. *Managing Information*, **6**(2), 38–39.

Muir, A. (1998) Publishers' views of electronic short-loan collections and copyright clearance issues. *Journal of Information Science*, **24**(4), 215–229.

Mulder, H. (1998) Het Utrechtse perspectief: het digitaliseren van bijzondere collecties. *Informatie Professional*, **2**(1), 27–29.

Mulvaney, T.K. and Lewis, E. (1998) Analysis of library services for distance learning students at the University of Birmingham. *Education Libraries Journal*, **41**(1), 29–34.

Nankivell, C. (1999) *The hybrid library and university strategy*. Birmingham: University of Birmingham, Builder Project. http://builder.bham.ac.uk/reports/html/strategic.asp

Niemitalo, J. (1998) Data envelopment analysis (DEA) as a method of evaluating libraries: a case study of Finnish academic libraries. In: *Proceedings* (1998), pp. 173–180.

Novak, J. and Robinson, G. (1998) 'You tell us': Indigenous students talk to a tertiary library. *Australian Academic and Research Libraries*, **29**(1), 13–22.

O'Daniel, H.B. (1999) Cataloguing the Internet. *Associates: the Electronic Library Support Journal*, **5**(3). http://raven.cc.ukans.edu/~assoc/heather399.htm

Ober, J. (1999) The California Digital Library. *D-Lib*, **5**(3). http://www.dlib.org/dlib/march99/03ober.html

Oberman, C. *et al.* (1998) Integrating information literacy into the curriculum: how is your library measuring up. *College and Research Libraries News*, **59**(5), 347–352.

Oehling, H. (1998) Wissenschaftlicher Bibliothekar 2000 – quo vadis? 12 Thesen zur Zukunft des Fachreferenten. *Bibliotheksdienst*, **32**(2), 247–254.

Ojiro, K. (1998) Electronic journals in an academic environment [in Japanese]. *Igaku Toshokan*, [Journal of the Japan Medical Library Association], **45**(2), 201–210.

Onwuegbuzie, A.J. and Jiao, Q.G. (1998) The relationship between library anxiety and learning styles among graduate students: implications for library instruction. *Library and Information Science Research*, **20**(3), 235–249.

Oppenheim, C. (1998) Beyond e-lib: how does e-lib fit into the wider context of electronic information research? *Library and Information Research News*, **21**(69), 17–23.

Oppenheim, C. and Smithson, D. (1999) What is the hybrid library? *Journal of Information Science*, **25**(2), 97–112.

Parker, S. and Jackson, M. (1998) The importance of the subject librarian in resource based learning: some findings of the IMPEL2 project. *Education Libraries Journal*, **41**(2), 21–26.

Pelowski, M. (1997) Examples of e-mail suggestion boxes. [to multiple recipients of list] *lis-link*, 28 October 1997, CDT 16:17:06.

Phillips, S. (1998) Irish university libraries: recent developments and future prospects. *Library Review*, **47**(5/6), 306–310.

Picci, L. (1998) La comunicazione scientifica e l'economia dell'informazione: nuove tendenze e scenari possibili. *Biblioteche Oggi*, **16**(3), 28–33.

Pinfield, S. (1998) Managing the hybrid library. *SCONUL Newsletter*, (14), 41–44.

Pinfield, S. *et al.* (1998) Realizing the hybrid library. *D-Lib*, **4**(10). http://www.dlib.org/dlib/october98/10pinfield.html

Pinfield, S. and McKenna, B. (1998) The builder project. *Electronic Library*, **16**(5), 305–307.

Proceedings (1998) *of the 2nd Northumbria International Conference on performance measurement in libraries and information services, September 1997*. Eds. P. Wressel and Associates. Newcastle upon Tyne: Information North.

Pullinger, D. (1999) Academics and the new information environment: the impact of local factors on use of electronic journals. *Journal of Information Science*, **25**(2), 164–172.

Ramsden, A. *et al.* (1998) *ELINOR Electronic Library Project*. East Grinstead: Bowker-Saur. [British Library Research & Innovation Report 22.]

Ray, K. and Day, J. (1998) Student attitudes towards electronic information resources. *Information Research*, **4**(2). http://www.shef.ac.uk/~is/publications/infres/paper54.html

Rettig, J. (1998) Designing scenarios to design effective buildings. In: C. LaGuardia (ed.), pp. 67–89.

Revill, D. (1998) Looking back in anger. *Ariadne*, (18), 4–6. http://www.ariadne.ac.uk/issue18/revill/

Robnett, B. (1998) Online journal pricing. In: Jones, W. (1998) (ed.), pp. 55–69.

Rose, P. *et al.* (1998) A focus group approach to assessing technostress at the reference desk. *Reference and User Services Quarterly*, **37**(4), 311–317.

Rosenberg, D. (1998) IT and university libraries in Africa. *Internet Research: Electronic Networking Applications and Policy*, **8**(1), 5–13.

Rusbridge, C. (1998) Towards the hybrid library. *D-Lib Magazine*, **4**(7/8). http://www.dlib.org/dlib/july98/rusbridge/07rusbridge.html

Sacchanand, C. (1998) Library networks for distance education: a case study of Sukhothai Thammathirat Open University in Thailand. *Asian Libraries*, **7**(10), 274–279.

Sandelands, E. (1998) Creating an online library to support a virtual learning environment *Internet Research: Electronic Networking Applications and Policy*, **8**(1), 75–80.

Santos, M.L. (1998) La aplicación del benchmarking en un sistema de información: un estudio de caso. *Ciencias de la Información*, **29**(2), 25–31.

Sarvilinna, M. (1998) Kurssikirja netissa, opiskelijat innokkaita. Kokemuksia elektronisesta oppimateriaalista, *Signum*, **31**(2), 36–37.

Savenije, B. (1998) De terugkeer van de betovering: bij de afronding de Elektronische Bibliotheek Utrecht. *Informatie Professional*, **2**(5), 30–34.

Schibel, W. (1998) 'Fachreferat 2000'. 13 Thesen zur Differenzierung des wissenschaftlichen Bibliotheksdienstes. *Bibliotheksdienst*, **32**(6), 1040–1047.

Schirdewahn, H.G. (1998) Das Freiburger Modell. *Bibliothek Forschung und Praxis*, **22**(1), 84–88.

Schlageter, G. (1998) Virtuelle Universität: eine neue Generation netzbasierter bildungssyteme. *Bibliothek Forschung und Praxis*, **22**(1), 45–50.

Schwartz, C. (1998) Restructuring academic libraries: organizational development in the wake of technological change. In: LaGuardia, C. and Mitchell, B.A. (1998) (eds), pp. 463–466.

Simpson, A.E. (1998) Information-finding and the education of scholars: teaching electronic access in disciplinary context. *Behavioural and Social Sciences Librarian*, **16**(2), 1–18.

Smith, C. and Phillips, C. (1999) Are our academic libraries ready for the Internet generation. *Cause/Effect*, **22**(1). http://www.educause.edu/ir/library/html/cem991a.htm

Staley, L. (1998) E-mail reference: experiences at City University. *PNLA Quarterly*, **62**(4), 20–21.

Stamatoplos, A. and Mackoy, R. (1998) Effects of library instruction university students' satisfaction with the library: a longitudinal study. *College and Research Libraries*, **59**(4), 323–334.

Stein, F. (1998) De markt in toom houden en veel meer publieke middelen beschikbaar stellen: Cees Hamelink beschouwt het recht op informatie als de toetssteen van alle mensenrechten. *BibliotheekBlad*, **2**(10/11), 18–20.

Stone, T. (1998) (De)convergence at Luton. *SCONUL Newsletter*, (14), 40–41.

Streatfield, D. and Markless, S. (1997) The effective college library. Coombe Lodge: Further Education Development Agency. [British Library Research and Innovation Reports 21.]

Tammaro, A.M. (1998) Dall' accesso alla conservazione: un 'infrastruttura nazionale per la gestione delle risorse elettroniche. *Biblioteche Oggi*, **16**(2), 72–75.

Tarvonen, S. (1998) Elektroninen kurssikirja opiskelun tukena. *Signum*, **31**(2), 37–38.

Tenner, E. *et al.* (1998) Electronic and traditional sources for a newly established branch library: product availability and user preferences. *Collection Building*, **17**(3), 123–128.

Thomas, C.F. and Griffin, L.S. (1998) Who will create the metadata for the Internet? *First Monday*, **3**(12). http://www.firstmonday.dk/issues/issue3_12/thomas/index.html

Thomas, P.S. and Jones, M. (1998) (eds) *Proceedings of the Eighth Off-Campus Library Services Conference, Providence, Rhode Island, 22–24 April, 1998*. Mount Pleasant, MI: Michigan University.

Tomney, H. and Burton, P.F. (1998) Electronic journals: a study of usage and attitudes among academics. *Journal of Information Science*, **24**(6), 419–429.

Tompkins, P. *et al.* (1998) New learning communities: collaboration, networking, and information literacy. *Information Technology and Libraries*, **17**(2), 100–107.

Treadwell, J.B. (1998) Travelling through the wilderness: the long transition to the digital library. In: LaGuardia, C. and Mitchell, B.A. (1998) (eds), pp. 74–79.

Tuck, B. and Grieves, M. (1998) *The impact of electronic journals on local network computing and printing (eLib supporting study commissioned by UKOLN)*. December 1998. http://www.ukoln.ac.uk/dlis/models/studies/printing/printing.html

Turunen, T. (1998) Elektroninen oppimisympäristö työseminaari Opiskelijakirjastossa. *Signum*, **31**(2), 32–34.

Unwin, L. *et al.* (1998) *The role of the library in distance learning: a study of postgraduate students, course providers, and librarians in the UK*. London: Bowker-Saur.

Valauskas, E.J. (1998) Electronic journals and their role on the Internet. In: Jones, W. (1998) (ed.), pp. 45–54.

Walters, W. *et al.* (1998) Guidelines for collecting aggregations of web resources. *Information Technology and Libraries*, **17**(3), 157–160.

Walton, G. and Edwards, C. (1998) The Impact of e-Lib: the emerging paradoxes. *Library and Information Research News*, **21**(69), 12–16.

Wefers, S. (1998) Thesen zur Zukunft des Fachreferenten. *Bibliotheksdienst*, **32**(5), 865–870.

West, C. (1998) User surveys in practice. In: D. Spiller (ed.) *Academic library surveys and statistics in practice: proceedings of a seminar held at Loughborough University, 2–3 June 1997*. Loughborough: Department of Information and Library Studies, Library and Information Statistics Unit, pp. 15–22.

West, L. (1999) Frequently asked questions and electronic enquiry services. [To multiple recipients of list] *lis-link*, 10 February 1999, CDT 10:42:00.

Whitmire, E. (1998) Development of critical thinking skills: an analysis of academic library experiences and other measures. *College and Research Libraries*, **59**(3), 266–273.

Widenius, M. (1998) Mahdollisuuksien verkosto. *Signum*, **31**(7), 138–142.

Willemse, J. (1998) Performance measurement in IFLA and United Kingdom academic libraries. *South African Journal of Library and Information Science*, **66**(4), 161–165.

Wilson, T. (1998) Redesigning the university library in the digital age. *Journal of Documentation*, **54**(1), 15–27.

Winkworth, I. (1998) Making performance measurement influential. In: *Proceedings* (1998), pp. 93–97.

Winston, M. (1998) The role of recruitment in achieving roles related to diversity. *College and Research Libraries*, **59**(3), 240–247.

Wolpert. A. (1998) Services to remote users: marketing the library's role. *Library Trends*, **47**(1), 21–41.

Yamada, T. (1998) User evaluation to develop the Jikei University Medical Library by questionnaire survey [in Japanese]. *Igaku Toshokan* [Journal of the Japan Medical Library Association], **45**(1), 97–104.

Younis, A.R. (1998) The use of Arabized software packages in Jordan university libraries. *International Information and Library Review*, **30**(4), 311–340.

Zongying, Y. *et al.* (1998) The China Education Research Network (CERNET) and library services. *Asian Libraries*, **7**(9), 210–214.

Public libraries and librarianship

4

Brigitte Kühne

Introduction

All over the world more and more people become aware of the fact that public libraries are the institutions where they can get information in order to participate in the democratic process and to develop their countries. Together with the new technologies this is the challenge for the future for public libraries. Another challenge is the new role of delivering distance education via the Internet. How is this to be done and how will this affect the role of librarians? When the Internet links public libraries throughout the world, international networks will become more and more important.

That said, the traditional public library roles of acquiring and disseminating books and other materials, conducting programmes for children, emphasizing reading and delivering special services to the culturally disadvantaged, will still be important. That is what the public and politicians want us to do, and of course these services will still be central for us. As Dempsey (1998) says: 'Libraries will continue to measure their missions against what the public wants, what the profession can offer and what the future of information access and retrieval will bring.'

Public libraries as information centres

Information is power for development. The right to information is therefore an important human right. There are, however, economic, cultural, social and political preconditions attached to achieving the right to information. It seems that developed countries have important opportunities to realize the right to information, while the least developed and developing countries are far from doing so (Yilmaz, 1999). The phrase 'the right to information' has no meaning for a person who is hungry, who does not have enough money, who is not educated and who does not have freedom. In the same way, a country that has problems of hunger, education, economic and political freedom cannot give priority to the right to information. On the other hand, information is a power that can play an important role in solving these problems. Governments and individuals generally are not aware of this power.

Public libraries have important responsibilities for safeguarding the public's right to information. When one looks at the distribution of public libraries in the world, one can see that there is a severe inequality and imbalance. In Uganda, for instance, the proportion of the population who were public library users in 1996 was 0.2%, compared with 57.6% in the UK (*UNESCO*, 1997). While as many as 1,145,611 people have the opportunity of using just one public library in Uganda, in Finland there is a public library for every 2,851 people. In the collections of public libraries in the UK there are 2.29 books per person, but only one book per 3,000 people in Uganda. It can be clearly seen that there is a strong relationship between the level of development and the use of public libraries: 'Development is the foundation which increases public library use and consequently the right to information' (Yilmaz, 1999).

The ideal of individuality – freedom from censorship, the right to read, the right to participate in lifelong learning, etc. – constitutes the basis for many public libraries and will also affect the public librarian's profession (Muswazi, 1999). Throughout the world, conferences have been held on the theme of libraries and freedom of information (Visby, 1996–; Muswazi, 1999). Nowacki-Chmielowic (1998) has described the feelings in Poland today in comparison with Poland under the influence of the Soviet Union. In South Africa (Sibanyoni, 1997), public libraries are regarded as a guarantee of democratic development. There were public libraries in the country before, but often they were reserved for white people's leisure reading, whereas now they are slowly changing into information centres, and new libraries are being built in areas where poorly educated and deprived people live. Lor (1998) described the new role of public libraries in South Africa in a speech at a Johannesburg conference. While the country has some excellent libraries and quite a sophisticated infrastructure for information provision, the vast majority of people do not have access to even the most rudimentary library and information services. At the same time a new and bold initiative has been taken to give citizens electronic access to the collective library resources of the country, and to enable them to access the global world of information (Leatt, 1998). This is the NVL, the National Virtual Library of South Africa; its goals are to provide citizens anywhere with access to electronic and print resources everywhere. Another idea comes from Schuler (1997), who argues that not only are public libraries at the foundation of the democratic society, but they are also natural partners in today's push to preserve a public sector in cyberspace. The solution for the future for public libraries and democracy may lie in linking libraries with community networks. However, there are still great problems with access to technology; for example, in Nigeria (Nwokocha, 1998) and Zimbabwe there are only 3,000 Internet users in the whole country (Cederqvist, 1997). This is comparable with levels of connection in the Baltic states of Estonia, Latvia and Lithuania, or in other former Soviet states.

Library services and the right to information can be regarded as part of a national information policy. However, many countries do not have such policies. The lack of a national policy in a country negatively affects library services and the right to information. Recently we have seen what happened in France where the extreme right National Front sought legitimacy by diffusing its ideas through libraries. This was at a time when library training excluded acquisition skills and budgets were under pressure. French law gives local councils responsibility over libraries, allowing National Front domination in towns they control. So how are librarians to act? As representatives of institutions, librarians need a clear policy to justify acquisitions decisions (Chourrot, 1997). On the other hand, Poulain (1997) argues that the public which the library serves includes that section of the population which voted for the Front, and the library belongs to its readers and not to the librarians (an argument that can be heard in many places worldwide). Acquisitions policy should therefore be made explicit and be displayed in libraries, and it should state the principles on which it is based. There is no universal model of a public library, but the values underpinning it can be harmonized, according to Poulain.

IFLA has set up a committee, FAIFE (Free Access to Information and Freedom of Expression), to speak for all libraries on their role regarding intellectual freedom. The committee, which has 23 members drawn from all over the world, has its office in Copenhagen. Its main task is to be an active instrument for IFLA to promote freedom of speech and to emphasize the vital role of the library as the entrance to information and knowledge. According to Ristarp (1999), FAIFE intends to work in three ways:

- to collect and disseminate as much information as possible about the practical possibilities for libraries to help citizens to gain information and give them freedom of speech;
- to work out a policy for IFLA on the role of public libraries in gaining information and giving citizens the right to freedom of speech;
- to help individual libraries, librarians and library associations if and when they are exposed to such injustice, or outrage, as the libraries in France by the National Front.

Public libraries as traditional lending libraries

The 'library romantics' who yearn for silence and old-fashioned books and who do not want to replace card catalogues with online bibliographic databases are as mistaken as those 'modern librarians' who cannot think in any other terms but technology. Public librarians must learn to think and work beyond their traditional boundaries. As McKee (1997) says, 'this is not easy – particularly for a profession seen with some justification to be overly inward-looking'. In the future, public information networks will be accessible to all citizens. Interactive services will bring government and citizens closer together, and networked opportunities for lifelong learning will be a reality for all who want to participate, but this means that public librarians will play a new role, additional to their traditional one of maintaining book stocks.

This is not to deny the need to revitalize old books, as in the DEBORA project in the Fourth Framework Programme of the Commission of the European Communities (CEC). DEBORA will develop tools for accessing collections of rare 16th century documents via networks. This includes the setting up of a production chain for digitizing the documents. Digitization will yield sets of images to be stored and indexed in an Image Based Management System, accessible via the WWW. The tools will also incorporate image recognition, and there will be supporting cooperative work. The DEBORA products will be tested and demonstrated in the participating libraries and at three further test sites: Munich, Barcelona and Geneva (DEBORA).

Our society needs libraries capable of acquiring and maintaining both print collections and electronic materials. Most public librarians have listened to the requests of users and try to maintain a good balance between them. Tipping the balance in either direction is a signal that the library has lost touch with its users and its mission (Dempsey, 1998). Others, however, think that with the increasing digitization of information the role of libraries as keepers and lenders of books will become so peripheral that librarians will soon be superfluous. Others again try to maintain some sort of a museum role in order to preserve the old collections.

Many researchers have noticed that more and more young people read less and do so less effectively. In Sweden, in more prosperous areas, only 76% of 14-year-olds are able to read easy texts 'without difficulties' (Josephson, 1999). In areas with many immigrants (e.g. Rinkeby, outside Stockholm), only 26% of this age group are able to read, despite all the reading campaigns that are carried out in the country with the help of school librarians and the government. In the UK, 1998–99 was designated the 'National Year of Reading' (Martin, 1999), a campaign supported by the Department of Education and Employment to encourage reading among the whole community. It was intended not only for children but also for parents, those with literacy problems, ethnic minorities, students, employees, etc. The European Union has also noticed this problem and launched a special programme called 'Culture 2000', by which the European Parliament wants to 'promote books and reading, in particular with young people and less favoured sectors of society' (Mouskouri, 1999). In some of these programmes it is hoped to raise standards of literacy generally through the promotion of reading, both for information and for personal enrichment. In a study by the Illinois Institute for Rural Affairs the extent to which libraries were actively engaged in local economic development efforts and how they perceived the benefits was demonstrated (Waizer and Gruidl, 1997). There is also a very important link to lifelong learning and distance education. Foster (1997) suggests that 'to argue that public libraries and learning are not joint entities is inconsistent with the past and denies their future'. The whole tradition of Scandinavian public libraries lies in their history of having emerged from a kind of education for 'the people', especially poor people and those who otherwise had no possibilities to participate in higher education (Folkbiblioteksutredningen, 1982). This aspect was also something that libraries in the former socialist countries of eastern Europe stressed (Górska, 1997; Marwinski, 1997). Arguably, some of the difficulties that German libraries face today stem from these differences in attitudes towards the role of public libraries in the former Bundesrepublik and GDR.

Public libraries and ICT development

Networking can transform and revitalize libraries but, according to McKee (1997), networking could also hasten their marginalization and decline. Partly for this reason, the CEC launched the Telematics for Libraries programme in the Fourth Framework Programme and now the Information Society Technologies programme in the Fifth Framework Programme (CEC). The Commission aims to make European citizens as well informed as possible. It has published a *Green paper on public sector information in the information society* (CEC, 1999), and has also promoted public library projects of different kinds (see Appendix) with a view to indicating the role of public libraries in the future. According to Raulff (1998), libraries must become media centres, stocking books and other media, and cooperating to convert old media into new where necessary; but he also says that the creation of a virtual world library is difficult to realize because of economic reasons.

In many other countries throughout the world, though, very few public libraries are yet equipped with computers. As long ago as 1995 the Thai government announced an IT Year to promote understanding of the role and importance of IT, but, as in many other countries, it was the academic libraries that were equipped first. As Premsit (1999) says, 'though many libraries were operating computerized library functions, no integrated system existed due to the fact that no integrated software was available at a reasonable cost', and 'in-house systems are still found in many libraries'. Similar things still apply in many countries – even Germany does not yet have a common database for its public libraries.

On the other hand, Finland has one of the most automated public library systems in the world. According to the Finnish Library Association, in 1997:

- 84% of all public library systems had automated library systems;
- 66% of main municipal libraries used external databases;
- the Internet was available in 47% of municipalities in January 1997, and it was estimated that in January 1999 between 80–90% of all main municipal public libraries would offer Internet access to their visitors.

The evidence suggests that Sweden is the country where the greatest number of computers are to be found in private homes. In 1998, 50% of all households had computers and in 1999 it was predicted to become 60%. Of these, around 60% are connected to the Internet (IT-Research, 1999). However, by turning the figures around it can be said that 30–40% of the population (even in a computer-dense country such as Sweden) do not have access to computers or the Internet. Consequently the pressure on computers in libraries will not decrease. Also, even if so many households have computers, does this say anything about how many actually are able to use them? Is it the case that only the young people in families use them, and older people tend to become a lost generation? If so, how can we help them in our libraries?

Well-stocked, well-staffed public libraries are essential if they are to play a significant role in the education of students and if they are to continue to serve as a catalyst for economic development and community improvement (Dempsey, 1998; Kühne, 1999). In this context, throughout the world library authorities are considering collaboration on:

- digitization programmes;
- networked community information;
- development of services promoting access to open learning, including strengthening links with the academic library sector;
- negotiation with suppliers including network partnerships.

In many countries, the strengthening of links between public and academic libraries seems to be of great importance. In Sweden, the newly adopted Library Act says that public and academic libraries are seen as partners and should cooperate, and that they should supply material from their collections free of charge to those who ask for it (*Svensk*, 1996). In the UK, the Joint Information Systems Committee (JISC) of the Higher Education Funding Councils has a programme of work, including the eLib research and development programme, to which considerable value could be added by involving the public library sector (McKee, 1997). In other countries both public and academic libraries work under extreme difficulties.

The Internet seems to offer many answers, but all who use it agree that chaos rules (Nielsen, 1999). The availability of electronic resources and references is constantly growing and changing, making it necessary for instructors as well as users to be familiar with various ways of accessing information, to possess the know-how to evaluate and organize information as well as the ability to synthesize and apply it in a coherent and correct way. For successful information retrieval one has to master the art of questioning. Organizing the Internet is in many ways the most important challenge we face at the moment. There have been several attempts to solve this problem; examples are the Michigan Electronic Library (Michigan), the Internet Public Library (Internet), the Finnish PULSE (Networked) and OCLC (OCLC).

The number of people using the Internet is growing steadily: in the USA it has grown from 18 million people in 1995 to 70.2 million aged over 16 in August 1998, so it is essential to make it more user friendly. According to Nielsen (1999), who cites Robert Kraus at Carnegie Mellon University, Pittsburgh, all those users seem to be extremely unhappy, and the more time they spend in front of their computers the more depressed they get. He also cites Karen Schneider, an Internet librarian in the USA, who says that if the problem is that the Internet makes people unhappy and alienated from the real world, then the solution could be to use computers in a socially valuable environment, e.g. in public libraries. Raulff (1998) argues that the creation of a 'great virtual world library', using electronic media, is impossible for economic reasons. However, since scientists increasingly rely on digital library services, it becomes more essential for public libraries also to get funds for access to electronic resources for bibliographic research, stock selection and databases all over the world.

Distance education, lifelong learning and information literacy

Distance education has gained popularity all over the world as a means of extending continuing education to all. It has benefited from rapid advances in electronic telecommunications in the 1980s and early 1990s. New communication technologies enable learning to take place outside the classroom. A number of colleges, universities and other institutions offer courses via distance education systems. Many of the participating students go to their nearest library (usually a public library) in order to get material or help from the library staff. The EU-funded project DERAL – Distance Education in Rural Areas via Libraries (see Appendix) explores the part that public libraries can play in this process.

According to Sacchanand (1999), distance education provides various opportunities for information professionals:

- It provides opportunities to acquire or update skills and knowledge in areas increasingly in demand.
- It enhances already acquired professional qualifications. Individual subjects may be taken as continuing education courses, without the need to meet formal entry requirements.

- It increases access to education and meets the needs of learners who are already in the workforce.
- It permits freedom from classroom limitations in location and time; time to learn is expanded to fit individual needs.
- It offers a chance to information professionals and people who live and work in remote areas and have no way of improving and continuing their education.
- It creates opportunities for people with families and work commitments who are unable to further their studies at conventional universities.

In Australia, libraries were already seen in Victorian times as the 'working man's university' (Foster, 1997). Foster suggests that 'the current trends in education could not emphasize this more with their focus on open learning, flexible service delivery, recognition of prior learning, and lifelong learning'. Not everyone wants to participate in academic courses; many want to take courses 'just for fun', in order to get better jobs, or for other personal reasons (Kühne, 1998). The Internet as a learning environment provides an outlet for searching for information within a specific subject area that can be incorporated into a distance education course and used by all kinds of people for personal lifelong learning.

Another potential way of using the library as a learning and resource centre is through the establishment of virtual classrooms as an aid in computer-based distance education (Attström, 1999). Modern technology and the Internet can revolutionize distance education by allowing students from varied backgrounds and countries to come together and study. A virtual classroom can, for instance, be built around a system of problem-based learning conducted online but with the aid of CDs containing images and films – a virtual library with references to recommended literature and qualified reviews, links to other sources, a Web board and a bulletin board. The success of online learning is based on the idea that participants stimulate learning, while teachers provide content as well as an agreed set of principles that will act as guidelines for both students and teachers. Students should influence the make-up and maintenance of the Web pages and preferably at some point meet their teachers and fellow course participants. Dowlin (1999), consultant and former head of the San Francisco public library, has shown how virtual schools and virtual libraries are fast becoming a reality.

Much of this leads to an emphasis on the importance of information literacy (IL). This means the ability to search, critically assess and use information. The initiatives that the ILL project (Oberman, 1999) has taken include providing immersion programmes that prepare librarians to become effective teachers of information literacy. They can promote 'community partnership programmes' and strategies for assisting individual institutions in creating and implementing effective information literacy programmes, and seek to ensure that information literate competencies are integrated into the instructional curriculum (Kühne, 1993).

When public librarians effectively become tutors or helpers for students who want to participate in distance education, they need to learn how to teach. A review of the literature on this subject indicates that most librarians learn to teach by attending workshops and conferences, reading literature (self-study), and discussing problems in discussion groups on the Internet; or they try to participate in distance education themselves (learning by doing). In the USA there are few courses in teaching in graduate schools of library and information science, but there are indications that this may be changing (Kilcullen, 1998).

Economics of public libraries

In many countries public libraries are the oldest existing cultural institutions. In some countries the libraries were built with private grant funds, in others governments provided the building. In both systems, however, the condition was usually that library services should be provided free of charge. Many early public leaders believed that free library services were the foundations of a literate population, an educated citizenry and a free and democratic society. Today throughout the world we hear that library budgets are being cut: in Hawaii by $3.5 million with five days' notice (Kane and Wallace, 1997); in Bucharest by half (Rotaru, 1999); and in France (Gabel, 1997), Germany (Bertelsmann Stiftung, 1997), Sweden (Ulvskog, 1999), Denmark (Alsmark, 1999), and the UK (LISU, 1998) by around 20–40%, to give a few examples. Libraries are increasingly turning to other sources to improve their financial situations: user fees, alternative funding, and co-sponsorship of activities and programmes with private companies. Fundraising, through lobbying and direct solicitation, has become a way of life for library directors. Professional staff in many libraries have also become innovative and assertive in seeking these outside funding sources (Kemp, 1999).

In various countries, librarians also try to find new ways to cope with reduced budgets by trying out new technologies and adopting more efficient ways of working. Library directors have used a number of innovative and cost-effective methods to hold down personnel costs – for example, hiring part-time employees, cross-training employees, contracting for services and increased use of citizen volunteers (Kemp, 1999). In Sweden and Denmark, some communities have been able to increase the number of opening hours and loans per person despite heavy cuts in their library budgets (Strandberg *et al.*, 1999). In Norway a research project started with Sunday opening for libraries in Steinkjer, Larvik and Trondheim (Markussen, 1999). It was difficult to draw any real conclusions from the figures, but if the aim was to offer families an extra cultural opportunity, the survey showed that Sunday opening for libraries was particularly attractive to them. In Helsinki, the City Library was open all year, even on Christmas Day and New Year's Eve, during a project that started in 1994. In the UK, Martin (1999) describes new and 'interesting times' since the change of government in 1997, even though budgets have been cut. Libraries, management of information, lifelong learning and the pursuit of knowledge are high on the agenda again. Reports in sectors such as disability discrimination, health service funding, the heritage lottery fund and homework centres have had an impact on libraries recently, and new strategies are being developed for a national information policy.

In many countries, new public libraries are being built despite the economic situation. In China, some new libraries were built in the early 1990s such as the Shanghai Library and large public libraries are under construction in the Shandong and Anhui Provinces and in the cities of Shenyang, Nanjung and Shenzhen (*Beijing Xinhua*, 1999). China now has more than 2,600 public libraries at county level or higher, with a total floor space of 4 million sq m, compared with 1,732 libraries with a floor space of 650,000 sq m around 1980. This growth rate is described as 'world leading'. Major American cities also, for example, Chicago, Los Angeles, San Francisco and Denver, continue to build new libraries (Dempsey, 1998); there are also examples in the UK (Nielsen, 1999). The Scandinavian countries have a large number of beautiful new library buildings with modern technological equipment (Statens kulturråd, 1998). Many of these libraries are built so that the customer can participate in distance education, look for information as easily as possible and use new technology even if unfamiliar with it. As Evald (1999) pointed out, all these changes and challenges are affecting the language of library architecture, and subsequently the shape and form of library buildings. The importance of integrating virtual possibilities into the physical space has been shown to be important, as has the balance between self-service possibilities for users and services provided by qualified staff.

In many countries, governments require users to pay fees in order to help the budget (Nielsen, 1999). However, in Sweden, the newly adopted Library Act says explicitly that library loans are to be free of charge (Svensk, 1996). Before the Act was adopted some Swedish communities tried to introduce charges for lending books or papers. The Library Act introduced in Finland in January 1999 also prohibits charging for basic services. In some countries, public library and information services tend to consume increasingly large budgets (Johnson, 1999), both for technical developments and for changes in management. The impact of technology on an organization demands top management attention and information professionals need to review their values in the light of those of the organization they serve. Yet in many countries, for example, Sweden and Germany, changes in political control have led to marginalization of the libraries and less money for them.

Changes in the public library profession

For many people in society (especially for many politicians), a librarian is still a person who lends books. In fact, members of the library profession exhibit a great awareness of the changes taking place in modern society, and they reveal a capacity to be intermediaries between the users of information and relevant information and communication technologies (Johnson, 1999). A relevant initiative is the National Information Literacy Institute, founded in 1997 at Plattsburgh State University of New York, and now known as the Institute for Information Literacy (Oberman, 1999). The institute's goals are to assist local libraries and schools in meeting people's needs, not only by helping them search for and access information, but also by teaching them how to evaluate information and use it wisely. One aspect of this work has been to redevelop the old concept of the 'teaching library', and thus a key component in the success of this project has been the role of the instructional librarian.

Another way of making librarians more effective in using the new technology is to give them opportunities in distance learning, so they can learn through participation. In Sweden such courses have been given to librarians (first by Kühne together with the University College of Kalmar in 1995, and most recently by a joint project involving the universities in Uppsala, Lund and Umeå). In the first course, 56 librarians learned about the Internet and how to seek information in databases. At that time, the Internet, e-mail, attaching files, etc. were still very new, so librarians had to learn the basics. In 1998–99, around 150 librarians participated in a diploma course, starting from a higher level. In Asia, the National Institute of Multimedia Education in Japan, in collaboration with UNESCO, carried out a survey of relevant distance education (Sacchanand, 1999). Seven countries in Asia and the Pacific region took part (Australia, China, India, Japan, New Zealand, Papua New Guinea and Thailand). Various levels of courses were offered, from diploma through to postgraduate degrees. Later Fiji and Pakistan also participated in the project.

We have seen that information professionals often have inadequate knowledge of modern management techniques and are rarely leaders or entrepreneurs. Johnson (1999) argues that schools of library and information science need to make greater efforts to promote career opportunities and to develop better management and leadership skills programmes in order to attract better students. The Bertelsmann Stiftung (1997) in Germany has carried out a study of strategic management, organization, development, marketing, etc., with the involvement of leading public librarians throughout the world. The conclusions stressed the need for management to be quality oriented, and for the rest of the library staff to think more in terms of quality. Unless library staff are involved, it is almost impossible to put the 'customer' in the centre (Klaassen and Wiersma, 1997).

Conclusion

Knowledge is the crucial competitive factor in the information society. The way in which we deal with information will therefore be increasingly important as the digital revolution affects our jobs and daily lives. Public libraries will therefore have to develop strategies for:

- providing access to information in a variety of formats in the spirit of democracy;
- promoting reading and literacy;
- offering lifelong learning opportunities;
- ensuring that our communities are able to cope with computers and have access to the equipment and systems they need;
- providing areas for 'social meeting';
- safeguarding cultural identity in a rapidly changing world;
- awareness of copyright and security questions (Skosana, 1998).

In order to be able to enhance the development of public libraries and to give them tools to participate in the rapid changes of the information society, public library research is of the utmost importance. Much has been said about the poor state of public library research in the literature, but less time has been invested in identifying and tackling the difficulties surrounding it (Goodall, 1998).

Some thinkers who work on these issues say that we now no longer live in the information society but are already in the 'polyoptic' society (Alsmark, 1999). This refers to a hyper-complex world in which we have to shift focus many times every hour. The world is developing all the time and we have to get used to that. One cannot explain the world from one angle, as there are so many different dimensions. If one sees the world from a thousand different angles all the time, one's personality might tend to dissolve. Here again public libraries can find a role in helping people to cope with complexity and meet the challenge of the polyoptic society.

References

Alsmark, A. (1999) Demokratirorelsen IT: ett polyoptiskt samtal med Knud Schulz på huvudbiblioteket i Århus. *Ciceron*, **3**(2), 10–13.

Attström, R. (1999) [Paper presented at the conference 'Creating Knowledge', Malmö University, Sweden, 15–16 April 1999.] http://www.bibl.mah.se/konferens/index.htm

Beijing Xinhua, (1999) 12 August.

Bertelsmann Stiftung (1997) *Internationales Netzwerk Öffentlicher Bibliotheken: Ergebnisse.* Gütersloh: Bertelsmann Stiftung.

CEC (1999) *Green paper on public sector information in the information society.* Brussels: CEC. http://www.cordis.lu/fp5/home.html

Cederqvist, G. (1997) Internet – ett dyrt äventyr. *Biblioteksbladet*, **82**(8), 16–17.

Chourrot, O. (1997) The place of the reader in the acquisitions process. [Abstract.] *Bulletin d'Informations de l'Association des Bibliothécaires Français*, **175**(2), 42–44.

DEBORA. http://www.cordis.lu/libraries/en/projects/debora.html

Dempsey, M.A. (1998) Tomorrow's library: the American view. *Illinois Libraries*, **80**(1), 5–10.

Dowlin, K. (1999) [Paper presented at the conference 'Creating Knowledge', Malmö University, Sweden, 15–16 April 1999.] http://www.bibl.mah.se/konferens/index.htm

Evald, P. (1999) [Paper presented at the conference 'Creating Knowledge', Malmö University, Sweden, 15–16 April 1999.] http://www.bibl.mah.se/konferens/index.htm

Folkbiblioteksutredningen (1982) *Folkbibliotek i tal och tankar*. En faktarapport från Folkbiblioteksutredningen. Malmö: Liber.

Foster, T. (1997) Libraries and learning: a partnership for life. *Australasian Public Libraries and Information Services*, **10**(4), 185–190.

Gabel, G.U. (1997) Aufbruch in den Bezirken mit Hindernissen. *Buch and Bibliothek*, **49**(12), 890–895.

Goodall, D. (1998) Public library research. *Public Library Journal*, **13**(4), 49–55.

Górska, E. (1997) *Organization and functioning of the Warsaw Public Library: the Central Library from 1907 to 1997*. [Paper presented at a symposium in Lübeck, Germany, 22–24 September.]

IT-Research (1999) *Dagens Nyheter*, 28 January.

Internet Public Library. http://www.ipl.org/

Johnson, I.M. (1999) Workshop on the management and use of human resources in Latin America, Chile, 6–9 April 1998. *IFLA Journal*, **25**(1), 42–46.

Josephson, C.O. (1999) Gästkrönikör. *Biblioteksbladet*, **84**(3), 30.

Kane, B. and Wallace, P. (1997) The outsourcing dilemma. *American Libraries*, **28**(5), 54–56.

Kemp, R.L. (1999) A city manager looks at trends affecting public libraries. *Public Libraries*, **38**(2), 116–119.

Kilcullen, M. (1998) Teaching librarians to teach: recommendations on what we need to know. *Reference Services Review*, **26**(2), 7–18.

Klaassen, U. and Wiersma, C. (1997) Qualitatsmanagement in öffentlichen Bibliotheken. *Internationales Netzwerk öffentlicher Bibliotheken*, Bd 2. Bertelsmann Stiftung.

Kühne, B. (1993) *Biblioteket skolans hjarna?* Stockholm: Almqvist and Wiksell International.

Kühne, B. (1998) *Deral, Workpackage 01, D1.1-2*. [Delivered to the EC Library Programme, Luxembourg, December 1998.]

Kühne, B. (1999) *Deral, first management report*. [Delivered to the EC Library Programme, Luxembourg, April 1999.]

Leatt, J. (1998) *The South African virtual library*. [Paper presented at the conference 'Telematics for Libraries', Johannesburg, 15–17 September 1998.] http://www.goethe.de/af/joh/tele/enindex.htm

LISU (1998) *Library and information statistics tables for the United Kingdom*. Loughborough: Loughborough University. [Booklet.]

Lor, P. (1998) *The national library of South Africa: powerhouse for a library and information renaissance in South Africa*. [Paper presented at the conference 'Telematics for Libraries', Johannesburg, 15–17 September 1998.] http://www.goethe.de/af/joh/tele/enindex.htm

McKee, B. (1997) Networking for the future. *Public Library Journal*, **12**(5), 101–104.

Markussen, S. (1999) Sunday opening for libraries – a research project at three Norwegian public libraries. *Scandinavian Public Library Quarterly*, **32**(1), 19–23.

Martin, J. (1999) Interesting times. *Information Europe*, **4**(1), 23–24.

Marwinski, F. (1997) *Die wissenschaftlichen Allgemeinbibliotheken in der DDR*. [Paper presented at a symposium in Lübeck, Germany, 22–24 September 1997.]

Michigan Electronic Library. http://mel.lib.mi.us/

Mouskouri, N. (1999) MEP's viewpoint: Culture 2000 programme. *Information Europe*, **4**(1), 27.

Muswazi, P. (1999) Freedom of information: in search of a niche for the library profession in Swaziland. *IFLA Journal*, **25**(1), 27–34.

Networked Public Library Services. PULSE Services. http://www.publiclibrary.fi/

Nielsen, J. (1999) Biblioteksudblik. *Bibliotekspressen*, (2), 61.

Nowacki-Chmielowic, C. (1998) Freedom of information, publications and libraries in the Polish People's Republic and in Poland today. *Focus on International and Comparative Librarianship*, **29**(3), 172–181.

Nwokocha, U. (1998) Public libraries in Nigeria: decades of persisting problems. *International Information and Library Review*, **30**(2), 97–104.

Oberman, C. (1999) [Paper presented at the conference 'Creating Knowledge', Malmö University, Sweden, 15–16 April 1999.] http://www.bibl.mah.se/konferens/index.htm

OCLC. http://www.oclc.org

Poulain, M. (1997) Acquisition in public libraries. Conclusion: a high quality of debate. [Abstract.] *Bulletin d'Informations de l'Association des Bibliothécaires Francais*, **175** (2), 58–64.

Premsit, P. (1999) Library and information services in Thailand. *IFLA Journal*, **25**(3), 137–142.

Raulff, U. (1998) Öffentliche Bibliotheken im neuen Europa. *Zeitschrift für Bibliothekswesen und Bibliographie*, **45**(1), 51–58.

Ristarp, J. (1999) Biblioteken och den intellektuella friheten. In: U. Ståhlberg *et al.* (eds) *Kunskapande i vår egen tid. Årsbok om folkbildning 1999*. Stockholm: Föreningen for folkbildningsforskning, pp. 27–32.

Rotaru, F. (1999) 'Lernen wir einander kennen': die Bibliotheken Süd-Ost-Europas haben viel in die Gemeinschaft der Bibliotheken einzubringen. *Buch und Bibliothek*, **51**(2), 123–125.

Sacchanand, C. (1999) Distance education in library and information science in Asia and the Pacific region. *IFLA Journal*, **25**(2), 97–100.

Schuler, D. (1997) Let's partner as patriots. *American Libraries*, **28**(8), 60–62.

Sibanyoni, E. (1997) A library for community development in Soshanguve. *IFLA Journal*, **23**(5/6), 362–364.

Skosana, P. (1998) [Opening speech at the conference 'Telematics for Libraries', Johannesburg, South Africa, 15–17 September 1998.] http://www.goethe.de/af/joh/tele/enindex.htm

Statens kulturråd (1998) *Tidernas bibliotek*. Stockholm: Fritzes AB.

Strandberg, H. *et al.* (1999) Bibliotek i 'kris' ökar öppethållandet. *Svensk Bokhandel*, **147**(6), 13–20.

Svensk (1996) *Forfattningssamling 1996:1596*. [Swedish library law]. *Bibliotekslag*. Stockholm: Department of Culture.

Ulvskog, M. (1999) [Speech by Minister of Culture, Swedish Parliament, 3 February 1999.]

UNESCO (1997) *Statistical Yearbook 1996.* Paris: UNESCO.

Visby (1996–) [Conferences held for the Baltic region on the theme 'Libraries and freedom of information', organized by Gotland County Library, Sweden, ongoing.]

Waizer, N. and Gruidl, J.J. (1997) Rural public libraries and community economic development. *Illinois Libraries,* **79**(4), 178–181.

Yilmaz, B. (1999) The right to information: is it possible for developing countries? *IFLA Journal,* **25**(2), 104–107.

Appendix Public libraries and EC-funded projects

Third Framework Programme

BIBDEL (*http://www.cordis.lu/libraries/en/projects/bibdel.htm*)
The completed project was designed to explore, identify and improve the availability and accessibility to remote users of modern libraries by demonstrating that library services can be delivered to users at a distance instead of users being required to visit libraries. It recognizes that many users who need to study do not have physical access to the library services they need. IT affords an opportunity to make service delivery both practical and cost effective, but experience of its utilization by libraries is spread very unevenly across the EU. The project brought together three very different models of provision through the medium of three universities. It demonstrated how technology and expertise can be transferred between libraries in different states and adapted to the needs of each. It aimed not to produce a single solution for EU-wide adoption, but rather a series of solutions each of which will find application in different geographical areas of different member states.

A large number of Community citizens would benefit from IT-related remote library services (over one million Europeans were in 1997 involved in distance education, with many more studying at universities with distributed sites). The three demonstration systems have shown, in three different countries and with three different sets of circumstances, the potential for technology-based means of access by remote users to a full range of library services. BIBDEL's key deliverable, the toolkit of techniques, provides a practical and cost-effective guide for distance learners throughout Europe.

Fourth Framework Programme

DEDICATE (*http://www.cordis.lu/libraries/en/projects/dedicate.html*)
The completed EDUCATE project clearly showed that scientific, technical and medical users have a need for access to information resources and assistance in how to handle them. Such assistance has become more necessary than ever because of the complexity of widely varying IT options. As a result, the DEDICATE project sets out to develop cost-effective distance education courses in information literacy. These will be based on programmes developed under the EDUCATE project and programmes for networked

learner support allowing both asynchronous and synchronous communication modes. Support will also be provided in the form of document supply.

The distance education courses will be demonstrated and tested at four library sites in technological universities in Estonia, Hungary, Latvia and Lithuania and at the International Centre for Information Management, Systems and Services in Torun, Poland. The distance education programmes will be directed initially at training library staff in the access and use of information resources in a networked environment. This will form part of a programme for training the trainers – with extension to scientists and engineers. The first group of application sites will be in the area of science and engineering. These demonstrator sites should act as catalysts for the development of user education programmes within the countries involved. The DEDICATE courses will thus encourage cooperation in the field between libraries in western and eastern Europe.

DERAL (*http://www.cordis.lu/libraries/en/projects/deral.html*)

DERAL sets out to encourage public libraries to play an increasingly important part in transferring information, knowledge and education to users who have difficulty in following normal courses of study. This frequently applies to those living in rural areas as well as to the unemployed and to elderly or disabled people who cannot normally attend university, college or high school.

Guidelines will be drawn up for librarians, and a set of tools based on Internet technology and video-conferencing will be developed to allow libraries to act as brokers between the providers of distance learning courses and users. The ultimate aim is to raise the level of education in rural areas and by doing so to help people to remain and work in their places of residence.

HERCULE (*http://www.cordis.lu/libraries/en/projects/hercule.html*)

HERCULE will develop the concept of young European citizens as information consumers and producers in the emerging information society. It will produce a website for European schoolchildren as library users. The site will contain signposts to learning resources linked to school curricula and validated by teachers and mapped by librarians. The website will also be a place for the viewing and exchange of multimedia cultural material produced by children and supported by arts workers. The project will thus provide opportunities for schoolchildren to share the local culture and heritage of their area with students from other European countries and explore how current issues concerning the environment and sustainable development are affecting this. Electronic newsgroups will be set up to allow HERCULE users to discuss, comment on and question the many exciting aspects of the HERCULE site.

LIBERATOR (*http://www.cordis.lu/libraries/en/projects/liberato.html*)

The objective is to establish and develop exemplary regional information services (RIS) in three diverse European regions. Relying on a combination of technical and human resources, networked public library services will be developed to provide independent and mediated information for the user. The project will set up new partnerships between information producers, mediators and end users and different kinds of libraries – academic, special and public. Critical legal and regulatory issues will be addressed, such as copyright and the implications of electronic commerce. A major element in RISs will be regional sites that coordinate all Web activity relevant to the needs of the participating regions. Sites will be multifunctional, offering mediated gateways to the Internet for citizens, virtual shop windows to stimulate regional economies, and new retrieval tools for information mediators. The sites will also address presentation and access by incorporating facilities such as localized searching, filters and security features. The project will achieve its goals through a high profile and energetic process of dissemination and exploitation activities. Charging mechanisms for certain information services will be considered with a view to generating income.

LISTED (*http://www.cordis.lu/libraries/en/projects/listed.htm*)
LISTED integrates Flexible and Distance Learning (FDL) solutions into a public library environment. Library users will gain access to a wide range of learning materials through a consistent interface: the library. The learning materials include a portfolio of interactive multimedia FDL titles, 'wrapped' with distant (via networks) or local mentor support. Six prototypes in four EU member states are envisaged. These will be linked for Europe-wide user support, feedback and discussion forums. Building on the PLAIL project (see below), LISTED includes an updated analysis of user needs and a market analysis for future exploitation. Pertinent copyright issues are also dealt with in depth.

From mid-1998 LISTED has entered into partnership with three Hungarian organizations to extend the testing of the LISTED service into central and eastern Europe. The objectives of this extension are as follows:

- to adapt existing Web-based service for use in Hungary;
- to install Internet-linked computer facilities in the two test sites;
- to train staff to support users;
- to test user reactions, both public users and library staff;
- to analyse and publish results;
- to demonstrate the service;
- to disseminate findings.

PLAIL (*http://www.cordis.lu/libraries/en/projects/plail.html*)
PLAIL arose from the rapidly growing customer demand (in terms of numbers, complexity and range) being experienced by public libraries throughout the European Union for the provision of information guidance and library materials support for independent learners. PLAIL aimed to help public libraries develop innovative and enhanced services, which would put them in a position to meet this demand. More specifically, the objects of the project were to improve professional expertise, to raise the level of competence of public library staff, and to apply and exploit new technologies in a public library setting in order to facilitate cost-effective access for customers to appropriate information and study support. PLAIL established replicable patterns for how innovative services can be introduced and developed in public libraries. Results included:

- a clear statement of norms and competency levels for public librarians;
- recommendations regarding the use of information technology to enable public librarians and public library services to attain such standards and levels of service;

- guidelines on the training needs of public librarians in responding to adult independent learners;
- a major dissemination programme both within the specific countries involved in this project and across the wider European Union.

The reports concluded that public libraries were ideally placed to serve the needs of adult independent learners, especially in view of the many barriers (identified by PLAIL) that prevent them from embarking on more formal courses of study.

Document access and supply

5

Edward Lim and
Janette Burke

Introduction

It is debatable whether the terms 'interlibrary lending', 'document supply' and 'document delivery' can be used interchangeably. Smith (1997) points out that in North America the term 'interlibrary loan' is used to mean lending between publicly funded libraries or institutions, while 'document delivery' is used for commercial document delivery services. However, he argues that this differentiation is artificial, since the distinction between the activities of public and private institutions and organizations in this area of supply has become blurred. He suggests further that the 'electronic environment is going to put the final nail in the coffin for any meaningful distinction between interlibrary loan and document supply'. Finnie (1998) uses the term 'document delivery' to cover interlibrary loan, commercial document supply, electronic document delivery and resource sharing. There is probably no benefit in embarking on a debate on definitions and this review will follow the definitions used by Lor (1996), where appropriate. Lor uses the term 'document supply' as the umbrella term for document delivery and interlibrary lending (DD/ILL for short) and limits the definition of document delivery to the supply of photocopies or electronic copies from fee-based commercial services, while interlending refers to the temporary loan of materials between libraries, even though the lending library might supply a copy instead of the original. However, this definition will not be rigidly applied and occasionally the terms document delivery, document supply and interlibrary loan will be used interchangeably, unless the context specifies otherwise.

Libraries are undergoing a period of exceptional changes and pressures, caused by developments in digital technology and the consequent revolution in scholarly communication and publishing, a large increase in the volume of publications, huge price increases in serials and monographs, reduced budgets and a tremendous increase in demand from their clients. In this environment, library managers must develop strategies which include 'planning for optimal performance; balancing resources and demands; creating effective and economic services; and anticipating new and changed demands, constraints and scenarios' (Davies, 1998).

As a result of these pressures, libraries are no longer able to build comprehensive collections which will meet most of their patrons' requirements, and they have attempted to make up for this deficiency through DD/ILL. Consequently, there has been an exponential increase in demand for document supply, and no area of library activity has witnessed more changes. Jackson (1998) points out that as recently as five years ago:

- few patrons could submit ILL requests electronically;
- virtually all ILL departments depended on paper files;
- most ILL units used fax for expedited delivery of photocopies, rather than the newly emerging ARIEL workstations;
- ILL managers lacked current knowledge of ILL transaction costs.

The literature on document supply in the past five years is extensive, made more so by the increasing availability of documents on the Web. A useful starting point is the Focused Investigation of Document Delivery Options Homepage (FIDDO, 1999). FIDDO was launched in 1995 with the primary purpose of providing information on 'the options, methods and management of document delivery' available to library managers (Davies and Morris, 1998). Other useful sources include the bibliographies and literature surveys published regularly in *Interlending and Document Supply*, e.g. Bibliography (1998a, 1998b) and Gould (1998b, 1998c). Another source of information is e-mail discussion lists, e.g. ILL-L, IFLA-L, DOCDEL-L, ARIE-L, LIS-ILL, DOCLIBS, AFLIB-L. Gould (1998a) classifies these lists as regional based, specific product focused and general.

For the purpose of this review, emphasis has been placed on documents published in 1997 and 1998. In general, these can be conveniently grouped into the following key categories:

- access versus ownership;
- commercial document suppliers versus national interlending systems;
- grey literature and non-print materials;
- unmediated document supply services;
- DD/ILL management systems;
- standards and protocols;
- copyright;
- quality and performance indicators;
- developing countries and international interlending;
- document supply and virtual library developments.

Access versus ownership

Faced with ever-diminishing resources and the inability to continue to build comprehensive collections, libraries are focusing on resource sharing through document delivery and interlibrary lending. Document supply, which used to be a peripheral activity of libraries, has become a mainstream activity; in fact, the American Library Association has suggested that 'interlibrary borrowing is an integral element of collection development for all libraries, not an ancillary option' (Fong, 1996). Thus the hoary debate on access versus holdings or ownership has taken on a new dimension and now includes document supply as an important component of the collection development policies of libraries.

This debate continues to rage in the literature. But now there is an increasing realistic view that just as ownership incurs costs, so too does access. There is therefore a need to undertake an economic analysis to determine an appropriate balance between the two models of just in case and just in time. This changed attitude has made libraries more conscious of the financial implications of document supply and of the need to establish budgets for such an activity.

McGrath (1998) provides a sceptic's view of the rhetoric that academic libraries have moved from a policy of collection building to one of providing access to their users. In fact, he points out that 'what is happening, at least in the UK higher and further education community, is that holdings are static or declining and access is being cut in most institutions'.

The jury is still out on this issue. Gould (1998a) points out: 'There is often the assumption that a library which cancels subscriptions and satisfies requests through interlibrary loan or document delivery . . . is somehow "freeloading" '. But Blagden (1997, 1998) shows that DD/ILL is not necessarily a cheaper option and that when all biotechnology journals were cancelled at Cranfield net costs rose by 37%. Other studies also reveal that not all materials can be obtained from commercial suppliers (Etschmaier and Bustion, 1997). Consequently some libraries would need to continue to play the role of holding institutions. But not many libraries will be prepared to play this role without additional funding, or at least some compensation from the borrowing institutions.

Fisher and Tuck (1997) examine some of the economic issues relating to document supply. They point out that, in the print environment, document delivery services are based on 'fair dealing' or 'fair use' principles, where no specific payment is made to the publisher. As a result, DD/ILL charges may be pitched at a lower level than what is realistic or economic. In fact, in some situations where DD/ILL is a 'free' service, there is a tendency for librarians to ignore the financial costs and to give it low priority. In his study of the economics of access versus ownership using the example of the SUNY Express consortium, Kingma (1997) argues that there are two potential financial savings for libraries within a consortium – the ability of the consortium to deliver lower interlibrary loan costs, and the possibility of achieving lower collection development costs from joint collection development. To justify access over ownership, libraries must determine the break-even level of use, which depends on 'the costs of interlibrary lending, the price of the journal subscription, the number of expected lifetime uses, and the costs of inhouse use of the journal'. This study is important because it provides guidelines to help libraries make decisions with respect to ownership or access through document delivery. It warns, however, that if all academic libraries were to cancel significant numbers of journal titles 'publishers would stop publishing some titles and increase prices on other titles in order to cover the lost revenue from journal cancellations'.

There are other questions about cooperative collection development that require answers. Newsome and Cook (1997) point out in their discussion of the Western North Carolina Library Network that these questions revolve around publishers' decisions relating to intellectual property, licence agreements, and pricing policies for consortia. They also state that there is both a negative and a positive impact on consortia agreements for cooperative collection development.

With the increasing migration of print to electronic formats, new issues arise in this debate. For example, publishers, who will have greater control over the distribution of their electronic publications, are likely to demand royalty payments for permission to distribute their publications, and this might not make document delivery economically viable. In other instances, they might even forbid through licensing arrangements the use of their electronic publications for document supply purposes.

The SAIL (1996) project undertaken by the US National Library of Medicine illustrates a general economic problem of electronic document delivery. In that project a database of some 23,000 scanned articles from more than 60 journals was created. But actual usage was confined to only one third of the documents stored and the basic delivery cost per item was relatively high.

Commercial document suppliers versus national interlending systems

The growth in demand for document delivery has led to an increasing number of commercial document suppliers entering the market to compete with libraries in document supply. Thus libraries now have a number of policy options to choose from. They can decide whether to:

- participate in national policies on access; *or*
- rely solely on commercial suppliers; *or*
- develop access policies based on a combination of participation in national resource-sharing programmes and usage of commercial suppliers.

Models of national interlending systems

Libraries should no longer develop their collection policies in isolation, but should collaborate to develop a national policy on access. The inability of many libraries to meet the needs of their clients because of the chronic inflation of serials prices, and substantial increases in the volume of information published as well as an exponential increase in demand, have led to the development of a number of interlibrary loan models for sharing information resources (Bjornshauge, 1998). They are all variations of the centralized or distributed/decentralized models.

Major examples of the centralized model are those in Canada and the UK. The Canadian system, the Canada Institute for Scientific and Technical Information (CISTI) provides three types of service: direct supply from its own collection and that of the Canada Agriculture Library; link supply via the British Library Document Supply Centre (BLDSC) and the Science and Technical Information Centre in Taipei (for Chinese documents); and global supply from anywhere in the world.

Prowse (1998) provides an overview of trends and developments in interlending and document delivery in the UK. The pre-eminent document supply service has always been the BLDSC. However, a number of decentralized systems also exist, including those developed under the eLib programme to support regional or local interlending. These initiatives include the London and Manchester Document Access (LAMDA, 1998), Sharing of Educational Resources in an Electronic Network, SEREN (Morris, 1997), Electronic Document Delivery (EDDIS, 1998) and COPAC (Davies and Morris, 1998).

During 1996 and early 1997 a survey of document delivery practices in UK academic libraries was undertaken under the aegis of FIDDO (Morris and Blagg, 1998). The survey revealed that 85% of the academic libraries relied on BLDSC for their document supply, and that only a small number used LAMDA, the British Medical Association (BMA) or local and regional sources. Little use was made of commercial document delivery services like UnCover and UMI, probably because of their higher charges. One pertinent finding was that the majority of document requesting and supply practices are still fairly traditional, in that requests from users are still paper based and notification and delivery of the documents still use the postal system, even though most libraries send their requests to suppliers using electronic means.

Another example of a centralized model is the one operating in Taiwan. Sung (1998) provides a description of the work of the National Central Library in Taipei, which has developed the READncl (Remote Electronic Access/Delivery service of the National Central Library) system. This makes available, among other things, a database of over one million records, three million pages of text images on CD-ROMs, and 246 full-text hyperlinked periodicals.

There are many examples of decentralized models, obviously because it would be too expensive to replicate the BLDSC model. One such model is the OhioLINK consortium, comprising all the academic libraries in the state of Ohio connected by a single library automated system (Kohl, 1998). Using this system, patrons from any of the libraries in the system are able to initiate a request for the loan of an item if that item is not available in the local collection. The development of resource-sharing models on such a large scale actually has serious implications for collection development. In the case of monographs, there has been a move towards better rationalization of collections. In the case of serials, the move has been towards the purchase of electronic serials on a consortial basis. Kohl claims that such an arrangement has been good for both sides in that libraries have vastly increased the range of titles available to them and have been able to ensure that inflation is kept to a minimum, while publishers have been able to receive a guaranteed revenue stream. What is interesting is that document supply for certain serial titles is no longer required since everyone has access to them.

The German system is a decentralized one based on the collections of several key institutions including Die Deutsche Bibliothek (an amalgamation in 1990 of the Deutsche Bibliothek, the former national library of West Germany in Frankfurt, and the Deutsche Bücherei in Leipzig), the State Library of the Prussian Cultural Foundation, the Bavarian State Library, and the four Central Special Libraries specializing in technology, economy, medicine and agriculture. In addition, there are 37 regional copyright libraries and several university and other tertiary libraries that provide document delivery services (Fuchs, 1998). The technology used to facilitate national document delivery is the Dutch PICA system and the Horizon system based on Dynix. The Dutch system, which includes the PICA Online Contents database of articles from 12,500 high-use journals connected to the RAPDOC document delivery system, is described by Bakker (Gould, 1998b). Germany has also embarked on developing a uniform document delivery system jointly funded by the federal and state governments called SUBITO, whose aims are as follows:

- online ordering on the basis of online holdings information;
- search and retrieval of library systems using the Z39.50 protocol;
- delivery to end users and where possible online;
- a standard fee structure;
- a guaranteed delivery time.

Denmark is the envy of many countries because of its ability to make accessible the entire library resources of the country to every user, 'no matter which library he or she enters' (Jensen, 1998). The successful cooperative model in Denmark is due not only to the existence of an appropriate infrastructure (the DanBib system, a national union catalogue and library network), but also to the organizational framework provided by the Danish Library Centre and the long tradition of cooperation in Danish society.

The Swiss Libraries and Librarians Association has established a computerized ILL system using the WWW, and involving some 60 libraries of all types (Mettraux, 1998).

There is a tendency to assume that all European countries have access to the most advanced technologies to facilitate document supply. Boza *et al.* (1998) describe interlending in one of the poorer regions of Spain – Andalusia – where no proper computerized infrastructure or union catalogues exist, and proposes a simple model using the telephone and postal service. Urbano's (1997) literature review of DD/ILL undertaken from the Spanish perspective shows the lack of a national document supply system in Spain. However, a successful cooperative project undertaken by the Consortium of Catalan University Libraries is described by Casares *et al.* (1997). Details of the project are also available at the Consortium's website (Consorci, 1999).

In Australia, the national interlending system is very decentralized and characterized by a high degree of cooperation, with nearly 1.5 million items transacted each year (Wells and Amos, 1998). The national system is underpinned by the interlibrary lending code developed by the Australian Council of Libraries and Information Services, a paper-based voucher system for payments, and the Australian Bibliographic Network (ABN, a bibliographic utility and database of 7 million records listing over 26 million holdings) which will be replaced in 1999 by Kinetica using the AMICUS software.

To improve the national document supply system, the National Library of Australia together with the Australian university libraries at one time promoted vigorously the concept of the Distributed National Collection – DNC for short (Byrne, 1997; Martin, 1997; Shipp, 1997). This is one model of access whereby libraries work together to develop cooperatively a national collection for resource sharing.

The economics of the distributed model have been explored by Chapman (1998), who suggests that since libraries no longer operate purely on altruism, some additional financial support might be necessary to support those libraries that may be obliged to buy some material which they might not otherwise purchase. Australia's DNC project has not got off the ground because no practical means has been found to finance this model of cooperative collection development. Lim (1998) suggests a means of extracting more funds from the higher education sector in order to build a national collection of serials. Access to this collection would be provided 'virtually' using a model of access and document delivery developed by Monash University called MEADS (Monash Electronic Access and Delivery of Serials).

In New Zealand the Joint Standing Committee on Interloan has produced a plan for 'a mixed model of commercial document supply operating alongside charged interlibrary loan in a more open, deregulated environment'. The New Zealand interlibrary loans scheme is a decentralized scheme jointly administered by the National Library of New Zealand and the New Zealand Library and Information Association (Interloans, 1998).

Some less developed countries are also exploring the development of a more formal national interlibrary lending network. In the Arabian Gulf countries, for example, a survey of thirteen libraries found that all were in favour of participating in an ILL network (Gould, 1997). While Saudi Arabia is developing policies based on the latest technology developments, Russian libraries face major problems in developing resource-sharing programmes because of the poor telecommunications infrastructure (Barwick, 1997). India also has a decentralized model of interlending and a recent description of library networks in India is provided by Vyas (1997). Unnikrishnan *et al.* (1997) describe the work of the Mahatma Gandhi University Library in supplying scientific information to its research community, and explore the problems encountered – mainly the lack of commitment to document delivery, the absence of a uniform procedure for payment and poor performance generally.

Olorunsola (1997) has found that Nigerian libraries do not use electronic information sources extensively. He identifies the inhibiting factors as an inadequate infrastructural base, an erratic supply of electricity and the poor state of the economy – with the consequent inability to make the large capital outlay needed for initial acquisition and maintenance. He points out that while most Nigerian universities have access to personal computers, these are not networked. Access to electronic information sources in Nigerian university libraries is mainly via stand-alone CD-ROMs. To move forward, he suggests that Nigerian library schools should incorporate library use of information technology in the curriculum. More use should be made of consultants to assist in the computerization of Nigerian libraries (most of whose earlier efforts have failed because of lack of expertise). Karaomerlioglu (1997) examines the pros and cons of document delivery versus ownership from the viewpoint of developing countries. Technological advances, particularly of the Internet, have changed the very nature of document delivery. The author argues that if users have direct access to remote libraries, then the role of the library in document supply transactions becomes questionable. Using Turkey as a case study, the author points out that of all the problems faced by developing countries, the lack of educated staff is the most significant.

Commercial suppliers

As indicated above, one of the options available to libraries is to rely exclusively on commercial suppliers to supply all the documents that they are unable to supply from their own collections. Is this option really viable?

Prabha and Marsh (1997) claim that commercial document suppliers are capturing an increasing share of the document supply market. They examine the services provided by five major suppliers: BLDSC, CISTI, the Institute for Scientific Information (ISI), University Microfilms Inc (UMI) and UnCover. Their findings are based on a sample of periodical requests processed through the OCLC PRISM

ILL, and suggest that these five suppliers can fulfil 92% of all article requests. Of course, one could argue that BLDSC and CISTI are not really commercial suppliers in the sense that they are more service- than profit-oriented organizations and receive substantial funding from their national governments. On the other hand, as their charges are not purely made on the basis of cost recovery, they resemble commercial suppliers in many respects. In other words, they straddle the chasm between the 'altruistic' public service and profit-motivated sectors.

Marcinko (1997) provides a study of the issues that commercial document delivery suppliers must deal with to be successful. Vendors have to keep up with the rapid advances in technology, grapple with the complex problems of intellectual property and provide good customer services that are cost effective and have a rapid turnaround time. At the same time as the industry matures, small individual companies have difficulty surviving and many have been taken over by large corporations.

The players who have entered the marketplace include a number of subscription agents (e.g. Swets and Blackwell's), publishers (e.g. ISI, Elsevier, Chemical Abstracts and Biosis) and database hosts (e.g. OCLC). OCLC has been dynamic in introducing its Electronic Collections Online (Nilges, 1998; Tenopir, 1998), as well as marketing its interlibrary loan system (Halgren, 1998; Ouyang and Sproat, 1998) and its SiteSearch suite of software, which allows libraries to integrate their electronic information resources by providing Web access to Z39.50 resources. The SiteSearch software suite includes WebZ, Database builder and Imaging Support Package (Hawk, 1998).

Turner (1997) predicts that the sheer volume of articles produced as well as the growth of electronic publishing will lead to the growth of intermediaries like Blackwell's. A list of commercial document suppliers is provided at the FIDDO site (FIDDO, 1999). Finnie (1998) also provides a list of the key document suppliers, which she categorizes as collection-based suppliers and non-collection-based suppliers, together with their subject, date coverage and formats.

UnCover (1998b) is a revolutionary document delivery service which allows users to search contents pages of periodicals and order articles directly. Originally it had a text-based interface. In September 1998, it released UnCoverWeb 2.0, which allows users to search and order periodical articles from a Web interface. A further development of the UnCover (1998a) service allows users to download TIFF images of full text articles from over 2,500 journals via the UnCover Desktop Image Delivery system.

Other suppliers are beginning to offer not only tables of contents service, but also searchable full text systems and images of print equivalents. CD-ROM products with full text images of key journals in specific disciplines, such as ADONIS and Business Periodicals Ondisc, continue to be popular and are used to support document supply services. In 1997, UMI produced Applied Science and Technology Plus (Zauha, 1998) and ProQuest Medical Library (ProQuest, 1998), both of which are CD-ROM image databases of key journals in these disciplines. Articles in ASTP are linked to the indexing and abstracting service of H.W. Wilson's Applied Science and Technology Index database while the ProQuest Medical Library is linked to the Medline database.

With the development of the Internet, full text products (some in ASCII rather than imaged pages) are migrating from CD-ROM to the Web. Examples include UMI's ProQuest Direct (UMI, 1999), which provides a common Web interface for a large range of databases, many of which continue to be available on CD-ROM, and InfoTrac's SearchBank (Mehta and Goodman, 1997).

The move towards the networked delivery of electronic journals was facilitated by TULIP (1997), a cooperative research project involving Elsevier and nine American universities which investigated the technical feasibility of networked distribution of electronic journals, appropriate organizational and economic models and user behaviour. What influence this research had on subsequent developments in electronic publishing, is hard to tell, but it certainly accelerated the development of Elsevier's Electronic Serials system (Mostert and Fransen, 1997), and subsequently ScienceDirect, which provides access via the Web to more than one thousand of Elsevier's full text journals (Osanai, 1998) and ScienceDirect OnSite (Elsevier, 1999). Other full text products offered via the Web include JSTOR (1999), an image database of the complete backfiles of more than one hundred journals, mainly in the humanities and social sciences (Deloughry, 1996; Dementi, 1998; Guthrie, 1998) and IDEAL (1998), an online electronic library containing 174 Academic Press journals. In the IDEAL system, abstracts and tables of contents are presented in HTML and full text articles are delivered in Adobe Acrobat format.

Finnie (1997) and Wettler (1998) have developed criteria for evaluating commercial document delivery services. These include factors such as charging, turnaround time, coverage or specialization in particular subject areas, fill rate, copyright, ease of use, ordering options, invoicing practices, format in which the document is supplied and availability of quantity discounts. Some studies have shown that commercial suppliers are not necessarily superior to traditional interlibrary loan systems in terms of speed of supply and turnaround time. They also tend to be more expensive (Morris and Blagg, 1998).

Grey literature and non-print materials

The dissemination of grey literature and non-print materials usually does not get much mention in the literature, as these are seen frequently to be peripheral to the main business of the library. However, there is no question that grey literature is very important for research in some disciplines, such as economics and mathematics. In the same way audiovisual materials, which have always been part of library collections but are seen to be subordinate to print-based materials, are now considered to be an important source of educational information, especially for the younger generation of scholars who are more 'visually and aurally' literate in this age of video hits and computer games.

There are a number of projects that attempt to disseminate grey literature in the field of economics using the World Wide Web. They include the DEGREE (Dissemination of Electronic GREy file on Economics) project (Stuyts, 1998), and WoPEc. A 'gateway' to these systems is provided through the RePEc archive (Krichel, 1999) which is a collection of mainly organization archives. In countries where there is less access to technology, the traditional manual method of delivering grey literature documents is still practised. One such initiative is described by Pavlov (1998), who outlines the activities of the Scientific and Technical Information Centre of Russia (VNTIC) in archiving and disseminating grey literature.

Improvements in WWW technology now enable sound and video files to be transmitted across the network. The major problem faced by projects such as JUKEBOX and Danish Audio History in making historical sound archives available via the Internet appears to be copyright, largely because intellectual property owners are reluctant to give permission for network transmission, and especially cross-border transmission, even though the technology permits this (Fønss-Jørgensen, 1998).

Unmediated document supply services

Jackson (1998) credits Paul Mosher, Vice-Provost and Director of Libraries, University of Pennsylvania, with the idea of user-initiated document requests. Mosher envisioned a future in which 80% of borrowing requests would be unmediated, with about 20% problem requests being processed by library staff. While many librarians were initially sceptical, this idea has caught on, partly as a result of the increased workload of document supply units, many of which do not have a corresponding increase in staffing, and partly because technology has facilitated this. A number of patron-initiated systems have been introduced in the past five years, including OCLC ILL Direct (OCLC, 1998a, 1998b), OhioLink and ORBIS, as well as commercial document delivery services like UnCover, ISI, UMI ProQuest Direct and CISTI (CISTI, 1998), which are now prepared to accept requests directly from end users. These services are generically known as CAS-IAS (Current Alerting Services – Individual Article Supply) services (Brunskill, 1997; Morris *et al.*, 1997).

Some locally developed systems tailored for unmediated usage are described in the literature (Douglas and Roth, 1997; Arkin, 1998). While user-initiated requests may result in saving the time of library staff, Arkin (1998) outlines some of the consequences of permitting them, following their introduction to faculty and employees of Aalborg University via UnCover. The major problem was the irresponsible and reckless ordering of articles from journals already owned by the library. However, UnCover now offers a customized gateway (for a relatively high charge) which will block orders for articles from journal titles held by the library. One interesting finding from the Aalborg University experiment is that the availability of user-initiated orders does not automatically reduce the burden of the DD/ILL department. In fact, the volume of requests processed by DD/ILL staff continued to increase, indicating that the library was expanding into a new service market. While user-initiated document requests appear to be the wave of the future, the major problem relates to the difficulty of controlling costs and inappropriate usage. Similar experiences have been reported by university libraries in the USA (Kleiner and Hamaker, 1997) and Australia (Orr and Appleton, 1998). UnCover has responded to the problem by announcing that it would soon be possible to impose limits on article ordering via their Web gateways, and thus allow libraries to impose quotas and contain costs.

It is interesting to note that while libraries assume that the facility to allow patron-initiated requests is desirable because it will speed up delivery time and also save staff costs, not all users like to take advantage of this option. In fact, Eastwood and Mornati (1998), reporting on a survey of user behaviour and perceptions of the ILL service at CERN (in high energy physics), state that:

- 53% do not wish to deal directly with a supplier;
- 55% do not believe that this would speed up delivery;
- 63% do not want documents to be delivered directly to them if they are required to deal with delivery problems;
- 43% do not like the idea of delivery as e-mail attachments.

Brunskill (1997) reports in her research considerable resistance to change by users, most of whom still want to rely on well-established methods of supplying their needs.

The acceptance or otherwise of unmediated document supply is very largely dependent on users' access to appropriate technology and computer literacy skills. Thus although there may be advantages for the user in terms of timeliness and benefits for the library in terms of staff savings, it cannot be assumed that users will naturally prefer unmediated services.

DD/ILL management systems

Document delivery/ILL has generally been a manual operation. But increasingly, electronic technology is being used to improve both the requesting and management processes. Libraries are beginning to take advantage of advances in digital technology for the following purposes:

- enabling users to search citation databases and then converting these citations to document delivery requests;
- using the Web to generate document delivery requests;
- using the online library catalogue interface to generate DD/ILL requests;
- permitting users unmediated access to commercial document delivery services;
- developing DD/ILL management systems to track requests, issue invoices, manage copyright and generally to assist DD/ILL departments to run their operations more efficiently and effectively;
- using technology to deliver articles and other documents in digital form.

Jackson (1997b) points out that while many libraries in the USA use at least one national messaging system (OCLC, RLIN, DOCLINE and WLN) for communicating with other libraries for document delivery purposes, and use fax or the ARIEL software to deliver documents, most DD/ILL processes continue to be very labour intensive. Even with the availability of e-mail based or Web-based request systems and the use of the proprietary ordering systems of commercial document delivery suppliers, the lack of integration of all these systems continues to make the DD/ILL operations inefficient and expensive. To promote the development of DD/ILL management systems, the North American Interlibrary Loan and Document Delivery (NAILDD) Project was initiated by the Association of Research Libraries (ARL) in 1993. The project works through the Developers/Implementors Group (DIG) and has established three developmental priorities: management software, accounting/financial tracking and standards. NAILDD has also established an ILL Protocol Implementors Group (IPIG) to encourage the use of the ISO ILL Protocol in the USA.

Although some interlibrary loan management systems are available commercially, a comparative analysis of these by Fong *et al.* (1996) shows that none of the systems are ideal and all fail to meet several important evaluation criteria. The criteria considered essential include:

- comprehensiveness (e.g. user friendliness, support for both borrowing and lending, automatically converting of records from OCLC and non-OCLC bibliographic records, patron database);
- reports (e.g. ability to customize reports, copyright compliance reports, collection management reports, statistical reports);
- accounting (e.g. invoicing, tracking payments, generating monthly statements);
- request management (e.g. tracking requests);
- technical requirements;
- technical support;
- costs.

Australia's initial involvement in improving DD/ILL software on an international scale was relatively modest. Some funding was provided in 1996 jointly with UK Joint Information Systems Committee under the JEDDS (Joint Electronic Document Delivery) project to enhance the ARIEL software, originally developed by the Research Libraries Group to allow scanned images to be transmitted over the Internet from one ARIEL workstation to another (Landes, 1997). The JEDDS-enhanced ARIEL software was completed in 1997. The increased functionalities include the ability to send scanned images using MIME-compliant e-mail, the provision for users to enter a request and add requestor information, preferred supply method and supplier information, and the ability to sort requests by type of request and supply preference (Greenaway and Blinco, 1997; *Come*, 1998; Rusbridge, 1998a).

The only Australian research report exploring the need for an integrated document delivery system for the research community was prepared by a research team led by Brittain (Brittain and Colmer, 1998). The report evaluates major resource discovery and retrieval tools available nationally and internationally and identifies projects aimed at improving access to electronic and print documents.

On a more practical level, Australian activity in this area has increased substantially with the launch of the CILLA (Coordinated Interlibrary Loan Administration) feasibility project, which found that no system currently exists which meets the requirements for a good DD/ILL management system (Greenaway, 1997, 1998; Greenaway and Blinco, 1997). As a result, a request for tender was issued under the auspices of the Australian Vice-Chancellors' Committee and the National Library of Australia to procure a system which would meet all the functionalities identified in the report. The new system, known as LIDDA (Local Interlending and Document Delivery Administration), will aim not only to automate the internal procedures relating to document delivery, but also to provide for unmediated access where feasible. The following features are planned (Sood, 1997; Wells and Amos, 1998):

- capability of retrieving bibliographic and location data from catalogues and databases;
- linkages with the National Library of Australia's ILL utility;
- linkages with other ILL utilities which conform to the ISO ILL protocol;
- linkages with local integrated library management systems.

The successful tenderer is Fretwell-Downing Informatics, whose OLIB VDX product will form the basis of the LIDDA system. This product has also been accepted as the system for the CAVAL (Cooperative Action by Victorian University Libraries) CIDER project (Tucker *et al.*, 1998). It is expected that beta testing and piloting will commence in 1999. The British Library has also awarded a contract to Fretwell-Downing to build a seamless gateway between its Document Supply Centre Automated Request Processing system and the ISO ILL Protocol.

Mention has already been made of document delivery projects which have been supported under the UK Electronic Libraries Programme (eLib, 1999). The project that most closely resembles the Australian LIDDA system is EDDIS, which will also use Fretwell-Downing Informatics' OLIB VDX software as the foundation for its document delivery system (Larbey, 1998). The system will 'allow users to search bibliographic databases, select items of interest, locate suppliers and their terms and conditions of supply, and place orders with suppliers of choice at a single session, and to receive documents electronically within 24 hours, or by traditional interlibrary lending channels; with all the administrative systems being handled transparently' (Larbey, 1997b).

Germany has the DBV-OSI II (1999) project and SUBITO, which is an initiative of German federal and regional governments 'to integrate search, ordering and delivery at the workplace of the user'.

Foo and Lim (1998) point out that even though Web-based request forms are used by a number of libraries, most of their back-end processing systems are still manually managed. They propose an integrated Web-based DD/ILL system and provide some details of the architecture, database development and Java development platform used to implement a new system. The advantages of their system include a reduction in human intervention by eliminating form filling and paperwork, improving the access and speed of the process by allowing participating libraries to update each other's databases directly, ensuring data integrity, simplifying status tracking and supporting instantaneous status and statistical reporting.

To ensure adequate compensation for intellectual property owners, a number of electronic devices and systems are being developed. One such system is the CopySmart intellectual property rights management for electronic documents, which is co-financed by the European Union. The system is intended to give controlled access to any digital information in a completely trusted environment (CopySmart, 1997).

Standards and protocols

The standards and protocols required for developing an integrated DD/ILL management system are many and complex. They include the Web interface (HTTP/HTML), Z39.50 for database search and retrieval, ISO ILL Protocol, GEDI agreement for electronic document interchange, SMTP/MIME e-mail for DD/ILL message and document transmission, and FTP for file transfer. Larbey (1997a) provides a detailed summary of three main categories of the standards and protocols:

- electronic document delivery and international standard network protocols;

- Group on Electronic Document Interchange (GEDI, 1999) standards for the electronic exchange of full text documents;
- ISO Interlibrary Loan Standard – sometimes called ISO ILL or ILL protocol for short (Interlibrary, 1997).

With the advances of technology, there has been a renewed interest in the development and implementation of the ILL Protocol. Shuh (1998) provides an historical overview of this protocol, starting with the first version developed by the National Library of Canada in 1987 and its subsequent adoption and modification by the international library community led by IFLA and other international bodies. In 1997 the National Library of Canada was officially designated as the ISO Interlibrary Loan Application Standards Maintenance Agency (Interlibrary, 1997) in recognition of its pioneering role in this area. Shuh (1998) attributes the 'renaissance' of the ILL Protocol to the worldwide presence of the Internet and the widespread availability of supporting protocols that have overcome the earlier problems created by proprietary networks. Implementation of the ISO ILL standard (Jackson, 1997a) has been slow because of cost. However, one version of the Protocol was released by the Library Corporation in 1997.

Europe (Moulton, 1997) and the UK (Larbey, 1997a) appear to be leading in the area of trialling systems that conform to the international standards, with an alphabetic soup of projects. Some major projects which have been funded by the European Commission under its Telematics for Libraries Programme include:

- Project ION (Interlending Open Systems Network), which has 'set up a demonstrator ISO ILL network for participants in the Netherlands, France and the UK'.
- Alternatives for International Document Availability (AIDA, 1995), which was a pilot project to provide document delivery services to Italy and Portugal.
- EDIL (1996), which trialled the GEDI (1999) model for electronic document delivery between the national libraries in France, Netherlands, UK and Germany.
- ELITE, which aimed to 'develop a generic model for distributed library services to users'.
- Document and Library Integration (DALI) Project which, among other things, developed an ILL-based management system using the Z39.50 Item Order service protocol to request documents. The importance of the DALI project also lies in its use of the ILL Protocol over TCP/IP rather than the ISO ISP format.
- UNIverse (1999) Project, which aims to develop a virtual union catalogue to deliver a number of library services, including document delivery services, to users using the ILL Protocol, TCP/IP and e-mail transport standards.

- Generic Architecture for Information Availability (GAIA, 199?), which aims to create a sector and supplier independent architecture to support 'multilateral information trading which will facilitate location and delivery of information, contents and digital services'.
- DECOMATE (Delivery of Copyright Materials to End-users), which is a joint project aimed at developing a generic system that offers end users a new electronic document delivery service in science (Dijkstra, 1997, 1998).

In the UK various document delivery projects such as EDDIS, SEREN, MODELS and LAMDA make use of agreed international standards, as does the German SUBITO project. The organizations that are very active in this area include the British Library, London and South Eastern Library Region (LASER), Consortium of University Research Libraries (CURL), Fretwell-Downing Informatics, GEDI and PICA (Netherlands). In addition, a number of projects using the Z39.50 standard are being undertaken. These include COPAC (CURL OPAC), which uses a web interface for the union catalogue, with a Z39.50 client under development (Cousins, 1997).

Copyright

Copyright, which was designed essentially for the print environment, has emerged as a major issue in the digital environment and has the potential to limit the benefits of resource sharing.

The growth of the Internet and developments in digital technology are creating new barriers for users as well as new problems for copyright owners. Of concern to copyright owners is that technology not only facilitates the rapid distribution of their protected works, but also allows reproduction without loss of quality. However, technology also permits publishers to place 'software locks' on their products, thus ensuring that they continue to maintain control over usage. As DD/ILL becomes more pervasive and extensive, librarians are finding that these barriers to resource sharing are becoming more difficult and expensive to cross. Norman (1998) has pointed out quite rightly that copyright is concerned with balancing the rights of creators with the rights of society to have fair access to ideas and knowledge. But because copyright is today an 'international tradeable commodity' and a major contributor of economic wealth, it is not surprising that greater emphasis is being given to the economic rights of intellectual property owners.

A number of countries have updated or are in the process of updating their copyright laws in response to advances in technology and to conform to the norms and standards spelt out in the WIPO treaties (WIPO, 1996, 1998). The WIPO (1996) treaties have strengthened the intellectual property rights of authors, performers and producers. However, because of the successful lobbying by library groups, signatory nations are allowed to make new exceptions, which are appropriate to the digital environment. Two questions then arise. First, what is the extent to which these exemptions are 'natural rights' and cannot be overridden by publishers' licences? Second, what is the value of these exceptions if digital technology will allow publishers to increase the protection of their works through controls, tracking and the use of 'electronic locks' such as encryption, tagging, digital fingerprinting, data identifiers and watermarking?

Thus, individual countries, within the constraints of the WIPO treaties, have to formulate policies to resolve issues such as the following:

- the nature of the digital rights of publishers;
- exceptions to these rights, e.g. fair dealing and the right to make temporary or incidental copies in the course of the technical process of transmission;
- liability of Internet service providers, libraries, archives and others with respect to copyright infringement by users;
- the use of technological copyright protection measures and the extent to which publishers should be compelled to give access to users of copyright materials;
- electronic rights management.

The Australian strategy is a good example of how these various issues will be resolved. The Australian government has canvassed views of a draft Bill to amend the Copyright Act, which if passed by parliament would implement the government's decision on the Digital Agenda copyright reforms it made in 1998 (Digital, 1999). The central aim of the reforms is 'to ensure that copyright law continues to promote creative endeavour whilst allowing reasonable access to copyright material on the Internet and through new communications technology'. The centrepiece of the draft Bill is a new technology-neutral right of communication to the public. This includes:

- applying the existing fair dealing exceptions to the proposed right of communication;
- applying the existing exceptions for library copying to the electronic reproduction and communication of copyright material for users and other libraries and archives;
- extending to the digital environment the provision that libraries and archives are not liable for authorizing the making of illegal copies simply because the copy was made on one of the machines in the library or archive;
- extending the statutory licence for educational institutions to make electronic copies of works;
- making it illegal to break 'software locks' except in certain circumstances.

An important provision relates to the decision to exclude from the scope of the existing reproduction right 'temporary reproductions made in the course of the technical process of both electronic communications and browsing (or simply viewing), copyright material on a computer screen'. This right would allow screen browsing and caching without infringing copyright and solve some of the current disputes in the print environment where an ARIEL or fax transmission of a copy, for example, is said to infringe copyright because multiple temporary copies are made in the course of the transmission.

The vast differences in the copyright laws of countries create barriers to international interlending. Publishers are generally hostile to the concept of fair dealing or fair use which, in most countries, allows some limited copying for private use, study and research. Publishers have generally tried to get around this in the digital environment through restrictive licensing arrangements (Hadley and Barrow, 1997). However, librarians have begun to take a more proactive stance on this issue. Outraged by the restrictive licensing arrangements proposed by many publishers relating to access of their electronic publications, a group of Dutch and German university librarians has drafted a common policy paper on access to electronic journals and licensing arrangements. The policy lays down terms which are considered to be acceptable with respect to access, use, storage and costs of electronic publications (Stoker, 1998). In the UK an alternative approach has been pursued, involving the negotiation of site licences which give unlimited and unrestricted access to materials from a publisher on a given site or campus. The Pilot Site Licence Initiative (PLSI) was implemented between 1996 and 1998 at the suggestion of Academic Press (Morrow, 1997). In this scheme the Higher Education Funding Council for England purchased a licence which made available to higher education institutions in the UK all of the journals published by Academic Press and other publishers who participated in the scheme. The PLSI demonstrated many benefits, since it facilitated the delivery of material more widely to the academic community and permitted academic staff to use the material more flexibly and in a less restrictive environment.

Some nations have more restrictive copyright laws than others. For example, while many European countries provide exceptions for private copying, the lending activities of libraries are more strictly regulated. The Rental and Lending Directive in the European Union requires authors to be remunerated (usually by the state) for the public lending of their works. In some countries, the lending of audiovisual material and multimedia can only be undertaken under licence.

Two other rights, which are not normally included in copyright legislation, are also covered in the European Union – Publication Right and Database Right (Cornish, 1998). Publication Right is a new and rather unusual right given to 'anyone who first makes available to the public a work which is out of copyright and has never been made publicly available before'. Databases whose contents are original have copyright protection. For other types of databases, publishers or producers can claim a Database Right if they can demonstrate that they have put a great deal of effort into creating it, and that the data is organized systematically. Bibliographies, the telephone directory or an anthology of poetry could qualify for Database Right even if they do not qualify for copyright protection. This obviously has major implications for document supply where a considerable amount of material is stored in databases.

Quality and performance indicators

The increasing tendency of libraries to focus on their clients or customers has resulted in a rising interest in total quality management (TQM) and performance indicators. Johannsen (1998) provides examples of how TQM can be applied to interlibrary loan processes. Continuous quality improvement is conditional upon management taking on responsibility to implement what has been called the PDCA cycle (Plan, Do, Check, Act) developed by Deming, the 'quality guru'.

Parry (1997) describes a study undertaken in 1996 which reveals that in the ten years to 1995 the volume of document delivery in UK and Ireland increased by nearly 17%, but unsatisfied or failed requests increased by 25%. Several reasons have been attributed to this failure including:

- insufficient verification and bibliographical checking before the requests are sent;
- certain types of materials (e.g. fiction and monographs) having a higher failure rate than other types (e.g. journal articles);
- failure of identified locations to supply items (site failure);
- slow speed of supply leading to cancellations;
- lower priority given to ILL by some libraries;
- copyright restrictions.

As document delivery operations become mainstream library operations, libraries must evaluate their operations in this area to ensure that they are efficient and cost effective. Waldhart (1985) outlines four performance indicators for interlibrary lending:

- satisfaction (or fill) rate;
- speed of supply;
- cost or efficiency;
- user satisfaction or user convenience.

The IFLA Section of University Libraries and Other General Research Libraries has developed guidelines for performance measures in academic libraries (Poll and Boekhorst, 1996). The criteria for measuring document delivery performance include speed, coverage and costs. The suggested primary indicator of success is defined as 'the proportion (%) of documents requested through local and international interlibrary loans that are supplied (availability) within a certain period of time' (Willemse, 1998).

However, a recent series of studies based on a survey of customer satisfaction relating to the services provided by the Greater Midwest Research Library Consortium (GMRLC) shows that speed is not always the most important factor in satisfying customers. (Fong, 1996; Levene and Pedersen, 1996; Weaver-Meyers and Stolt, 1996). While costs and patron convenience (including the ability to issue unmediated requests electronically via the WWW) are important, customers continue to give high value to their ability to interact with library staff. The presence or absence of this interaction, more than anything else, seems to affect customer perceptions of the interlibrary loan service, perhaps because this interaction helps patrons to understand the limitations that characterize a particular request thus 'reducing negative interpretations of delays'.

Fill rate is also a measure of the effectiveness of a library's DD/ILL service. Based on the American experience, a 61% fill rate for lending and an 84% fill rate for borrowing is seen to represent a minimal level of effectiveness (Paine and Ward, 1996). The GMRLC study reveals that while borrowing fill rates are rising, supply fill rates are falling, leading to the conclusion that libraries are giving greater priority to borrowing for their clients as resources diminish.

In the USA the ARL has conducted a study of interlibrary lending and document delivery in North American research libraries. Of the 97 research libraries and 22 college libraries surveyed, eight were identified as being high performance operations and a number of best practices were identified (ARL, 1998; *Measuring*, 1998). The study analysed four performance indicators:

- *direct costs of fulfilling a borrowing or lending request*: the study found that for research libraries the unit costs of borrowing ranged from $9.76 to $27.84 and of lending from $4.87 to $16.34, while the comparable figures for college libraries were $6.39–$18.50 and $4.75–$10.08;
- *percentage fill rate*: the average fill rate for borrowing was 85% for research libraries and 91% for college libraries, while the lending fill rate was 58% and 65% respectively;
- *turnaround time*;
- *user satisfaction*: with timeliness, quality and completeness of material and interaction with staff.

International assistance to developing countries

There is generally a paucity of literature relating to document delivery in developing countries and most of it is quite out of date (e.g. Smith, 1987; John, 1989; Dimitroff, 1993; Ferguson, 1995; Alemna, 1997). Developing countries have always had problems in accessing hard copy information because their libraries are usually not well supported and many have traditionally relied on the resources of libraries in the developed world to supply their information needs (Constantin, 1998). In the digital environment, their problems are compounded by the fact that they have difficulty using information technology and the Internet to access electronic information resources. The reasons are the usual ones of affordability, poor telecommunications facilities, lack of bandwidth and lack of technical skills to take advantage of the new technologies. The new model of scholarly communication using digital technology will increase their costs, as it will require the creation of an extensive network infrastructure, acquisition of appropriate hardware and software, training of users and the employment of systems personnel. In addition, the premium that publishers of print usually demand for access to their electronic versions will add to the costs.

Thus, while the move towards the digital environment will help greatly to improve access for users in the developed world, it may also prove to be a barrier for developing countries. The need for international assistance is therefore unquestionable and libraries in the developed world have put in place a number of strategies in order to help.

Liu (1997) provides a description of the work of Bridge to Asia, an international non-profit organization, based in California and Hong Kong, which supports the educational and research activities of developing countries, making use of the Internet. There are several barriers to the use of the new technology such as costs, lack of local skills and the consequent need for mediated assistance. To overcome these barriers, Bridge to Asia has established several 'Information Transfer Stations' which provide a combination of information specialists and technology to deliver information to end users.

A study by Dobson and Pedersen (1998) shows that libraries supporting international document delivery and interlending to developing countries have to deal with the problems caused by uneven levels of technology in these countries, and hence the need to develop workflows to deal with different methods of communication. The problems of developing countries have led IFLA to support libraries which are actively involved in international lending through the development of the IFLA Voucher Scheme. This is an alternative method of payment for interloans and applies to countries that face foreign exchange difficulties (Gould and Watkins, 1998). Kisiedu (1998) provides a description of the IFLA-initiated project to improve document delivery in developing countries, funded by the Danish and Norwegian governments. The objectives of the project are assisting in the establishment of electronic networking links, training of personnel, obtaining favourable terms for document supply from western libraries and developing a model which can be adopted by other Third World countries. The project covers two countries: Ghana, funded by DANIDA (Kondrup, 1998) and Kenya, funded by NORAD.

Canada's International Development Research Centre (IDRC) has provided assistance through the Pan (1997) Asia Networking programme to improve the communications infrastructure of a number of developing countries in Asia. This programme has contributed to the strengthening in some countries and creation in others of affordable computer-based communications (e-mail, conferencing and information retrieval) services to a range of clients, including individuals, non-government and government organizations and businesses. The primary objective is to promote the sharing of information resources and the research and development of Internet systems, technologies and policies.

Document delivery and virtual library developments

What is the future for document delivery services? As more and more print moves into the electronic environment, there is a view that this will make DD/ILL redundant, since users can gain access to full text resources without any mediation. The current trend to purchase electronic journals and other aggregated databases on a consortial basis so that all users have unlimited access to these resources will not only transform the nature of DD/ILL, but will also allow the evolution of a new vision of the future library. Kohl (1998) states that this will allow librarians to move away from the 'traditional concept of the library as basically a stand-alone institution limited primarily to a local collection which is only modestly supplemented by DD/ILL use, to a developing view of the local library as an integrated part of a larger entity'.

There is no doubt that the Internet has had a tremendous impact on the delivery of information services. A number of writers have examined this impact critically and described systems using the Internet and the Web to deliver information to users (Nye, 1997; Ugolini *et al.*, 1997; Johnston, 1998).

Smith (1998) is of the view that the future of document delivery is closely bound up with the future growth of electronic publishing using the Internet for delivery. Although there has been significant growth in this area, he points out that the vast majority of documents supplied are still paper based and use photocopying, fax, the post and courier delivery systems. Nevertheless, as networks and other technologies encourage a move from paper distribution to electronic delivery, the central role of document supply services must be reassessed.

More specifically, libraries have explored alternative delivery and access methods to bring the required resources to their researchers. Bancroft *et al.* (1998) have listed these alternatives as the 'promotion of electronic journals, the upgrading of print capabilities for electronic publications, the development of document delivery projects to determine the efficacy of giving users direct access to journal literature vendors, and the fostering of consortial alliances to reduce the cost and/or increase access to resources'.

The issues that document supply services must face in the electronic environment are ably outlined in the papers by Tuck (1997) and Fisher and Tuck

(1997). These are quite complex issues and represent important aspects of electronic document delivery. Each issue or aspect has a conflicting or competing element which must be resolved for successful electronic document delivery. The issues concerned include the following:

- ordering and supply of documents (mainly paper based) by electronic means, as opposed to the delivery of purely electronic documents;
- for digitized documents, whether one should store at source as in Beilstein's FASTDOC system, or scan-on-demand as in EDIL (Deschamps, 1995; Braid, 1996), or combine the two as in EURILIA (O'Flaherty, 1995);
- subscription versus pay per view;
- centralized supply (e.g. BLDSC) versus distributed supply (PICA, ARIEL) models;
- single media versus multimedia documents;
- standards approach (e.g. ISO-ILL or Z39.50) versus proprietary systems;
- delivery using e-mail, WWW or FTP versus fax;
- mediated versus unmediated requesting/ordering.

The pros and cons as well as the costs of the above are also explored in some detail.

A number of broad-based initiatives have been undertaken in the past five years, mainly in Europe and North America, to explore the possibilities of the new digital environment and improve access for users. Many of these projects are aimed at creating new library models and new ways of information delivery integrating both analogue (print) and digital information resources. The major initiatives include:

- The eLIB (1999) programme, which aims to develop models of the electronic library through a programme of more than 60 projects (Russell, 1997). Rusbridge (1998b) provides an evaluation of phases 1 and 2 of the programme and concludes: 'There are many general lessons, including problems of inexperience in project management, difficulties of communication in consortium projects, and many difficulties in dissemination. However, the most outstanding lesson from this phase and from JISC's other work in provision of datasets is the need for integration.'
- The NSF/DARPA/NASA (1998) Digital Libraries Initiative (DLI) Projects. Unlike the British, the Americans focus on six large projects rather than a number of small ones. While the British projects tend to assume that digital library initiatives will continue to help traditional libraries to expand into new functional areas, the Americans work on the assumption that future libraries will be purely digital. Because of the success of DLI, further funding has been provided under DLI – Phase 2, with the National Library of Medicine, the Library of Congress, and the National Endowment for the Humanities joining NSF, DARPA and NASA as primary sponsors.

Descriptions of the Phase 1 DLI projects are provided by Bishop (1995), Schatz and Chen (1996), and Griffin (1998).

* The European Libraries Programme (Johnson, 1996) or the Telematics for Libraries Programme was conceived in the early 1980s to make available Europe's diverse and rich information and cultural resources to its citizens. The programme has seen the development of numerous systems to support document delivery, many of which have already been mentioned in the section on standards and protocols above.

Developments in electronic technologies for document delivery will have an impact on the future role of libraries. Many commercial players – subscription agents, publishers, database hosts – will compete with libraries in the area of document supply. Already there are some reports in the literature of companies outsourcing their document supply (Barth *et al.*, 1998). Libraries play a valuable social role which none of these suppliers perform. This role is to ensure equitable access to information for scholarship, education and the creation of an informed citizenry. If libraries cease to play a role in the dissemination of information in the future, society will be the poorer for it.

References

AIDA (1995) *Alternatives for international document availability: edited progress report.* http://www.cib.unibo.it/aida/ (accessed 15.05.2000).

Alemna, A. (1997) The future of document delivery for developing countries: a view from West Africa. *Interlending and Document Supply,* 25(1), 5–7.

Arkin, E. (1998) User initiated interlibrary loan. *Interlending and Document Supply,* 26(3), 119–122.

ARL (1998) identifies best practices in ILL operations. *Advanced Technology Libraries,* 27(9), 1–2.

Bancroft, A.F. *et al.* (1998) A forward-looking library use survey: WSU libraries in the 21st century. *Journal of Academic Librarianship,* 24(3), 216–223.

Barth, A. *et al.* (1998) AutoDoc: an automated document delivery broker system at FIZ Karlsruhe. *Program,* 32(4), 403–412.

Barwick, M. (1997) Interlending and document supply: a review of recent literature – XXXII. *Interlending and Document Supply,* 25(3), 126–132.

Bibliography (1998a) of interlending and document supply: 39. *Interlending and Document Supply,* 26(2), 93–97.

Bibliography (1998b) of interlending and document supply: 40. *Interlending and Document Supply,* 26(4), 178–181.

Bishop, A.P. (1995) Working toward an understanding of digital library use: a report on the user research efforts of the NSF/ARPA/NASA DLI Projects. *D-Lib Magazine,* (October). http://www.dlib.org/dlib/october95/10bishop.html/ (accessed 15.05.2000).

Bjornshauge, L. (1998) From document delivery and interlending to document access and interlibrary collection. In: *64th IFLA General Conference August 16-21, 1998. Proceedings.* http://www.ifla.org/IV/ifla64/146-142e.htm/ (accessed 15.05.2000).

Blagden, J. (1997) Opinion paper: access versus holdings. *Interlending and Document Supply*, **25**(4), 179–182.

Blagden, J. (1998) Opinion paper: access versus holdings. *Interlending and Document Supply*, **26**(3), 140–143.

Boza, O.J. *et al.* (1998) El préstamo entre bibliotecas públicas municipales: mas servicio aprovechando recursos. Una propuesta de trabajo. [Lending between municipal public libraries: better services by maximizing resources. A work proposal.] *Boletín de la Asociación Andaluza de Bibliotecarios*, **13**(50), 37–51.

Braid, A. (1996) Standardization in electronic document delivery: a practical example. *Interlending and Document Supply*, **24**(4), 12–18.

Brittain, J.M. and Colmer, M. (1998) Access to information – new directions. *International Journal of Information Management*, **18**(2), 81–90.

Brunskill, K. (1997) The issue surrounding the provision of CASIAS services in libraries. *Interlending and Document Supply*, **25**(2), 57–63.

Byrne, A. (1997) *After the DNBC: establishing a sustainable information environment for research and scholarship in Australia.* [Keynote paper; presented at the National Scholarly Communications Forum Round Table no. 7: The Distributed National Collection.] http://www.anu.edu.au/caul/nscf/byrne.htm/ (accessed: 15.05.2000)

Casares, L., *et al.* (1997) Projectes de cooperació en matèria de préstec interbibliotecari dins el marc del Consorci de Biblioteques Universitàries de Catalunya. In: Jornades Catalanes de Documentació (6es.: 1997: Barcelona). *Cap a la societat digital: un món en contínua transformació.* Barcelona: Societat Catalana de Documentació i Informació: Collegi Oficial de Bibliotecaris-Documentalistes de Catalunya, pp. 213–223.

Chapman, E. (1998) Buying shares in libraries: the economics of cooperative collection development. *IFLA Journal*, **24**(2), 102–106.

CISTI [website] *NRC's Canada Institute for Scientific and Technical Information: document delivery.* http://www.cisti.nrc.ca/cisti/docdel/docdel.html/ (accessed 15.05.2000).

CISTI (1998) implements INNOPAC Millenium Catalog for document delivery. *Advanced Technology Libraries*, **27**(1), 8.

Come (1998) fly with JEDDS-enhanced Ariel. http://www.nla.gov.au/ntwkpubs/gw/33/33.html#JEDDS (accessed 15.05.2000).

Consorci (1999) de Bibliotheques Universitàries de Catalunya. http://www.cbuc.es (accessed 16.04.1999).

Constantin, O. (1998) International interlibrary lending activity in Romania and cooperation with other countries. *Interlending and Document Supply*, **26**(3), 115–118.

CopySmart (1997) intellectual property rights management for electronic documents. *Interlending and Document Supply*, **25**(1), 36.

Cornish, G.P. (1998) Copyright and document delivery in the electronic environment. *Interlending and Document Supply*, **26**(3), 123–129.

Cousins, S.A. (1997) COPAC: the new national OPAC service based on the CURL database. *Program*, **31**(1), 1–21.

DALI [website] Document and library integration.

http://www.cordis.lu/libraries/en/projects/dali.html

Davies, J.E. (1998) Strategic issues in managing information and document supply in academic libraries. *Library Management*, **19**(5), 318–326.

Davies, J.E. and Morris, A. (1998) Weighing up the options for document delivery supply: a description and discussion of the FIDDO project. *Interlending and Document Supply*, **26**(2), 76–82.

DBV-OSI II (1999) project.
http://www.ddb.de/partner/dbv-osi_ii.htm// (accessed 15.05.2000).

Deloughry, T.J. (1996) Journal articles dating back as far as a century are being put on line. *Chronicle of Higher Education*, **43**(15), A30, A32, A34–A36.

Dementi, M.A.E. (1998) Access and archiving as a new paradigm. *Journal of Electronic Publishing*, (March).
http://www.press.umich.edu:80/jep/03-03/dementi.html/ (accessed 15.05.2000).

Deschamps, C. (1995) The ION and EDIL projects. *Inspel*, **29**(2), 133–134.

Digital (1999) Agenda copyright amendments.
http://www.dcita.gov.au/cgi-bin/graphics.pl?path=3562 (accessed 15.05.2000).

Dijkstra, J. (1997) A generic approach to the electronic access of scientific journals: the DECOMATE project. *Library Acquisitions: Practice and Theory*, **21**(3), 393–402.

Dijkstra, J (1998) Journals in transition: from paper to electronic access: the Decomate Project. *Serials Librarian*, **33**(3/4), 243–270.

Dimitroff, A. (1993) Information access in a developing country: special libraries in Egypt (problems of document delivery; report of a 1992 study tour). *Special Libraries*, **84**(1), 25–29.

Dobson, C. and Pedersen, W.A. (1998) Document delivery to developing countries. *Interlending and Document Supply*, **26**(1), 3–9.

Douglas, K. and Roth, D.L. (1997) TOC/DOC: 'it has changed the way I do science'. *Science and Technology Libraries*, **16**(3/4), 131–146.

Eastwood, E.J. and Mornati, S. (1998) Behaviour and perceptions of interlibrary loan and document delivery service users: high energy physics at CERN a case study. In: Gould, S. and Johnson, D. (1998) (eds), pp. 147–165.

EDDIS (1998) Electronic Document Delivery – the integrated solution.
http://www.ukoln.ac.uk/services/elib/projects/eddis/intro.html (accessed 15.05.2000).

EDIL (1996) http://www.lboro.ac.uk/department/dils/fiddo/edil.html/ (accessed 15.05.2000).

eLib (1999) Electronic Libraries Programme.
http://www.ukoln.ac.uk/services/elib/ (accessed: 15.05.2000).

Elsevier (1999) Website. http://www.elsevier.nl. (accessed: 15.05.2000).

Etschmaier, G. and Bustion, M. (1997) Document delivery and collection development: an evolving relationship. *Serials Librarian*, **31**(3), 13–27.

Ferguson, S.W.L. (1995) Interlibrary lending and document delivery in the Caribbean: the perplexing reality. *Interlending and Document Supply*, **23**(2), 4–9.

FIDDO (1999) Focused Investigation of Document Delivery Options Project.
http://www.lboro.ac.uk/departments/dils/fiddo/finalreport.html (accessed 15.05.2000).

Finnie, E. (1997) Selection and evaluation of document suppliers. *Managing Information*, **4**(3), 25–32.

Finnie, E. (1998) *Document delivery*. London: Aslib.

Fisher, R.A. and Tuck, B. (1997) Issues in electronic document delivery. *Interlending and Document Supply*, 25(1), 18–24.

Fong, Y.S. (1996) The value of interlibrary loan: an analysis of customer satisfaction survey comments. In: Weaver-Meyers, P.L. *et al.* (1996) (eds), pp. 43–54.

Fong, Y.S. *et al.* (1996) Interlibrary loan management software: a comparative analysis of SAVEIT, AVISO and PRS. In: Weaver-Meyers, P.L. *et al.* (1996) (eds), pp. 95–124.

Fønss-Jørgensen, E. (1998) Network access to the audiovisual cultural heritage – possibilities and problems. *Interlending and Document Supply*, 26(4), 171–174.

Foo, S. and Lim, E.P. (1998) An integrated Web-based ILL system for Singapore libraries. *Interlending and Document Supply*, 26(1), 10–20.

Fuchs, H. (1998) German interlending and document delivery in the nineties. In: Gould, S. and Johnson, D. (1998) (eds), pp. 45–56.

GAIA [website] http://www.syspace.co.uk/GAIA/ (accessed 15.05.2000).

GEDI (1999) http://www2.echo.lu/oii/en/library.html#GEDI (accessed 15.05.2000).

Gould, S. (1997). Interlending and document supply: a review of recent literature – XXXI. *Interlending and Document Supply*, 25(1), 27–35.

Gould, S. (1998a) Apologies for cross-posting a brief look at Internet discussion lists in interlibrary loans and document delivery. *Interlending and Document Supply*, 26(1), 21–24.

Gould, S (1998b) Interlending and document supply: a review of recent literature – XXXIII. *Interlending and Document Supply*, 26(1), 36–43.

Gould, S (1998c) Interlending and document supply: a review of recent literature – XXXIV. *Interlending and Document Supply*, 26(3) 144–151.

Gould, S. and Johnson, D. (1998) (eds) *Interlending and document supply: resource sharing possibilities and barriers; proceedings of the 5th Interlending and Document Supply International Conference, Aarhus, Denmark, 24–28 August 1997.* Boston Spa: IFLA Offices for UAP and International Lending.

Gould, S and Watkins, J. (1998) International cooperation: the role of the IFLA Offices for UAP and international lending. *Journal of Librarianship and Information Science*, 30(3), 195–199.

Greenaway, J. (1997) *The Coordinated Interlibrary Loan Administration Project: final report and recommendations of the feasibility study.*
http://www.gu.edu.au/alib/iii/docdel/cilla (accessed 15.05.2000).

Greenaway, J. (1998) Interlending and document delivery: the way forward. In: *Robots* (1998), pp. 39–55.

Greenaway, J. and Blinco, K. (1997) Creating an integrated document delivery environment in Australia: the role of JEDDS and CILLA. In: *'On the edge': proceedings of the 7th Asian Pacific Specials, Health and Law Librarians' Conference Perth 12–17 October 1997*, Perth: Australian Library and Information Association Special Libraries Section and Health Libraries Section; Australian Law Librarians Group, pp. 393–402.

Griffin, S.M. (1998). NSF/DARPA/NASA Digital Library Initiative. *D-Lib Magazine*, (July/August).
http://www.dlib.org/dlib/july98/07griffin.html/ (accessed 15.05.2000).

Guthrie, K.M. (1998) JSTOR and the University of Michigan: an evolving collaboration. *Library Hi Tech*, 16(1), 9–15.

Hadley, C. and Barrow, E. (1997) Licensed document supply: the role of IFFRO. *Interlending and Document Supply*, 25(2), 73–76.

Halgren, J.V. (1998) The University of Oregan saves staff time with ILL direct request. *OCLC Newsletter*, (232), 13–14.

Hawk, J. (1998) The OCLC SiteSearch suite allows libraries to integrate information resources. *OCLC Newsletter*, (231), 28–30.

IDEAL (1998) International Digital Electronic Access Library. http://www.idealibrary.com/ (accessed 15.04.1999).

Interlibrary (1997) Loan Application Standards Maintenance Agency. http://www.nlc-bnc.ca/iso/ill (accessed 15.04.1999).

Interloans (1998) handbook. The New Zealand interlibrary loan system: operation guidelines. http://www.lianza.org.nz/interloans_handbook.htm (accessed 15.05.2000).

Jackson, M.E. (1997a) The application of the ILL Protocol to existing ILL systems. In: *63rd IFLA General Conference, August 31–September 5, 1997. Conference programme and proceedings.* http://www.ifla.org/IV/ifla63/63jacm2.htm/ (accessed 15.05.2000).

Jackson, M.E. (1997b) The North American Interlibrary Loan and Document Delivery project: improving ILL/DD services. *Interlending and Document Supply*, 25(1), 8–10.

Jackson, M. E. (1998) Loan stars: ILL comes of age. *Library Journal*, 123(2), 44–47.

Jensen, M.B. (1998) The collaborative library community – a Danish reality. *Library Review*, 47(3), 60–65.

Johannsen, C.G. (1998) A TQM perspective on interlibrary loan processes. In: Gould, S. and Johnson, D. (1998) (eds), pp. 123–129.

John, S. (1989) INFONET [Organization of Eastern Caribbean States information network] in the Eastern Caribbean. *Interlending and Document Supply*, 17(1), 20–21.

Johnson, R. (1996) European Libraries Programme. *Ariadne*, (5). http://www.ariadne.ac.uk/issue5/european-libraries/intro.html/ (accessed 15.05.2000).

Johnston, C. (1998) Electronic technology and its impact on libraries. *Journal of Librarianship and Information Science*, 30(1), 7–24.

JSTOR (1999) Journal storage. http://www.jstor.org (accessed 15.05.2000).

Karaomerlioglu, D.C. (1997) Technology and new means of information: windows of opportunity for developing countries? *Resource Sharing and Information Networks*, 12(2), 59–65.

Kingma, B.R. (1997) Interlibrary loan and resource sharing: the economics of the SUNY Express Consortium. *Library Trends*, 45(3), 518–530.

Kisiedu, C.O. (1998) Barriers in using new information technology in document delivery in the Third World: prospect for the IFLA Project in Ghana. In: Gould, S. and Johnson, D. (1998) (eds), pp. 99–113.

Kleiner, J.P. and Hamaker, A. (1997) Libraries 2000: transforming libraries using document delivery, needs assessment, and networked resources. *College and Research Libraries*, 58(4), 355–374.

Kohl, D.F. (1998) How the virtual library transforms interlibrary loans – the Ohiolink experience. *Interlending and Document Supply*, 26(2), 65–69.

Kondrup, R. (1998) Project report: Interlibrary lending and document delivery in developing countries, the IFLA/Danida pilot project in Ghana. *Newsletter of the IFLA Section on Document Delivery and Interlending*, July 1998. http://www.nlc-bnc.ca/ifla/VII/s15/pubs/news9807.htm/ (accessed 15.05.2000).

Krichel, T. (1999) RePEc. http://netec.mcc.ac.uk/RePEc (accessed 15.05.2000).

LAMDA (1998) http://www.man-bus.mmu.ac.uk/lamda/ (accessed 15.05.2000).

Landes, S. (1997) ARIEL document delivery: a cost effective alternative to fax. *Journal of Interlibrary Loan, Document Delivery and Information Supply*, **7**(3), 61–72.

Larbey, D. (1997a). Electronic document delivery (including overviews of network standards, GEDI, ISO, ILL and Z39.50). *Library and Information Briefings*, (77/78), 2–30.

Larbey, D. (1997b) Project EDDIS: an approach to integrating document discovery, location, request and supply. *Interlending and Document Supply*, **25**(3), 96–102.

Larbey, D. (1998). Project EDDIS. *Ariadne*, (14).
http://www.ariadne.ac.uk/issue14/eddis (accessed 15.05.2000).

Levene, L.A. and Pedersen, W. (1996) Patron satisfaction at any cost? a case study of interlibrary loan in two U.S. research libraries. In: Weaver-Meyers, P.L. *et al.* (1996) (eds), pp. 55–71.

Lim, E. (1998). Building a virtual national serials collection using the MEADS system. *AARL*, **29**(4), 165–175.

Liu, N.X. (1997) Using the Internet to share information between China and the west. *Inspel*, **31**(2), 103–109.

Lor, P.J. (1996) Document supply. In: M.B. Line (ed.) *Librarianship and Information Work Worldwide 1995*. East Grinstead: Bowker Saur, pp. 259–298.

McGrath, M. (1998) The current state of ILL: some realities behind the hype. *Librarian Career Development*, **6**(2), 17–25.

Marcinko, R.W. (1997) Issues in commercial document delivery. *Library Trends*, **45**(3), 531–550.

Martin, A. (1997) *Identifying the issues*. [Paper presented at the National Scholarly Communications Forum Round Table no. 7: The Distributed National Collection.]
http://www.anu.edu.au/caul/nscf/martin.htm/ (accessed 15.05.2000).

Measuring (1998) *the performance of interlibrary loan operations in North American research and college libraries: results of a study funded by the Andrew W. Mellon Foundation*. Washington, DC: Association of Research Libraries.

Mehta, U. and Goodman, B. (1997) InfoTrac's SearchBank databases: business information and more. *Journal of Business and Finance Librarianship*, **2**(3), 23–37.

Mettraux, B. (1998) Réalisation du système de prêt interbibliothéques global. Realization of the global interlibrary loan system. *Arbido*, **13**(1), 9–11.

Morris, A. and Blagg, E. (1998) Current document delivery practices in UK academic libraries. *Library Management*, **19**(4), 271–280.

Morris, A. *et al.* (1997) Options in electronic document delivery. *Managing Information*, **4**(3), 21, 23–24.

Morris, P. (1997) *SEREN sharing educational resources in electronic network*.
http://seren.newi.ac.uk/ (accessed 15.05.2000).

Morrow, T. (1997) Infobike – delivering electronic full text to the end-user. *Library and Information Briefings*, **79**, 2–13.

Mostert, P. and Fransen, P. (1997) Technical and functional aspects of electronic journals systems developed in TULIP and EES projects. *Library Acquisitions: Practice and Theory*, **21**(3), 347–353.

Moulton, R. (1997) ILL protocol related activities in the UK, Europe and Australia. In: *63rd IFLA General Conference, Conference programme and proceedings, August 31–September 5, 1997*.
http://www.ifla.org/IV/ifla63/63mour.htm/ (accessed 15.05.2000).

Newsome, N. and Cook, E.I. (1997) More questions than answers: transition from print document delivery to electronic document delivery; one consortium's dilemma. *Serials Librarian*, **31**(3), 49–65.

Nilges, C. (1998) Evolving an integrated electronic journals solution: OCLC Firstsearch Electronic Collections Online. *Serials Librarian*, **33**(3/4), 299–318.

Norman, S. (1998) Copyright issues in document supply. In: Gould, S. and Johnson, D. (1998) (eds), pp. 77–87.

NSF/DARPA/NASA. (1998) Digital Libraries Initiative Projects. http://www.cise.nsf.gov/iis/dli_home.html/ (accessed 15.05.2000).

Nye, J.B. (1997) Integrating serials into the Triangle Research Libraries network document delivery system. *Serials Librarian*, **31**(3), 29–47.

OCLC (1998a) direct request allows user initiated, library controlled ILL. *Advanced Technology Libraries*, (January), 6.

OCLC (1998b) ILL direct request offers direct patron initiated document delivery. *Online Libraries and Microcomputers*, **16**(2), 6.

O'Flaherty, J.J. (1995) European initiative in library and information in Aerospace: EURILIA. *Program*, **29**(4), 407–416.

Olorunsola, R. (1997) Electronic delivery of information in Nigeria: situation and suggestions for future directions. *OCLC Systems and Services*, **13**(1), 12–16.

Orr, D. and Appleton, M. (1998) Management issues surrounding unmediated document delivery at Central Queensland University. In: *Robots* (1998), pp. 57–66.

Osanai, M. (1998) Electronic journals for practical use [in Japanese]. *Igaku-Toshokan*, **45**(2), 211–216.

Ouyang, G. and Sproat, E. (1998) Chinese library begins using OCLC Interlibrary Loan. *OCLC Newsletter*, (232), 28.

Pan (1997) Asia Networking Programme. http://www.PanAsia.org.sg/ (accessed 15.05.2000).

Paine, N.E. and Ward, J. (1996) Changing workloads and productivity in interlibrary loans. In: Weaver-Meyers, P.L. *et al.* (1996) (eds), pp. 73–93.

Parry, D. (1997) Why requests fail. *Interlending and Document Supply*, **25**(4), 147–156.

Pavlov, L.P. (1998) The state and development of the Russian grey literature collection and dissemination centre. *Interlending and Document Supply*, **26**(4), 168–170.

Poll, R. and Boekhorst, P. (1996) *Measuring quality: international guidelines for performance measurement in academic libraries*. [Prepared by IFLA Section of University Libraries & Other General Research Libraries.] München: K.G. Saur. [IFLA Publications 76.]

Prabha, C. and Marsh, E.C. (1997) Commercial document suppliers; how many of the ILL/DD periodical article requests can they fulfil? *Library Trends*, **45**(3), 551–568.

ProQuest (1998) Applied Science and Technology Plus. *Interlending and Document Supply*, **26**(1), 53.

Prowse, S. (1998) Trends and developments in interlending and document delivery in the UK. *Interlending and Document Supply*, **26**(2), 883–892.

Robots (1998) *to knowbots: the wider automation agenda: proceedings of the Victorian Association for Library Automation 9th biennial conference, Melbourne, 28–30 January 1998*. Melbourne: Victorian Association for Library Automation.

Rusbridge, C. (1998a) eLib goes down under: the National ILL utility. *Ariadne*, (16). http://www.ariadne.ac.uk/issue16/ill/intro.html/ (accessed 15.05.2000).

Rusbridge, C. (1998b) Towards the hybrid library. *D-Lib Magazine,* July/August. http://www.dlib.org/dlib/july98/rusbridge/07rusbridge.html/ (accessed 15.05.2000).

Russell, K. (1997) The eLib Phase 3 Programme: Hybrid Libraries and Large Scale Resource Discovery (Clumps).
http://www.ukoln.ac.uk/services/elib/background/pressreleases/summary2 (accessed 15.05.2000).

SAIL (1996) System for Automated Interlibrary Loan Programme.
http://archive.nlm.nih.gov/proj/sail.html/ (accessed 15.05.2000).

Schatz, B. and Chen, H. (1996) *Building large-scale digital libraries.*
http://computer.org/computer/dli (accessed 15.05.2000).

Shipp, J. (1997) *Identifying the issues.* [Paper presented at the National Scholarly Communications Forum Round Table no. 7: The Distributed National Collection.]
http://www.anu.edu.au/caul/nscf/shipp7.htm/ (accessed 15.05.2000).

Shuh, B. (1998) The renaissance of the interlibrary loan protocol: developments in open systems for interlibrary loan message management. *Interlending and Document Supply,* **26**(1), 25–33.

Smith, E.S. (1987) Document supply: developments and problems. *Quarterly Bulletin of the International Association of Agricultural Librarians and Documentalists,* **32**(1), 19–24.

Smith, M. (1997) Interlibrary loan and document supply: time for a merger? *Interlending and Document Supply,* **25**(1), 3–4.

Smith, M. (1998) The next five years – World Wide Web, Internet, and . . .? In: Gould, S. and Johnson, D. (1998) (eds), pp. 179–196.

Sood, C. (1997) *Interlending and document supply infrastructure developments in Australia.* [Paper presented at the Interlending and Document Supply, 5th International Conference, Aarhus, Denmark.]
http://www.nla.gov.au/nla/staffpaper/ids5spe.html/ (accessed 15.05.2000).

Stoker, D. (1998) Commercial pressures upon electronic publishing. *Journal of Librarianship and Information Science,* **30**(2), 83–85.

Stuyts, C. (1998) The project DEGREE: dissemination of electronic GRey files on economics. *Interlending and Document Supply,* **26**(4), 163–167.

Sung, C.C. (1998) The national library in the era of digital libraries: the remote access/delivery of the National Central Library [in Chinese]. *Journal of Library and Information Science* [Taiwan], **23**(2), 41–50.

Tenopir, C. (1998) Linking to full texts. *Library Journal,* **123**(6), 34–36.

Tuck, B. (1997) Document delivery in an electronic world. *Interlending and Document Supply,* **25**(1), 11–17.

Tucker, J. *et al.* (1998) CIDER: CAVAL Information delivery and electronic reporting. In: *Robots* (1998), pp. 67–78.

TULIP (1997) The University Licensing Program.
http://www.elsevier.nl/inca/homepage/about/resproj/tulip.shtml (accessed 15.05.2000).

Turner, R. (1997) Document delivery: the publisher, the librarian and the intermediary. *Managing Information,* **4**(3), 33–35.

Ugolini, D. *et al.* (1997) ViCLib – creating a hypertext library information system. *Journal of Librarianship and Information Science,* **29**(4), 205–210.

UMI (1999) http://www.umi.com/proquest/ (accessed 15.05.2000).

UnCover (1998a) desktop image delivery. *Interlending and Document Supply*, **26**(3), 152.

UnCover (1998b) unveils UnCoverWeb 2.0. *Advanced Technology Libraries*, **27**(9), 3.

UNIverse (1999) project.
http://www.fdgroup.co.uk/research/universe/ (accessed 15.05.2000).

Unnikrishnan, S. *et al.* (1997) Document delivery service through NUCSSI: a case study of Mahatma Gandhi University Library. *Library Science with a Slant to Documentation and Information Studies*, **34**(2), 101–109.

Urbano, C. (1997). Obtención de documentos: una lectura de las últimas revisiones bibliográficas desde la situación española. In: *Amiari SOCADI de documentació informació*. Barcelona: Societat Catalana de Documentació i Informació, pp. 191–201.

Vyas, S.D. (1997) Library automation and networking in India: problems and prospects. *World Libraries*, **8**(1), 27–35.

Waldhart, T.J. (1985) Performance evaluation of interlibrary loan in the United States: a review of research. *Library and Information Science Research*, **7**(4), 313–331.

Weaver-Meyers, P.L. and Stolt, W.A. (1996) Delivery speed, timelines and satisfaction: patrons' perceptions about ILL services. In: Weaver-Meyers, P.L. *et al.* (1996) (eds), pp. 23–40.

Weaver-Meyers, P.L. *et al.* (1996) (eds) *Interlibrary loan/document delivery and customer satisfaction: strategies for redesigning services*. New York: Haworth Press. Also published as *Journal of Library Administration*, **23**(1/2).

Wells, A. and Amos, H. (1998) *Developing a new resource sharing infrastructure in Australia*. [Paper presented at the Document Delivery Beyond 2000 conference, London.] http://www.nla.gov.au/nla/staffpaper/awells3.html/ (accessed 15.05.2000).

Wettler, M.A. (1998) Evaluating document delivery services. *Database*, (21), 73–74.

Willemse, J. (1998) Measuring quality: international guidelines for performance measure in academic libraries. In: Gould, S. and Johnson, D. (1998) (eds), pp. 115–122.

WIPO (1996) Copyright Treaty.
http://www.wipo.org/eng/diplconf/distrib/94dc.htm/ (accessed 15.05.2000).

WIPO (1998) World Intellectual Property Organization.
http://www.wipo.int/ (accessed 15.05.2000).

WoPEc [website]. http://netec.mcc.ac.uk/WoPEc.html/ (accessed 15.05.2000).

Zauha, J. (1998) Applied science and technology plus. *Database*, **21**(2), 56–58, 60.

National information policy and planning

6

Giuseppe Vitiello

Introduction

If we compare the definition of national information policy and planning in the mid-1960s and 1970s with today's elaborations of national plans for the information (digital, knowledge or intelligent) society, the profound transformations that have taken place in the last decades and the different objectives that are now assigned to public and private organizations carrying out policies at a national and international level become obvious. In earlier times, national information policies were a concept limited in scope and nature. Under the influence of Machlup (1962) and Porat (1978), information was considered mainly as a commodity. National information policy was a specialized concept including, within a single chain, information originators (such as research institutes, press agencies, etc.), mediators (among others brokers, librarians and archivists) and users. Information actors were to be found both in the private and public sectors, although planning was essentially a public business and a fundamental component of the welfare system. At its hottest, the debate was focused on political choices: on centralization versus decentralization of information distribution and the levels of its institutionalization, and on technical solutions, i.e. methods and standards in data processing. Planning was mainly done through state intervention, a position at that time defended by the UNESCO General Information Programme, perhaps the only major international programme on information.

Today's concept of information policy and planning is the result of the sweeping effects of the technological revolution and of a society based on intelligence. In the USA in the 1960s there were twice as many people in goods handling employment (mining, construction, manufacturing, transportation, wholesale/ retail trade) as in information-handling employment (communications, finance, insurance, services, government). By the 1990s, the information sector had almost caught up and further growth is to be expected (Castells, 1996). The concept of information has a granular nature, inherent to all human activities and no longer confined to specialized institutions: it is a fundamental component of human life, closely intertwined with one's ability to communicate through networks and networking. Information is also a shared value, a peace-making (or trouble-making) tool, and a parcel of individual identities. The political, economic, societal and cultural implications of such assumptions have been widely investigated.

Less known is the role that governments play in devising and developing national strategies for building up the information society. Some current grand statements seemingly supporting an unregulated process of development, free from state interference, may give the impression that Hayek's prediction was right when he indicated that the marketplace was the only regulator of knowledge distribution in society (Machlup, 1984). In reality, especially in the western world, even countries having no tradition of state intervention have formed national plans for an information society that is fair and open to all. The debate on whether information societies should be the result of an all-encompassing framework of information policies or of developments shaped by market forces seems no longer topical, so great is the number of activities that governments have set in motion and for which public expenditure has been earmarked.

This chapter reviews the different visions of the information society put forward by several countries, in an attempt to identify objectives and areas set as priorities for governmental intervention. It explores the terms of the political discourse on the information society through official documents dealing with intervention by public powers. While being aware of general literature concerning the perceived and hidden effects of information and communication technologies (ICT) on society, it concentrates on national information policy and planning from the viewpoint of government agencies and international organizations – a discourse and rhetoric usually known as National Information Plans (NIPs).

The chapter deals first with the respective roles of national governments and international organizations in creating information plans. Although written rules codify the core missions of international organizations, the pervasive nature of the information society puts well-established norms and behaviours under strain. There are fields in which national public authorities are not willing to cede their competences to international bodies. Second, a thematic approach investigates recurrent topics within NIPs, such as the question of values, intellectual property, education, employment (with special reference to jobs in the content industry) and culture. Third, some overarching concepts are briefly examined that underpin the philosophy of governmental action and constitute the societal dilemmas any information policy has to confront: sustainability, convergence and globalization. The conclusion will assess the impact of national information policy and planning and to what extent the notion of nation-state seems to have lost its significance in favour of more worldwide arrangements.

National and international information plans

The role of national governments

The introduction to this chapter departed from the assumption that governments play an active role in elaborating NIPs. However, what is 'government', and what are the specialized agencies and ministerial bodies in charge of drafting, coordinating, implementing, monitoring and most likely assessing NIPs? In the 1970s, UNESCO documents were unanimously recommending the Office of the Prime Minister, or a ministry responsible for the information and communication infrastructure, as the institutional location for the elaboration of national strategies (UNESCO, 1984). Apart from some countries – e.g. the remarkable case of South Korea – this recommendation was seldom followed closely. It has now experienced a revival, for many governments, according to different national traditions, have created specialized units or departments within the prime minister's office or have left the responsibility to the Ministry of Telecommunications or Scientific Research, or even, in the case of the Netherlands and Finland, the Ministry for Economic Affairs. At least institutionally, the value of information as an economic resource, providing a competitive advantage for those who hold it, is fully acknowledged.

In general, the role of government in the implementation of NIPs is cautiously defined, taking into account disparate political and administrative traditions and different rates of economic growth and levels of telecommunication infrastructure. High-level political gatherings have often been instrumental in setting up NIPs and providing shared objectives within a common framework. Politically significant are the 'Bangemann report' (CEC, 1994), and the 1995 G7 Ministerial Conference in Brussels (CEC, 1995). In another part of the globe, equally important was the African Information Society Initiative, started in 1996 and officially submitted to the 22nd meeting of the Economic Commission for Africa (AISI, 1996).

It is clear that the developments envisaged by NIPs are highly disparate, although they mainly concentrate on setting up proper frameworks and empowering people within the information society. While actual implementation is left to individual and collective initiatives, direct involvement of the government is usually focused on projects intending to regulate the telecommunication sector, to find a balance between the various operators, to reform public administration and to provide direct access to public information. In the international arena, governmental action is aimed at protecting national interests and providing vigilance of the government's standing on cultural and ethical values. NIPs may well go into more detail in areas such as education and culture, where governments feel that national interests are at stake. The level of comprehensiveness of the different NIPs, however, is highly disparate.

Take, for example, the Republic of Mauritius, which has a population of just over one million and a per capita GDP of about US$3,700 per year: in the government *White paper* aimed at fostering the info-communications society, the formulation of appropriate strategies for the development of the telecommunications sector over the decade 1997–2007 is the main concern (Mauritius, 1997). The proposed solution is to keep separate the roles of the government, the regulator and the operator.

In India (1999), a telecommunications plan aims to redirect the 1994 National Telecom Policy with a view to introducing elements of connectivity, accessibility, resource availability and networked facilities in the light of the progress of ICT. Such a limited ambition is rare. In most western states the rule that an independent agency is in charge of the telecommunication policy, with the government providing resources and the operator managing the telecommunication infrastructure, is well established, and the completion of a telecommunication infrastructure is achieved almost everywhere. NIPs therefore aim to fulfil less basic needs.

In spite or perhaps because of their tradition of state non-interference, the USA and Netherlands are examples of how NIPs can describe quite accurately the role of the government in the implementation of the information society. In the USA, the action of the administration envisages complementing and enhancing the efforts of the private sector, through appropriate tax and regulatory policies, research and development programmes, and acting as a catalyst to promote technological innovation and new applications. In the legal field, the US government is eager to ensure information security and network reliability and to protect intellectual property. The promotion of a universal service aimed at ensuring that information resources are available to all at affordable prices and access to government information are also high priorities on the government's agenda (US, 1997, 1998).

The Dutch government policy consists of ensuring a wide variety of pluriform sources of information, to be reflected in policies for information supply, public information and education. It devises a new framework for (self)-regulation, in particular in the field of intellectual property rights and privacy. The government intends to make the most of its indirect influence exerted as major user of information and telecom services, and plans to foster research and development and a progressive approach involving deregulation and liberalization (Netherlands, 1995).

The regulatory role of the state is clearly described in the Italian NIP where it is recommended that the government should regulate:

- access to the market of new operators;
- interconnection among operators;
- cost identification and sharing of the Universal Service;
- a price system and mechanisms for tariff readjustments;
- interoperability of the various services made available by the operators on interconnected networks (Italy, 1997).

The role of international organizations

Reference has already been made to the 1995 G-7 Ministerial Conference in Brussels, often designated as the inspirational muse and putative father of many NIPs in Europe. For the historical record, the G7 Conference endorsed the following principles:

- providing open access to networks;
- ensuring universal provision of, and access to, services;
- encouraging private investment;
- promoting diversity of content;
- promoting equality of opportunities;
- promoting dynamic competition;
- defining an adaptable regulatory framework;
- recognizing the necessity of worldwide cooperation with particular attention to less developed countries.

The recently issued *Final report* on the pilot projects carried out by the G8 global information society highlights the results obtained in areas such as commerce, culture (with the two grand projects of the Electronic library and Access to world cultural heritage), education, environment, health and public administration (G8, 1999).

Mention has also been made of AISI (1996), an action framework aimed at building Africa's information and communications infrastructure. The governments of 53 African countries were asked to provide a vision and a strategy which would promote, together with the use of information and communication technologies, the adoption of national policies and plans, and establish the appropriate framework and mechanisms. Governments were also requested to develop the legislative/regulatory framework on issues such as the cost and accessibility of telecommunications, universal service objectives, intellectual property, privacy, free flow of information and convergence of broadcasting with telecommunications. The number of projects that have taken place since then shows how important this gathering was (AISI, 1999).

Other international organizations have undertaken various initiatives as a serious attempt to set the rules of global governance, at least in some areas of the information society. A few of them are worth mentioning. One is the World Trade Organization initiative in the field of basic telecommunication services and electronic commerce, although the Third Ministerial Conference in Seattle in November 1999 failed to reach even a starting point for negotiations (WTO, 1999). Other initiatives include the World Intellectual Property Organization Treaties (WIPO, 1996), the OECD (1997) studies on the impact of communication networks in industrial sectors, the UNESCO (1997) Forum on Ethical Issues, and the Council of Europe (1999a) programme in the areas of culture and human rights. Attention will be drawn to such initiatives within the thematic section of this article.

The most ambitious supranational policy on the information society is certainly that pursued by the Commission of the European Communities (or European Commission) (CEC). A vast array of initiatives, programmes, policy documents, and inter-ministerial conferences has endeavoured to identify a European policy able to deal on an equal footing with the American counterpart and to challenge its supremacy on communication networks. The CEC initiatives are well documented in the website of the CEC Information Society Promotion Office (CEC, 2000). They include programmes of data interchange between European Union (EU) administrations, security in telecommunication and information services, support for trans-European telecommunication networks and cultural and educational initiatives, not to mention the various streams and action lines of the huge Fifth framework programme on research and development.

The aim of these initiatives is twofold. On the one hand, there is a need to coordinate the activities undertaken by the CEC and member states and, within the CEC, those of its different Directorates. On the other hand, clustering all initiatives on the information society should eventually lead to the development of a single European policy in the global electronic marketplace. This policy should find solutions and agreements on technical issues such as the connection and interoperability of national networks, standards and frequencies. A consistent legal framework has to support electronic transactions so that public interest is safeguarded in areas such as indirect taxation, labour law, copyright, data protection, authentication, and many others. It is equally understandable that conflicting policies, rules and regulations have to be overcome for they are now a barrier to the realization of the economic, social and cultural benefits of the online economy (CEC, 1998a).

Former Commissioner Bangemann has often (and loudly) called attention to such stringent needs. In 1997 he suggested an international charter for global communication that could provide a suitable framework for online communication (Bangemann, 1997). This proposal was followed by a Business Round Table in Brussels in 1998, where business leaders from around the world discussed global communication issues, and by a Global Business Dialogue on issues related to the online economy in the framework of the information society (CEC, 1998c). Under the energetic lead of Bangemann, CEC action has been dynamic and equal to the level of its ambition of strengthening international cooperation among regional players in the information society, thus balancing the otherwise indisputable US supremacy. Nevertheless, such activism is not without criticism.

In spite of its leading role, Directorate General XIII initiatives (CEC, 2000) have been paralleled in recent years by similar activities undertaken by other directorates of the CEC with different priorities, methodology and objectives. The European Parliament has sometimes been grudging in its acceptance of Bangemann's initiative, in particular the controversial concept, very often endorsed by DG XIII, that there is no separation between network industries (telecoms, cable, Internet) and content providers (broadcasters, publishers). The corollary concept is that current regulatory frameworks governing telecommunications and the media must be transformed in order to allow new business to take off. This view has infuriated supporters of a culture- and education-oriented information society and has resulted in lingering suspicion between organizations of the civil society and technocrats and/or eurocrats in Brussels. The subsequent creation of an Information Society Forum in 1995, where different stances and actors of the civil society are represented, has not dissipated the initial mistrust (Information Society Forum, 2000). After all, the prospective results do not seem so far to have matched initial ambitions. The proposal of an International Charter for global communication has certainly led to the practice, still to be implemented, of a Global Business Dialogue. Negotiations have started, but much talking has still to be done before the dialogue leads to any form of international agreement or charter.

Thematic issues

A question of values

The question of values and the emphasis on ethical issues are especially stressed in more recent NIPs, thus showing an evolution in the consideration of the citizen's point of view. In general, the core values of an information society are those stemming from the constitutional legacy. The Portuguese NIP (Portugal, 1997), for instance, asserts that the information society should develop in conformity with constitutional principles, and new technologies should make the exercise of fundamental rights easier. Individual freedoms and ethical principles are overtly mentioned in the Icelandic *Vision of the information society*, where the 'utilization of information technology ... should be made to harmonize in every way with ethical values and not damage the interests of individuals and groups' (Iceland, 1997). Reference is made in particular to child pornography, propaganda promoting racism and other forms of material that clearly undermine public good. Occupational groups and institutions are invited to set clear rules of use and assist other parties in making them. This sensitive issue – freedom of expression on communication networks – is extensively reviewed in a report recently issued by the Council of Europe (1998).

NIPs outline three ways in which ICT is considered to be conducive to the full exercise of democracy and of shared human values. The first is to reduce the distance between politics and citizens and to empower the latter to participate in the decision-making process. Within this stream are included initiatives aimed at creating permanent consultation with citizens, such as electronic polls. The second is to reinforce political interaction between central and local government.

This is an objective in NIPS of Belgium (1997), Denmark (1997) and South Korea (Korea, 1998), although it has to be said that communication between the two tiers of government is not always an explicit aim.

The third and most ambitious way of using ICT in order to fully implement democracy is by enabling the 'right to know' about governmental action through public registers and legislative schemes, thus meeting the requirements of transparency, accountancy and ease of access. This principle is overtly expressed in the report of a committee on information management set up by the Australian government (Australia, 1997). The Australian 'open government' calls for the following objectives:

- to enable people to participate in the policy, accountability and decision making processes of government;
- to open the government's activity to scrutiny, discussion, comment and review;
- to increase the accountability of the executive.

The implementation of such principles requires a reversal of the usual rules governing access to information, from not disclosing information unless absolutely necessary to disclosure unless there is a very good reason not to. 'From government's to people's property' – this is the policy for government information resolutely pursued in the Anglo-Saxon world as well as in Scandinavian countries. It is a policy that is now being given careful consideration in other NIPs and may result in the establishment of international legal instruments.

In the Danish Information Technology Policy Plan 1997/1998 (Denmark, 1997), the 'right to know' as a citizen's right sets further requirements. Technology must be user-friendly, not require advanced education, be inexpensive to use and accessible to everybody. Free Internet access for everyone in all public libraries is among the main measures envisaged to ensure this right is respected.

In some NIPs the examination of the 'right to know' can go into even more detail and include a thorough discussion on the principle of free-of-charge access to government information. In the Australian NIP, information is seen as a national resource, of potential value to individuals, the private sector and others. Therefore it ought to be processed and stocked by specialized agencies, which should make it freely available at no more than the cost of dissemination. Government agencies are not expected to gain a competitive advantage in their business activities, but should play a custodial role respecting privacy and security legislation (Australia, 1997). The risk, however, that government information will be offered at a high price to citizens exists, especially in a climate of reduced public budgets. The Canadian plan proposes that 'in developing plans to digitize federal collections, the government should strike an appropriate balance between providing equitable and universal access to materials of public interest and importance, and facilitating the commercial exploitation of materials in federal collections' (Industry Canada, 1997).

In concluding this paragraph, mention must be made of the UNESCO INFO-ETHICS Programme, launched in 1997 with the principal objective of reaffirming the importance of universal access to information in the public domain and defining ways in which it may be achieved and maintained in the Global Information Infrastructure. Although the Programme has so far failed to set up international legal instruments, it provides for a high level Forum on:

- promotion of the principles of equality, justice and mutual respect in the emerging information society;
- identification of major ethical issues in the production, access, dissemination, preservation and use of information in the electronic environment;
- provision of assistance to member states in the formulation of strategies and policies on these issues (UNESCO, 1997).

Intellectual property

The introduction of digital technology has made possible the transformation of protected works into a format which can be transmitted worldwide. Information originators are at the moment almost without protection, although international legal instruments are starting to be put in place. Particularly important in this context are the Copyright Treaty and the Performances and Phonograms Treaty adopted by the December 1996 Diplomatic Conference of the World Intellectual Property Organization (WIPO, 1996). All NIPs consider the integration of such treaties in their domestic legislation as a priority and are aware that the exclusive rights of authors and holders related property rights must also be preserved and if necessary extended. The German NIP proposes that the term 'public', as defined in national legislation, should be amended to the extent that a transmission to several unrelated individuals is public even when only one person is reached in each case (Germany, 1998).

The current debate is dominated by the issue of copyright for digital works and, in particular, by the recent CEC proposal for a directive on the harmonization of certain aspects of copyright and related rights in the information society (CEC, 1998f), aimed at bringing about a coherent and favourable environment for creativity and investment in the framework of the internal market. This EU initiative provides for the exclusive right to authorize or prohibit direct or indirect, temporary or permanent reproduction by any means and in any form, in whole or in part, the original and copies of copyright protected works.

Two lobbies have crossed swords for approximately two years: on the one hand, there are artist associations and organizations of cultural industries (publishing, audiovisual, music industries), interested in restricting as much as possible the free use of protected content; on the other, there are organizations of telecommunications, software producers and users' associations, among which are libraries, rallying to extend the number of possible uses of protected material. Telecom industries and information providers are keen on offering value-added services with the provision of useful and free-of-charge content, and libraries are interested in offering free access to the electronic material they make available. On 10 February 1999, in adopting the draft Directive, the European Parliament reinforced copyright in the information society. Authors and producers are now on the way to being given the exclusive right to authorize the diffusion of their work on communication networks and will very likely be remunerated for private copying. National legislation will decide whether to make exceptions for educational and cultural institutions such as schools, libraries, etc.

Once adopted, one of the consequences of the draft Directive will be a generalized shift from the traditional copyright framework to the licensing system. The system of licensing in the Directive provides for levies of different kinds for calculating fees and different methods of identification for rights management, which will probably include some form of watermarking or use of digital object identifiers with sanctions against digital piracy and misuse.

The development of licences for scientific texts is particularly important in the field of STM (Scientific-Technical-Medical) publications, where costs are rising both for publishers, who take risks in producing and disseminating electronic publications, and information institutions, whose general costs and expenditure for acquisitions are also inexorably increasing. Licensing may therefore represent the optimal solution for groups or consortia of libraries.

Although it is not an intergovernmental resolution, mention has to be made of the EBLIDA/ECUP/STM Joint Statement on incidental digitization and storage of STM print journal articles, a list of principles set out by EBLIDA and the international Association of STM publishers, currently uniting 240 publishing imprints in 26 countries (Rösner, 1998). The Statement makes an important distinction between material collected on an 'incidental basis', i.e. individual articles from journals, and material acquired and held by libraries on a 'permanent basis'. For this kind of material, libraries have preferential treatment even when the publisher terminates a licence or withdraws from participating in the uses contemplated in the Statement.

The interesting thing about intellectual property is that the elaboration of international legal instruments is preceding policy formulation. In this respect, it is true that relevant international legislative bodies have reacted unusually fast to the technological challenge. If principles for the harmonization of copyright laws in the electronic environment are set up at international level, NIPs may make an attempt to strike a balance between the rights of content creators and users, so as to equalize the interests of commercial and non-commercial intermediaries. In Canada, for instance, new legislation passed in 1997 provides for exceptions and special provisions for non-profit educational institutions, libraries, archives and museums (Canada, 1997).

Some organizations, such as the Council of Europe (2000), are indeed attempting to make strategic links between legal deposit schemes for electronic publications and copyright regulations. Apart from preservation, the most ambitious objective is to establish national repositories as copyright clearance centres working for the whole library community of a country. This arrangement may be ideal for smaller countries that can opt for agreements with publishers at national level, which also imply authors' remuneration. If not linked with legal deposit libraries, bargaining agencies – such as library consortia, a library association or another non-governmental agency – should be established in order to contract licence agreements on behalf of libraries within a country. In this way, general solutions made on a collective basis would put non-commercial users in a stronger position in relation to suppliers.

Employment and the social dimension

The 'impact' metaphor which originally depicted the way ICT is embedded in the society described an exogenous phenomenon with sweeping effects on employment working structures and living conditions. These effects were portrayed as particularly gloomy in the field of employment, with a number of traditional jobs suddenly becoming obsolete and a smaller number of professionals emerging with new skills and competencies.

With hindsight, we can now see that such fears were exaggerated. The notion of 'pervasiveness' and continuity with existing social structures has taken the place of the 'flood' image. Patterns of integration of new technologies in society remain unclear, however. The case of former socialist countries in eastern Europe, where large investments in science, technology and education did not bring significant growth and development or facilitate the emergence of a civil society, is often mentioned as an example of lack of 'social embeddedness' (CEC, 1997a).

The most widespread concern is that ICT would reinforce, rather than reduce, existing inequalities, with the risk of creating a two-tier information society divided into the information 'haves' and 'have nots'. The people who would not benefit from the positive effects of ICT are 'less favoured' groups of disabled, elderly, unemployed people and immigrants. The debate is politically sensitive. In an almost Freudian manner, however, NIPs tend to emphasize the tremendous opportunities provided by ICT and the amount of IT jobs which remain unfilled. Evidence for this mounts up. According to recent OECD estimates quoted by the British NIP (UK, 1998), the number of jobs that are currently unfilled owing to skill shortage are as follows:

World	600,000
USA	346,000
Germany	60,000
Canada	20,000/30,000
United Kingdom	20,000

The same NIP also quotes figures provided by the International Data Corporation for Microsoft:

- In the UK, demand for IT professionals is forecast to grow by up to a third (250,000 people) by 2002.
- By the end of 2002 there will be an estimated deficit of 1.6 million IT skilled employees across Europe.
- The US Bureau of Labor Statistics predicts the need for over two million extra employees in the US ICT sector by 2006.

The Portuguese NIP stresses the quality of change in working structures and the fact that a rational production process as a mechanism to generate wealth tends to be replaced by a creativity mechanism, with knowledge originators able to invent their work according to circumstances (Portugal, 1997). Many (though not all) of the professions actively building up the information society belong to the category of persons that Reich (1991) defined as 'symbolic analysts', whose work consists in problem solving, problem identifying and strategic brokering activities.

In 1996, the AISI initiative foresaw increasing demand for skilled employees in information services, software development, translation services, data entry, data housing, data conversion, system maintenance, training and other information technology related areas (AISI, 1996). The final policy report of the high level expert group set up by the EU also considered that ICT provides plenty of opportunities for new forms of employment: 'in high value, high skill occupations; in new information-intensive industries such as the multimedia sector; in new micro-business where creative entrepreneurship thrives; in new information-intensive jobs; and in many more traditional person-to-person occupations focusing on some of the communal and caring aspects of work and non-work' (CEC, 1997a). The Dutch NIP rightly identifies spectacular job growth in content production (professional information, audiovisual productions, educational programmes, games) (Netherlands, 1995).

The emphasis of the Dutch NIP on cultural industries leads us to consider the rapid development of the so-called 'content industry'. An OECD report (1996) analyses the current expansion of two sectors. On the one hand, there is audiovisual and music content that is being developed on digitized networks with the offer of new services, such as video-on-demand. On the other hand, there are multimedia services, combining digitized text, data, audio and visual content distributed through CD-ROM or the Internet – also called new media. In Europe, the growth of cultural employment over the past ten years has been strong, going up in Spain, France and the UK respectively by 24% between 1987 and 1994, 36% between 1982 and 1990, and 34% between 1981 and 1991. In some regions the growth in the number of cultural businesses and jobs rose at a spectacular rate – in the case of North-Rhine-Westphalia, 161% between 1980 and 1992 (CEC, 1998b). Most of these new jobs are to be found in the area of electronic publishing, digital audiovisual media and the new media. It is no urprise that countries holding the EU presidency have since 1997 prioritized mployment in their cultural programmes.

The weight of the cultural sector in the digital media and communication nvironment depends very much on the pace of change of conventional cultural ndustries into digital industries. The challenge is not so much technical or financial s organizational and political. The OECD report puts it clearly: 'First, changes n the traditional financing, pricing and structuring of the final consumption need o be facilitated to support future product and market development. Second, governments will need to ensure regulatory frameworks are in place which support these structures' (OECD, 1996).

New work structures and employees' skills are therefore needed for cultural workers to thrive in the information society. A recent draft Recommendation of he Council of Europe (1999c) deals with new professional profiles and competencies for information professionals and knowledge workers operating n cultural industries and institutions. Four broad categories are identified:

- *content and technology*, which concerns those professionals who prepare, select and produce content within a technological environment for use in digital products and services;
- *design and technology*, relating to professionals designing the presentation and effects of digital products and services;
- *management and technology*, in relation to professionals who supervise the overall production of digital and multimedia products and services, in particular from an administrative and financial viewpoint;
- *distribution and technology*, concerning professionals responsible for the distribution, dissemination and conservation of digital information, cultural products and services (Council of Europe, 1999c).

Education

No NIP fails to mention education as one of the priority areas for the development of a national information society. As a topical issue, education is dealt with at two evels. On the one hand, it concerns computer literacy (also called information iteracy or technological literacy). This new form of literacy can take different forms, well identified in a white paper on communications in Japan (1997), which makes a distinction between basic information literacy, PC literacy (the ability to use a computer) and network literacy (the ability to use networks such as the Internet).

Information literacy is a prerequisite for an intensive use of PCs and networks and is a fundamental parameter in detecting gaps between 'haves' and 'have nots', the latter being today found more in age ranges, gender and/or geographical areas than in levels of instruction. All investigations mentioned by NIPs, whether from Japan, the EU or USA, agree that highest levels of information literacy are to be found among males in the age range 20–50, resident in urban areas.

On the other hand, ICT is an essential factor in the general shift from a 'once and for all' education to a permanent renewal of one's competencies within a lifelong learning environment. ICT application in schools is strongly encouraged and supported, but results are not unequivocal. As a rule, NIPs put emphasis on infrastructure, personnel, content and learning methods.

The call for a good infrastructure is to be found very clearly in the recommendations of the African Information Society Initiative (AISI, 1999), which states that IT should provide equitable remote access to resources in support of both distance education and strengthening of local educational capacity. In some countries, plans for a fully networked school infrastructure are in a quite advanced stage. In the USA, school interconnection was started in 1996 after the launch of the 'technological literacy challenge', a national initiative intending to connect all American schools (US, 1997). In Japan (1997), the white paper emphasizes the development of multimedia applications in teaching; but this is part of a long term strategy initiated with a nine-year action plan which was introduced as long ago as 1990. Incorporating telecommunication networks and new applications into schools requires a large initial capital investment, to which the maintenance and update of online services should be added. Therefore all NIPs encourage cooperation between schools, universities, libraries and the private sector in the provision of computer stations and network infrastructure. In order to be cost effective, such huge investments have to be expanded beyond classroom walls – hence the need to provide remote teaching from resource centres established in schools, universities and libraries.

Early experiments in the 1990s failed because computers were used in education as an add-on, which did not fundamentally change curricula and teaching methods. Investment in technology was wasted and did not result in widespread computer literacy. No wonder, therefore, that most NIPs focus on retraining the main players in the teaching process: teachers and pupils. In fact, while many institutions and businesses have been forced to reskill their employees in order to maintain their level of competitiveness, school instructional methods have not changed appreciably over the past hundred years. It is important to train actors involved in the educational process to use ICT for what have been considered the four pillars of knowledge: learn to know, learn to do, learn to live together, learn to be (CEC, 1997c).

Another fundamental aspect of education is content. The grammar of graphics or the rhetoric of combined text, sound, graphics has replaced text organized in a sequential way. This aspect, well illustrated by the NIP Iceland (1997), consists in creating hyperlinks and net-specific forms of exchange and expression and in totally revising the three traditional Rs (reading, writing and arithmetic). Even if content may be the same, it is not organized in the same way as traditional textbooks and other educational material. Information literacy needs to build up new patterns of understanding, which are based on different rules of rhetoric.

The educational infrastructure is improved by the creation of data banks, educational projects, distance learning, continual education and other offerings. The fourth aspect of education through ICTs is therefore: access. The networked education system needs to create 'competence' centres in schools, universities, libraries and municipalities. These centres are not just working for the education offered in schools, but go to provide material for third-level education providers; i.e. private firms transforming themselves into learning organizations. This revolutionary aspect is singled out by various NIPs and the importance of creating interchange between information producers and originators, on the one hand, and consumers, on the other, is often stressed.

Access regulation implies preferential rules for educational institutions and fair rules of use for the content disseminated on communication networks. Access can be improved through cooperative projects involving publishers and schools, publishers and resource/technological centres, as well as publishers and libraries, and a focus on the dissemination of information and on information retrieval. In defining the national information infrastructure, the USA rightly stresses the copyright problem. Today there are different rules for accessing educational material in the classroom. For instance, showing a videotape in a classroom is clearly permitted in a US classroom, but showing the same videotape to remote students in a 'virtual' classroom via satellite is not permitted (US, 1997).

Culture

NIPs set up by offices of the prime minister, ministries of finance and economics or of research and telecommunications are expected to prioritize economic growth; they assign little space for culture. In fact when, in July 1997, 25 heads of state and government convened in Bonn to discuss the role that official public bodies should play in the development of communication networks, many areas for action were designated such as protection of creativity and investment, security and confidentiality, digital signatures, electronic literacy and education and data protection (*Global Information Networks*, 1997). The cultural dimension was clearly overlooked.

This has since become less of a matter for concern. Also in 1997, heads of state and government resolved in their Second Council of Europe Summit to 'develop a European policy for the application of the new information technologies, with a view to ensuring respect for human rights and cultural diversity, fostering freedom of expression and information and maximizing the educational and cultural potential of these technologies'. Two years later, in May 1999, at a meeting in Budapest, ministers of foreign affairs of Council of Europe member states were adamant in prioritizing culture as a key area of development for new technologies, when they made a Declaration on a European policy in this field (Council of Europe, 1999a).

It is well known that culture has different interpretations according to historical tradition and people's identity. The development of a cultural infrastructure, especially when supported by public powers, not only corresponds to a social demand, but it aims to nurture a sense of belonging and a reinterpretation of common values through the legacy of history and cultural heritage. It also creates new patterns of mutual understanding and social cohesion. In the 'intelligent' island of Singapore (1997), for instance, improving quality of life means that 'Singaporeans will have more time to spend on leisure, kinship, social and civic pursuits'. In the Japanese *White paper*, info-communication for entertainment and leisure is seen as a strategic goal, with the development of satellite television and Internet used as a means to collect information and provide access to entertainment (Japan, 1997).

A different interpretation of the use of the Internet, and certainly of culture, is adumbrated in the NIP set up by the French Inter-Ministerial Committee on the Information Society (France, 1999). France has initiated a far-reaching scheme for the digitization of the French cultural heritage, with the object of diffusing cultural content on the Internet. This plan involves both the public and private sectors, and grants are given for research and development in cultural technologies applied to multimedia as well as for fostering creativity in art, science and technology. It also aims to foster professional empowerment in cultural information technologies and update equipment. Moreover, free-of-charge availability to the public of digital cultural data is strongly recommended.

In many other plans, especially in those of smaller countries such as Finland (1996), Iceland (1997) or Portugal (1997), much concern is expressed about preservation of the national language and identity. In the Finnish and Icelandic plans, great emphasis is put on independent production and national programming against the incumbent threat of US programming. The aim is to preserve Finnish and Icelandic cultural and linguistic identity in a globalized environment. Digitization of cultural heritage through the development of a digital ALM (archives, libraries and museums) system is strongly encouraged. Even in countries like the UK (1998) where the cultural mission of the information highway is overlooked or absent altogether, initiatives relating to the information society do not neglect the completion of the national information and cultural infrastructure with massive cash boosts for museums, libraries and archives.

A country that is developing a solid and well structured policy on development of cultural content on the Internet is Canada. The reason is easy to understand: the proximity of the USA, which holds the most powerful content industry in the world, exposes Canadian cultural products and services to market failure. Therefore, a series of measures facilitating the production and distribution of Canadian content has been enforced for some years. A report produced by the Information Highway Advisory Council (Industry Canada, 1997), sets out a strategy that enlarges the traditional scope for aid to cultural industries and encompasses both new and traditional media. In the report, various areas for development are identified, oriented to creative work, production and distribution of content reflecting the distinctive character of Canadian society, its heritage and the work of Canadian creators. Artists, information industries, universities and research centres should be linked to one another. A Canadian Multimedia Fund should be established, to assist in the generation of new services and products for the information highways produced by cultural institutions. Measures concerning distribution should be targeted at the development and use of Canadian navigational systems in both English and French, providing meaningful access to Canadian content on the information highway and promoting Canadian culture through government web sites, heritage institutions, cultural agencies and publications. Apart from special incentives for French language projects, it is suggested that Canadian advertisers should be able to deduct the cost of advertising aimed at Canadians, if the advertisements are placed in Canadian new media.

If so much emphasis has been placed here on the Canadian NIP, it is because it reflects well-grounded fears of loss of local and diverse identity under the threat of global trends in culture – and it invites the government to develop a strategy. The direct prescriptions of the Canadian NIP illustrate very well the attitude of national administrations and their reaction to what are to be considered the three crucial issues which any fair and open-to-all information society has to confront: sustainability, convergence and globalization.

Overarching issues

Sustainability

Paraphrasing Proust, one could say that sustainability is a word of good taste, worthy of being launched. According to standard dictionaries, 'sustainable' is the characteristic of something that can be maintained or prolonged. Associated with development, sustainability is the challenge to current generations to satisfy their needs, without diminishing the chances of future generations. The concept of ecological sustainability, a relatively new concept introduced by Lester Brown in 1981 (Capra and Pauli, 1995), has become the key principle for the ecological movement and the core theme of the Earth Summit on Environment and Development in Rio de Janeiro in 1992. Applied to ICT, it includes all sorts of ecological as well as societal concerns.

One of the main aspects of a sustainable information society is 'de-materialization'. Dematerialization of activities takes place when a 'unit good or a unit service can be produced and consumed with less material than before, counting the entire material used over the entire life circle, that is producing more goods and more services from fewer resources and with less burden on the environment' (CEC, 1998e). The case of a library illustrates well the process o gradual dematerialization of work processes and flows. In a library, automatec cataloguing and indexing have put an end to the old paper catalogue. Texts ar preserved in digital form and document delivery is frequently done throug] electronic networks.

The main consequence of dematerialization is a reengineering of industria activities within an environment friendly framework. Industrial reengineering at the same time as restructuring firms and organizations, has an impact on loca communities and individuals. The traditional industrial model was based on th concept of territorial loyalty, large office facilities, workers commuting, bi; industrial plants and offices in congested areas. Dematerialization consists ii reducing the amount of material extracted, processed, used and dispersed an in the widespread application of teleworking and electronic commerce Teleworking is a form of dematerialization of work within organizations, whil electronic commerce dematerializes economic transactions.

Both concepts are seminal in NIPs. A vast array of facilitating measures an accompanying activities is envisaged in order to encourage social and economi players to eliminate physical intermediaries, to transform offices into meetin; places and occasional bases for a nomadic and decentralized workforce, and t convert economic transaction into electronic exchanges through communicatioı networks. While the sustainability of such a process for the environment i undisputed, there is concern about the effects of such policy on social objectives

Take labour legislation, for instance. For many specialists, teleworking is contract service, for which the rules of conventional labour legislation are nc applicable. While this may be a convenient and desirable solution for highly skillec workers, for whom contingent work can offer freedom and mobility, it may resul in insecurity for less skilled workers. In many NIPs a sustainable informatioı society is seen to exist when innovative concepts do not damage traditional link of social solidarity. The Canadian Information Highway Advisory Council, fo instance, was unable to find any agreement on this issue (Industry Canada, 1997) In other countries, for example, Germany (1998), it is recommended that restrain should be exercised in terms of legislation concerning telecommuting in order t prevent such work. We are at the heart of the sustainability dilemma: to wha extent can spontaneous economic growth be reoriented, or diverted from it natural course, without suffocating the impetus for further development on th one hand and links of social solidarity and cohesion on the other? Consensus oı strategies is far from being reached.

A curious example of this can be found in a report issued by the CEC, whicl combines various theses on the sustainable information society. It is stated tha an approach on global environmental sustainability should not diverge fron continued economic growth, in stark contrast to the 'current debate oı sustainability, notably in Rio and Kyoto where the goals of sustainability ar seen to be in conflict with economic growth, employment and industria nterests' (CEC, 1998e). Some pages later, however, another author claims that Europeans 'should fight stronger for that point of view [respect for every human on the planet] even if, for the time being, they have to and will adapt to the world market as it is, even if we play the "world market game" presently to the wrong rules ... [and Europe should] find agreement with Asian partners on such a new world and global governance [rather] than with the US, a picture that can be observed in the Rio+5 and Kyoto Summits, where Europe took a clear lead'.

The aggressive reference to the USA and to those organizations, such as the World Trade Organization, that are allegedly under strong US influence, is not isolated. Rightly or wrongly, the USA is often considered to be the champion of an economic-oriented approach which overlooks the political demand for collective wealth and eludes the needs and the expectations of the 'have nots' within advanced societies and on the planet.

Convergence

The many mergers and alliances that are reshaping the existing ICT industries seem to provide evidence of convergence between telecommunications, audiovisual production and publishing. Horizontal and vertical alliances between the giants of the industry of convergence (such as those between America On Line and Time Warner or Vivendi and Vodaphone) have made the headlines in newspapers and television.

Feeling a sense of urgency at the magnitude of the phenomenon, the EC issued a green paper on convergence which sets out options for regulatory provisions and policy issues in the convergence age (CEC, 1997b). The paper set up a number of questions concerning

- the nature and pace of convergence;
- its economic and social impact;
- barriers to the coming together of the convergent sectors;
- approach to regulation.

It was meant to be merely a discussion paper, but no organization understood it in that way. All considered it to be a policy document, paving the way for future CEC action. Submitted to public consultation, it attracted a large number of answers that showed a broad range of approaches and different views on the meaning, impact and magnitude of the convergence phenomenon (CEC, 1998g).

The crux of the document is the search for a regulatory policy framework. At the moment, regulatory practices in the three converging sectors – telecommunications, audiovisual production and the media – differ greatly. In the publishing sector, for instance, there should be no regulation for those entering the market, but instead incentive-based policies that guarantee diverse and pluralistic opportunities. In other words, the emphasis is on policy measures (reduced VAT rate, massive acquisitions by libraries, etc.), not on regulatory provision.

The situation is different for telecommunication and broadcasting policies. In traditional telecommunication regulation, the democratic impetus finds its primary expression in the effort to provide universal access to a basic level of communication services (for telephone providers, for instance, the obligation to cover the whole national territory, including sparsely populated areas where traffic is low). In traditional broadcast regulation, democratic values are pursued through the imposition of content regulations aimed at assuring that broadcasts provide the types of information necessary for an informed citizenry.

In the search for a regulatory policy framework in the information society many issues are at stake:

- a policy that can suit the needs of the convergent players, but keeps alive public, social and political concerns;
- diversity in the supply of content and information which will adequately represent European culture;
- the possible shift from the current time-based quotas (in the broadcasting sector) to investment-related incentives;
- control over information flow;
- a model for a democratic and culture oriented information society (Benkler, 1998).

Critics of the green paper on convergence do not accept the linear and economic-oriented approach chosen by the CEC. They object to the deterministic vision of the 'Great Convergence', as they ironically call it, on philosophical, legal and economic grounds (Council of Europe, 1999b).

First, blurring different systems of communication does not mean achieving the same performance. Historians of cultural practices have shown that different 'protocols' of reception are applied by users to different media. In other words, reading from a book is not the same as reading from a screen. Therefore, convergence between media, if any, can only result in hybrid forms, which will keep alive former modes of expression and traditional media.

Second, media systems are not the outcome of genuine market forces, but the result of policy-oriented choices. Each media sector has its own policy framework, which permeates the related market and creates the rules for competition among actors. New media do require a proper framework; therefore, strategies solely shaped by market forces may only result in delaying a necessary process of market regulation.

Finally, mergers and alliances among economic players do not have to take place exclusively within the media sector, but may be more effective and more profitable if they go beyond the media sector. An alliance between two or three cultural industries may be less than, or just as, strategic as alliances between cultural industries and other businesses, for example, tourism. On the other hand, industries having different traditions and corporate cultures do not necessarily merge successfully. After all, the world of publishing, albeit electronic, is not the same as the world of audiovisual, albeit digital. It is true that Mediaset, a major audiovisual Italian group, took control of Mondadori, the biggest Italian publishing house. But the acquisition of Havas, a major publishing group in France, by Vivendi, a multisector conglomerate, has proved to be just as successful. Whether convergence among cultural industries is going to be a major trend for the new millennium remains an open question.

Globalization

Recent advances in technologies are not only making movement of physical objects, money and ideas far easier and cheaper than ever before, but are doing it in ways that governments find it hard to interfere with. Convergence of telecommunications and computers has meant that national boundaries are not a barrier to international exchanges. The concept of GII-GIS (Global Information Infrastructures – Global Information Societies) emerged within the framework of the G7 and of OECD countries and has been taken up by the EU as the GIN (Global Information Networks) initiative. Globalization seems to be a characteristic feature of the information society; perhaps there is no information society if it is not global.

The globalization of economies is strongly encouraged; it is seen as a positive factor for the liberalization of economies and political systems and a decisive step towards democracy. More debatable is whether a global society can fully meet the needs of human beings. Globalization of events, of symbols, of icons of our modern life impact on people's identity and cultures and provoke substantial alterations and breaks with their traditions. Is this process as straightforward and inexorable as it is portrayed? Where is the trend and where is the political rhetoric?

The problem of identity has become crucial as a form of struggle against and response to global forces and all-embracing symbols. Conflicts all over the world are seen as clashes of civilizations, very often taking the shape of people's resistance to western values. Global trends are often regarded as processes that contrast with the emergence of national identities and destroy the concept that the state should create a unified culture within its territory.

There is indeed evidence that globalization has affected the market for cultural products and services. It is visible in cultural production, where the top six music corporations take 81% of the market. A few audiovisual players have stakes in a broad range of satellite and terrestrial television. Print publishers go beyond national boundaries and languages, and create multinational companies and alliances. Globalization is also obvious in the distribution sector, where a programme like *Dallas* enjoys an international audience in over ninety countries. The technologies of cultural distribution seem to enhance a new global order based on the presence of the same product tailored to different audiences. Globalized consumption assimilates popular singers and film and TV actors into popular tradition without limitation of frontiers. The growth of the content industry through ICT accelerates such trends (Street, 1997).

Nevertheless, communication without boundaries has internal limitations. One can argue that, even if the product is the same, the way in which it is interpreted changes and produces hybrid configurations with local cultures and myths. Another body of criticism of this theory is that it is inherent in the very nature of development of multinational cultural industries to find national 'niches' for further expansion and to find 'new' products for new audiences in new countries. Rather than imposing a product, the marketing strategies of globalized industries consist more in mediating what they offer with local assumptions and tastes.

At present, however, the most effective way to resist, and interact with, the global cultural offering is still through national cultural policies. It is argued that, because of the sensitive nature of the cultural issue and the implications of homogenization of cultural content for national identities and cultural diversity, regulations intending to support the production and distribution of cultural content should be excluded from global economic negotiations.

The international legitimacy of this argument is today becoming weaker. Global political governance is reducing the state's autonomy and increasing the search for free trade areas or general agreements. In an attempt to settle disputes and litigation concerning their economic relationship, the EU and the USA initiated negotiations as early as 1995 aimed at reducing or eliminating barriers which hinder the transatlantic flow of goods, services and capital. These negotiations eventually led to the New Transatlantic Marketplace (NTM), a programme of activities which was presented in a Communication to the European Council of the EU on 11 March 1998 by three EU Commissioners. After the London EU–US Summit of 18 May 1998, NTM has been reinforced by TEP (Transatlantic Economic Partnership), which tackles those trade issues, mainly regulatory barriers, that are now the main obstacle to transatlantic business. The overall aim of the initiative is to stimulate further multilateral liberalization, and develop a framework for convergence of law, procedure and practice between the EU and the USA (CEC, 1998d).

Such negotiations have raised concern in many states, where culture is strongly supported by state intervention. In 1998, a lobby of artists, creators and film directors mobilized successfully against the MAI (Multilateral Agreement on Investment) Treaty, which has the objective of liberalizing access to investments within OECD countries (OECD, 1998). They feared that it would threaten public support schemes for national cultural industries. In general, the world of arts and culture feels threatened by the globalization of trade, where public funds devoted to promoting national culture may be considered forms of market distortion and a challenge to competition laws. The same applies to the state aid provided to organizations that work as servers and provide high-capacity leased lines in universities and research institutes.

The lack of technical solutions concerning culture is often used as an argument to discredit international organizations engaged in global negotiations. The World Trade Organization (WTO) has undergone overwhelming criticism both from the advocates of downright liberalism, who consider that these negotiations are excessively politicized, and from the champions of economic interventionism, who consider that on issues such as intellectual property, investment and environment, a purely market-based approach would be unsustainable. Such opinions have influenced negotiations within the WTO Ministerial Conference in Seattle in November 1999 which should have led to a general agreement called GATS (General Agreement on Tariffs and Services) (WTO, 1999).

Conclusion

Finally, it may be useful to look at ways in which NIPs can be assessed. The lack of monitoring systems and the absence of updated lists of activities available on websites cast some doubt on the ways they are assessed and, even more, on the operability of such plans (the French and Dutch NIPs represent noteworthy exceptions). Some rapid conclusions, however, can be drawn. First, the identification of boundaries to the information sector, difficult at the time of Machlup and Porat, has now become an impossible exercise. Because of the multitude of agencies, sectors and participants, the assessment of a national information policy would be a judgement on the society itself. Moreover, the shift from tangible products to intangible production and consumption creates a virtual value chain where added value is often dematerialized and difficult to evaluate. Any kind of traditional measurement risks being based on outdated and/or biased industrial concepts. It has been proposed, for instance, that the transformation of tacit knowledge into codified knowledge is one of the key performance indicators of the virtual value chain (CEC, 1997a).

A second conclusion is the decline of the belief that free market forces alone might shape the information society. This assumption, originally advocated in the 1994 Bangemann report (CEC, 1994), is not only narrow in its approach, but has arguably proved to be wrong. Though limited in its scope by a framework approach, the role of national and international public authorities in regulating emerging information society markets and in acting as engines of growth is recognized by NIPs. Pauli (Capra and Pauli, 1995), an advocate of the sustainability argument, has maintained that: 'the first step in developing technologies that are technologically sustainable must be to transform the very nature of technology from a totalitarian "megatechnology" to a tool, the use of which is restricted by cultural norms'.

The third conclusion is that the concept of nation-state is resilient even though many of the decisions in selected areas (intellectual property, cultural exception, secrecy, etc.) seem to be left to international bodies. Planetary economies are looking for international guidance. Paradoxical though it may seem, the work carried out by international organizations such as WTO, WIPO, UNESCO, OECD or the Council of Europe seems nevertheless too specialized to nurture any aspiration for global governance. On the other hand, supranational regional institutions such as the EU disperse their efforts across too many directorates, giving the impression of lacking a unitary vision. At any rate, the need to strike a balance between the rich and the poor of the globe makes it desirable to recast the notion of national sovereignty in the political scene.

Happiness within (or without) information societies will not therefore be global. In spite of common tenets describing the information society as *par excellence* global, we will have in the future different models of information society, just as we have today many models of growth, development and society itself. The difference lies in the way in which new technologies are integrated not only into the mainstream of economic growth, but also into policies designed to enhance human solidarity, social cohesion, lifelong learning, local identity, cultural diversity. This is why, even if the information society's life is global, national information policy and planning will not die.

All of this assumes that NIPs work. The Icelandic information plan casts (self-) ironic but well-grounded doubt on the grand ambitions exhibited by NIPs: 'the lore of policy formulation tells us that it is easier to talk about twelve mountains than to climb one' (Iceland, 1997).

Note

This chapter expresses the author's views, which are not necessarily those of the organization for which he works. The author wishes to thank Mrs Gesa Buttner, Information Manager at the Council of Europe, for her invaluable assistance.

References

AISI (1996) *Meeting of ECA Conference of Ministers, May 1996. Resolution 812 (XXXI). Implementation of the African Information Society Initiative (AISI)*.
http://www.bellanet.org/partners/aisi/confr/812xxxi.htm
AISI (1999) *Programme areas*. http://www.bellanet.org/partners/aisi/prog/index.htm

Australia (1997). Information Management Steering Committee on Information Management in the Commonwealth Government. *Management of government information as a national strategic resource.*
http://www.ogit.gov.au/publications/imsc/imscrept.htm

Bangemann, M. (1997) A new world order for global communications. The need for an international charter. In: *Telecom Inter@ctive '97.* Geneva: International Telecommunications Union, 8 September.
http://www.ispo.cec.be/infosoc/promo/speech/geneva.html

Belgium (1997). Service Fédéral d'Information. *Un plan d'actions coordonnées pour la société de l'information au sein des Autorités fédérales, 1997–1999.*
http://belgium.fgov.be/pa/fra_frame.htm

Benkler, Y. (1998) Communication infrastructure regulation and the distribution of control over content. *Telecommunication Policy,* **22**(3), 183–196.

Canada (1997) Preparing Canada for a digital world. *Final report of the Information Highway Advisory Council.* http://strategis.ic.gc.ca/ihac

Capra, F. and Pauli, G. (1995) (eds) Industrial clusters of the twenty-first century. In: *Steering business towards sustainability.* Toronto: United Nations University Press.

Castells, M. (1996) *The information age: economy and culture. Vol. 1: The rise of the network society.* Oxford: Blackwell.

CEC (1994) *Recommendations to the European Council. Europe and the global information society.* http://www.ispo.cec.be/infosoc/backg/bangeman.html

CEC (1995) *The G7 Information Society conference.* [Brussels, 25–26 February 1995.]
http://www.ispo.cec.be/g7/g7main.html

CEC (1997a) *Building the European information society for us all. Final policy report of the high-level expert group.* Luxembourg: Office for Official Publications.

CEC (1997b) *Green paper on the convergence of the telecommunications, media and information technology sectors, and the implications for regulations. Towards an information society approach.* Brussels: European Commission. [4.12.1997. COM(97)623.]

CEC (1997c) *Teaching, learning, information: towards an open Socratic school. Proceedings of the AMPERE seminar, February 1997.* Brussels: European Commission.

CEC (1998a) *Communication from the Commission to the European Parliament, the Council, the Economic and Social Committee and the Committee of Regions.* [Adopted by the Commission 4 February 1998. COM(98)(50).]
http://www.ispo.cec.be/eif/policy/com9850en.html

CEC (1998b) *Culture, the cultural industries and employment.* Brussels: European Commission. [14 May 1998 SEC(98)837.]

CEC (1998c) *Launching a global business dialogue: Business Round Table on global communications.* http://www.ispo.cec.be/eif/policy/brtlaunch.html

CEC (1998d) *The new transatlantic marketplace. Communication from the Commission to the Council, the European Parliament and the Economic and Social Committee communication.* [11 March 1998.] http://www.eurunion.org/partner/ntm/annex.htm

CEC (1998e) *1998 status report. Towards a sustainable information society. DG XIII-B, November 1998.* Brussels: European Commission.

CEC (1998f) *Proposal for a European Parliament and Council directive on the harmonization of certain aspects of copyright and related rights in the information society.* Brussels: European Commission. [COM(97)628 final – 97/0359(COD).]

CEC (1998g) *Summary of the results of the public consultation on the green paper on the convergence of the telecommunications, media and information technology sectors: areas for further reflection.* Brussels: European Commission. [Commission working document, 29 July 1998, SEC(1998)1284 final.]

CEC (2000) *The EC information society promotion office.* http://www.ispo.cec.be

Council of Europe (1998) *Freedom of expression and the communication networks.* Strasbourg: Council of Europe. [CC-CULT(98)18.]

Council of Europe (1999a) *Action plan for the new technologies project.* Strasbourg: Council of Europe.
http://culture.coe.fr/postsummit/nti/en/project/eselection.texts.htm

Council of Europe (1999b) *The cultural work within the information society: a critical perspective.* Strasbourg: Council of Europe.
http://culture.coe.fr/postsummit/nti/en/project/eselection.texts.htm

Council of Europe (1999c) *Draft recommendation on cultural work within the information society.* Strasbourg: Council of Europe.
http://culture.coe.fr/postsummit/nti/en/project/eselection.texts.htm

Council of Europe (2000) *Council of Europe – EBLIDA guidelines on library legislation and policy in Europe.* Strasbourg: Council of Europe. [DECS/CULT/POL/book (2000)1.]

Denmark (1997). Ministry of Research and Information Technology. *Action for change: IT policy plan 97/98.* http://www.fsk.dk/fsk/publ/1997/action97

Finland (1996). Ministry of Finance. *Finland's way to the information society – the national strategy and its implementation.* http://www.tieke.fi/english/index.htm

France (1999). Comité Interministériel pour la Société de l'Information (CISI). *Mise en oeuvre du programme d'action gouvernemental pour la société de l'information.*
http://www.internet.gouv.fr/francais/textesref/cisi190199/accueil.htm

G8 (1999) Global Information Society Pilot Projects. *Towards a global information society.* http://www.gip.int/mainreport.htm

Germany (1998). Bundesministerium für Bildung und Forschung. *Rat für Forschung, Technologie und Innovation Thema 'Informationsgesellschaft'.*
http://www.iid.de/rat/index.html

Global information networks (1997) Ministerial conference, Bonn, 6–8 July 1997, ministerial declaration. http://www2.echo.lu/bonn/final.html

Iceland (1997). *The Icelandic government's vision of the information society.*
http://www.stjr.is/framt/vision00.htm

India (1999). Department of Telecommunications. *Perspective plan for telecom services (1997–2007).* http://wwwdel.vsnl.net.in/tec

Industry Canada (1997) *Preparing Canada for a digital world. Final report of the Information Highway Advisory Council.* http://strategis.ic.gc.ca/ihac

Information Society Forum (2000) [Website]. http://www.ispo.cec.be/infoforum

Italy (1997). Presidenza del Consiglio dei Ministri. *Promuovere lo sviluppo della societa dell'informazione in Italia: uno schema di riferimento.*
http://www.comunicazioni.it/dossier/pcmdoc.htm

Japan (1997). Ministry of Posts and Telecommunications. *White paper: communications in Japan.* http://www.mpt.go.jp/policyreports/english/papers/WhitePaper1998.pdf

Korea (1998). Information Society Development Institute. *Building an information society in the 21st century.* http://www.kisdi.re.kr/kisdi/event/build.htm

Machlup, F. (1962) *The production and distribution of knowledge in the United States*. Princeton, NJ: Princeton University Press.

Machlup, F. (1984) *The economics of information and human capital. Vol. III: Knowledge: its creation, distribution and economic significance*. Princeton, NJ: Princeton University Press.

Mauritius (1997). Ministry of Telecommunications and Information Technology. *White paper on the telecommunications sector: fostering the info-communications society*. http://ncb.intnet.mu/mtit/ministry/whitepap.htm

Netherlands (1995). Ministry of Economic Affairs. *Information superhighway: from metaphor to action*. http://minez.nl/docs/nap-en.htm

OECD (1996) Working Party on Information Economy. *Content as a new growth industry*. DSTI/ICCP/IE(96)6/Final. Paris: OECD.

OECD (1997) *Towards a global information society*. Paris: OECD.

OECD (1998) *The Multilateral Agreement on Investment*. http://www.oecd.org/daf/investment/fdi/mai/ukreport.pdf

Pauli, G. (1995) Industrial clusters of the twenty-first century. In: F. Capra and G. Pauli (eds) *Steering business towards sustainability*. Tokyo: United Nations University Press.

Porat, M.U. (1978) *The information economy: definition and measurement*. 9 vols. Washington, DC: US Department of Commerce, Office of Telecommunications.

Portugal (1997). Ministry of Science and Technology. Mission for the Information Society. *The green paper on the information society in Portugal*. http://www.missao-si.mct.pt/english/greenpaper/green.htm

Reich, R. (1991) *The work of nations: preparing ourselves for 21st century capitalism*. New York: Knopf.

Rösner, H. (1998) Electronic copyright and digital licensing. [EBLIDA conference, Rome.] *Bibliotheksdienst*, **32**(12), 2143–2156.

Singapore (1997). National Computer Board. *Singapore's IT masterplan: IT 2000*. http://www.ncb.gov.sg/ncb/it2000.asp

Street, J. (1997) 'Across the universe': the limits of global popular culture. In: A. Scott (ed.) *The limits of globalization: cases and arguments*. London: Routledge, pp. 75–89.

UK (1998). Department of Trade and Industry. Information Society Initiative. *Our competitive future: building the knowledge driven economy*. [White paper.] http://www.dti.gov.uk/comp/competitive/wh_int1.htm

UNESCO (1984) *National information policy: scope, formulation and implementation. Dubrovnik, Yugoslavia, 25–29 June 1984*. Paris: UNESCO. [PGI-84/WS/17.]

UNESCO (1997) *Legal and ethical issues. Infoethics*. http://www.unesco.org/webworld/public_domain/legal.html

US (1997). Information Infrastructure Task Force. *National information infrastructure (NII): general information*. http://nii.nist.gov/nii/niiinfo.html

US (1998). *National information infrastructure: virtual library*. http://nii.nist.gov

WIPO (1996) *Diplomatic conference on certain copyright and neighboring rights questions, Geneva 2–20 December, 1996*. http://www.wipo.org/eng/diplconf/distrib/94dc.htm

WTO (1999) *The 3rd WTO ministerial conference 30 November – 3 December*. http://www.wto-ministerial.org

Bibliographic control and access

7

Ann Matheson

Introduction

The most marked new factor in the period of this review is the increased recognition of the expansion of electronic resources as a permanent feature of the future of libraries. Significantly more attention is being paid to considering how the abundance of information in a wide range of formats (paper, video, audio and digital) can be handled effectively in libraries so that users can have good quality services. Already noted trends and developments in bibliographic control and access have continued to be discussed during this period, and some new perspectives have been highlighted. The general thrust of all these developments has been to increase the global view of bibliographic access and control; to encourage cooperative effort among libraries and others; and to underline the 'internationalism' of information and those involved in its creation or provision of access to it. The emerging factors during the period include:

- First and foremost, a significant increase in references to electronic resources and strategies for dealing with them.
- A movement among libraries and professional practitioners towards consideration of national strategies for bibliographic control and access.
- An increasing awareness that national bibliographic aims should fit within an international framework.
- Increased scale and emphasis on electronic materials and Web resources and their implications.
- Evolution of standards for the electronic environment.
- A reassessment and re-evaluation of the role of the cataloguer in an increasingly complex information age.
- A growing recognition of the need to seek harmonization of standards and cataloguing rules to assist the convenient exchange of information and easier access for researchers.

Cataloguing staff in libraries worldwide continue to face change. Oddy (1996) in her excellent work on libraries of the future and catalogues of the future points to this climate of change. Cataloguers also continue to increase their personal contacts with their colleagues in other countries, assisted by the ease of use of the Internet. This has been accompanied by a growing realization that national standards, originally developed with the best of intentions and subsequently guarded with national pride, can act as impediments to the international exchange of data. As a result this period has been marked by steps in the direction of harmonization of standards and cataloguing rules, as well as rising support for the 'internationalizing' of the standards developed in the Anglo-American world, and the neutralizing of their 'Anglo-American' provenance. Others (Ayres 1995) challenge the present direction of bibliographic control, arguing that the basic principles must be re-examined and that the traditional cataloguing methods of the past are too narrow for the multiplicity of formats that online catalogues must now present to users.

Another major feature of the period has been the effect of falling library budgets in most areas of the world and the dilemmas faced by librarians in balancing the provision of good quality access to the traditional materials they acquire and the requirements of new areas such as electronic resources, while having to cope with both with reduced staffing levels. There are a number of attempts to develop solutions, including flexible working: Black and Hyslop (1996), for example, describe an experiment in 'telecommuting' or 'flexible workplace' in Michigan State University Libraries and assess the advantages and the limitations of this type of approach: and Pappas (1996) describes a project among a number of RLIN libraries to speed copy cataloguing workflow.

Cooperation and sharing of tasks by libraries are one major response to the 20th century conundrum of increased workloads and declining staff numbers. It is not surprising, therefore, to find that during this period the number of cooperative cataloguing programmes and consortia involving libraries working together to share this task has increased significantly. Greater knowledge of the scale – and the instability – of online information has also underlined the view that the only realistic means to address this information explosion nationally and internationally is through cooperative effort.

It is clear that this is now the information age, if not the digital age, and the single most challenging issue for libraries is how they can find a coherent and effective method of dealing with the vast amount of information that is now generated, organize it and make it conveniently navigable to all who seek access to it – and do so with significantly fewer resources than they have had. Assessing the position from the perspective of a library director, the response of Meyer (1997) is to implore cataloguers to 'observe, learn, and innovate', while Thomas (1997) reviews traditional ways of approaching cataloguing in libraries, and the declining interest in cataloguing among library managers, and advances a more holistic approach to library practice starting within library schools.

Cooperation and sharing of records

Cooperative initiatives

As a result of rising levels of publishing outputs, allied with a whole new range of electronic resources to be acquired and made available to users, libraries are scrutinizing afresh the level of resources that they make available for labour-intensive activities such as cataloguing, and thinking about innovative ways of dealing with the 'crisis in cataloguing'. Tabb (1997) outlines LC's response to these trends through the setting up of the Program for Cooperative Cataloging (PCC), a coalition of US libraries working together to create individual records to mutually acceptable standards. This initiative has led to simplification of some LC rule interpretations and the identification of a core-level bibliographic record.

S.E. Thomas (1996) deals in detail with the concept of the PCC 'core bibliographic record', which is aimed at embodying principles of usefulness, cost effectiveness and dynamism and plays a critical role in achieving the PCC goal of increasing the availability of unique records created in a decentralized fashion by a network of libraries to mutually acceptable standards. The Program is backed up by a strong training programme for participants, a clear essential for all cooperative cataloguing endeavour. From a Canadian perspective, McKeen (1998) outlines how levels of cataloguing treatment have been determined for Canadiana. Chervinko (1995) describes a cooperative initiative for the cataloguing of foreign-language materials among a group of 27 academic and research libraries in the USA; and Fineberg (1998) promotes the case for cooperation in cataloguing Asian materials. Gorman (1998) underlines the importance of the principle of shared cataloguing by reaffirming that the ideal of Universal Bibliographic Control (UBC) is that each document should be catalogued once in the country of origin, and that cataloguing thus created should be made available to libraries round the world. Recognition of the importance of cooperative effort is springing up in many areas of the world. For example, Lee-Smeltzerk (1996) proposes that the development of Chinese MARC and the establishment of the national online bibliographic database (NBINet) have affected cataloguing processes in libraries in Taiwan, offering the prospect of greater cooperation in the cataloguing of Chinese-language materials at the international level. Oddy (1997) underlines that all cataloguing strategies should have as their basis recognition of the need to 'remind, reassure, reward', a timely reminder that the successes of cooperation are achieved through people, not just through machines.

Retroconversion of catalogues

The retroconversion of printed catalogues continues to be written about in the literature of the period. De Gennaro *et al.* (1997) describe Harvard's retroconversion strategy, which is aimed at positioning Harvard's libraries for the electronic age; and Danskin (1997c) gives an account of the retroconversion of the British Library's Catalogue of Printed Books.

Bibliographic formats

A considerable amount of the literature of this period has been devoted to examining developments in bibliographic formats. Spicher (1996) provides a historical résumé of the development of the MARC format from its inception in the 1960s to the 1990s; and Hill (1998) provides a further edition of his guide to the MARC format. A number of articles, such as Ede's (1995), have emphasized the urgent need for simplification of formats which would minimize differences and make international exchange of data easier to accomplish. A survey by McKercher and Xin Chang (1995), undertaken to identify the use of MARC bibliographic formats in national libraries worldwide, demonstrated that USMARC and UNIMARC, and their derivatives, were the most commonly implemented. The expansion of USMARC (now MARC21) is attributed to the wide availability of USMARC format cataloguing records, along with the spread of American library systems into new markets in the developing and developed world. UNIMARC, on the other hand, is promoted by IFLA and by a number of aid agencies internationally in countries across the world.

Format harmonization

National formats, once jealously guarded as national symbols, are now increasingly regarded in some areas of the world as an impediment to the easy exchange of cataloguing data among libraries and across national boundaries. Ede (1995) outlines the transatlantic initiative to harmonize UKMARC, USMARC and CANMARC in order to assist the international exchange of records. Tabb (1997) records that LC and NLC have succeeded in harmonizing their formats (MARC21), but notes that there are some remaining issues to be overcome in aligning UKMARC. Hendrix (1997) argues strongly for speedy action to be taken to harmonize UKMARC and USMARC, and for the professional skills of cataloguers to be utilized to harness and describe the resources of this ever more complex and demanding electronic world.

UNIMARC

UNIMARC was designed and promoted by IFLA almost twenty years ago as the proposed universal MARC format to provide a way of permitting the transfer of data among different national MARC formats without any loss of information. A decisive step taken in Florence in 1991 was the creation of the Permanent UNIMARC Committee (PUC). A new edition of the *UNIMARC Manual* was published in 1996. Holt (1997) highlights its main points and also summarizes the future proposals of PUC. Numerous accounts of the use of UNIMARC in countries in Europe exist in the literature of the period: for example, Scandinavia (Salomonsen, 1995); Lithuania (Varniené, 1995); France (Lahary, 1999); and the Czech Republic (Lichtenbergova and Stoklasova, 1999). Willer (1996a) outlines experience with the UNIMARC format over fifteen years and provides a very useful bibliography. Arising out of the work of the Consortium of European Research Libraries (CERL), Curwen and Kirk (1999) have published the results of a research project into the application of UNIMARC to the multinational databases of its members, a study carried out in close cooperation with PUC. Meanwhile, European libraries continue variously to select UNIMARC or USMARC, or remain with national formats. Tsvetkova and Skvortsov (1999) describe the adoption of UNIMARC as the Russian exchange format; and Masevich and Zakharov (1995) outline the role of UNIMARC in the investigation of automated systems by the National Library of Russia and the Russian Academy of Sciences. Chkhenkeli and Garibashvili (1998) give an account of the implementation of UNIMARC in libraries in Georgia. Supported by UNESCO and the Eurasia Foundation, these libraries previously had only a very rudimentary knowledge of bibliographic description or online cataloguing. Campos (1998) urges that USMARC and UNIMARC should not become a battlefield between American and European interests and argues the case for greater cooperation between the two formats, an approach also advocated by McCallum (1996). An update in 1998 confirms that there are 51 institutions (in, for example, India, Iran, Italy, Lithuania, Namibia, Portugal, Russia and Slovakia) utilizing UNIMARC, with a further ten (in Albania, Bangladesh, Cuba, Korea and Peru) planning to implement it within the next three years.

Record exchange

Different formats are not the only factor militating against easy exchange of records. The CoBRA (Computerised Bibliographic Records Action) initiative, part of the European Libraries Programme, was established to advance projects that promote record exchange, including the application of UNIMARC to multinational databases; bibliographic data and service provision in Europe; the investigation of the feasibility of a European name authority network; and the AUTHOR project separately described by Bourdon and Zillhardt (1997). It is hoped that the Programme will lead on to the development of further functional models that will enable different levels of electronic information, e.g. bibliographic records with abstracts, tables of contents, etc. to be linked. Parmeggiani (1995) outlines the issues that had to be resolved in setting up the Servizio Bibliotecario Nazionale, the Italian library network, for shared cataloguing and record exchange. Pinedo and Magliano (1997) give an update on this programme, which is under the governance of the Istituto Centrale per il Catalogo Unico delle Biblioteche Italiane e per le Informazioni Bibliografiche, and on its involvement with CERL's Hand Press Book database.

New national strategy models

A striking development within the period of this review is the increased evidence that internationally more countries are seeking to evolve national strategies for bibliographic control. Holley (1998) discusses the results of a survey on bibliographic control and national bibliography, conducted by the IFLA Section on Bibliography. In some areas of the world, such as Australia and the Nordic countries, the process has been well described in earlier literature, but information about new developments continues to be published. Ralli (1996) describes the impact of the Australian Bibliographic Network on Australian libraries. Waneck and Hansen (1997) demonstrate the high level of achievement in Denmark on national strategies: a national bibliography with a high level of currency and coverage; more than 50 years of experience of central cataloguing for public and school libraries; and widespread cataloguing cooperation among Danish research libraries. The next objective for this advanced country is to solve the question of national bibliographic registration of Internet resources for inclusion in the national bibliography. The Netherlands is at exactly the same point in its development of effective national bibliographic control: Berg (1998) explains the steps that are being taken by the Royal Library to establish a depot for electronic publications to extend bibliographic control to this field. Chapman (1995, 1997) examines the availability of national library bibliographic records in the UK and considers what further can be achieved from the data collected. Vitiello (1996) gives an overview of the production and marketing of national bibliographic services in Europe; and Lenart (1996) provides extremely useful information on the various models that exist across Europe for the provision of national bibliographic services.

But there is also now quite extensive evidence of a similar drive to develop national strategies for bibliographic control in other countries, some with little history or previous experience of library cooperation. Katuscák (1996) outlines new developments in Slovak librarianship and the development of new cataloguing rules based on international standards in order to achieve better national bibliographic control. The situation in the Baltic countries is covered by Varniené (1999), who stresses the decision taken there to opt for integrated library systems with the aim, from the outset, of firm bibliographic control within these countries through a shared vision. Baydur (1995) reviews general aspects of bibliographic control in Turkish librarianship; and Atilgan (1996) describes steps being taken in Turkey towards the creation of a national MARC format and a national strategy for cataloguing among different sectors of Turkish libraries. A similar aim is explored by Kucuk and Hartley (1996) in their proposed scheme for a national cooperative cataloguing system for manuscripts in Turkey. Equal effort is being advanced in South Africa: Behrens (1996) sets out recommendations for a national strategy on the improvement of national bibliographic services and bibliographic control in South Africa. In Uganda, by comparison, there are many complex issues to be addressed: Kasajja (1995) deals with the steps that must be taken to enable the national bibliographic agency to conform to international standards; and Kigongo-Bukenya (1998) sets out a strategy for the 21st century, pinpointing the creation of a national library, or a distributed system of several libraries, as an essential prerequisite for effective bibliographic control. Ouyporn (1998) provides a country report on national bibliographic control activities and current priorities in Thailand.

Bibliographic standards

With the globalization of information comes a renewed concern with bibliographic standards, both in terms of how successfully they meet users' needs and also with regard to the issue of how standards will be formulated in the future, in comparison with the speed being utilized in developing Internet standards. The World Wide Web is increasingly being used to host online information about standards: for example, IFLA's (1996, 1998b) *Functional requirements for bibliographic records*, first made available on the IFLA Website in 1996. Madison (1998a, 1998b) deals in some detail with issues relating to standards for international bibliographic control. IFLA (1998a) sets out its Medium Term Programme for 1998 to 2001. The editor of this document, Sally McCallum (1996), describes the characteristics of standards (defined as 'the backbone of bibliographic control') developed by the formal standards organizations (ISO, ANSI and NISO), and the key standards for the Library community. She points to the comparative speed with which standards are being formulated for the Internet (for example, by the industry group called the Internet Engineering Task Force (IETF)), since the Internet community takes the view that the formal standards processes are too slow and bureaucratic. Holley (1996) raises the question of whether the importance of IFLA as a standards setting body is likely to be reduced by the increasing importance of library networks and the internationalization of bibliographic control: he speculates on the need for a new more international model that takes less account of national boundaries.

One essential aspect of promoting international standards is that they must be accessible and acceptable for use within the global library community. AACR2 has been internationally adopted in a range of countries (and translated into fourteen languages), and is the nearest thing to an international code, as Stern (1996) points out. But if it is to have potential as a universal code, it will have to reflect the requirements of non-English speaking environments and will need to divest itself of its present nomenclature and bias towards the English-speaking world.

Descriptive cataloguing rules

The most significant event during the period was the decision by the Joint Steering Committee for Revision of AACR to hold an International Conference on the Principles and Future Development of AACR, in Toronto, 23 to 25 October 1997 (*Report*, 1997), and the subsequent published proceedings (Weihs, 1997). The main outcomes of this important conference included decisions to undertake a logical analysis (using a data modelling technique) of the principles and structures on which AACR is based, work which has been undertaken by Tom Delsey of the National Library of Canada; to formalize the recommendations on seriality and introduce them into the rule revision process; and to solicit a proposal to revise rule 0.24 to advance the discussion on the primacy of intellectual content over physical format. IFLA (1996) also published the final results of its study on the functional requirements for bibliographic records. Individual rules have continued to attract attention: Bowman (1996) proposes changes in rules to assist the cataloguing of certain categories of printed material (for example, anonymous works, edited works and conference proceedings). His study shows that between 1841 and the 1990s there has been a decrease in anonymous works and works of personal authorship, but this is offset by a sharp rise in works of multiple authorship, edited works and conference proceedings.

Comparative studies

The greater availability of MARC records from countries internationally has led to comparative studies of cataloguing rules. Jacobowitz (1995) compares French

(AFNOR) cataloguing rules with AACR2. Münnich (1997) describes an initiative aimed at harmonizing AACR2 and RAK-WB, the German rules for descriptive cataloguing. The similarities and differences between the Russian Rules for Bibliographic Description (1986) and AACR2 are examined by Montviloff (1997). All stress the need for developing a common standard for descriptive cataloguing. Edmunds (1995), on the other hand, points out the limitations of AACR2 in addressing issues raised by legal deposit, since under French law all French-language materials described must bear the date of legal deposit as well as any dates relating to publication. The particular requirements of older books have received attention during this period: in the UK the Library Association (1997) Rare Books Group published *Guidelines for the cataloguing of rare books*. Willer (1996a) describes the implementation of international cataloguing standards in the cataloguing of old and rare books in Slovenia and Croatia; and Katić (1997) describes a project on retrospective cataloguing of older books in Croatia, using UNIMARC. Taking an international view of the subject, Snyder (1998) stresses the impact of information technology on the bibliography of early printed books and the advances in terms of access to material of this period that it has facilitated. The requirements of other special groups have also received attention during the period through, for example, the work by Intner and Weihs (1996) on standard cataloguing for schools and public libraries. Making further progress, the electronic version of AACR (*Anglo-American*, 1999) was made available; and with the aim of assisting cataloguing staff, and recognizing the utility of the World Wide Web, Molto and Svenonius (1998) describe a project aimed at designing an interface to the newly emerging electronic AACR2.

Serials cataloguing

A considerable amount of work has been carried out in the field of serials cataloguing during the period of this review. Leibowitz (1995) discusses the use of form and genre headings in the cataloguing of serials and outlines the positive benefits and the pitfalls. Leazer (1996) queries whether USMARC formats will ever be able effectively to accommodate information on sequential bibliographic relationships and advocates a more complex concept of the 'bibliographic family'. One of the results of the 1997 Toronto International Conference on the future of AACR was to formalize the Conference's recommendations on seriality and introduce them into the rule revision process. The most extensive treatment of serials is given in the work by Boydston and his fellow contributors (1997) on serials cataloguing at the turn of the 20th century.

Authority control

Internationalization

Increasing internationalization is also the theme in the field of authority control
Danskin (1996) outlines the background to the Anglo-American Authority File
the working title for an ambitious undertaking between the British Library and
the Library of Congress to develop a single shared authority file in place of the
existing British Library Name Authority List and the US National Authority File
with completion of the project scheduled for 1999. Two further articles by Danskin
(1997a, 1998) describe the implementation and completion of Phase 2 of the project
In a separate paper on respective costs and benefits (1997b), Danskin links the
exchange of authority information with improved productivity. Bourdon and
Zillhardt (1997) describe the AUTHOR project – part of the European CoBRA
programme, which is aimed at developing remote access to multiple authority
files. The project is predicated on the understanding that each project partner
will have access through the Internet to the authority files of other partners, and
that each will be able to reuse research carried out by colleagues in other European
countries. On the other hand, Tillett (1995) has advocated a different approach in
a new form of access control record – International Standard Authority Data
Number (ISADN) – which would act as a node for the collocation of all variant
forms of a particular name. The ONE (Opac Network in Europe) project, funded
by the European Commission, started in January 1995 and was completed in
December 1997. The outcome of its findings, as outlined by Holm (1999b), favours
the development of the ISADN on the basis of the project's experience in searching
remote databases using Z39.50 protocols. Holm (1999a) also examines authority
control in an international context in the new 'global' environment and concludes
that authority control is more important in a network of systems than in a single
system. This issue is also dealt with by Merrick (1998), in an article on Z39.50
and the virtual distributed catalogue.

National authority files

A number of articles in the literature deal with experience gained from planning
national authority files. Murtomaa (1996) describes the Finnish experience and
queries why it is desirable to have a single standard name form to which all
works are linked rather than giving equivalent treatment to all forms of the name
Kuhagen (1996) examines the transition from the national authority file developed
from an LC-orientated file to one attempting to serve a wide and diverse group
of contributors and users. The experience in France of preparing for the new
Bibliothèque nationale de France is dealt with by Guy (1996). Selivanova and

Extrem (1996) describe the creation and implementation of a national authority file in the Russian National Library; and Terekhova (1996) deals with the development of authority files in the Rudomino Library for Foreign Literature in Moscow.

Subject headings

The Library of Congress Subject Headings (LCSH) system has a long history, dating back to the beginning of the 20th century. Matheson (1996) argues for the position of LCSH as the most internationally accepted system currently available to us, while recommending a name change to signify its international scope and acceptance. McEwen (1996) also raises the prospect of an international subject authority database and stresses that the same economic necessity unites all users of LCSH. Burton (1998) gives an overview of the issues and challenges of subject access. McGarry (1996) describes the *Guidelines for subject authority and reference entries*, which were prepared to provide guidelines for creating subject authority records that could be easily consulted and exchanged internationally. An account of the work carried out by a working group of IFLA's Section on Classification and Indexing in taking an international approach to the investigation of principles for the construction of subject headings is given by Lopes (1996). The position in Germany is dealt with by Heiner-Freiling (1995) and by Kelm (1996), who also describes the proposed Multilingual Subject Authority File, which was intended to become the focal point for international cooperative work with partners from France, Italy, the Netherlands, Austria, the UK and Germany. Unfortunately, the project had to be postponed until the turn of the millennium for funding reasons. Baydur (1996) reviews the current position of subject indexing in libraries in Turkey, which he describes as transitional, and highlights the lack of user input into the development of subject access for Turkish sources.

Williamson (1996) argues strongly for standardization of subject access to bibliographic information systems as vital in national and international networking, cooperation and exchange of bibliographic data. She underlines the need for standards and guidelines to ensure consistency and quality in the design, development and application of indexing languages to documents and their citations; and the article offers definitions of the terms 'standards' and 'guidelines' as they apply to subject analysis used in library catalogues and bibliographic databases. Down (1995) describes the OCLC/LC Fiction Project and examines the types of access (form/genre, character, geographical setting, and topical) to individual works of fiction. This topic is expanded upon by Hidderley and Rafferty (1997) in a chapter on 'democratic indexing' as an approach to the retrieval of fiction.

Classification

New roles

The subject of classification is extensively dealt with during the period of the review. The literature relating to new roles for classification in libraries and networks is covered by A.R.S. Thomas (1996), who has collected articles which argue the case that classification has an important role to play as technology changes the way in which information is stored and retrieved from libraries and information networks. Riemer (1996) has assembled a number of articles on aspects of cataloguing and classification standards and rules. He clarifies potential uses for classification data in machine-readable form, and advances reasons for the development of a standard, drawing on experience at Library of Congress with the implementation of USMARC classification. Shearer and Thomas (1997) deal extensively with current and future trends in classification. Albrechtsen and Jacob (1997) argue that classification research today takes place not only within the framework of traditional research and development (for example, in LIS schools) but also in modern libraries. In a separate article Albrechtsen (1998) explains how the role of classification systems in public libraries is evolving into a form of social instrument, facilitating communication and cooperation in the open distributed environment of the modern electronic library. The general theme of the treatment of classification during the period of the review is summed up by Thomas (1995) as 'options and opportunities'.

National solutions

Numerous articles deal with the national situation on classification in a range of countries. Soltani (1996) describes the use of LC and DDC systems in the Arab countries and Iran; and Traiser (1995) covers the policies adopted in Die Deutsche Bibliothek. Increased internationalism is another strong theme: the international use of DDC is covered by Sweeney (1995) and Chan and Mitchell (1997); and Geisselmann (1997) highlights the range of classification issues in Germany that require tackling (e.g. better joint national development) to ensure that international cooperation can be promoted effectively. Mahmood (1997) gives an account of subject cataloguing in Pakistani libraries and the complexities of this issue in his country.

Future trends

Burton (1997) argues that classification (along with cataloguing) should no longer be part of the curriculum for information professionals, since with the growth of electronic creation, storage and dissemination of information such skills will be largely redundant. Brunt (1997) disagrees with this view, contending that indexing and description will continue to be necessary in the information age. This theme is expanded upon in a number of articles in the literature during this period. McIlwaine (1996) provides a thorough approach to adapting traditional classifications for the future. Riesthuis (1995) makes some interesting comments on the sociological aspects of classification, arguing that many features of classification schemes are sociological in origin and that 'prejudice' can play a significant part, so that a library's choice of classification scheme is often made on the basis of sociological reasoning rather than by scientific means; while Pollitt (1998) makes a strong case for the role of classification and indexing as crucial to the continuing development of view-based searching, since systems that take advantage of evolving ways to represent knowledge structures at the user interface will ensure better quality results for users.

Internet resources

One of the major new trends in this period is the increased emphasis on online resources and how to deal with them. Much of the most interesting work has come from a seminar held in Lithuania in 1998 on the function of bibliographic control in the global information infrastructure. Ede (1999) refers to 'digital indigestion' through the overload of information that libraries have to tackle in order to assert control and because of the particular complexities of searching for information on the Internet. He offers some remedies for the alleviation or cure of 'digital indigestion'. The level of debate on the issue of dealing with electronic resources is quite intense: Hakala (1999) describes the Nordic Metadata initiative in detail; it is clear that the Nordic countries are well advanced in this field and hope to remain so. Hopkinson (1999) puts the case for the retention of MARC, which he argues serves a different but complementary purpose from the later generation of formats such as Dublin Core. Banerjee (1997) examines issues arising from the need to describe electronic resources in online catalogues and concludes that it is only practicable to provide minimal descriptive information for remote resources in the catalogue record. Poulter (1997b) describes the effects of the Internet on the work of descriptive cataloguers by putting them in closer contact with suppliers and publishers and by making available a vast range of reference or cataloguing information. He argues that these factors will have a profound effect on the practice of descriptive cataloguing. Dunsire (1999a) believes it is essential for the library community to assert more effectively its professional competence in contributing to the debate on managing global electronic information. He is critical of Day (1998b) for the weakness of the language used in the ROADS cataloguing guidelines. Libraries' cataloguing skills and techniques, he asserts, are the key to ensuring the maximum benefit to the global information society. His arguments are very convincing – provided that libraries seize the challenge.

Cataloguing the Internet

Dunsire (1996, 1999b) contributes two interesting articles about the Cataloguing and Retrieval of Information over Networks Applications (CATRIONA) project in Scotland, which was set up to investigate the cataloguing of electronic information objects (EIOs) and then retrieving the EIO from a wide area network, such as the Internet, for display and manipulation on a local public access catalogue computer (PAC). The implementation of this project followed an earlier feasibility study on 'cataloguing the Internet' described by Nicholson *et al*. (1996). The CATRIONA project was able to demonstrate that the facility to go from the local viewer to the electronic resource and then come back without operator invention (which is what users require) can be implemented with the new generation of client/server library management systems. A report on a project to produce a unified information access system in California State University is described by Pollard (1998); and Kellermann and Lor (1997) give an account of a seminar on accessing information resources in South Africa. Beaney and Carpenter (1996) deal extensively with the indexing and retrieval of digital items; and Olson (1995) offers a practical guide and manual for cataloguing Internet resources. Ellis *et al*. (1998), in an article focusing on searching for the 'unknown user', examine indexing, hypertext and the World Wide Web; while Davies (1996) makes a case for thesaurus-aided searching in search and retrieval protocols.

Tools for describing electronic resources

Electronic resources and the tools for describing them appear frequently in the literature of this period. Stoker (1998) provides a beginner's guide to metadata; Sha (1995) concentrates on library approaches to cataloguing Internet resources; Pattie and Cox (1996) examine selection and bibliographic control of electronic resources; and Dempsey and Heery (1998) offer a wide-ranging review of metadata practice and issues. Metadata, generally defined as 'data about data', is a prominent issue in the literature of this period: the arguments for and against the main initiatives (Dublin Core and Warwick Frame) are rehearsed exhaustively but without resolution. Day (1998a) sets out guidelines for mapping from Dublin Core to UNIMARC; and Day *et al*. (1999) deal more extensively with national bibliographic records in the digital information environment. There are a number of articles during the period on the specific topic of Dublin Core and its suitability and use as a standard. Powell (1998) provides some useful notes on the use of Dublin Core. Electronic access to the core metadata fields has been provided (*Dublin*, 1998); and they are also mounted by UKOLN (1998).

National initiatives

There is also a significant amount of literature on national initiatives in this field. In Germany, for example, a multi-partner project called MetaLib (involving Göttingen University Library, Die Deutsche Bibliothek and the Bayerische Staatsbibliothek, Munich) has been set up to consider metadata issues. In the UK the Distributed National Electronic Resource has been established by the Joint Information Systems Committee (JISC), with a technical and service infrastructure which will address, among other issues, the development of standards for metadata. Also in the UK, Strutt (1997) outlines the British Library's current policies on cataloguing Internet resources. Poulter (1997a) describes CIGnet, the CIG guide to the Internet; and OCLC offers online guidance on how to build a catalogue of Internet-accessible materials (*Dublin*, 1998). Noordermeer (1999) describes the DONOR project established by the Dutch Royal Library in 1998 to provide tools for creating and managing Internet metadata and to promote the use of metadata standards by authors of Internet publications in the Netherlands. This is linked to the development of an integrated workstation, the Advanced Information Workstation, described by Niet (1998) and Noordermeer (1999). Brisson (1995a, 1995b) deals in two articles with the cataloguer's workstation in the transition of cataloguing to a fully electronic environment and gives an overview of the many facets that make up the cataloguer's workstation. An excellent overview of electronic library developments in the Netherlands is given by Noordermeer *et al.* (1998); this dwells in particular on developments in relation to the national (voluntary) deposit of electronic publications and on the virtual library for research and education.

The national electronic library

A great deal of the most constructive progress on building national electronic libraries seems to be taking place in small countries in Europe; but one of the most ambitious schemes is being promoted in a large country: Australia. In 1996, the National Library of Australia established the PANDORA (Preserving and

Accessing Networked Documentary Resources of Australia) Project, described by Smith (1998), with the specific aim of establishing procedures and standards for maintaining long-term access to Australian online electronic publications, for both current and future users. The PANDORA Project follows standard procedures for cataloguing online electronic publications: the 856 field is used to record the URL of the publication, both at the publisher's site and in the PANDORA archive, while in the library's OPACs, these URLs are maintained as active links via Webpac, subject to conditions of access to the publication. Ma *et al.* (1997) describe a project based on cataloguing non-print resources in the USA and compare the organization and provision of access to selected electronic and audiovisual resources.

The 'format' debate

Substantial debate is taking place on the question of traditional communication formats versus metadata, Dublin Core, etc; or, to put it in the words of Hopkinson (1999), ' Do we still need MARC?'. No consensus has yet been reached on this important question. Hopkinson argues strongly that the new formats are complementary to MARC and that MARC continues to serve a useful purpose in promoting the building of catalogues. Ollier (1996) poses the rhetorical question 'MARC in time'. At the Toronto Conference on the future of AACR, Gorman made a strong plea for a 'flexible MARC', which he argued was quite capable of accommodating all formats. There is similar debate about the usefulness of AACR in the online environment. Heaney (1998) conducts an analysis of AACR as a model. Fattahi (1995) examines the thinking on AACR2 in the online environment on the basis of the available literature at that time. He concludes that the literature demonstrates that the majority of authors consider radical change of AACR2 impossible and undesirable because of the large number of catalogues already created according to the existing rules; and he draws attention to the absence of empirical research on the suitability of the rules for the online environment.

The future of cataloguing

This has been a volatile period for the question of the future of cataloguing. The debate has ranged from projecting virtually no future for cataloguing or cataloguers at the beginning of the period to a new realization that the advent of the online global information world will create a new and challenging prospect for cataloguers. Electronic resources, like other resources, must be described for users, and who better to do this – given a little flexibility and vision – than skilled and expert cataloguers? Perhaps a new nomenclature should be introduced to define their new status and responsibilities.

In the sceptical camp, Barnes (1995), then President of the (UK) Library Association, points to the decline in the number of specialist cataloguers and suggests that this is detrimental because it limits the ability of libraries to respond effectively to local needs; and Harmon (1996) deplores the death of quality cataloguing. Towsey (1995), in an analysis of cataloguing jobs over a period of a year in the UK, highlights the decline in professional posts. Velluci (1996) sums it up in a title: 'Future cataloguers: essential colleagues or anachronisms?'; and Ayres (1996) asks the question 'What is the future for catalogues and cataloguers?'.

On the other side of the argument, Bryant (1995) invokes the example of a 14th-century monk, John Whytefeld, an admirable cataloguer of his day, to reinforce the case for the importance of cataloguing. Gorman (1998), in a philosophical treatise on the future of cataloguing and cataloguers delivered at the IFLA Conference in Copenhagen, argues vehemently that the bibliographic structure is essential to the future of libraries, that libraries are an essential component of education, learning and literacy, and that society needs learning and educated citizens in order to develop, thrive and survive. He is convinced that, for cataloguers particularly, 'the future is challenging and bright'. Gorman's sane credo is that libraries must maintain the bibliographic structures that have been built, and develop them in two main directions: first, by ensuring that worthwhile electronic documents are organized and preserved for future generations; second, by improving bibliographic standards worldwide and ensuring that they reach a level of standardization that makes possible a new level of global cooperation. Dunsire (1999a) concurs with this view, urging cataloguing staff to seize the opportunities that now present themselves. In the USA the drift seems to be in the direction of 'catalogue librarians', who are more involved with technology, management, training and education and who possess skills broadened beyond the actual cataloguing of materials. Meyer (1997), for example, believes that cataloguers must develop expanded skills with automation networks and modern software systems if they are to maintain control.

Conclusion

Overall the outlook for cataloguing and cataloguers over the period of this review is more optimistic than pessimistic. Admittedly, it must be said that funding pressures, bringing the inevitable prospect of retrenchment, are still affecting most libraries. There does not seem to be any realistic expectation that the situation is going to improve significantly over the next few years. Without question, the worldwide explosion of information in such a variety of formats, as Lowenberg

(1998) outlines, is a daunting prospect to control, especially with limited resources. But, equally, technology is solving more and more of the barriers to the exchange of information in our global world. Cooperation and the sharing of tasks among libraries are gaining recognition internationally as the direction in which we must all travel; and there are encouraging prospects that cataloguing staff – if they can reassess their roles and grasp the opportunities now before them – will play an increasingly significant part in the online world of the 21st century.

References

Albrechtsen, H. (1998) The order of catalogues – towards democratic classification and indexing in public libraries. *International Cataloguing and Bibliographic Control*, **27**(2), 41–43.

Albrechtsen, H. and Jacob, E. (1997) Classification systems as boundary objects in diverse information ecologies. In: E. Efthimiadis (ed.) *Proceedings of the 8th ASIS SIG/CR workshop, 1 November 1997, Washington (D.C). Anglo-American (1999) Cataloguing Rules*. 2nd edn. 1999 revision. Electronic Version 1.0 CD-ROM.

Atilgan, D. (1996) The state of the art in cataloguing in Turkey. *International Cataloguing and Bibliographic Control*, **25**(3), 49–50.

Ayres, F.H. (1995) Bibliographic control at the crossroads. *Cataloging and Classification Quarterly*, **20**(3), 5–18.

Ayres, F.H. (1996) What is the future for catalogues and cataloguers? *Catalogue and Index*, (122), 1–5.

Banerjee, K. (1997) Describing remote electronic documents in the online catalog: current issues. *International Cataloguing and Bibliographic Control*, **25**(1), 5–20.

Barnes, M. (1995) Will the last cataloguer to leave please turn out the light? *Catalogue and Index*, (116), 4.

Baydur, G. (1995) Bibliographic control in Turkey. *International Cataloguing and Bibliographic Control*, **24**(2), 19–21.

Baydur, G. (1996) Subject indexing practices in Turkey. *International Cataloguing and Bibliographic Control*, **25**(1), 8–9.

Beaney, S. and Carpenter, L. (1996) The indexing and retrieval of digital items. *Information Services*, **16**(3/4), 209–221.

Behrens, S.J. (1996) Recommendations for the improvement of national bibliographic services in South Africa. *South African Journal of Library and Information Science*, **64**(2), 81–85.

Berg, K. van den (1998) Bibliographic control in the Netherlands. *International Cataloguing and Bibliographic Control*, **27**(2), 31–33.

Black, L. and Hyslop, C. (1996) Cataloguing from home: telecommuting at the Michigan State University Libraries. *International Cataloguing and Bibliographic Control*, **25**(2), 37–39.

Bourdon, F. and Zillhardt, S. (1997) AUTHOR: vers une base européenne de notice d'autorité auteurs. *International Cataloguing and Bibliographic Control*, **26**(2), 34–37.

Bowman, J.H. (1996) Changing cataloging rules in relation to changing patterns of publication. *Cataloging and Classification Quarterly*, **22**(2), 29–50.

Boydston, J.M.K. *et al.* (1997) *Serials cataloging at the turn of the century.* New York: Haworth Press.

Brisson, R. (1995a) The cataloguer's workstation and the continuing transformation of cataloging: part I. *Cataloging and Classification Quarterly*, **20**(1), 3–23.

Brisson, R. (1995b) The cataloguer's workstation and the continuing transformation of cataloging: part II. *Cataloging and Classification Quarterly*, **20**(2), 89–105.

Brunt, R.M. (1997) The decline and fall of 'Cat. & Class.' *Catalogue and Index*, (125), 9.

Bryant, P. (1995) Quality of a national bibliographic service: in the steps of John Whytefeld – an admirable cataloguer. *International Cataloguing and Bibliographic Control*, **24**(2), 29–32.

Building (1998), a catalog of Internet-accessible materials.
  http://www.oclc.org/oclc/man/catproj/overview.htm

Burton, P.F. (1997) The decline and fall of 'Cat. & Class'. *Catalogue and Index*, (124), 9.

Burton, P.F. (1998) Issues and challenges of subject access. *Catalogue and Index*, (128), 1–6.

Campos, F.M. (1998) UNIMARC: the virtual format in the virtual age. *International Cataloguing and Bibliographic Control*, **27**(4), 74–75.

Chan, L.M. and Mitchell, J.S. (1997) *Dewey Decimal Classification Edition 21 and international perspectives. Papers from a workshop held at the IFLA Conference, Beijing, China, August 29, 1996.* Albany, NY: OCLC Forest Press.

Chapman, A. (1995) National library bibliographic record availability: a long-term survey. *Library Resources and Technical Services*, **39**(4), 345–357.

Chapman, A. (1997) 1994 revisited: a year in the life of the BNBMARC currency survey. *International Cataloguing and Bibliographic Control*, **26**(2), 41–46.

Chervinko, J.S. (1995) Cooperative and contract cataloging of foreign-language materials in academic and research libraries. *Cataloging and Classification Quarterly*, **21**(1), 29–65.

Chkhenkeli, T. and Garibashvili, I. (1998) Implementation of the UNIMARC format in Georgian libraries. *International Cataloguing and Bibliographic Control*, **27**(1), 21–23.

Curwen, A.G. and Kirk, C. (1999) *Application of UNIMARC to multinational databases.* [Coordinated by Claudia Fabian.] München: K.G. Saur. [UBCIM Publications, n.s.20.]

Danskin, A. (1996) The Anglo-American Authority File: an idea whose time has come? *International Cataloguing and Bibliographic Control*, **25**(3), 57–59.

Danskin, A. (1997a) The Anglo-American Authority File – completion of phase 2. *Select: the Newsletter of the* [BL] *National Bibliographic Service*, (20), 13.

Danskin, A. (1997b) International standards in authority control data: costs and benefits. *International Cataloguing and Bibliographic Control*, **26**(2), 31–34.

Danskin, A. (1997c) The retrospective conversion of the British Library Catalogue of Printed Books. *International Cataloguing and Bibliographic Control*, **26**(4), 91.

Danskin, A. (1998) The Anglo-American Authority File: implementation of Phase 2. *International Cataloguing and Bibliographic Control*, **27**(4), 72–73.

Davies, R. (1996) Thesaurus-aided searching in search and retrieval protocols. In: R. Green (ed.) *Knowledge organization and change. Proceedings of the Fourth International ISKO Conference, 5–18 July 1996.* Washington, DC. [Advances in Knowledge Organization, 5.]

Day, M. (1998a) *Mapping Dublin Core to UNIMARC.*
  http://www.ukoln.ac.uk/metadata/interoperability/dc_unimarc.html

Day, M. (1998b) *ROADS cataloguing guidelines – Draft (v.0.1).* UK Office for Library and Information Networking.
http://www.ukoln.ac.uk/metadata/roads/cataloguing/cataloguing-rules.html

Day, M. *et al.* (1999) National bibliographic records in the digital information environment metadata, links and standards. *Journal of Documentation,* **55**(1), 16–32.

De Gennaro, R. *et al.* (1997) Positioning Harvard's libraries for the electronic age *International Cataloguing and Bibliographic Control,* **26**(4), 92–94.

Dempsey, L. and Heery, R. (1998) Metadata: a current review of practice and issues. *Journal of Documentation,* **54**(2), 145–172.

Down, N. (1995) Subject access to individual works of fiction: participating in the OCLC/LC Fiction Project. *Cataloging and Classification Quarterly,* **20**(2), 61–69.

Dublin (1998) *Core metadata: metadata for electronic resources.*
http://purl.oclc.org/dc

Dunsire, G. (1996) CATRIONA, serials and the Internet. *Serials,* **9**(2), 182–188.

Dunsire, G. (1999a) Bringing it all back home: retrieval and access for the globa information society. *International Cataloguing and Bibliographic Control,* **28**(1), 13–14.

Dunsire, G. (1999b) CATRIONA: netting the cat and PACing the Net. *Catalogue and Index* (115), 1–3.

Ede, S. (1995) Fitness for purpose: the future evolution of bibliographic records and their delivery. *Catalogue and Index,* (116), 1–3.

Ede, S. (1999) Digital indigestion – is there a cure? *International Cataloguing and Bibliographic Control,* **28**(1), 3–7.

Edmunds, J. (1995) Le dépot légal: implications for cataloging. *Cataloging and Classification Quarterly,* **21**(1), 19–28.

Ellis, D. *et al.* (1998) In search of the unknown user: indexing, hypertext and the World Wide Web. *Journal of Documentation,* **54**(1), 28–47.

Fattahi, R. (1995) Anglo-American cataloguing rules in the online environment: a literature review. *Cataloging and Classification Quarterly,* **20**(2), 25–50.

Fineberg, G. 1998) Cooperative cataloging: LC promotes cooperation at Asian materials seminar. *Library of Congress Information Bulletin,* **57**(5), 120–121.

Geisselmann, F. (1997) National problems and international cooperation in classification *International Cataloguing and Bibliographic Control,* **26**(1), 21–23.

Gorman, M. (1998) The future of cataloguing and cataloguers. *International Cataloguing and Bibliographic Control,* **27**(4), 68–71.

Guy, M. (1996) The Bibliothèque Nationale de France and authority files: advances and perspectives in cooperation. *International Cataloguing and Bibliographic Control,* **25**(3) 59–62.

Hakala, J. (1999) Internet metadata and library cataloguing. *International Cataloguing and Bibliographic Control,* **28**(1), 21–25.

Harmon, J.C. (1996) The death of quality cataloging. *Journal of Academic Librarianship* **22**(4), 306–307.

Heaney, M. (1998) Models, materials and moments: the model of AACR. *Catalogue and Index,* (129), 1–3.

Heiner-Freiling, M. (1995) Subject indexing in the nineties: the situation in Germany. In *Subject indexing: principles and practices in the 90s. Proceedings of the IFLA satellite meeting held in Lisbon, Portugal, 17–18 August 1993.* München: K.G. Saur.

Hendrix, F. (1997) MARC harmonisation: strategies for the future. *Catalogue and Index*, (124), 1–5.

Hidderley, R. and Rafferty, P. (1997) Democratic indexing: an approach to the retrieval of fiction. In: H. Albrechtsen and C. Beghtol (eds) *Fiction, OPACs, networks. Proceedings of the 1st Research Seminar on Electronic Access to Fiction, Multicultural Knowledge Interaction, and Communication of Culture via Networks, Copenhagen, 11–13 November 1996.* Copenhagen: Royal School of Librarianship.

Hill, R.W. (1998) *Setting the record straight: a guide to the MARC format.* 3rd edn. Boston Spa: British Library National Bibliographic Service.

Holley, R.P. (1996) IFLA and international standards in the area of bibliographic control. *Cataloging and Classification Quarterly*, **21**(3/4), 17–36.

Holley, R.P. (1998) Results of a survey on bibliographic control and national bibliography, IFLA Section on Bibliography. *International Cataloguing and Bibliographic Control*, **27**(1), 3–7.

Holm, L.A. (1999a) Authority control in an international context in the new environment. *International Cataloguing and Bibliographic Control*, **28**(1), 11–13.

Holm, L.A. (1999b) ONE Project – results and experiences. *International Cataloguing and Bibliographic Control*, **28**(1), 29–33.

Holt, B. (1997) The new edition of the *UNIMARC Manual* and future work related to UNIMARC. *International Cataloguing and Bibliographic Control*, **26**(1), 20.

Hopkinson, A. (1999) Traditional communication formats: MARC is far from dead. *International Cataloguing and Bibliographic Control*, **28**(1), 17–21.

IFLA (1996) *Functional requirements for bibliographic records.* http://www.ifla.org/V11

IFLA (1998a) *Medium Term Programme 1998–2001.* The Hague: IFLA.

IFLA (1998b) Study group on the functional requirements for bibliographic records. *Functional requirements for bibliographic records. Final report.* München: K.G. Saur. [UBCIM Publications, 19.] http://www.ifla.org/V11/s13/frbr/frbr.htm

Intner, S.S. and Weihs, J. (1996) *Standard cataloging for school and public libraries.* Englewood Cliffs, NJ: Libraries Unlimited.

Jacobowitz, N.A. (1995) A comparison of AACR2R and French cataloging rules. *Cataloging and Classification Quarterly*, **20**(1), 47–49.

Kasajja, K.J. (1995) *A study of practices at the National Bibliographic Agency in the light of international bibliographic standards.* Dissertation for the degree of Bachelor of Library and Information Science, East African School of Library and Information Science, Makerere University.

Katić, T. (1997) Retrospective cataloguing of Croatian older books in UNIMARC. *International Cataloguing and Bibliographic Control*, **26**(4), 82–84.

Katuscák, D. (1996) New developments in librarianship and bibliographic control in Slovakia. *International Cataloguing and Bibliographic Control*, **25**(1), 16–19.

Kellermann, B.C. and Lor, P.J. (1997) *Report on the Seminar* [on accessing information resources in South Africa] *and Gauteng Declaration.* Pretoria: State Library.

Kelm, B. (1996) The subject authority file in Germany. *International Cataloguing and Bibliographic Control*, **25**(3), 62–67.

Kigongo-Bukenya, I.M.N. (1998) The state of Uganda bibliographic control and strategies into the 21st century. *International Cataloguing and Bibliographic Control*, **27**(2), 34–36.

Kucuk, M.E. and Hartley, R.J. (1996) Towards a national cooperative cataloguing system for manuscripts in Turkey. *International Cataloguing and Bibliographic Control*, **25**(3), 54–56.

Kuhagen, J.A. (1996) Standards for name and series authority records. *Cataloging and Classification Quarterly*, **21**(3/4), 131–154.

Lahary, D. (1999) UNIMARC as a cataloguing format in France. *International Cataloguing and Bibliographic Control*, **28**(2), 50–52.

Leazer, G.H. (1996) Recent research on the sequential bibliographic relationship and its implications for standards and the library catalog: an examination of serials. *Cataloging and Classification Quarterly*, **21**(3/4), 205–220.

Lee-Smeltzerk, J. (1996) Exploring the potential for cooperative cataloging of Chinese-language materials on an international basis: the role of library automation in Taiwan. *International Cataloguing and Bibliographic Control*, **23**(2), 41–56.

Leibowitz, F.R. (1995) Form and genre headings in serials cataloging. *Cataloging and Classification Quarterly*, **20**(3), 19–41.

Lenart, M. (1996) *Models for the provision of national bibliographic services in Europe. Final report. Translated and edited by the British Library.* Brussels, Luxembourg: European Commission. [DGXII-E/4.]

Library Association (1997) Rare Books Group. *Guidelines for the cataloguing of rare books.* London: RBG.

Lichtenbergova, E. and Stoklasova, B. (1999) UNIMARC in Czech libraries. *International Cataloguing and Bibliographic Control*, **28**(1), 52–54.

Lopes, M.I. (1996) Principles underlying subject heading languages: an international approach. *International Cataloguing and Bibliographic Control*, **25**(1), 10–12.

Lowenberg, E. (1998) The expanding world of alternative formats. *National Library [of Canada] News*, **30**(1), 7–8.

Ma, Y. *et al.* (1997) Cataloguing non-print resources in the United States and China: a comparative study of organization and access for selected electronic and audiovisual resources. *International Cataloguing and Bibliographic Control*, **26**(2), 46–49.

McCallum, S. (1996) What makes a standard? *International Cataloguing and Bibliographic Control*, **21**(3/4), 5–15.

McEwen, A. (1996) LCSH and the British Library: an international subject authority database? *Catalogue and Index*, (120), 1–6.

McGarry, D. (1996) Guidelines for subject authority and reference entries. *International Cataloguing and Bibliographic Control*, **25**(3), 67–68.

McIlwaine, I. (1996) Preparing traditional classifications for the future: universal decimal classification. *Cataloging and Classification Quarterly*, **21**(2), 49–58.

McKeen, L. (1998) Canadiana levels of cataloguing. *National Library [of Canada] News*, **30**(6), 1.

McKercher, B. and Xin Chang, P. (1995) A survey of the use of MARC formats in national libraries. *International Cataloguing and Bibliographic Control*, **24**(4), 57–59.

Madison, O.M.A. (1998a) *IFLA functional requirements for bibliographic records.* [Paper presented at the American Library Association's ALCTS PreConference, Washington DC, 26 June 1998.]

Madison, O.M.A. (1998b) *Standards for international bibliographic control: proposed basic data requirements for the national bibliographic record.* [Paper presented at the 1998

International Conference on National Bibliographic Services, Copenhagen, 25 November 1998.]

Mahmood, K. (1997) Subject cataloguing in Pakistani libraries. *International Cataloguing and Bibliographic Control*, **26**(3), 68–70.

Masevich, A.C and Zakharov, V.P. (1995) The role of machine-readable format in planning an electronic catalogue in the two largest libraries of Saint Petersburg. *International Cataloguing and Bibliographic Control*, **24**(1), 10–12.

Matheson, A. (1996) LCSH: the future for subject access. *Catalogue and Index*, (119), 1–9.

Merrick, M. (1998) Z39.50 and the virtual distributed catalogue. *Catalogue and Index*, (130), 1–4.

Meyer, R.W. (1997) The cataloger's future: a director's view. *Cataloging and Classification Quarterly*, **24**(1/2), 195–204.

Molto, M. and Svenonius, E. (1998) An electronic interface to AACR2. *Cataloging and Classification Quarterly*, **26**(1), 3–19.

Montviloff, N. (1997) An overview of the Anglo-American Cataloguing Code and comparison between the Code and Russian bibliographic standards. *International Cataloging and Bibliographic Control*, **26**(1), 17–19.

Münnich, M. (1997) Approach to AACR2 and RAK-WB or: no problems in future data exchange. *Cataloging and Classification Quarterly*, **24**(3/4), 3–16.

Murtomaa, E. (1996) Planning and creating name authority control: the Finnish experience. *International Cataloguing and Bibliographic Control*, **25**(3), 68–71.

Nicholson, D. *et al.* (1996) *Cataloguing the Internet: CATRIONA feasibility study*. London: The British Library. http://bubl.ac.uk/org/catriona/cat1rep.htm

Niet, M. de (1998) A single access point to information resources: the advanced information workstation of the National Library of the Netherlands. *Resource Sharing and Information Networks*, **13**(2), 29–37.

Noordermeer, T. (1999) A bibliographic link between publishers and national bibliographic agencies concerning electronic publications: Project BIBLINK. *International Cataloguing and Bibliographic Control*, **28**(1), 26–29.

Noordermeer, T. *et al.* (1998) Electronic library developments in the Netherlands. *LIBER Quarterly*, **8**(1), 57–80.

Oddy, P. (1996) *Future libraries, future catalogues*. London: Library Association Publishing.

Oddy, P. (1997) Remind, reassure, reward; issues in developing a cataloguing strategy. *Catalogue and Index*, (125), 1–6.

Ollier, A. (1996) MARC in time. *Catalogue and Index*, (119), 9.

Olson, N.B. (1995) *Cataloging Internet resources: a manual and practical guide*. Dublin, OH: OCLC.

Ouyporn, S. (1998) *National bibliographic control activities in Thailand: a county report*. [Paper presented at the IFLA/UBCIM Seminar on Bibliographic Control, Kuala Lumpur, 9–12 March 1988.]

Pappas, E. (1996) An analysis of eight RLIN-members' authority-controlled access points for purposes of speeding copy cataloging work flow. *Cataloging and Classification Quarterly*, **22**(1), 29–47.

Parmeggiani, C. (1995) Cooperative cataloguing in Italy. *Catalogue and Index*, (117), 1–3.

Pattie, L.W. and Cox, B.J. (1996) (eds) *Electronic resources: selection and bibliographic control*. New York: Haworth Press.

Pinedo, I. de and Magliano, C. (1997) Cooperative cataloguing: supply and exchange of data through a European project and a European Union feasibility study: the Italian experience. *International Cataloguing and Bibliographic Control*, **26**(2), 38–41.

Pollard, M. (1998) *California State University unified information access system: project report* http://uias.calstate.edu/uiasproject.html (27.08.98).

Pollitt, A.S. (1998) The key role of classification and indexing in view-based searching *International Cataloguing and Bibliographic Control*, **27**(2), 37–40.

Poulter, A. (1997a) CIGnet: the CIG guide to the Internet. *Catalogue and Index*, (125), 10.

Poulter, A. (1997b) The Internet as a tool for descriptive cataloguing. *Cataloging and Classification Quarterly*, **24**(1/2), 187–193.

Powell, A. (1998) *NewsAgent for libraries: notes on the use of Dublin Core.*
http://www.ukoln.ac.uk/metadata/newsagent/dcusage.html

Ralli, T. (1996) The impact of the Australian bibliographic network on Australian libraries *Alexandria*, **8**(1), 35–49.

Report (1997) on the international conference on the principles and future development of AACR held Toronto, October 23–25, 1997.

Riemer, J.J. (1996) (ed.) *Cataloging and classification standards and rules.* New York: Haworth Press.

Riesthuis, G.J.A. (1995) Sociological aspects of classification. *International Cataloguing and Bibliographic Control*, **24**(2), 35–37.

Salomonsen, A. (1995) Bibliographic control and UNIMARC activities in Scandinavia *International Cataloguing and Bibliographic Control*, **24**(1), 9–10.

Selivanova, J.G. and Extrem, M.V. (1996) Creation of an authority file system in the National Library of Russia. *International Cataloguing and Bibliographic Control*, **25**(4), 83–84.

Sha, V.T. (1995) Cataloguing Internet resources: the library approach. *Electronic Library* **13**(5), 467–476.

Shearer, J.R. and Thomas, A.R. (1997) *Cataloging and classification: trends, transformations teaching and training.* New York: Haworth Press.

Smith, W. (1998) PANDORA: providing long term access to Australia's online electronic publications. *Alexandria*, **10**(1), 63–75.

Snyder, H.L. (1998) The application of information technology to the bibliography of early printed books. *International Cataloguing and Bibliographic Control*, **27**(1), 8–12.

Soltani, P. (1996) Translation and expansion of classification systems in the Arab countries and Iran. *International Cataloguing and Bibliographic Control*, **25**(1), 13–15.

Spicher, K.M. (1996) The development of the MARC format. *Cataloging and Classification Quarterly*, **21**(3/4), 75–90.

Stern, B. (1996) Internationalizing the rules in AACR2: adopting and translating AACR2 for use in non-Anglo-American and non-English-speaking cataloging environments *Cataloging and Classification Quarterly*, **21**(3/4), 37–60.

Stoker, D. (1998) A beginner's guide to metadata. *CIQM Newsletter*, **3**(1), 1–30.

Strutt, S E. (1997) Cataloguing and the Internet: considerations at the British Library *Library Review*, **46**(7), 490–499.

Sweeney, R. (1995) The international use of the Dewey Decimal Classification. *International Cataloguing and Bibliographic Control*, 24(4), 61–64.

Tabb, W. (1997) The Program for Cooperative Cataloging: mission, goals, and potential for international cooperation. *International Cataloguing and Bibliographic Control*, **26**(4) 75–78.

Terekhova, L.A. (1996) Generating authority files for the multi-lingual database of the Rudomino Library for Foreign Literature. *International Cataloguing and Bibliographic Control*, **25**(4), 84–86.

Thomas, A.R. (1995) (ed.) *Classification: options and opportunities*. New York: Haworth Press.

Thomas, A.R. (1997) The work-wide Web: a cataloging career for every librarian? *International Cataloguing and Bibliographic Control*, **24**(1/2), 5–22.

Thomas, A.R.S. (1996) New roles for classification in libraries and information networks: an excerpt bibliography. *Cataloging and Classification Quarterly*, 21 (2), 91–118.

Thomas, S.E. (1996) The core bibliographic record and the program for cooperative cataloging. *Cataloging and Classification Quarterly*, **21**(3/4), 91–108.

Tillett, B. (1995) *21st century authority control: what is it and how do we get there?* [Paper presented at OCLC Preconference Seminar, ALA Midsummer, Chicago.]

Towsey, M. (1995) Does anyone out there want a cataloguer? *Catalogue and Index*, (117), 4–5.

Traiser, W. (1995) Die Deutsche Bibliothek und die Basis-klassifikation. *Dialog mit Bibliotheken*, **7**, H.2, 37–44.

Tsvetkova, I. and Skvortsov, V. (1999) Adaptation of UNIMARC as Russian exchange format. *International Cataloguing and Bibliographic Control*, **28**(2), 54–55.

UKOLN (1998) *Metadata resources: Dublin Core*.
    http://www.ukoln.ac.uk/metadata/resources/dc.html

Varniené, R. (1995) UBC and UNIMARC activities in Lithuania. *International Cataloguing and Bibliographic Control*, **24**(1), 8–9.

Varniené, R. (1999) Bibliographic control in the context of the integrated library systems of the Baltic countries. *International Cataloguing and Bibliographic Control*, **28**(1), 33–35.

Velluci, S.L. (1996) Future catalogers: essential colleagues or anachronisms. *College and Research Libraries News*, **57**(), 442–443.

Vitiello, G (1996) The production and the marketing of national bibliographic services in Europe. *Alexandria*, **8**(2), 97–116.

Waneck, K. and Hansen, R.D. (1997) Bibliographic control in Denmark. *International Cataloguing and Bibliographic Control*, **26**(2), 28–31.

Weihs, J. (1997) (ed.) *The principles and future of AACR: proceedings of the International Conference on the Principles and Future Development of AACR, Toronto, Ontario, Canada*. Ottawa: Canadian Library Association.

Willer, M. (1996a) International and national standards in old and rare book cataloguing. In: *International cataloguing standards: their implementation in Slovenia and Croatia*. Praha: Narodni knihovna.

Willer, M. (1996b) *UNIMARC u teoriji i praski* [UNIMARC in theory and practice]. Rijeka: Naklada Benja.

Williamson, N.J. (1996) Standards and rules for subject access. *Cataloging and Classification Quarterly*, **21**(3/4), 155–176.

Knowledge management

8

Michael Koenig

Introduction

This chapter aims to cover the birth and growth of the concept of knowledge management (KM) and considers among other things its relationship to librarianship. Knowledge management has taken the business world by storm. Although it is a recent phenomenon, this field is burgeoning more rapidly than any other information and management enthusiasm of the second half of the 20th century. This enthusiasm for KM is also evidenced by hundreds of published books and more than a thousand articles in the periodical literature, innumerable websites, numerous conferences, workshops and symposia organized by professional associations, and various studies on many of the Fortune 500 companies. In the USA alone, knowledge management consulting firms have been paid $1.5 billion in 1996; this figure is projected to be $5 billion by 2001. The potential of KM for changing the world of corporate librarianship in particular, and librarianship in general, is dramatic. However, the connection between KM and librarianship is not as direct as one might expect or infer from its name. To see why that is so, we must trace the rapid and complex evolution of the term and of the concept(s) which it now represents.

Knowledge management is a surprisingly recent phenomenon, developing only in the mid-1990s. It is however true that the term appears to have been used first in the context of library and information work: Marchand (1985), then Dean of the School of Information Studies at Syracuse University, coined it in the 1980s as a descriptor for the final level in his stage hypothesis of information systems development (Koenig, 1992). However, the term as presently used appears to have been re-coined more or less anonymously somewhere in the big six (now big five) accountancy consulting firms.

In somewhat metaphorical and equestrian terms KM may be described as the intranet out of intellectual capital. 'Intellectual Capital represents the awareness that information is a factor of production, as economists would phrase it, in a category with land, labour, capital and energy' (Talero and Gaudette, 1995) – in short the awareness in the business community that knowledge was an important organizational resource that needed to be nurtured, sustained and, if possible, accounted for. Peter Drucker, as he commonly does, put it perhaps most compellingly:

> We now know that the source of wealth is something, specifically human knowledge. If we apply knowledge to tasks that we obviously know how to do, we call it productivity. If we apply knowledge to tasks that are new and different, we call it innovation. Only knowledge allows us to achieve those two goals.
> (quoted in Hibbard, 1997)

Intellectual capital as it was first defined had two major components: Information and knowledge capital, and structural capital.

INFORMATION AND KNOWLEDGE CAPITAL	STRUCTURAL CAPITAL

Information and knowledge capital was of course the organization's information and knowledge, but the informal and unstructured as well as the formal. This was the first major contribution of intellectual capital: the recognition of the importance of unstructured knowledge, tacit knowledge as it later came to be called, knowledge that is customarily and traditionally outside the domain of the librarian.

The structural capital comprised, of course, the mechanisms in place to take advantage of the information and knowledge capital, the mechanisms to capture, store, retrieve and communicate that information and knowledge – library and information work – at least potentially so, though it was often unrecognized as such in the business community, primarily because of the focus on unstructured and tacit knowledge, items not generally seen as within the librarian's domain.

What was also new within the intellectual capital movement, the second major contribution, was the attempt not just to recognize the importance of knowledge, but also to quantify and measure it in some utilitarian fashion. This is also an activity not customarily undertaken by librarians, as acidly noted and commented on by Matarazzo and Prusak (1996). The attempt to quantify knowledge and information proved very difficult, not at all a surprisingly result. Information, let alone knowledge, is an extraordinarily amorphous and diffuse notion to measure, and consequently relatively little progress was made in that direction. A few companies, e.g. Scandia corporation with its intellectual capital supplement to its annual report being the most famous example (Edvinsson, 1995), made and still makes noble efforts to quantify, or at least to chart progress and changes in, the organization's intellectual capital. But very few other companies have followed its lead, at least for external reporting as Scandia does. Edvinsson (1997) elaborated further and described the Scandia model in detail, and this continues to be the most developed model of intellectual capital.

The intellectual capital movement was however very successful in obtaining publicity for the importance of information and for being aware of the importance of valuing and nurturing intellectual capital. Stewart wrote a number of prominently featured articles (Stewart, 1991a, 1991b, 1994, 1995) in *Fortune*, of which probably the most compelling was 'Your company's most valuable asset: intellectual capital' (Stewart, 1994). In the same period, the Conference Board seized on the theme and initiated a sequence of high profile meetings at which intellectual capital (and now KM) is the central theme.

In that same period, the Internet, hitherto solely an academic and not-for-profit enthusiasm, burst into the consciousness of the business community. The realization rapidly followed that Internet technology could be used to build an internal network, an intranet to link an organization together, using the Internet and its conventions for data display and access, but limiting access to the members of one's own organization. Local Area Networks (LANS) and Wide Area Networks (WANS) had been used for some time for that purpose. However Internet-based intranets were far easier to set up and administer and, even more importantly, the tools for employees to put information on the Net and to access it were far superior.

What followed next was an extension of the intranet concept, the awareness that the same Internet technology could be used to facilitate communications with one's customers, as well as within the organization itself. In short the intranet could be extended to include customers and/or suppliers, in which case it becomes an extranet. Of course, electronic communications with suppliers and customers had been increasing since the 1970s – EDI (electronic data interchange) and JIT (just-in-time inventory) being examples – but the intranet/extranet very much accelerated that process. Thus the definition of intellectual capital expanded to include the customer's knowledge and input, customer capital.

Information and Knowledge Capital		Structural Capital
	Customer Capital	

The inclusion of customer capital was not unrelated to the popularity of total quality management (TQM), in which responding to customer needs and demands and soliciting customer input were key components.

Concurrent with intellectual capital, and very much reinforcing it, was the notion of the 'balanced score card' (Kaplan and Norton, 1992): the thesis that traditional financial reporting was too narrow in its outlook and that in particular it focused only on the present and the past, with little or no thought to the future. It was argued that instead there should be a 'balanced score card', which included not only the traditional financial measures, but also measured other things such as comparative product quality, customer satisfaction and customer turnover; things that were more indicative of current performance and better indicators of likely future performance. Intellectual capital was of course one of the obvious items that begged to be included in the balanced score card.

KM was also one consequence of the dramatic increase in the volume of data and information made available to the typical office or professional (knowledge) worker, yet much information also exists as tacit knowledge, unknown and unavailable to most people. The paradox is that much of the available information is of poor quality and poorly organized, while much of the most useful information remains invisible. Information and knowledge assets can seem overwhelming and very confusing to the user, as almost every knowledge worker now relies on electronic access to information via WWW, the Internet, groupware and similar technologies. KM is an attempt to resolve this problem, this paradox.

The new paradigm: knowledge management

The first organizations fully to realize the potential of intranets were typically the larger, worldwide consulting firms which had long realized that the commodity they dealt in was information and knowledge. An example of a central concern to such organizations is: How can a consultant in Valparaiso, working for a company based in Chicago, be made aware of work by another consultant in Stockholm, work that the Valparaiso consultant could use to respond authoritatively and convincingly to a request for a proposal, and be awarded the contract?

These firms saw the intranet as an ideal tool with which to share and disseminate knowledge throughout their organization's scattered offices. They recognized that the confluence of the intranet with the treatment of information and knowledge as an asset was substantially more than just an expansion of the concept of intellectual capital. The phrase they chose to describe this new confluence, and in particular the intranet-based systems they were developing, was 'knowledge management'. Whether the re-coiners of the term were aware of Marchand's (1983, 1985) earlier use is not clear.

From there the concept of KM continued to expand. Senge's (1990) *The fifth discipline: the art and practice of the learning organization* had established something of a cult following, but it had not made a major impact. With the intranet driven KM, however, it meshed perfectly. The thesis of the learning organization, somewhat oversimplified, is that what ultimately creates and distinguishes a successful organization is its success in creating and sharing information and knowledge, in short its success at learning. The obvious corollary is that to be successful an organization must create a culture that fosters learning. One can say, to summarize perhaps too briefly, that the concept of the learning organization focused on the creation of knowledge, while KM as it was originally construed, focused on the acquisition, structuring, retention and dissemination of that knowledge. What has happened is that KM has expanded explicitly to include the concept of the learning organization, expanded to include knowledge creation as well as knowledge sharing.

A new term that has recently emerged, representing an extension of KM further in that same direction, is the faster learning organization (FLO). This is the goal of KM: to create a FLO that will thereby have a major competitive advantage over other organizations. In the words of LeFauve (1998), Senior Vice-President of General Motors, President of General Motors University and previously Chairman of GM's Saturn Division: 'The only long-term competitive advantage that a company has is how effectively it manages its company knowledge.'

Another important perception that has accelerated the enthusiasm for KM has been the 'richness versus reach' thesis of Evans and Wurster (1997). They point out that the nature of communications has drastically changed: until now, one had a choice of richness or reach in communication, but one could not achieve both simultaneously. A face-to-face conversation, for example, was rich in content, nuance and interactivity, but its reach was small, one or at most a few persons. A mass mailing, radio or TV broadcast had great reach, but was thin on content, nuance, and interactivity. Communication strategies were always an either–or choice.

Now with the Internet, the argument runs, we can craft systems that simultaneously provide both richness and reach. This transforms not only how we think about communications, but also how we think about organizations and how they do business. This thesis, which is in a sense an instantiation of Gibson and Jackson's (1987) 'Domain III, transformation' and Koenig's (1986, 1992) 'Stage III', has been incorporated into the canon of KM as a very persuasive argument on why the time is right for a thorough rethink of methods of sharing information and knowledge in the organization. Further, it can be argued that the removal of the richness or reach dichotomy means that changes will not be gradual and incremental, but major and dramatic, and that an organization which does not keep up not only risks being left very far behind, but risks being put out of business very quickly.

Knowledge management – the portmanteau term

Those dramatic changes harken back to the vision of business process reengineering. However, the relationship between KM and business process reengineering is subtle and fascinating. The latter, stripped to its essentials, simply meant redesigning the operations and workflow of organizations to take advantage of the capabilities of information technology and electronic communications. However, as it was implemented, business process reengineering came to have a sub-theme of not only making organizations more efficient and more effective, but also leaner and meaner, with the dark side to that definition – at least to the employees affected – of downsizing, euphemistically referred to as rightsizing and not always so beneficial to the organization either.

Both KM and business process reengineering are in one sense derived from the same foundation – that we are no longer bound by the constraints of print-on-paper technology. In a response to the argument that there was a 'productivity paradox' (Banks, 1989), the economist David (1990) pointed out that there is a fascinating parallel between information technology and the introduction of electric power and the electric motor, and reveals how surprisingly long it took for that technology to have a measurable impact on industrial productivity.

Koenig and Wilson (1996) extend the David observation and link it to business process reengineering. The reason posited by David as to why the dynamo and the grid took so long to have an effect was that major industrial redesign, manufacturing process redesign as it were, had to be accomplished first. New factories that were built to take advantage of unit drive capability (machines being driven directly by an electric motor, rather than connected by belts and pulleys and shafts to a central mechanical power source) had to be constructed before a dramatic productivity effect was seen. Koenig and Wilson (1996) argue that business process redesign is the factory rebuilding of the computer age and the corollary is that when this has been accomplished, we will then enter an era of noticeably improved productivity. They draw the analogy that business process reengineering is to the limitations of delivering information via print-on-paper technology as the manufacturing process redesign that was necessary to take advantage of electric motors and the electric process distribution network (and which, if you will, produced a productivity paradox in the late 19th century between the introduction of electric power and the subsequent dramatic productivity gains of the early 20th century) was to the limitation of delivering power by shafts, gears, pulleys and belts.

Business process reengineering		manufacturing process redesign
– is to –	as	– was to –
print-on-paper technology		shaft, gear, pulley and belt technology
	or	
Business process reengineering		manufacturing process redesign
– is to –	as	– was to –
computer and information technology		the dynamo and electrical technology

Similarly, it can be argued that KM came about because of the same awareness of the limitations of previous communication technologies, particularly print on paper. The 'richness and reach' observations of Evans and Wurster (1997) make precisely that point.

Despite the joint parentage of business process redesign and KM however, a key thrust of what KM has come to mean in the business community is that it is to a large degree a rejection of, or at least a partial rejection of and a reaction against, the excesses of business process reengineering, which may lead to corporate downsizing with its combination of human suffering among those downsized and insecurity among those remaining, and knowledge lost, carried away by those who were downsized. The word now being mentioned, often in the same breath with KM, is 'trust'.

This is perhaps a trifle surprising, but it is also in fact quite logical. Good communication and extensive knowledge sharing are not likely to happen unless there is an atmosphere of trust and some organizational commitment to the employee. KM is in effect being presented as the antidote to the trust and the knowledge lost in ill-conceived and ill-executed rightsizings when valuable employees were let go. Their knowledge went with them and a reservoir of mistrust and insecurity was left behind. As Prusak (1998) bluntly puts it, 'reengineering is the enemy of knowledge'.

Social capital is another frequently mentioned facet of the same recognition. In this business context, social capital is operationally defined as those behavioral norms that lower transaction costs and enable cooperation. What norm better to enhance communications, transactions and cooperation than trust? It is interesting to observe that at the same time there is an increasing recognition at the macroeconomic level of the importance of trust, consistency, and predictability in facilitating international trade and for inducing foreign direct investment (*Economist*, 1998; World Bank, 1998).

In another sense, social capital is what has been added to intellectual capital to create KM. Prusak (1998) of IBM employs the following graphic:

Knowledge resources	Social capital	Infrastructure
Explicit	Culture	Processes
Tacit	Trust	Resources
Formal	Knowledge Behaviour	Technology
Informal	Human capital issues	Metrics

It is very similar to the graphic for intellectual capital, but with the 'customer capital' component replaced by 'social capital'. It is now assumed that customer capital is included in all of the above, the infrastructure extended to include the customer, the knowledge resources including the customer, and the social capital embracing the relationships, not just within the organization, but with the customer (and the supplier to whom one is a customer) as well.

Two of the best articles relating to social capital are by Ulrich (1998), whose article's title is particularly pithy 'Intellectual capital = competence x commitment'; and by Kim and Maubourgne (1997) who state the importance of ensuring that in the information economy employees perceive that the process as well as the outcome is fair. In fact, it is perhaps not too strong to say that KM has expanded to become a portmanteau term intended to include all of the positive aspects of the management fads of the last decade and a half, while avoiding their excesses.

Another very useful graphic visualization of the expanded concept of KM depicts the knowledge management framework.

KNOWLEDGE MANAGEMENT FRAMEWORK

C	HIGH	INNOVATION	RESPONSIVENESS
O	INTERACTIVITY		
L			
L			
A			
B			
O			
R			
A			
T			
I			
O	LOW	COMPETENCY	PRODUCTIVITY
N	INTERACTIVITY		

INDIVIDUAL   GROUP

KNOWLEDGE

What this is intended to represent is that as KM enhances knowledge sharing and collaboration, the results achieved are:

- innovation: in areas of high interaction and individual knowledge;
- competency: in areas of low interaction and individual knowledge;
- responsiveness: in areas of high interaction and group knowledge;
- productivity: in areas of low interaction and group knowledge.

This graphic, promoted by IBM, conveys particularly well how broad the concept of KM has become in the business community.

Another useful graphic aid to thinking about KM depicts the knowledge management progression.

> THE KNOWLEDGE MANAGEMENT PROGRESSION
>
> KNOWLEDGE MANAGEMENT
> GROUPWARE
> E-MAIL

The idea here is that typically the first extensive use of information technology to enhance knowledge sharing is the widespread use of e-mail. Then comes broad use of groupware, software designed to help teams work together in an electronic environment, and then the apex is true KM, including transformation in the culture of the organization to encourage and reward information creation and sharing.

For a quick background on current KM thinking, the best source is probably the twelve-part series carried by the Monday editions of the *Financial Times* from 1 February to 19 April, 1999, covering KM and related areas. The series was aimed at fostering the management of information and of the technology that captures, stores, and distributes and processes it inside and outside their organization.

Davenport and Marchand (1999) stressed that KM projects have a significant element of information management, but beyond that KM facilitates the creation of knowledge and requires management that facilitates the way people share and apply it. An end note is that the companies which prosper with KM will be those that realize it is as much about managing people as information. Despres and Chauvel (1999) point out that as the number of KM books, articles, software products and potential applications increase massively, mapping (plotting) different KM activities can help companies plan how best to extend them in the future. Earl and Scott (1999a), in analysing the role of the chief knowledge officer (CKO), stress that his/her job is to maximize the creation, discovery and dissemination of knowledge within the organization. According to them the best CKOs fulfill four roles:

- willing to champion risky new initiatives (entrepreneur);
- able to match new ideas with business needs (consultant);
- fully information technology literate (technologist);
- able to design settings and processes to maximize knowledge and its utilization (environmentalist).

Prusak (1999), on the other hand, argues that people value many things without expecting to be able to measure their value, and companies should make knowledge visible through knowledge activities, outcomes and investments. Murray (1999) suggests that first companies should know the desired results and then concentrate on how to achieve them. He argues further that KM is primarily a 'people and process' issue, and an effective strategy is to create and nurture 'virtual teams' which can leverage knowledge across geographical and organizational boundaries. The consensus of the series is clearly that KM may be a product of the information age, but there is far more to it than information technology (Manchester, 1999) because it involves employees sharing their know-how with each other, via networked databases and other means.

In summary so far, KM has grown into a far broader, more pervasive, more powerful notion than it started out to be or than its name would suggest. In fact, there is beginning to be a reaction in some circles that the term knowledge management is not the appropriate phrase. It is argued that it is too specific for a concept that is really much broader and also that it is perhaps somewhat impolitic, in that users, employees and customers do not particularly relish the implication that their knowledge is being managed; rather they would prefer terminology which would imply that they are being supported in their undertakings. Three of many phrases that have been suggested to replace knowledge management are 'knowledge-sharing', 'knowledge networking' and 'knowledge mobilization'. All three terms are certainly more descriptive of what the phrase knowledge management now means.

Whether any substitute term will replace knowledge management, even if substantially more descriptive, is another matter. It may be that the term knowledge management will be replaced by a more descriptive term, just as the term management information systems (MIS) was at least partially replaced by decision support systems (DSS). However, this only came about because MIS got something of a black eye. The authors suspect that a more likely parallel is the history of the term 'word processing'; a term which we now take for granted, but which in its nascent period provoked much discussion and numerous suggested alternatives. The term 'word processing' became the standard through its use and promotion by IBM. A similar standardization is likely to unfold for knowledge management. For those with an interest in epistemology and with the antecedents of KM, the article by Pemberton (1998) 'Knowledge management (KM) and the epistemic tradition', is a fascinating read.

Unlike some recent developments which appeared like a flash in the pan and then faded (for example, business process reengineering, information resource management, total quality management), KM appears to be on solid ground and demonstrating staying power. While KM has evolved as a product of the information age, it has clearly added value during its evolution. It is hard to find fault with the thesis that, other factors being equal, the organization that learns faster will be more competitive and more successful.

Knowledge management themes

Having sketched the evolution and current domain of KM, the domain can be filled in by briefly discussing some of the major themes running through what the business community understands as knowledge management.

Communities and collaboration versus silos

'Silo' is the hot new buzzword – as in 'how do you integrate the silos?'. The silo here is a metaphor for the unit which is too self-contained, into which stuff gets dumped in and taken out, but which has little or no communication with the other silos (products, regions, divisions, units, etc.) that constitute the organization. The solution to the silo problem is to create communities and thereby further collaboration. This is part of the reaction against the excesses of business process reengineering. The silos are, if you will, what was left after business process reengineering removed much of middle management and flattened the organization. That middle management had provided much of the connective tissue of the organization. They provided the communication channels that kept the units from becoming silos. KM is now seen as the repair mechanism for business process reengineering, presumably both more effective and less expensive than replacing those middle management and staff positions.

Most of the concrete applications of KM described to date consist of creating and supporting communities of shared interest and information need. These communities might be the sales representatives of a pharmaceutical company or those persons at the World Bank and their clients interested in road transport and logistics. In some cases, as in the former, the community already to a degree exists formally and hierarchically or, as in the latter, it exists informally and horizontally. At the World Bank, for example, there are now some 70 'knowledge areas' grouped into fifteen large sections; at IBM there are more than 50 'competency networks'. The intended consequence of these communities is not only knowledge sharing, but also collaboration and thereby, of course, enhanced productivity.

Tacit knowledge

Tacit knowledge is now the term for the knowledge that is in people's heads or in their own files, as distinguished from explicit knowledge that exists in documents or databases. Current KM thinking is focused on establishing the structure and climate to enable and encourage those who have knowledge, to share it. There is close to no mention of capturing that knowledge, particularly in the now somewhat tarnished sense of artificial intelligence and the 'knowledge engineer' who would capture the expertise of the expert on diesel/electric locomotive repair trouble shooting before he retired. What exists is the encouragement and establishment of systems to enable employees to submit a 'best practices' description of how they accomplish something so that others can use it. The information may be screened and edited before it goes on the systems (particularly, for example, in pharmaceutical companies which are subject to Food and Drug Administration approval concerning what they may say about a therapeutic agent), but the knowledge is input by the user, not by a 'knowledge engineer' or 'knowledge manager'. This is an important point for information professionals to recognize: that there has been substantial disillusionment in the business community with the over-hyped 'artificial intelligence' and 'expert systems', and with the software packages and consulting firms that promised to set up AI systems for companies. There have been AI successes to be sure, but they have been at the tactical and near clerical level, for example, monitoring credit card transactions for plausibility or likely misuse. They have not been at the strategic level envisioned by the proponents of KM, nor have they been of the collaborative synergistic kind yielding new knowledge or faster learning.

One frustrating problem is that while KM puts great emphasis upon tacit knowledge (Hibbard, 1997; Kleiner and Ruth, 1997; Liedtka *et al.*, 1997; Davenport, 1998; Duhon, 1998), there is very little reported upon in the literature that is concrete. A good system to capture and exploit tacit knowledge is inevitably rather specific to the culture and context of that organization and it is also (even more important) a significant competitive advantage, not something that the organization wants made public. The two most useful discussions are by Davenport (1998), who focuses on customers' knowledge, and by Kleiner and Ruth (1997), who describe a process they call a learning history to capture important project-related tacit knowledge within the organization. Despite the paucity of concrete reports, tacit knowledge is heavily emphasized. Paying insufficient attention to tacit knowledge is Fahey and Prusak's (1998) deadly sin number five.

Incentives and rewards

Effective knowledge sharing requires rewarding those who input information into the system and contribute something useful. Otherwise, what motivation do employees have to contribute information that will, for example, improve the performance of other sales representatives relative to their own, thereby decreasing their own year-end bonus? Changing compensation and incentive systems is not something that organizations do readily, or lightly; it is an undertaking fraught with peril and with unintended and often unfortunate consequences. A frequent complaint among knowledge management system implementers is how slow and difficult it is to get top management to make such changes.

Customer knowledge

A pervasive theme in business discussion of KM is the importance of including the customer in the scope of KM systems so as to incorporate and leverage this expertise. This is considered key for a number of reasons:

- better and more timely design of new products and services;
- early warning and competitive intelligence;
- customer commitment and loyalty;
- the synergy of collaboration.

The emphasis here is upon the exchange of knowledge, ideas and opinions, for example, not just the transaction data currently exchanged with just-in-time inventory or supply chain management systems.

Top management support and change agentry

Another major theme is that KM is about a whole new way of operating, indeed the transformation of the organization. As such, it requires knowledge management professionals to be change agents, which in turn requires top management support. Better yet is the direct involvement of top management if the effort is to be successful.

One of the best techniques to get a feel for the nature of KM is to examine the 'perils and pitfalls' and 'golden rules' class of articles that caution the practitioner about what not to do and what to be sure to do. KM already has several excellent articles in this genre. Fahey and Prusack (1998) delineate the eleven deadliest sins of knowledge management:

- Not developing a working definition of knowledge.
- Emphasizing knowledge stock to the detriment of knowledge flow.
- Viewing knowledge as existing predominantly outside the heads of individuals.
- Not understanding that a fundamental intermediate purpose of management knowledge is to create shared context.
- Paying little heed to the role and importance of tacit knowledge.
- Disentangling knowledge for its uses.
- Downplaying thinking and reasoning.
- Focusing on the past and the present and not the future.
- Failing to recognize the importance of experimentation.
- Substituting technological contact for human interface.
- Seeking to develop direct measures of knowledge.

Davenport (1997) lists only seven 'known evils':

- If we build it . . .
- Let's put the personnel manual online!

- None dare call it knowledge.
- Every man a knowledge manager.
- Justification by faith.
- Restricted access.
- Bottoms up!

In a later and influential article, Davenport *et al.* (1998) examine successful knowledge management projects and argue that they tend to have eight factors in common:

- Link to economic performance or industry value.
- Technical and organization infrastructure.
- Standard flexible knowledge structure.
- Knowledge-friendly culture.
- Clear purpose and language.
- Change in motivational practices.
- Multiple channels for knowledge transfer.
- Senior management support.

Careful perusal of these three articles is strongly recommended for anyone interested in KM. The names of the errors and success factors above are often cryptic and reading them in context is essential.

In a report prepared for the World Bank (KM is not after all the exclusive province of the for-profit sector), Arthur Andersen Consulting (1996) enumerated six 'characteristics of world class knowledge management systems':

- Leadership.
- Culture.
- Organizational structure.
- Knowledge collection and sharing processes.
- Measurement.
- Technology.

These are rather too generic and therefore rather less useful than the lists above.

Hansen *et al.* (1999) argue that there are basically two fundamental approaches to KM – codification and personalization – and that knowledge management systems are typically an 80–20 balance, with some firms emphasizing the codification, for example Andersen Consulting and Dell, while others, for example, McKinney and Hewlett-Packard, emphasizing the personalization. They point out that a firm must think carefully about its knowledge management strategy and align this strategy with its business operations and goods; codification if an organization's products are standardized and mature and if people rely primarily on explicit knowledge; and personalization if an organization's products are customized and innovative, and if people rely primarily on tacit knowledge. This distinction is in fact the vertical dimensions in a graphic (below) that IBM has used for some time.

KNOWLEDGE MANAGEMENT STRATEGIES

	EXPLOIT	EXPLORE
COLLECT (stuff)	HARVEST Example: Best practices	HUNTING Example: Data mining
CONNECT (people)	HARNESS Example: Response teams	HYPOTHESIZE Examples: Brainstorming Scenario analysis

The obvious point for librarians is that they have most to offer when the codification strategy is the more appropriate and more emphasized. Indeed, the authorities describe the codification model thus: 'In the codification model, managers need to implement a system that is much like a traditional library.' The larger point is of course that one size does not fit all, and that librarians or everyone else should not recommend a KM solution without thoroughly understanding the context in which it is going to be employed.

Hansen *et al.* (1999) go on to present a further point that KM systems are almost invariably fish (80% codification, 20% personalization) or fowl (80% personalization, 20% codification) and that straddles – something like a 50–50 mix – are a sign of a lack of focus and are to be avoided. The advice is very specific: 'Do not straddle.' The author of this chapter would argue that while the advice to match the strategy with the context is admirable, the 'do not straddle' advice is simple minded. One can think, for example, of the pharmaceutical industry, where a heavy emphasis on codification is required: codified access to compounds synthesized, screening results, research notebooks, etc., is *de rigeur*. The difference, however, between the less successful and the successful pharmaceutical companies in terms of their research revenues, as revealed by Koenig (1983), is that the less successful companies do indeed have an 80–20 emphasis upon codification, while the more successful companies, though putting no less emphasis upon codification, place an equal emphasis upon personalization and have deliberately adopted a 50–50 approach, precisely the straddle that Hansen *et al.* (1999) advise wielding. A related concern is that different parts of different levels of the same organization may need different strategies. The basic advice to carefully match strategy with context is however incontestable.

Another good view of the context specificity of KM is the graphic approach of Despres and Chauvel (1999). They class KM into five stages: scan and map; capture and create; package and store; share and apply; transform and innovate. These stages are one dimension of a matrix. The second is the content dimension, individual, group or organization content, and for each of these, whether explicit or tacit content. Various KM endeavours can then be placed on this matrix. Of course KM should ideally span all five stages, but the map does allow one to place and compare different emphases.

This section has emphasized the evolution of KM and what it has come to mean, precisely because this meaning has become such a broad and inclusive term. It means so much more and has acquired so much more baggage than professionals with a background in library and information work would expect. It is important for us to understand what the business community means by KM and what it expects. A good example of the often too narrow view of KM is a recent article (Field, 1998) in *Information Outlook* (the former *Special Libraries*). This is correct in what it says, but is rather too limited and narrow. There is, for example, no examination of tacit knowledge and the discussion of and examples of collaboration are far more limited than what is aimed for in practice.

The transformation of library and information work

KM has impacted the LIS area in two specific ways: the transformation of the work of library and other information workers in the corporate arena; and the transformation of education for library and information work. Predictably, the first transformation is proceeding much more rapidly than the latter.

An excellent overview of what KM is, how it relates to librarianship and the roles of the librarian in KM is that by Broadbent (1998), someone familiar with both the general business and the library contexts. She makes the same point that we emphasize in the introduction explaining the evolution of KM – the breadth of the term and how much more it encompasses than we librarians, with our specific cultural background and experience, would expect:

> Knowledge management is not owned by any one group in an organization, nor by any one profession or industry. But if librarians and information specialists want to be key players in the emerging knowledge management phenomenon, they need to understand the multiple perspectives of the other players.

Knowledge management requires a holistic and multidisciplinary approach to management processes and an understanding of the dimensions of knowledge work.

A similar work, but not so grounded in specifics, is by Stear and Wecksell (1997) on 'information resource center management', which is far more *au courant* than its title would indicate. Good discussions of the relationship between intellectual capital, knowledge management and corporate planning are by Wiig (1997) and Demarest (1997). Another useful review of the potential role of librarians is by Cropley (1998).

A pertinent analysis of the possible ranges of roles for library and information workers is contained in the article by Chase (1998), which reviews a delineation of information roles emanating from Arthur Andersen (Williams and Bukowitz, 1997) and from Skyrme and Amidon (1998); Chase concludes that a role he describes as knowledge navigator, which could be 'likened to a spider at the center of a gigantic "knowledge web" ' offers librarians a once-in-a-lifetime opportunity to reinvent themselves as value-adding professionals.

The most direct effect of KM is in the transformation of library and information work. The easiest place to see that effect is in the organization or reorganization of corporate libraries and information centres.

Many articles discuss in the abstract the transformation of the library/ information centre to a virtual workspace and the accompanying trans-formation of the librarian's role (Ghilardi, 1994; Pigott, 1996; Marshall, 1997). More instructive are articles that give concrete examples of change and transformation.

One of the more detailed and revealing accounts of the transformation of a specific corporate library/information centre is by Steele (1998), recounting how United Technologies Corporation (UTC) changed the way it delivered information services. Ten libraries were closed, with the librarians becoming 'information managers', moved closer to the customer and linked electronically with the customers and among themselves. In addition 'research analyst' positions were created to summarize and filter information, write reports and point out trends and make recommendations. As part of the publicity campaign for the new organization, about 16,000 letters were sent out. The metaphor for the new organization was that the information network was the user's toolbox, with the three components of the toolbox being desktop access, global information support (with reference service provided via the UTC intranet) and on-site research and analysis. The toolbox metaphor is supported by a small toolbox-shaped box of chocolates, with each chocolate wrapped in foil with a logo reflecting one of the icons from the information network home page. The thrust of these changes is to transform the provision of information services from the reactive, the 'we're ready when you are' (Steele, 1998) style, to the participatory style with information managers and analysts participating in project teams.

Remeikis and Koska (1996) describe in comparable detail the building of a KM infrastructure at Booz Allen and Hamilton. They stress both the creation of an IPC, the information professional community, the renamed research library and the creation of KOL, knowledge online, the repository not only of documents and information but of Booz Allen success stories; the tacit knowledge of how 'it' was done well under previous circumstances. A new job category of 'information manager' was created, the job requirement being people who 'have deep industry knowledge combined with an information science background and an in-depth understanding of their role as change agents within the firm'. The account is striking in the extent to which Booz Allen was ahead of the curve in recognizing the organization dynamics aspects of knowledge management, and the degree to which the potential contributions of information professionals were recognized early on.

Another excellent view of change occasioned by KM is by Ryske and Sebastian (1999), reporting on a change in role of a library at Andersen Consulting, which used to focus on information technology issues but has become a knowledge centre adding value to consultants working in information technology. The phrase 'value added' rather than 'service provider' is a key descriptor of the cultural change involved; a change which included measuring performance by the satisfaction of customers and by their willingness to pay. The value proposition and the key marketing message of the knowledge centre is:

> Professional researchers provide **better results** because they have knowledge of more information sources, better skills in using a variety of information tools, access to additional information sources, are networked with content experts, networked with other researchers within and outside the organization, and use professional experience and perspective to analyse the results.

At first glance this is not so major a change from traditional library and information work; the key change is the 'professional experience and perspective to analyse the results'. Therein lies the heart of the value added. Ryske and Sebastian, 1999) describe the changes as having three major components or shifts:

- from *cost centre* to *value-added centre*;
- from *offering a service* to *meeting the needs of customers*;
- from *information provider* to *knowledge partner*.

Precisely this change was advocated and predicted by Drotas (1994). An article by Williams and Bukowitz (1997) is in effect a report on and confirmation of Drotas's predictions, though they never cite him. The article describes the emergence of just such positions (though the terminology has morphed slightly to 'knowledge manager') in a large number of contexts, with specific descriptions of developments within Arthur Andersen, Hewlett-Packard, Dow Chemical and Buckman Laboratories International. What these developments have in common is that the librarian has become a facilitator as well as a researcher, and a knowledge organizer and selector who uses the network to 'push' information out to the users. This combination of 'select' and 'push' seems to be emerging as a key role for library and information work in the corporate domain. Selective dissemination of information (SDI) was reinvented on the Net environment in 1994 (Glynn and Koenig, 1995). SDI was received with great enthusiasm, but the realization soon set in that algorithmic selection was too insensitive to recognize high priority items and to filter and rank items appropriately. The logical response has been to use the Net and SDI packages to provide a 'push' substrate to which the librarian can add value by filtering, selecting and highlighting the high value items. The required components on the part of the knowledge manager/librarian are:

- a thorough knowledge of information sources;
- a thorough knowledge of Net techniques and technology;
- a thorough knowledge of the organization and its context;
- a high degree of common sense;
- a high degree of business sense.

DiMattia and Oder (1997) describe the reaction to KM and the perceptions of corporate librarians in organizations moving to such techniques. DiMattia and Blumenstein (1999) follow by discussing the changes in six corporate libraries, specifically those of the Ernst and Young Center for Business Knowledge (also described by Hibbard, 1998a, b); Messner Vetere Berger NcNamee Schmetterer (an advertising agency); the Knowledge Center at Turner Broadcast Sales; Piper and Marbury (a law firm); Sprint; and Newsday. The common themes reported here are much the same as above: the shrinkage in physical size of corporate libraries; the change to a more proactive 'push' stance; and greater and closer integration with the companies' core functions. One interesting and pervasive theme is the large amount of time that the information managers spend negotiating licences and access conditions for electronic information. In the print-on-paper world, information was typically provided in bundles (books or journals) of a fixed size and at a fixed price, with a fixed and common set of access rules, known as copyright, fair use, and first purchase doctrine. For the electronic world, all that has become flexible and negotiable. The information manager must be a skilled broker and negotiator. Here again, the need arises for business background, skills and acumen.

Further descriptives of KM applications and implementations include Caulkin (1997) who somewhat superficially describes implementations at 3M and ICI. Elliott (1997) describes Arthur Andersen's (distinct from Andersen Consulting) implementations of KM. Her article contains a pragmatic list of the following top ten lessons learned in Arthur Andersen's knowledge journey:

- Importance of leadership – vision, values, and behaviours.
- Focus on strategy – 'Knowledge to do what?'
- Focus on user needs – 'How will this improve my day?'
- Need to create a network of experts.

- Need to create a network of knowledge managers.
- Need a common organizing framework, e.g. a content classification scheme.
- Need a common content authoring and publishing template.
- Need human support, e.g. a call hotline.
- Need a flexible technology platform.
- Remember – 'Focus on what works, not perfection'.

Hibbard (1997) describes KM implementations at Dow, Monsanto, and Freightliner. Fishenden (1997) reviews what would now be considered proto-knowledge management systems at Albion Oil, the UK Parliament and the Securities and Investment Board of the UK. Roos (1998) examines knowledge management developments at Caterpillar. Graham *et al.* (1998) describe knowledge management developments within the educational consulting group at Andersen Consulting. This is a particularly good descriptive account of a 'community at practice'. Boeri and Hensel (1988) discuss the role of special librarians in general and report, particularly on intranet and web development, at Esperian Corporation (credit reporting). Sherwell (1997) reports from a library perspective on the development of KM at Smith Kline Beecham, but unfortunately the report is very superficial. An article well worth reading for its insights is Prokesch's (1997) interview with John Browne of British Petroleum (BP). It not only describes BP's KM initiatives in some detail, it is also an insightful discussion of the role of information in the operations of a major multinational organization.

Case studies also furnish good descriptions of KM implementations, the problems and problem solutions arising within those implementations, and how they lead to precepts about how to do it right. Notable examples are Alavi's (1997) description of KM implementation at KPMG and Chard's (1997) similar description of developments at Ernst and Young.

By contrast, Marshall *et al.* (1996) write a fascinating and detailed study of how Barings Bank, Kidder Peabody, and Metallgesallschaft all got themselves into major difficulties through lack of KM.

Solomon (1997) gives a chatty but very informative review of some of the standard retrieval tools (as opposed to the glitzy 'information space mapping' search tools such as SemioMap that are featured at Knowledge Managed trade shows) which are appropriate for KM applications.

Another change unfolding is that IT user support and help desk functions in larger organizations are increasingly being assumed by the part of the organization that historically derives from the library. Overleaf are sections of the organizational charts of two large multinational pharmaceutical companies that illustrate this phenomenon.

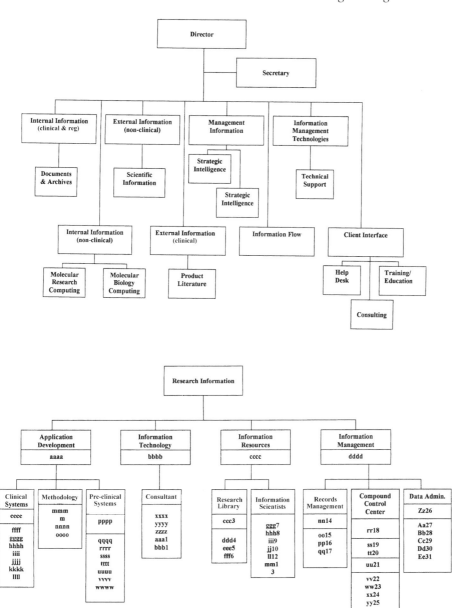

This phenomenon is remarkably, little recognized in the literature, but it appears to be rather widespread. Such reorganizations are, however, not often documented in the open literature but are often regarded as confidential. It is only through 'insider trading' that the two charts above are available.

Another aspect of KM, a direct descendant from its parentage out of intellectual capital, is the need to try to qualify the effect and impact of knowledge management. The seminal article in this field remains the 'balanced score card' article of Kaplan and Norton (1992). Two good articles describing some of the possible ways this could be done are by Skyrme (1997), and Skyrme and Amidon (1998). Another, aimed specifically at librarians and advocating how they can use the hunger for quantitative results to increase their leverage in the organization, is by Koenig (1997). This also contains a selective bibliography of key articles in both the LIS and business literature, and highlights those which examine the (positive) relationships between library and information services and organizational productivity and effectiveness. Note however that Fahey and Prusak (1998) list 'Seeking to develop direct measures of knowledge' as one of their eleven deadly sins of KM. They argue, first, that given the difficulty of measuring information, this threatens to put the measurement cart before the management horse; and second, that what should be measured is outcomes not the information or the knowledge itself. At the same time, Davenport (1997) lists 'justification by faith' as one of the known evils and argues that quantifiable results of KM must be demonstrated if it is to continue to be supported. Since both pieces of advice ultimately focus on demonstrable outcomes, they are not as orthogonal as they seem at first glance, but they do serve to illustrate the difficulty of the question of metrics for KM.

One of the more interesting and more compelling predictions, or projections as they would prefer to call it, is one by the Gartner Group, a well-known IT consultancy firm, in a study entitled 'IRC 2001 – a value-added service provider' (Jurek, 1997). IRC stands for Information Resource Center, which was previously more commonly known as the corporate library. Gartner reports that in 1995 IRCs spent about half, 48%, of their time searching electronic databases, but that by 2001, as end users do more of their own searching, the figure will fall to only 5%, with the remainder being high value KM (45%), specialized research (25%), Internet/intranet content consulting (15%) and training/education (10%). The report is interesting and compelling because of Gartner's relative lack of bias and (presumed) objectivity – they are not members of the LIS community. Admittedly some of the change may be more apparent than real – some of that 48% now spent searching electronic databases is probably the same as that 25% of time spent doing specialized research in the future – but nonetheless the projected change is rapid, dramatic, and exciting. Some of the changes are clearly revealed in the literature discussed above. It is the extent of the transformation projected by Gartner that is notable.

The transformation of LIS education

KM is similarly forcing a transformation in education for library and information work, or in the shorthand frequently used, LIS education. The reasons for that transformation are clear: the importance of KM and the overlap between KM and LIS. This overlap notwithstanding, there are however very large differences in emphasis between the two traditions, if we can call something as recent as KM a tradition. Koenig and Srikantaiah (1999) delineate the differences thus:

COMPARATIVE EMPHASIS

KNOWLEDGE MANAGEMENT	TRADITIONAL LIBRARY AND INFORMATION WORK
• Emphasis on unstructured and informal information/knowledge	• Emphasis on structured and formal information/knowledge
• Emphasis on internal information	• Emphasis on external information
• Corporate culture	• Neutrality within the organization
• Transformation and change agentry	
• Information and knowledge sharing: a dense web structure	• Information and knowledge delivery: a hub (library) and spoke structure
• A loose, unformed, poorly developed appreciation for information/knowledge structuring	• Syndetic structures, information structuring, cataloging, etc. as a central concern
• Knowledge of the context, organization and sectoral (industry)	• Growing contextual knowledge, but not well recognized within the organization
• An awareness of knowledge as text, but a background in non-textual information	• Information as text
• Linking knowledge sharing with compensation policy	• Never thought about this before

One of the most discussed topics in the literature is what constitutes the appropriate qualifications for a chief knowledge officer (Davenport, 1994, 1996; Corcoran and Jones, 1997; Pemberton, 1997; Hibbard, 1998a, b; Stuller, 1998; Earl and Scott, 1999a, 1999b). As Koenig and Srikantaiah (1999) point out, most CKOs will be recruited from the ranks of line managers within the organization: managers who know the context, who are familiar with IT and its capabilities, who have a proven track record, and who have the support and respect of their peers in senior management. They will not be recruited from the ranks of information professionals. Noteworthy however is that the chief knowledge officer for Ernst and Young describes his job as 'part evangelist, part librarian, and part publisher' (Stuller, 1998).

While almost all commonalities are agreed that there is now no standard set of qualifications for a CKO (Hibbard, 1998a, b), a good summary of what is expected of a CKO is given by Pemberton (1998):

- The CKO is a staff rather than a line position, without support staff.
- CKOs are to be the organization's primary advocate for learning and knowledge development.
- The CKO will design and have implemented the organization's knowledge infrastructure, including training, knowledge bases, libraries, data warehouses, research groups, and relationships with external academic organizations.
- The CKO will be the liaison between the organization and external suppliers of knowledge; e.g. consultants, publishers, information providers, database vendors, and the like.
- This position will help the organization find ways to 'milk' organizational information resources, including 'documents in libraries and file cabinets', so that they yield the maximum useable knowledge.
- The CKO will ensure that computer systems and networks are designed for effective round-the-clock use by employees regardless of location and will see that materials put into the organization's systems are organized, edited and indexed for maximum usefulness.
- The CKO will work to break down the natural reluctance to share information within what were once competitive units in the organization and will foster an environment in which collaboration and teaming can thrive.

While many LIS graduate schools have courses on KM, there are only a few degree programmes in the field. The School of Information Management and Systems (formerly the School of Library and Information Studies) at the University of California, Berkeley, offers masters and PhD degrees for knowledge managers, and RMIT (formerly Royal Melbourne Institute of Technology) University in Australia has a degree programme, Master of Business in information innovations (Hibbard, 1998b).

There is beginning to be a greater appreciation in the KM literature of the contributions that librarians can make. Prusak (1995) recommends that businesses should consider librarians, journalists and anthropologists for KM appointments. Peetz, CKO at Ernst and Young, reports that even though staffers do more of their own researching than in the past, KM has caused the firm to hire more librarians, not less (DiMattia and Oder, 1997).

One asset that the librarians have in the typical organization is their perceived neutrality. This is an asset because of the issue of who owns the information. Librarians have long been perceived as information owners, but neutral information owners. If a party is to lose information ownership because of KM implementations, then the party needs to be rewarded for relinquishing and sharing. But in any case this may be an easier pill to swallow if perceived ownership moves to a neutral organization, and not to a competitor. The problems occasioned by perceived information ownership are often mentioned (Davenport, 1997; Murray, 1999). Unfortunately the contribution of the librarian as a neutral location is seldom explicitly recognized.

KM is also unusual in that it is not only not 'owned' by any one discipline, but there is not even a majority shareholder. No one has as much as 50% ownership: not management or administration; not information technology; not human resources; and not library/information science. KM has generally tended to undervalue the LIS field and continues somewhat to do so, although not as markedly as in the past. However, the more the interdisciplinary nature of KM becomes recognized, the greater is the recognition that successful KM implementations require a team, and the easier it becomes for the information professional to become a member of that team.

It is quite common, indeed almost customary these days, to open an article with a quotation from Peter Drucker; he has after all not only been right but also ahead of the curve on so many issues. We shall instead close with Drucker (1998) – in fact with two quotations. In his recent article 'The next information revolution' he makes two major points; both are extraordinarily positive about the potential future of library and information work.

The first point is about the importance of information external to the organization, the librarian's bailiwick: 'In the next 10 to 15 years, collecting *outside* information is going to be the next frontier' [italics his]. The second point is about the shift in emphasis from the T of IT, information technology, to the I, a point also made by Koenig (1992). Drucker reviews the rise of the great printing princes technologists, of the 16th century, Aldus and Plantin, and concludes his article:

> By 1580 or so, the printers, with their focus on technology, had become ordinary craftsmen, respectable tradesmen to be sure, but definitely not of the upper class. Their place was soon taken by what we now call publishers (though the term wasn't coined until much later), people and firms whose focus was no longer on the 'T' in IT but on the 'I.'

This shift got under way the moment the new technology began to have an impact on the MEANING of information, and with it, on the meaning and function of the 15th century's key institutions such as the church and the universities. It thus began at the same juncture at which we now find ourselves in the present information revolution as we undergo the shift in business information and, with it, the redefinition of the function and purpose of business. Is there a lesson in this for today's information technologists, the CIOs in organizations, the software designers and developers, the devotees of Moore's Law?

References

Alavi, M. (1997) *KPMG Peat Marwick U.S.: one giant brain.* Boston: Harvard Business School Publishing.

Arthur Andersen Consulting (1996) *World Bank knowledge management concept paper: a practical approach.* Chicago: Arthur Andersen Business Consulting.

Banks, H. (1989) The productivity paradox. *Forbes*, **144**(2), 15.

Boeri, R.J. and Hensel, M. (1998) Special librarians and enterprise knowledge management. *EMedia Professional*, **11**(4), 36.

Broadbent, M. (1998) The phenomenon of knowledge management: what does it mean to the library profession? *Information Outlook*, **2**(5), 23–36.

Caulkin, S. (1997) The knowledge within. *Management Today*, (August), 28–32.

Chard, A.M. (1997) *Knowledge management at Ernst and Young.* Palo Alto, CA: Graduate School of Business Stanford University.

Chase, R.L. (1998) Knowledge navigators. *Information Outlook*, **2**(9), 12–26.

Corcoran, M. and Jones, R. (1997) Chief knowledge officers? Perceptions, pitfalls, and potential. *Information Outlook*, **1**(6), 30–36.

Cropley, J. (1998) Knowledge management: a dilemma. *Business Information Review*, **15**(1), 27–34.

Davenport, T. (1994) Coming soon: the CKO. *Information Week*, (491), 95.

Davenport, T. H. (1996) Knowledge roles, the CKO and beyond. *CIO*, **9**(12) 24–29.

Davenport, T. (1997) Known evils: seven fallacies that can hamper development of knowledge management in a company. *CIO*, **10**(17), 34–36.

Davenport, T. (1998) Managing customer knowledge. *CIO*, **11**(15), 32–34.

Davenport, T.H. and Marchard, D.A. (1999) Is KM just good information management? *Financial Times*, (8 March), 2.

Davenport, T.H. *et al.* (1998) Successful knowledge management projects. *Sloan Management Review*, **39**(1), 43–57.

David, P.A. (1990) The dynamo and the computer: an historical perspective on the modern productivity paradox. *American Economic Review*, **80**(2), 355–361.

Demarest, M. (1997) Understanding knowledge management. *Long Range Planning*, **30**(3), 374–384.

Despres, C. and Chauvel, C. (1999) How to map knowledge management. *Financial Times*, (8 March), 1.

DiMattia, S.S. and Blumenstein, L.C. (1999) Virtual libraries: meeting the corporate challenge. *Library Journal*, **124**(4), 42–44.

DiMattia, S. and Oder, N. (1997) Knowledge management: hope, hype, or harbinger? *Library Journal*, **122**(15), 33–35.

Drotas, P.V. (1994) From online specialist to research manager – changing with the times. *Online*, **18**(1), 54–58.

Drucker, P.F. (1998) The next information revolution. *Forbes ASAP*, (24 August), 47–58.

Duhon, B. (1998) It's all in our heads. *Inform*, **12**(8), 9–13.

Earl, M.J. and Scott, I.A. (1999a) The role of chief knowledge officer. *Financial Times*, (8 March), 5.

Earl, M.J. and Scott, I.A. (1999b) What is a chief knowledge officer? *Sloan_Management Review*, **40**(2), 38–39.

Economist (1998) Making aid work. *Economist*, **349**(8094), 806.

Edvinsson, L. (1995) Visualizing intellectual capital in Skandia. *Skandia's 1994 Annual Report*. Stockholm: Skandia AFS.

Edvinsson, L. (1997) Developing intellectual capital at Skandia. *Long Range Planning*, **30**(3), 366–373.

Elliott, S. (1997) Arthur Andersen maximizes its core commodity through comprehensive knowledge management. *Practice*, (August/September), 1–7.

Evans, P.B. and Wurster, T.S. (1997) Strategy and the new economics of information. *Harvard Business Review*, **75**(5), 70–82.

Fahey, L. and Prusak, L. (1998) The eleven deadliest sins of knowledge management. *California Management Review*, **40**(3), 265–276.

Field, J.J. (1998) Knowledge management: a new competitive asset. *Information Outlook*, **2**(9), 27–30.

Fishenden, J. (1997) Managing intranets to improve business process. *ASLIB Proceedings*, **49**(4), 90–96.

Ghilardi, F.J.M. (1994) The information center of the future? The professional's role. *Online*, **18**(6), 8–9.

Gibson, C.F. and Jackson, B.B. (1987) *The information imperative: managing the impact of information technology on business and people*. Lexington, MA: D.C. Heath.

Glynn, K. and Koenig, M.E.D. (1995) Small business and information. In: M.E. Williams (ed.) *Annual review of information science and technology. Vol. 30*. Medford, NJ: Information Today, pp. 251–280.

Graham, W. *et al.* (1998) A real-life community of practice. *Training and Development*, **52**(5), 15–22.

Hansen, M.T. *et al.* (1999) What's your strategy for managing knowledge? *Harvard Business Review*, **75**(2), 106–116.

Hibbard, J. (1997) Knowing what we know. *InformationWeek*, (20 October), 46–64.

Hibbard, J. (1998a) Knowledge and learning officers find big paydays. *InformationWeek*, (15 June), 170.

Hibbard, J. (1998b) Lotus takes on knowledge management. *InformationWeek*, (2 February), 26.

Jurek, R.J. (1997) An argument for change. *Marketing Research*, **9**(4), 56.

Kaplan, R.S. and Norton, D.P. (1992) The balanced scorecard – measures that drive performance. *Harvard Business Review*, **70**(1), 71–91.

Kim, W.C. and Maubourgne, R. (1997) Fair process: managing in the knowledge economy *Harvard Business Review*, **75**(4), 65–75.

Kleiner, A. and Ruth, G. (1997) How to make experience your company's best teacher *Harvard Business Review*, **75**(5), 172–177.

Koenig, M.E.D. (1983) Bibliometric indicators versus expert judgement in assessing research performance. *Journal of the American Society for Information Science*, **43**(2), 136–145.

Koenig, M.E.D. (1992) Entering stage III – the convergence of the stage hypotheses. *Journal of the American Society for Information Science*, **43**(3), 204–207.

Koenig, M.E.D. (1983a) A bibliometric analysis of pharmaceutical research. *Research Policy* **12**(1), 15–36.

Koenig, M.E.D. (1983b) Bibliometric indicators versus expert judgement in assessing research performance. *Journal of the American Society for Information Sciences,* **43**(2) 136–145.

Koenig, M.E.D. (1997) Intellectual capital and how to leverage it. *The Bottom Line Managing Library Finances*, **10**(3), 112–118.

Koenig, M.E.D. and Srikantaiah, T. (1999) Education for knowledge management *Information Services and Use*, **19**(1), 17–31.

Koenig, M.E.D. and Wilson, T.D. (1996) Productivity growth, the take-off point. *Information Processing and Management*, **32**(2), 247–254.

LeFauve, S. (1998) *The 1998 conference on knowledge management and organization learning* [Presentation to the Conference Board, Chicago, 15 April.]

Liedtka, J.M. *et al.* (1997) The generative cycle: linking knowledge and relationships *Sloan Management Review*, **39**(1), 47–59.

Manchester, P. (1999) Tools for knowledge management. *Financial Times*, (8 March), 11.

Marchand, D.A. (1985) Information management: strategies and tools in transition *Information Management Review*, **1**(1), 27–37.

Marshall, C. *et al.* (1996) Financial risk and the need for superior knowledge management *California Management Review*, **38**(3), 77–101.

Marshall, L. (1997) Facilitating knowledge management and knowledge sharing: new opportunities for information professionals. *Online*, **21**(5), 92–98.

Matarazzo, J.M. and Prusak, L. (1996) The value of corporate libraries. *Online*, **20**(2) 101–109.

Murray, P. (1999) How smarter companies get results from KM. *Financial Times*, (8 March) 12–13.

Pemberton, J.M. (1997) Chief knowledge officer: the climax of your career? *Record Management Quarterly*, **31**(2), 66–69.

Pemberton, J.M. (1998) Knowledge management (KM) and the epistemic tradition. *Record Management Quarterly*, **32**(3), 58–62.

Pigott, S. (1996) New roles for the information professional. *SLA Specialist*, **19**(9), 8.

Prokesch, S.E. (1997) Unleashing the power of learning: an interview with British Petroleum's John Browne. *Harvard Business Review*, **75**(5), 146–148.

Prusak, L. (1995) Hiring outside the box. *CIO*, **8**(18), 98.

Prusak, L. (1998) *Managing principal, IBM global services, consulting group presentation t the conference board.* [Paper presented at the 1998 Conference on Knowledg Management and Organizational Learning, Chicago, 16 April.]

Prusak, L. (1999) Making knowledge visible. *Financial Times*, (8 March), 3.

Remeikis, L.A. and Koska, E. (1996) Organizing for knowledge: developing a knowledge management system. In: M. Williams (ed.) *Proceedings of the 17th national online meeting, 14–16 May 1996.* Medford, NJ: Information Today, pp. 315–318.

Roos, J. (1998) Exploring the concept of intellectual capital. *Long Range Planning,* **31**(1), 150–153.

Ryske, E.J. and Sebastian, T. (1999) From library to knowledge center – the evolution of a 'corporate' infocenter. In T. Srikantaiah and M.E.D. Koenig (eds) *Knowledge management for the information professional.* Medford, NJ: Information Today.

Senge, P.M. (1990) *The fifth discipline: the art and practice of the learning organization.* New York: Doubleday/Currency.

Sherwell, J. (1997) Building the virtual library: the case of SmithKline Beecham. *Managing Information,* **4**(5), 35–36.

Skyrme, D.J. (1997) From information to knowledge management: are you prepared? www.skyrme.com/pubs/on97full.htm.

Skyrme, D.J. (1998) Valuing knowledge: is it worth it? *Managing Information,* **5**(3), 24–26.

Skyrme, D.J. and Amidon, D.M. (1998) New measures of success. *Journal of Business Strategy,* **19**(1), 20–24.

Solomon, M. (1997) Knowledge management tools for knowledge managers: filling the gap between finding information and applying it. *Searcher,* **5**(3), 10–17.

Stear, E.B. and Wecksell, J. (1997) Information resource center management (IRCM). *Bulletin of the American Society for Information Science,* **23**(4), 15–17.

Steele, N. (1998) United Technologies Corporation moves to virtual information services. *Bulletin of the American Society for Information Science,* **24**(6), 13–16.

Stewart, T.A. (1991a) Brainpower. *Fortune,* (3 June), 44–60.

Stewart, T.A. (1991b) Now capital means brains, not just bucks. *Fortune,* (14 January), 31–32.

Stewart, T.A. (1994) Your company's most valuable asset: intellectual capital. *Fortune,* (3 October), 68–74.

Stewart, T.A. (1995) Getting real about brainpower. *Fortune,* (27 November), 201–203.

Stuller, J. (1998) Chief of corporate smarts. *Training,* **35**(4), 28–34.

Talero, E. and Gaudette, P. (1995) *Harnessing information for development: World Bank group vision and strategy.* Washington, DC: World Bank.

Ulrich, D. (1998) Intellectual capital equals competence x commitment. *Sloan Management Review,* **39**(2), 15–26.

Wiig, K.M. (1997) Integrating intellectual capital and knowledge management. *Long Range Planning,* **30**(3), 399–405.

Williams, R.L. and Bukowitz, W.R. (1997) Knowledge managers guide information seekers. *HR Magazine,* **42**(1), 76–81.

World Bank. (1998) *Assessing aid, what works, what doesn't and why.* Oxford: Oxford University Press.

Management

9

Michael Cotta-Schønberg

Introduction

The area of management is a naturally fertile ground for theory making, development of models and . . . fads! Moreover, gurus, consultant firms and publishers alike have vested interests in keeping the management mill going. Finally, our political lords and masters regularly come up with new trendy demands on public managers. So, it is no wonder that library managers may sometimes despair of discerning what is valuable and relevant in this confusion of management trends.

Some library managers give up altogether and may actually find support in yet another management trend according to which management is obsolete. Most of us believe that the fate of a business depends on management. It will thrive with good management and die with bad management. Not so: you can now read in *Harvard Business Review* that all companies die, but they do it at different times. Good management can make a difference only for a short time (Hout, 1999). Once librarians could feel safe since libraries do not die. But today disintermediation looms high on the horizon, and the question of libraries' survival as well as the role of management in this process is asked not only by the doomsayers among us but also by solid, positively interested librarians who simply project the present trends to their logical end and wonder where our traditional institutions fit in.

To those – probably most of us – who believe that management matters, this situation gives management a special relevance and the question of what is good management in this transitional period has become urgent (McBeth, 1997). Whereas formerly library management reflected the dominant management culture, though after a significant time lag, the process has now speeded up and 'academic library administrators are adopting the latest organizational fashions almost as quickly as their corporate counterparts' (Day, 1998).

The present chapter reports on recent developments in the area of management taken in the general sense and excluding specific areas like management of information technology, as well as human resource management. The period covered is mainly 1996–1998.

Two basic handbooks have appeared in the period: a Gower handbook edited by Prytherch (1998a) and another by Bryson (1997) in a new edition. A small introduction for beginners has been published by Morris (1996).

Strategic management

Strategy, strategic management and strategic planning cover one of those basic concepts on which it is difficult to get a terminological handle. One difficulty is that publishers and authors with abandon affix the epithet 'strategic' to any moving object out there in the word-jungle in order to make it alluring and eatable. The same thing happened earlier to 'competitive'. Another difficulty is that the concept of strategic planning became unfashionable overnight when the super-guru published his book on the 'rise and fall of strategic planning' (Mintzberg, 1994) and many of us discreetly buried our own strategic plan in the bottom drawer on the left. However, strategy was too important to let go and Mintzberg's critique really had to do with the planning-thing, not with the strategy-thing. So strategic management gained predominance instead of strategic planning.

For some library authors, reflecting one trend in general management literature, strategic management means management informed by strategy, i.e. major long-term goals. For others, strategic management is that part of management which is concerned with developing and implementing specific strategy. Other authors again seem to be using the two terms interchangeably.

In the second of two major volumes on strategic management in academic and public libraries (Hayes, 1993 and Hayes and Walter, 1996) the authors define strategic management as 'that part of general management of organizations that emphasizes the relationships to external environments, evaluates the current status of them and the effects of future changes in them, and determines the most appropriate response of the organization to them. Strategic management is oriented toward long-range institutional goals and objectives'. As a definition, I think this focuses too much on the effect of the environment on the library and too little on the independent drive in the library to change the environment.

The Hayes–Walter definition is taken up by Prytherch (1998b), who examines a number of definitions of strategic management in the management literature and concludes: strategic management can be viewed as the overall process of longer-term achievement; the organization needs to be considered as a whole – although it may be split into segments for accurate appraisal – and decisions should be made, by managers at all levels, in line with the future pattern that is agreed through the strategic process. The focus is on what the organization is aiming to achieve (its objectives), when it should achieve those objectives, and how it should achieve those objectives.

Another definition is given by Chalmers (1997): 'Strategic management is considered to be concerned with the formulation, development, implementation and evaluation of strategy. Strategy is considered to be about the choice of direction for an organization and the achievement of aspects of that direction.' In a questionnaire-based study of fifteen key aspects of strategic management in eleven national libraries, she found that respondents considered the following aspects to be the most important:

- the ongoing development of electronic systems and services for the access and use of information;
- a match between the organization's budget priorities and strategic priorities;
- a written document of strategic intent;
- a written mission statement;
- the identification of user groups for whom services or products will be provided.

On the question of respondents' satisfaction with the aspects of strategic management, she found that they were most satisfied with those that involved thinking, planning and documenting and least satisfied with those involving changes in human behaviour sustainable over the medium term.

Values

Defining one's values before declaring visions and mission has become important in recent years. A strong indictment of the development or degradation of public library values during the Thatcher years has been published by Usherwood (1996). The application of new managerialism and private sector management techniques to public libraries in the UK, with contracting out, privatization and performance-related pay as just three examples, is inappropriate. It is an example of how important the question of values and ideology is to management and of how serious this clash of values is to the realization of the basic mission of libraries as public service institutions.

Instead of taking over value sets and management methods from private manufacturing industry, libraries may profit from concepts developed in the service sector. How service management might be used in a South African library setting is described by de Bruin (1996).

Goal setting

However it is defined, strategy has as its first stage the setting of goals. The formulation of vision and mission statements (e.g. What, 1996) and of strategic objectives seem now to be fairly well understood and generally practised in libraries which work systematically with strategic management and planning.

A particular form of goal setting on the operational level is represented by service charters or service level agreements (SLA), emanating from the charter movement initiated by the British government in 1991 and fairly widespread in the UK. Such charters and agreements are really contracts between the library and bodies that represent the users (university authorities, local government). Among the advantages of the use of an SLA are that it provides an opportunity to examine rigorously the nature and level of the library's service and to develop a dialogue with users on their needs and expectations. Among the disadvantages are that the agreed level may become a maximum level rather than a minimum level of service and that flexibility and long-term change may be impeded (Steward, 1997; see also Barton, 1996; Ford, 1996; Smith, 1998; and – for an Italian approach – Solimine, 1997a).

Another form of goal setting in the guise of contract management is currently being tried out in Denmark, where the two national libraries were the first libraries to have contracts with their ministry, the Ministry of Culture. The contracts covered four-year periods and specified the major development goals of the institutions to be reached during the contract period. Budgets were fixed for the whole period, with possibilities for supplementary allocation for special purposes. From the libraries' point of view, the advantages of this system are a framework which is conducive to organizational change, that planning conditions are improved by virtue of fixed budgets and clear priorities and that the targets are agreed upon by both parties, i.e. the library and the political-administrative system. From the point of view of the ministry the system's advantages are that it reduces discussion of administrative and financial details and makes it possible, during the negotiation period, to exert pressure on the institution to demonstrate effectiveness and relevance (Larsen, 1998).

Planning

Strategic planning is of course treated extensively in the more general works on strategic management (see above). As a specific area of strategic management it has moreover been the subject of general articles (Hipsman, 1996; Pitkin, 1997; Dougherty, 1998a; Prytherch, 1998c). Published case studies range from academic libraries in Australia and the USA (Mackenzie, 1997; Simpson, 1997) and public libraries in Ghana and the USA (Badu, 1997; Birdsall, 1997), through national libraries in the USA and Russia (Bryant, 1998; Savenije, 1998), to special libraries in Scandinavia (Johannsen, 1996b) and medical libraries in the USA (Gall *et al.*, 1997). The Ghana study showed that among five environmental segments of relevance to Ghanaian university libraries the most important were the economic and political segments, with socio-cultural, technological and international segments being of lesser importance (Badu, 1997).

During the period under review, scenario planning seemed to be gaining importance as a planning tool for libraries. An introductory text with cases has been published by Giesecke (1998) and two case studies from Australia and the UK have been published by O'Connor *et al.* (1997) and Corrall (1998). Whereas some views of strategic planning seem to focus heavily on the influence of environmental factors on the library, it is basic to scenario thinking that 'the future is unknown' and that 'multiple futures exist out there' (Giesecke, 1998). O'Connor nicely illustrates the techniques of creating various scenarios by telling stories about them ('the *Star wars* scenario', 'the *Empire strikes back* scenario', 'the *Return of the Jedi* scenario'), and of making a conscious choice, where the library does not just decide which of the scenarios it prefers, but commits itself to a course where it will imprint its own stamp on the future.

Management of change

Recent library literature is replete with statements to the effect that major change is a must and a condition for survival for libraries today (e.g. Line, 1996), indeed that change is becoming a continuous way of life and not just a sequence of periodical upheavals leading to new stable institutional forms (e.g. Dougherty, 1998a). The revolution in information technology is unanimously considered to be a major reason for this development, with shrinking funds, new forms of public management and new mindsets of users and employees coming in as important seconds. All agree that the reasons for change are external developments, which necessitate radical adjustment on the part of libraries.

A broad historical view of the situation of academic libraries is taken by Day (1998). In a remarkable article on ideologies of organizational change in the LIS literature he makes the following statement:

> All civilizations exhibit fissures in their cultural foundation. These breaches are caused by contradictions in the structural principles upon which they were founded. The social tensions that build along these fault lines usually are controlled or dissipated in ways that prevent major dislocations from occurring. Sometimes, however, a major realignment occurs and triggers the release of tremendous cultural energy which transforms the social landscape. Academic libraries currently are caught up in a cultural tsunami caused by just such a realignment in the principles upon which modern Western civilization was founded.

Here Day places the texts he investigates in two groups: technocratic and managerial. The former emphasize a traditional systems rationalization approach or focus on the social design of life with computers in which organizations are treated as open natural systems. Within the managerial texts three major strategies stand out. The first, represented by the work of Lewis (1984, 1986, 1994), reaffirms the traditional values of librarians and the strengthening of their professional power, while improving staff conditions and rewards. The second is represented by Stoffle of the University of Arizona (Stoffle *et al.*, 1996). This merges staff and all types of professionals into flexible work teams within a strong corporate culture. The third, implemented in many libraries and represented by Harvard (Lee and

Clack, 1996), merges human relations and general systems to create a learning organization. Despite their strategic differences, nearly all the texts encountered, according to Day, use a grammar of ideological motives that stays within a consensus paradigm which regards the prevailing order in working life and society as for the most part inevitable with regard to type of economic system, private ownership and technology of development. 'To this extent,' he adds, 'librarians' transformational discourse involves little true transformation.' Many librarians will probably breathe a sigh of relief at this statement, though some may wonder what the author would have us do! It is, however, the privilege of critical scholarship to raise questions for others to wonder about and be stimulated by, whether to reaffirm basic values or to create new things.

To return to a more mundane sphere, two well-known specialists of transformational library discourse offer coherent perspectives and solid advice on change in libraries. Line (1996) summarized his thinking on the matter, with special emphasis on institutional mindsets, barriers to change and leadership. With fourteen years of experience as a library boss, I still wonder about Line's assertion that it is especially hard 'for a boss to assume a new style after more than, say, five years at the head of an organization'. It is probably true, though.

For his part, Dougherty (1998a) offers cogent observations on the trans-formational situation of the university: 'Campus visions of the future aren't truly shared visions'; 'faculty are customarily focused on their own work'. Does it sound familiar? Dougherty therefore does not realistically expect transformational change in universities to occur in the foreseeable future. As for libraries, he is convinced that the most commonly used strategy is still a top-down incremental approach, but with growing tendency to empower staff groups through a team approach to problem solving. Though a great deal of change has actually occurred through slow incremental processes, Dougherty generally warns against them: 'More powerful processes are needed for this era of constant and turbulent change.' Among the special themes treated in the literature on management change are: innovation, business process reengineering and the learning organization.

Innovation

Change and innovation are evidently not the same thing. All innovation is change, but not all change is innovation. For one author at least, librarians have always been innovators in the sense that they were among the first to adapt to and use the latest information handling and communications technology: e.g. the Sumerian librarians who in 2000 BC made catalogues using clay tablets, the most advanced medium of the time for record keeping (Malinconico, 1997). He goes on to note that libraries generally seem to be on the front edge of applying new information technology in their local environment. This seems actually to be a widespread experience.

Line (1996) may not quite agree with so rosy a picture: at least, he quotes an IFLA study, published in 1995, which concluded that libraries are not fast-moving dynamic organizations (Prins and Geer, 1995). Dougherty (1998a) claims that the non-profit sector is lacking the sense of urgency of the private sector. As an example he gives librarians who talk endlessly about change, but almost always it turns out to be incremental change. Moreover, he points to the lack of 'pain or dissatisfaction' with prevailing conditions as an explanation of why librarians have been slow to embrace the need for change.

Whether innovation is carried out incrementally or in quantum leaps, leadership and management are necessary. To those who believe that innovation management is simply a technique, Hersberger (1997) has a salutary reminder concerning the role of intuition in successful leadership: 'Experience and advice influence one's intuition, but often the successful leader "knows" or "feels" when a possible program is appropriate in a particular library setting and offers enough value to risk being implemented.'

A proper academic dissertation on organizational innovation in libraries comes from Australia, where Clayton (1997) studied four cases – warts and all – and defined a model for innovation. The model comprises a set of enabling conditions (characteristics of innovation, resources available, nature of the organization, leadership) and intervening variables (implementation strategies and intervening circumstances) whose interplay determines the degree of implementation, i.e. the actual innovation that takes place.

Business process reengineering

From Germany, Ceynowa (1997) reports on a project at the Universitäts- und Landesbibliothek Münster, where the management of business processes was combined with a thorough exercise in activity-based costing. Apart from a tightly reasoned argumentation against the concept of library 'products' ('Bibliotheken produzieren nichts, sie leisten Dienste'), the study shows how to analyse the processes of a library using a hierarchy of processes. Combined with activity-based costing procedures, this process model provides a powerful tool for the analysis of work functions and costs and a method for optimizing resources. The model was applied in a pilot exercise in business process reengineering where the computer department of the library was transformed into a service-oriented team structure. Also from Germany is an academic study on BPR and chaos management. To some the very concept of 'chaos management' may seem to be a contradiction in terms, as chaos generally is conceived of as wild, unpredictable, untameable and therefore unmanageable. However, the proper definition of chaos appears to be 'the empty room', and in this sense chaos becomes a privileged room for creativity (Janke, 1997).

The learning organization

Goble (1997) presents a framework for translating Senge's 'learning organization' into library concepts – and argues, convincingly, for the use of banks as a private sector model for library development. Rowley (1997) stresses the elusive character of the learning organization. Apart from all the plus concepts of the later years, the basic condition for becoming a learning organization seems to be continuously concerned with becoming one, just as a good monk is a monk who every day asks himself what is a good monk (as a Cistercian abbot once said). Rowley also has a pertinent observation on the 'tensions between public service, political agendas and business efficiency which leave the public sector with an ambiguity in their mission that might undermine effective learning'. If this is a chaste reminder that implementing the learning organization may cause a drop in library productivity which our political masters may not approve of, many library directors will recognize a familiar worry (see also Marcum, 1996; Fowler, 1998).

Quality management

Fortunately, defining quality management is not within the scope of this chapter. Definitions vary, from broad ones that make quality management a comprehensive system of management, to narrower ones that see quality management as a management tool with rather specific objectives.

An important example of quality management as a general strategic (in the broad sense) management system or theory is provided by a Danish specialist, Johannsen (1996a). In a careful theoretical study he examines the similarities and differences between strategic management and quality management in the library and information sector. He concludes that the typical strategic management and quality management methodologies are likely to produce the same type of beneficial organizational learning processes and that there is a cyclical relation between the two methodologies which inform one another. He proceeds to construct an integrated model of strategic quality management which is really a comprehensive management model, integrating both strategy and quality.

That QM today is an important subject for libraries is witnessed by the number of books and articles published in the later years. As a result of national developments in the whole area of public service, the British appear to be leading the movement (e.g. Brockman, 1997; Milner *et al.*, 1997; see also Crawford, 1996; Dow, 1998), but a number of publications show that it is a subject of interest in many other countries: e.g. India (Jain and Gupta, 1996; Mulye and Deshpande, 1998); Spain (Izquierdo Alonso *et al.*, 1996; Pardo, 1997); Slovenia (Trzan-Herman and Kiauta, 1996); Italy (Solimine, 1997b; Tammaro, 1997); South Africa (Viljoen and Underwood, 1997); Australia (McGregor, 1997); Scandinavia (Johannsen, 1996a, 1996b); and France (Sutter, 1997; see also Girard-Billon and Giappiconi, 1997; Giappiconi, 1998).

For general overviews of the subject of QM in libraries see Brophy (1996, 1997); Shaughnessy (1996a); Brophy and Coulling (1997); Mayere and Muet (1997); Sutter (1997); St. Clair (1997b).

Models of quality management

One of the first comprehensive models of QM to be implemented in libraries was the ISO 9000 standard (Ellis and Norton, 1996; White and Mack, 1996; see also Dawes, 1997). Obviously this model has a special attraction for corporate libraries belonging to firms which otherwise implement the standard and make use of the ISO certification for marketing purposes. Some academic libraries have been working with the standard, but it would appear that it has lost its momentum in the library quality movement, possibly because of its being perceived as rigid and prescriptive (Garrod and Kinnell, 1997b).

Another comprehensive quality model is the European Business Excellence Model, a quality model underlying the European Quality Award (for a short description of this model see Brophy and Coulling, 1997). This model is really a comprehensive model of management including leadership and strategy, resource management, processes, etc. among its main criteria. It is also a model based on a stakeholder approach: the customer is of course very important, but other stakeholder groups are important too, e.g. employees and subcontractors. In this sense it may be a more balanced model than service quality models where the customer is the only king and it may be more in tune with European workplace values and culture. As it is pushed by European governments as a management model for public service institutions, we shall probably hear more about it in the library sector, but it is too early to say whether a general model of this type is the most appropriate one for a large and specific public service sector as the library sector. Possibly, quality models developed specifically for the library sector but based on systems known and acceptable to governments might prove more rewarding.

In 1996 the University Library of Wollongong, Australia, obtained an Achievement in Business Excellence Award from the Australian Quality organization. The Australian quality model is in several respects similar to the European one (McGregor, 1997).

A general model of quality management applicable across the spectrum of organizations from industry to public service institutions has been developed by the team at the Centre for Research in Library and Information Management at the University of Central Lancashire. The model is a generalized model or map of quality management showing how key quality concepts relate to each other and incorporating them into a broad process model including inputs, processes and outputs and – very importantly – review and improvement conceived as a continuous process (Brophy, 1997). In my experience, the proof of a library's quality commitment is in the tedious process of follow-up: having nice goals is easy, making them work in the long run is hard, unglamorous work.

Service quality has become an important concept in the literature on library quality and the contributions of Hernon and Altman have attracted widespread and well-merited attention, both as a philosophy of library work and as a model of library service assessment (Hernon and Altman, 1996, 1998). Insofar as it is considered to be a proper model of library quality, it may be remarked that its exclusive focus on service makes it less appropriate for libraries wanting to implement a comprehensive quality model, including management and processes. Moreover, the identification of 'user satisfaction' with 'quality' and of 'perceived quality' with 'objective quality' is problematic and has been criticized fairly by Quinn (1997), who opposes another model, of didactic service, to the quality service model (see also Cram, 1996).

Performance measurement

Every two years since 1995 the Department of Information and Library Management at the University of Northumbria at Newcastle has arranged an international conference on performance measurement in libraries and information services. These conferences and the conference proceedings are today the most important international vehicle of information on the subject. Proceedings of the Second conference, held in September 1997, were published in 1998 (*Proceedings*, 1998). In the first keynote paper of the conference, Cullen of Victoria University, New Zealand, applied postmodern thinking to performance measurement in libraries and asked: Why is there so little uptake of scholarship and research on performance measurement in the library profession and so little agreement on the best approach to take, when library services are in so many other ways becoming more and more standardized? It sounds like criticism, but happily she concludes – like a good postmodernist – that any library is free to choose the system of measurement which best serves its purposes: 'There are no absolutes, no gurus to follow, no guarantees' (Cullen, 1998). I would highlight also a paper from the conference by that eminent German veteran-practitioner of performance measurement, Poll of Münster University and State Library, who gives excellent advice and makes the process of performance measurement a practical proposition for librarians, where scholarship and research make it a rather daunting affair, fraught with methodological difficulties and theoretical impossibilities (Poll, 1998). Others of the conference papers are referred to below but the whole volume of proceedings is a must for theoreticians and practitioners alike.

On the theoretical side, one might also consult a paper by Cram (1996), in which she stresses the stakeholder approach to performance measurement (see also Brophy and Coulling, 1997; Crawford *et al.*, 1998), presents a critique of current interpretations of satisfaction measures and proposes a hierarchical performance measurement model (see also Wood, 1998).

So many sets of performance measures and indicators have been compiled and used in individual studies from 1996 to 1998 that only a broad selection of them can be listed here: official ones are the provisional ISO *Standard on library performance indicators* (ISO 11620) (see Harnesk, 1998) and the long-awaited IFLA guidelines (Poll and Boekhorst, 1996). The [US] Association of Research Libraries has published a set of *Indicators for academic library performance*, based on ratios from ARL statistics, 1993–95 (Kyrillidou, 1996) and the Council of Australian University Libraries has issued its first three indicators on satisfaction, document delivery, and availability (Byrne, 1997). For the EU project, EQLIPSE, a set of indicators was developed and tested in six European libraries (Brophy *et al.*, 1997a) and a manual on performance indicators for African university librarians has been published by the International African Institute (Abbott and Rosenberg, 1996).

Preeminent among individual studies are those on service quality by Hernon and Altman (1996, 1998), as followed up by studies in New Zealand (Hernon and Calvert, 1996; Calvert, 1997; Calvert and Hernon, 1997) and Singapore (Calvert, 1998). An Italian set of performance indicators selected from the official sets was developed at the University of Sassari, taking as its point of departure the universally applicable fiat of politicians: 'Creare una pubblica amministrazione che lavori meglio e costi meno' (Pilia, 1997). Instruments of library quality measurement have also been developed in Spain – University of Granada (Pardo, 1997); Portugal – public libraries (Pinto, 1998); Finland – public libraries (Ruth, 1998); Wales and Malaysia – national libraries (Baba and Broady, 1998). From the USA comes a study on a measuring instrument based on SERVQUAL and used at the Sterling C. Evans Library, Texas (Coleman *et al.*, 1997; see also Nitecki, 1998), a report on the development of a user satisfaction survey instrument at the Odum Library, Valdosta (Davis and Bernstein, 1997) and a stakeholder based study of library units' quality comprising a client satisfaction survey, a peer review and an operations review developed at the Library at Central Missouri State University (Littlejohn and Wales, 1998; see also M.D. White, 1997). In Taiwan a method for assessing performance of libraries has been developed, using a data envelopment analysis and being so mathematical in its method that the authors themselves comment that 'it is difficult to communicate our results to relevant library managers because it is a complicated quantitative process' (Chen, 1997). From the UK a study by Crawford *et al.* (1998) has been referred to above, and a team consisting of Philip Brooks, Don Revill and Tony Shelton has developed a scale to measure the quality of an academic library from the perspective of its users (Brooks *et al.*, 1997). At John Moores University in Liverpool – in true stakeholder spirit – a questionnaire was used to assess library staff's own perception of the library's service. It concluded that users' perception would appear to be more positive than that of the staff (Revill, 1997), a phenomenon that is probably be fairly common. Last but not least should be mentioned a study of user satisfaction survey from Australia, with the tantalizing title 'Measuring customer satisfaction: myth or reality?' (Garlick and Hoegh-Guldberg, 1998). The most noteworthy trends in the studies listed above seem to me:

- an increasing stress on stakeholders – as opposed to an exclusive customer focus;
- the inclusion of input, process and outcome parameters;

- a blend of 'subjective' and 'objective' data;
- the development of larger sets of indicators and measures from which the individual library may choose whatever seems most relevant in the given context.

Generally, it would appear that we are in the middle of a blooming period of experimentation and creativity and that the time for standardization is somewhere in the future, if ever. However, a number of indicators and measures do recur in the various studies and possibly some consensus will be formed around these, aided by the efforts of international organizations (IFLA and ISO).

Benchmarking

Benchmarking is one tool of quality management which has attracted much attention in industry and the service sector, including libraries. The harvest of literature on benchmarking in libraries in the period 1996–98 is rather meagre, however and does not measure up to the literature on quality management generally.

Research at Loughborough University's Department of Information and Library Studies with the help of funding from British Library Research and Innovation Centre (BLRIC) has been reported (Garrod and Kinnell, 1997a, b). Using a combination of questionnaire and telephone survey, literature searching, demonstrator projects and workshop, the team concluded that 'despite interest in quality management techniques, including performance measurement, there is little evidence of any formal comparative analyses of the processes which make up library services'. However, 25% of libraries responding to the questionnaire survey did reply in the affirmative to the question whether or not they compared any of their activities with those of other organizations. The researchers identified six key issues concerning library benchmarking:

1. A definition of benchmarking is required.
2. A concrete model or approach should be developed.
3. Library processes are considered to be the most suitable subject for benchmarking.
4. Training and skills are required for all staff.
5. Timescales should be realistically estimated.
6. Effective communication is essential (see also Gohlke, 1997).

Library benchmarking cases have been reported from Hong Kong using measures of customer satisfaction and impact on users (Cheng, 1996). In the UK, a Loughborough study compared indicators on income per capita, income from fines and fees, expenditure on books per capita, book issues per capita, staff per 1,000 population – across public libraries (Spiller, 1998). From Australia, two articles report on the establishment of a benchmarking database for public libraries in New South Wales with comparisons between – in the first phase – ten public libraries in terms of 22 indicators like expenditure per capita, circulation per capita and percentage of library resources less than 5.5 years old. One of the indicators, expenditure per visit, was originally to have been expenditure per issue, but was changed in order more accurately to reflect the changes in library use, particularly the use of new technologies (Garlick, 1997; Ellis, 1998). In the USA, a study was made of benchmarking in the context of restructuring (St. Clair, 1997a).

Also from Australia comes the only report identified for this chapter on a full-scale benchmarking exercise, i.e. including a proper comparative analysis on best practice in various processes. Queensland University of Technology compared its acquisitions and cataloguing, document delivery and research support services with those of the University of New South Wales. The report on this pioneering venture in library benchmarking will be helpful to all who are wondering whether or not to enter into a full-scale benchmarking exercise. Among the basic difficulties were the problems of comparing measures. Even apparently simple data proved to be difficult. In some areas the productivity measure proved critical and at the same time very problematic. Sometimes difference in performance was obvious, in other cases much less so, and even when there was agreement on the difference there might be disagreement about causes and remedies (Robertson and Trahn, 1997).

Resource management

For the purpose of this chapter, the main resources of libraries are considered to be financial resources, human resources, collections of materials, information technology and space resources. To these should now be added external resources of various types: collections which are co-owned through consortium-type constructions; online resources which are leased or subscribed to (e.g. electronic periodicals); Web resources which are made available to users through interface systems developed specifically for that purpose by the library (Hamilton, 1998). In a broader view, all information resources available on the Net may be considered as resources, but a distinction may be made between those Web resources that are properly resources of a given library in the sense of being produced or somehow paid for by the library, and those that are merely used by it, though this distinction may become more and more difficult to uphold as the local library merges with the global library.

Not only 'has' the library resources, it 'is' also, on another level, a resource. It is an intellectual resource or a knowledge resource for citizens nationally or regionally or for institutions and organizations of various types, educational institutions, corporations. This means that resource management in libraries should not be aimed at growth or impressiveness or even survival of the library, but at usefulness to those whom it is set to serve (Baker, 1997).

Baker, a veteran in the field from the University of East Anglia, has published an important overview of resource management, concentrating on academic libraries, but also of general interest to the whole library sector (Baker, 1997). A basic introduction to the field came out recently in a revised edition (Roberts, 1998). For surveys of various domains of resource management in libraries, see Bryson (1998) on financial management, Pluse (1998) on human resource management, Lovecy (1997) on IT management, and McDonald (1997) on space management.

Major themes in the literature on resource management in libraries during the period 1996–98 were basic issues, better use of resources, and how to get better funding.

Basic issues

Formerly, libraries had very little freedom in the administration of the resources allocated to them (Wätjen, 1996). However, in a number of countries this situation is rapidly changing as politicians and state authorities impose new forms of management on the public service sector and as models of block grants are introduced. Librarians should of course be happy with the greater room for manoeuvre they have been given, but they are learning to be wary of authorities bringing gifts: the counterpart of this greater freedom is budget cuts and increased demands for accountability (Baker, 1997) and value for money (Bryson, 1998), with all that this implies. Häkli (1996) has given a very good survey of this development with a keen eye not only to the increased burden on library managers, but also to the upheaval in their traditional values when competencies such as cataloguing, formerly considered to be at the core, have to be shunted aside in favour of fundamental priorities of service.

In some parts of the world such concerns may seem to be problems of affluence. African libraries, in particular university libraries, are not so much worried about how to spend their money as about whether they will get any at all. As a result of two decades of economic crisis public financing, even of great libraries, has been to an unhealthy degree replaced with donor financing and even that largely insufficient. The result is 'a marginalization of the library in the life of the university and a growing use of alternative methods of accessing and acquiring information. Universities and their academic staff and students are seemingly managing to exist without the benefit of a library in any real sense of the word' (Rosenberg, 1998).

Germany does not have that problem, though funds may be short. In an article comparing German and British university libraries Cockrill (1997) has described how the budgets of German university libraries have come under pressure in the wake of the reunification of Germany. East German universities and university libraries proved to be in a sorry state due to antiquated technology, unsound buildings and a lack of western literature but a plethora of ideologically correct socialist literature. The costs of developing eastern Germany together with a general recession has put pressure on the public finances of Germany and led to a reduction of funds available for libraries in western Germany. A new system for funding higher education institutions based on annual block grants is being introduced, but how it will affect library budgets remains uncertain. One thing is certain to continue, though: Besitzstandswahrung, i.e. protecting and defending what you already have. And another thing is going to become more important, i.e. Begründungszwang, meaning that everyone will have to substantiate requests carefully (Gattermann, 1996); see also Griebel (1996) on model budgets for university libraries, and Poll (1996) on income generation in academic libraries.

The effects of recession have been felt in the UK too, with important decreases in government grants for the established universities. This development has led universities to search for new sources of income (Wilkinson, 1996) and to focus on formulae, devolved budgets and overheads (Graham, 1996). Even if their libraries are only a little more involved in income generation than they used to be, they are more influenced by the income generating patterns of their parent institutions (Cockrill, 1997). Public libraries have fared no better. Scarcity of public money as well as local government restructuring has thrown the public library system in Great Britain into a financial crisis – worsened by public libraries' ineligibility to compete for national lottery funding (Almeida, 1997)! Mr Blair may have done something about that.

In a careful US study, Cummings *et al.* (1996b) have documented long-term budget trends for academic libraries. During the happy 1960s there was a sharp rise in library funding with indications that research libraries participated more than fully in the rapid growth of university budgets. During the 1970s libraries essentially held their own; since then the typical research library has seen its funding relatively decline. As for the components of library expenditures, there have been some noteworthy shifts in relative shares over the last decades. In the study by Cummings *et al.* (1996a) salaries fell from 62% of total expenditure in 1963 to 52% in 1991; library materials remained stationary around 34%; other operating expenditures rose from 6% to 14%, with computerization as the driving force.

Budget cuts are not news, of course: libraries have been living with them for some time. What seems different now is the way they are reported by libraries. Whereas there was formerly much moaning and gnashing of teeth, a different, more entrepreneurial spirit seems to have taken over (Fatzer, 1996). Scarce resources are more accepted as a fact of life, and the interesting thing is what libraries do about it.

Two basic strategies for dealing with this situation dominate the literature: better use of funds through costing, controlling and outsourcing, and getting more funds through fees and fund-raising.

Costing

Together with controlling and pricing, costing is one way of achieving better use of the resources allocated to the library. A general introduction to costing and pricing has been published by the (UK) Library Association (Snyder and Davenport, 1997), as well as a number of individual studies (Broady, 1997; Cooper, 1997; Forrest and Cawasjee, 1997; Hart, 1997; Hutchins, 1997; Moeske, 1997; Snyder, 1997). For a proper German exercise in activity-based costing see the above-mentioned study (p. 229) by Ceynowa (1997).

Outsourcing

In 1995 someone listed 'outsourcing' as a buzzword that would soon fall out of favour, both in the library jargon and practice – like other passé terms such as total quality management, information superhighway and ownership vs. access! This prediction did not prove to be true: outsourcing is still very much with us and it does not seem that it will leave us soon. At least it is definitely a major trend in the literature 1996–98, though there is a heavy US slant to it, probably because conditions of American librarianship are in several ways more propitious to outsourcing than in most other countries. A sensible how-to-do-it manual has been published (Hirshon and Winters, 1996), together with a volume of case studies concerning outsourcing in technical services (Wilson and Colver, 1997) and a full-scale, state-of-the-art monograph on outsourcing in academic libraries with an important bibliography (Bénaud and Bordeianu, 1998). Among the periodical articles, several are concerned with individual cases, some of them remarkable examples from the public sector like the total outsourcing/privatization of Riverside County's public library system and Hawaii State Public Library's wholesale outsourcing of collection development and technical services (Helfer, 1997; Leiserson and Montgomery, 1997; Baker, 1998; Dubberly, 1998; Holt, 1998; Schneider, 1998). Other studies cover the outsourcing of corporate sector libraries (Agada, 1996; Miles, 1996). Insourcing of previously outsourced library functions now occurs (Dobb, 1998; Hill, C., 1998), as does library-to-library outsourcing (Quinn and Coffman, 1996) and co-sourcing (Bates, 1997). Two important theoretical papers deal with outsourcing in the context of high strategy (Marcum, 1998) and competition and the value chain (Renaud, 1997), and an article on the situation in Italy proves that outsourcing is not just an Anglo-American issue (Cerri, 1996).

The slightly hysterical overtones of former debates seem now to give way to the realization that libraries have always to some extent outsourced a number of functions (Schneider, 1998). Surveys show that the present trend towards outsourcing does not present a radical break with established library practices, but that apart from some highly publicized exceptions, 'libraries' adoption of outsourcing is deliberate, incremental, and cautious, and focused . . . on collection development and technical services' (Bénaud and Bordeianu, 1998, see also Libby and Caudle, 1997, on cataloguing).

Three issues seem to me especially important. The first has to do with the library's core mission or core competence: the basic task even of the traditional library was never to perform technical services as such – these were always support functions. Rather, it is effectively to bring 'people with the need to know in touch with the information or knowledge they need, in a discerning and informed way', including intelligent selection of materials (Abel, 1998). When technical services can be provided better and cheaper by private companies without indirect deleterious effect on the basic work of the library, well for heaven's sake let them! The earlier uproar over the outsourcing of technical services raises the question whether outsourcing was not a timely reminder to libraries of what their proper mission is.

This leads to the second issue: why private companies can perform certain traditional library functions better than libraries themselves. There are some good reasons of course. Large companies serving a great number of libraries may very well have the competence and resources needed for innovative developments and large-scale rationalizations which single libraries – even large ones – cannot carry out. There are, however, some bad reasons, succinctly stated by Dubberley (1998): 'Although many governmental entities are relatively effective, far more are ineffective in their traditional modes. They are cumbersome and complicated – enmeshed in Byzantine rules and procedures'; not to mention how difficult it is for the public sector to get rid of even grossly inefficient employees. The outsourcing trend may thus be a testimony to the inadequacy of public management.

Third, the whole migration to online resources not 'owned' or physically present in the library may be conceived of as one enormous outsourcing venture which will eventually make the present move towards the outsourcing of technical services seem unimportant and possibly useless. As my own head of acquisitions asked me recently: 'If we are moving full-speed towards substituting electronic periodicals for paper periodicals, then why should we waste time on outsourcing the handling of paper periodicals first?'

Fees

An obvious internal strategy for raising a library's income is to introduce new fees and raise existing fees. Formerly, this issue caused violent debate among librarians, but today fees seem more and more to be taken for granted. The question is rather how they affect use and whether or not certain core services should be excepted from charging or not.

Two cases from eastern Europe have been reported. One concerns the Library for Foreign Literature in Moscow. Traditionally, Russian libraries had no other funding sources than state or local budgets and the very idea of charging for library services was 'shocking and indecent'. In 1989, however, the state stopped providing the Library of Foreign Literature with hard currency and salaries fell below the official standard of living. So new sources of income had to be found. Charges were introduced for a number of services considered to be additional or supplementary, e.g. photocopying, but the heavy money earner has shown to be a bibliographic and iconographic search service, some subjects being more spiritually edifying for the librarian ('The world of the Holy Bible') and some less so ('Cruelty in modern art') (Sinitsyna, 1997).

The other case, from a similar background, is the Cluj Medical Library, Romania. Fees for a number of formerly free services, e.g. photocopying, were introduced and fees today generate an important income for a library in a very difficult situation. Initially, users and local staff reacted in opposite ways to the changes, perceived as a way of making extra money for the staff. When the income was used ostentatiously for the benefit of the library and readers, attitudes changed. The introduction of fee-based services thus became a stimulus for an institutional culture change. In connection with borrowing cards it was helped by the card itself becoming a status symbol for students as evidence of their being a medical student (Lamont and Robu, 1997).

These cases are concerned with charging for 'additional services'. Other libraries have transgressed that sacred threshold of charging for essential services, i.e. book loans. Reports from Germany show that charging for book loans is quite common and systematized (Rossoll, 1997). A study from Heidelberg performed with proper German Gründlichkeit documents the effects of introduction of fee-based user cards vs. fees for individual loans. The introduction of fees led to a fall in the number of active users, the fall being biggest in the group of 18–25 year olds. The successive decisions concerning the size of fees for the annual user's card vs. the fees for individual book loans appear to have been a case of advanced library experimentation with market forces (Heimann, 1997).

The relationship between library use and size of library fees has also been investigated in public libraries in Israel, where annual fees for library use are quite common. No statistical correlation was found (Shoham, 1998): ordinary market forces may not apply in the Holy Land.

An Irish case is reported by Latimer (1997) and an investigation of charging for ILL in UK university libraries was performed by Clinton (1996).

Fund-raising

Fund-raising, sponsoring and friend-raising are very much an American thing, arising out of a social system not founded on a European welfare state model, but leaving a number of social and cultural issues to be dealt with by private charity. Articles with cases and good advice abound (e.g. Lapsley, 1996; Marino and Cooney, 1996; Hannah, 1997). Apparently, American universities are now beginning to use the word 'development' in preference to 'fund-raising'. It is unclear whether this is in consideration of the delicate sensibilities of academics or of donors.

Nonetheless, fund-raising and sponsoring now seem to be spreading to other parts of the world, for example, Germany (Klut, 1996). Libraries active in this area should be aware of tax complications (Dörpinghaus, 1998; Snyder, 1998), and the Internet may of course be used for fund-raising and friend-raising on the Web (Franken and Rau, 1997; Corson-Finnertyand Blanchard, 1998).

Library directors wondering what all this may mean to them personally will be left in no doubt by Martin's very informative article (1998) on the changing role of the library director in relation to fund-raising. In maturing a development programme, i.e. a fund-raising programme, the library director will be required to travel up to one week a month making appointments with leadership prospects and also some 'discovery' calls. This precious advice is added: 'A sponsorship prospect with serious intentions of making a gift should normally be visited at least three times before the "ask".' Many library directors would probably not like to be transmogrified into fund-raisers and would rather agree with African university librarians that 'the responsibility for funding libraries rests squarely with the university, and, in the public sector, ultimately with the government' (Rosenberg, 1998).

The future

The basic future prospect for library budgeting as of today has been formulated by Martin and Wolf (1998) in *Budgeting for information access*:

> The first, and possibly the most drastic, effect [of the electronic revolution] on libraries will be further shifts between categories of budget expenditure . . . Although, for some time to come, libraries will continue to spend substantial amounts on printed and similar resources, gradually there will be a move to spend more and more on electronic materials and access. The shift will be controlled by the degree to which the publishing community moves towards electronic publication. (Bowen, 1996; Pastine, 1996; Ray, 1996; see also Baker, 1997).

Organizational structure

The basic text on libraries as organizations would still appear to be Martin's *Organizational structure of libraries*, published first in 1984 and in a revised edition in 1996. In the chapter on the internal structure of the library, he points out that the predominant structure in the traditional library is the functional one, where departments are defined by a main function (e.g. acquisitions). In various library types and individual libraries, the functional structure is supplemented to a greater or lesser extent by departments based on subjects, user groups, geography, form of materials, language (Martin, 1996).

Evidently, in a period of organizational turmoil such as libraries are undergoing nowadays, the issue of structure ought not to be neglected and has not been. A first question asked in the literature is whether there is an ideal structure (Haka, 1996). The question, of course, is a logical and rhetorical one and it is effortlessly and emphatically answered with a no: 'No existe un modelo de organización bueno y todos los demás malos' (Angulo, 1996). In Plato's world of ideas there might have been an ideal library with an ideal structure, but in this postmodernistic age where there is nothing ideal at all, it would be truly strange to discuss the ideal library structure. The broad consensus among authors is very well expressed by Angulo: 'lo importante es contar con una estructura orgánica que permita a la Biblioteca cumplir sus objetivos . . . que contribuya a que el personal se sienta motivado con su trabajo, involucrado en los proyectos e integrado en la institución; que sea flexible, es decir, capaz de responder a los cambios que se produzcan'.

Even if it is generally agreed that there is no ideal library structure, there is a strong US trend in the development of library structure today which is propagated almost as if the true gospel or at least the library philosophers' stone had finally been found. The message is that the traditional hierarchical structure is bad and that libraries should move towards flatter structures (Boissé, 1996). Hewitt (1997) did a study which showed that librarians' dissatisfaction with traditional structure was focused on insufficient flexibility, too little external or client-centred orientation, too little staff empowerment and specific problems with the management process. According to Honea (1997), a basic problem with the typical administrative structure in academic libraries is that it is in conflict with academic culture. This culture respects expertise power, i.e. power accruing to individual by virtue of special knowledge. In academic libraries, to the contrary, the structure is based on position power, i.e. power accruing to an individual by virtue of a particular position in the formal organization. Although Honea is not blind to certain strengths of the traditional system, she maintains that it is not conducive to the self-actualization connected with expertise power, that it is inflexible, formalized and tends to generate 'parochial' attitudes. Honea therefore advocates a transformation of traditional library structure by creating a balance between the two types of organizational structure: expertise-based structure representing the individual and position structure representing the formal organization (see also Campbell, 1996).

A Norwegian study focuses on how the traditional bureaucratic-rational structure in libraries naturally fosters rigidity. This inevitably becomes counterproductive with regard to the larger goals and leads to pathological states like super-control, super-complexity and super-stability (Olaisen *et al.*, 1996).

What to do? Apart from flatter structures, generally, the major themes of the US literature on the development of library structure are participatory management, empowerment and team structure. These trends may be seen as manifestations of deeper cultural forces (cf. Day, 1998) which are shaping the workplace today. Empowerment and added value 'are two important, irreversible, universal trends, occurring throughout business, industry, and all of society . . . We might think of these two trends as huge waves flowing across the ocean getting larger as they progress' (Sweeney, 1997). Interestingly, most writers on the subject and promoters of this cause seem to belong to the managerial class.

One veteran of the movement from Duke University has interesting comments on this movement in an article called 'How can something that sounds so good make me feel so bad? The Dilbertian dilemma' (Lubans, 1998). Workers want adequate elbow room for decision making, opportunity to learn continually on the job, an optimum level of variety, mutual support and respect, meaningfulness and a desirable future. Managers would like workers to have these things. But even in libraries where managers and employees have wholeheartedly espoused these ideas, the success rate is not impressive. Barriers to success are still, according to Lubans, the intractability of the existing systems, structure and some incumbents, generational and 'genetic' factors, perceived expense in terms of diminished productivity and the 'kudzu' hierarchy, meaning that the dominant organizational structure and culture can smother positive motives and results. Day (1998) also points to the Dilbertian dilemma, claiming – not without malice – that empowerment may be just another management ploy designed to improve productivity.

To a radical proponent of empowerment in libraries, Sweeney (1997), it is much more than delegation: 'It means that someone is . . . given the power of a full partner in making important decisions . . . Teams of employees may be given budgetary control over their own work and the authority to hire new team members without prior consultation with management.' However, empowerment is not even in Sweeney's view unlimited, it extends so far as responsibility allows. 'Empowerment . . . means nothing without corresponding responsibility . . . This full partnership is not unrestricted freedom to make decisions without regard to consequences.'

Team structure as a 'humanistic' management system is the subject of Baldwin and Migneault (1996), both of the University of New Mexico General Library, where teamwork was implemented as an organizational alternative to traditional hierarchic library management as far back as 1986. The whole book is a jubilant celebration of teamworking, but the authors have, fairly, summarized some disadvantages of such a structure: there is an illusion of unanimity, a view of the 'opposition' as inept, avoidance of disagreements, collective rationalization in the case of clearly unworkable decisions, self-appointed mind guards, pressure on dissenting members, self-righteousness and a shared feeling of unassailability. Among the advantages are: great adaptability, individual empowerment in flattened hierarchies, powerful teams, emphasis on humanistic values based on Douglas McGregor's Theory X.

For two case studies on participatory management and empowerment in Ghana and the USA see Akpena (1997) and Pitkin (1997). For a manual on team structure see Bluck (1996) and for four more US cases see Bender (1997), Butcher (1997), De Vries (1997) and Echt (1997).

Managers

That library managers have different personal styles is no surprise. A taxonomy of library managers in the form of a field guide might be useful reading to managers who innocently wonder whether they have personal styles or foibles which staff might notice. An example:

> Elbow-patched therapist trasher: Known for its incessant call, 'Yes, I understand your feelings on this', the therapist manager is a non-indigenous species, imported from the human relations movement of the 1970s. Its well-meaning but misguided adherents believe that the purpose of management is to make everyone feel better. Unique in silhouette, always perched in an easy chair, leaning forward with hand under chin, listening attentively to subordinates. Not known for conflict resolution skills or problem solving; nonetheless a very friendly bird. Coloration of plumage always soothing; earthy browns, tans, and deep red. (Lichtenstein, 1997).

A first issue reflected in the predominantly American literature on the subject is the difference between managers and leaders. Managers seemingly do the old POSDCORB thing – planning, organizing, staffing, directing, coordinating, reporting and budgeting – they command and control (Giesecke *et al.*, 1997; H.S. White, 1997). Leaders, it seems, do something completely different. They are change agents (Shaughnessy, 1996b), who motivate, inspire and energize (H.S. White, 1997), who provide support for staff to help them adapt to the uncertain environment (Giesecke *et al.*, 1997), who bring the best out in people (Sweeney, 1997) and who are visionaries (Riggs, 1997).

On a discordant note, H.S. White (1997) challenges the general axiom that managers should become leaders. Both are needed: leaders for unfettered creativity and independent action and managers for doing that which is necessary in an environment circumscribed by all the normal constraints of institutional life.

As for desirable leadership traits, Sweeney (1997) gives the following list: wisdom, knowledge, understanding, vision, resourcefulness, performance, collaboration, courage, energy, flexibility, persistence, initiative, creativity, communication, influence, empathy for other human beings, and even a sense of humour. Maybe one should add: a generous tolerance of one's own shortcomings.

Sweeney's article highlights the paradox of leadership: on the one hand, libraries need stronger, more visionary leadership; on the other hand, each staff member should be given more power over his or her own work life through empowerment.

This paradox can only be unravelled, he claims, by realizing that leadership is not about control. To some the paradox may not be that easily resolved: 'the leader must develop a vision', 'the leader must decide on what is most important to the organization', Sweeney says. But if empowerment is truly making employees full partners, why must they not develop the vision together, on an equal basis, in a consensus process which is not inspired and led by the leader, but sustained by all the full, equal partners in Sweeney's ideal, empowered and reengineered library?

Apart from the general discussion on managers and leaders, the following specific issues have been treated in the literature: the changing role of associate directors and department heads (Bloss and Lanier, 1997; Giesecke *et al.*, 1997); the pivotal role of the library director/provost relationship (Dougherty, 1998b; White, 1998); the situation of new college library directors (Hardesty, 1997; O'Keeffe, 1998); the missing women library directors in India (Dasgupta, 1998) and the USA (Fisher, 1997, 1998; Kirkland, 1997); evaluation of public library leaders (Osborne, 1996); demands on library managers in the new South Africa (Swanepoel, 1996); and the situation of academic library directors in the USA (D'Andraia, 1997).

References

Abbott, C. and Rosenberg, D. (1996) *Performance indicators: a training aid for university librarians.* London: International African Institute.

Abel, R. (1998) The return of the native. *American Libraries*, **29**(1), 76–78.

Agada, J. (1996) Outsourcing of corporate information services: implications for redesigning corporate library services. *International Information and Library Review*, **28**(2), 157–176.

Akpena, J.E. (1997) Participative management in a university library: the case of Abubakar Tafawa Balewa University Library, Bauchi, Nigeria. *Aslib Proceedings*, **49**(7), 190–193.

Almeida, C. de (1997) Is there a public library funding crisis? *New Library World*, **98**(1135/1136), 144–155.

Angulo, S.C. (1996) Organización interna de la biblioteca universitaria y puesta al día de su personal. *Boletín de la Asociación Andaluza de Bibliotecarios*, **12**(45), 9–17.

Baba, Z. and Broady, J. (1998) Organisational effectiveness assessment: case studies of the National Library of Wales and the Perpustakaan Negara Malaysia. In: *Proceedings* (1998), pp. 319–342.

Badu, E.E. (1997) Strategic planning in an uncertain environment: the case of Ghana's university libraries. *Information Development*, **13**(4), 172–178.

Baker, D. (1997) (ed.) *Resource management in academic libraries.* London: Library Association Publishing.

Baker, R.J. (1998) Outsourcing in Riverside County: anomaly, not prophecy. *Library Journal*, **123**(5), 34–37.

Baldwin, D.A. and Migneault, R.L. (1996) *Humanistic management by teamwork: an organizational and administrative alternative for academic libraries.* Englewood, CO: Libraries Unlimited.

Barton, D. (1996) (ed.) *Library contracts in a post-NBA environment.* Bruton: Capital Planning.

Bates, M.E. (1997) Outsourcing, co-sourcing, and core competencies: what's an information professional to do? *Information Outlook*, 1(12), 35–37.

Bénaud, C.-L. and Bordeianu, S. (1998) *Outsourcing library operations in academic libraries: an overview of issues and outcomes.* Englewood, CO: Libraries Unlimited.

Bender, L.J. (1997) Team organization – learning organization: the University of Arizona four years into it. *Information Outlook*, 1(9), 19–22.

Birdsall, D.G. (1997) Strategic planning in academic libraries: a political perspective. In: C.A. Schwartz (ed.) *Restructuring academic libraries: organizational development in the wake of technological change.* Chicago: Association of College and Research Libraries, pp. 253–265.

Bloss, A. and Lanier, D. (1997) The library department head in the context of matrix management and reengineering. *College and Research Libraries*, 58(6), 499–508.

Bluck, R. (1996) *Team management.* London: Library Association Publishing. [Library Training Guides.]

Boissé, J.A. (1996) Adjusting the horizontal hold: flattening the organization. *Library Administration and Management*, 10(2), 77–81.

Bowen, W.G. (1996) How libraries can help to pay their way in the future. *Logos*, 7(3), 237–241.

Broady, J.E. (1997) Costing of bibliographic services. *Journal of Librarianship and Information Science*, 29(2), 89–94.

Brockman, J. (1997) (ed.) *Quality management and benchmarking in the information sector: results of recent research.* London: Bowker-Saur. [British Library Research and Innovation Report 47.]

Brooks, P. *et al.* (1997) The development of a scale to measure the quality of an academic library from the perspective of its users. In: Brockman, J. (1997) (ed.), pp. 263–304.

Brophy, P. (1996) *Quality management for information and library managers.* Aldershot: Aslib.

Brophy, P. (1997) Total quality management. In: Baker, D. (1997) (ed.), pp. 74–84.

Brophy, P. *et al.* (1997) *Eqlipse evaluation and quality in library performance: system for Europe. Final report.* Preston: University of Lancashire, Centre for Research in Library and Information Management.

Brophy, P. and Coulling, K. (1997) Quality management in libraries. In: Brockman, J. (1997) (ed.), pp. 33–119.

Bryant, T. (1998) Strategic planning at the Library of Congress. *Liber Quarterly*, 8(4), 370–372.

Bryson, J. (1997) *Managing information services: an integrated approach.* Aldershot: Gower.

Bryson, J. (1998) Financial planning. In: Prytherch, R. (1998a) (ed.), pp. 52–75.

Butcher, K.S. (1997) Decision making in a team environment. *Library Administration and Management*, 11(4), 222–230.

Byrne, A. (1997) CAUL's interest in performance measurement. *Australian Academic and Research Libraries*, 28(4), 252–258.

Calvert, P.J. (1997) Measuring service quality: from theory into practice. *Australian Academic and Research Libraries*, 28(3), 198–204.

Calvert, P.J. (1998) A different time, a different country: an instrument for measuring service quality in Singapore's polytechnic libraries. *Journal of Academic Librarianship*, **24**(4), 296–299.

Calvert, P.J. and Hernon, P. (1997) Surveying quality within university libraries. *Journal of Academic Librarianship*, **23**(5), 408–415.

Campbell, J.D. (1996) Building an effectiveness pyramid for leading successful organizational transformation. *Library Administration and Management*, **10**(2), 82–86.

Cerri, R. (1996) Perché bibliotecari e archivisti hanno paura delle privatizzazioni? *Archivi and Computer*, (3/4), 289–295.

Ceynowa, K. (1997) Geschäftsprozessmanagement für wissenschaftliche Bibliotheken. *Zeitschrift für Bibliothekswesen und Bibliographie*, **44**(3), 241–263.

Chalmers, A. (1997) Strategic management in eleven national libraries: a report on a research study. *Alexandria*, **9**(2), 101–113.

Chen, T.-Y. (1997) An evaluation of the relative performance of university libraries in Taipei. *Library Review*, **46**(3/4), 190–201.

Cheng, G.Y.T. (1996) The use of benchmarking in improving the library service quality of devolved management. *Journal of the Hong Kong Library Association*, (18), 1–14.

Clayton, P. (1997) *Implementation of organizational innovation: studies of academic and research libraries*. San Diego, CA: Academic Press.

Clinton, P. (1996) Charging users for remote document supply in UK university libraries. *OCLC Systems and Services*, **12**(3), 12–17.

Cockrill, A. (1997) Coping with change: issues facing British and German university libraries in the 1990s. *Journal of Librarianship and Information Science*, **29**(2), 77–88.

Coleman, V. *et al.* (1997) Toward a TQM paradigm: using SERVQUAL to measure library service quality. *College and Research Libraries*, **58**(3), 237–251.

Cooper, L. (1997) How much should it cost? An introduction to management use of costing information. *Health Libraries Review*, **14**(4), 209–217.

Corrall, S. (1998) Scenario planning: a strategic management tool for the future. *Managing Information*, **5**(9), 34–37.

Corson-Finnerty, A. and Blanchard, L. (1998) *Fundraising and friend-raising on the web*. Chicago: American Library Association.

Cram, J. (1996) Performance management, measurement and reporting in a time of information-centred change. *Australian Library Journal*, **45**(3), 225–238.

Crawford, J. (1996) *Evaluation of library and information services*. London: Aslib.

Crawford, J. *et al.* (1998) The stakeholder approach to the construction of performance measures. *Journal of Librarianship and Information Science*, **30**(2), 87–112.

Cullen, R. (1998) Does performance measurement improve organizational effectiveness? A postmodern analysis. In: *Proceedings* (1998), pp. 3–20.

Cummings, A.M. *et al.* (1996a) Components of library expenditures. *Journal of Library Administration*, **23**(3/4), 29–48.

Cummings, A.M. *et al.* (1996b) Growth of library expenditures. *Journal of Library Administration*, **23**(3/4), 49–70.

D'Andraia, F. (1997) (ed.) *The academic library director: reflections on a position in transition*. New York: Haworth Press. Also published as *Journal of Library Administration*, 24(3).

Dasgupta, K. (1998) Women as managers of libraries: a developmental process in India. *IFLA Journal*, **24**(4), 245–249.

Davis, D.S. and Bernstein, A.M. (1997) From survey to service: using patron input to improve customer satisfaction. *Technical Services Quarterly*, **14**(3), 47–62.

Dawes, S. (1997) Managing with quality assurance. *Library Management*, **18**(2), 73–79.

Day, M.T. (1998) Transformational discourse: ideologies of organizational change in the academic library and information science literature. *Library Trends*, **46**(4), 635–667.

de Bruin, H. (1996) Strategic information services management under conditions of financial restraint: a perspective from service management theory. *South African Journal of Library and Information Science*, **64**(3), 167–176.

De Vries, J. (1997) Teamwork: getting results in Minnesota. *Quarterly Bulletin of the International Association of Agricultural Information Specialists*, **42**(3/4), 257–259.

Dobb, L.S. (1998) Bringing it all back home: insourcing what you do well. *Bottom Line*, **11**(3), 105–110.

Dörpinghaus, H.J. (1998) Sponsoring für wissenschaftliche Bibliotheken in öffentlicher Trägerschaft: steuerrechtliche Aspekte. *Zeitschrift für Bibliothekswesen und Bibliographie*, **45**(3), 279–294.

Dougherty, R.M. (1998a) Inside Pandora's box: navigating permanent 'white-water' of organizational change. *Against the Grain*, **9**(6), 68–74.

Dougherty, R.M. (1998b) Library director/provost relationships and faculty attitudes toward changes in libraries. *Library Issues*, **18**(3), 1–2.

Dow, R.F. (1998) Using assessment criteria to determine library quality. *Journal of Academic Librarianship*, **24**(4), 277–281.

Dubberley, R.A. (1998) Why outsourcing is our friend. *American Libraries*, **29**(1), 72–74.

Echt, R. (1997) The realities of teams in technical services at Michigan State University Libraries. *Library Acquisitions*, **21**(2), 179–187.

Ellis, D. and Norton, B. (1996) *Implementing BS EN ISO 9000 in libraries*. London: Aslib.

Ellis, M. (1998) Benchmarking public libraries: comparisons in context. *Australasian Public Libraries and Information Services*, **11**(2), 56–60.

Fatzer, J.B. (1996) Budget stringency as a stimulus to innovation: the cases of Louisiana and Ohio. *Journal of Library Administration*, **22**(2/3), 57–77.

Fisher, W. (1997) The question of gender in library management. *Library Administration and Management*, **11**(4), 231–236.

Ford, G. (1996) Service level agreements. *New Review of Academic Librarianship*, **2**, 49–58.

Forrest, M. and Cawasjee, A.-M. (1997) Costing the library services: Cairns Library – case study. *Health Libraries Review*, **14**(4), 219–232.

Fowler, R.K. (1998) The university library as learning organization for innovation: an exploratory study. *College and Research Libraries*, **59**(3), 220–231.

Franken, K. and Rau, G. (1997) Werbung von Sponsoren über das Internet: ein Versuch an der Bibliothek der Universität Konstanz. *Bibliotheksdienst*, **31**(3), 446–451.

Gall, C.F. *et al.* (1997) Strategic planning with multitype libraries in the community: a model with extra funding as the main goal. *Bulletin of the Medical Library Association*, **85**(3), 252–259.

Garlick, M. (1997) The public libraries (New South Wales) benchmarking database. *LASIE*, **28**(4), 35–39.

Garlick, M. and Hoegh-Guldberg, H. (1998) Measuring customer satisfaction: myth or reality? *Australasian Public Libraries and Information Services*, **11**(2), 61–74.

Garrod, P. and Kinnell, M. (1997a) Benchmarking development needs in the LIS sector. *Journal of Information Science*, **23**(2), 111–118.

Garrod, P. and Kinnell, M. (1997b) Towards library excellence: best practice benchmarking in the library and information sector. In: Brockman, J. (1997) (ed.), pp. 305–398.

Gattermann, G. (1996) Budgeting – pros and cons. *New Review of Academic Librarianship*, **2**, 41–48.

Giapicconi, T. (1998) Performance measurement and management strategy: a public library perspective from France. In: *Proceedings* (1998), pp. 21–30.

Giesecke, J. (1998) (ed.) *Scenario planning for libraries*. Chicago: American Library Association.

Giesecke, J. *et al.* (1997) Changing management roles for associate directors in libraries. *Library Administration and Management*, **11**(3), 172–180.

Girard-Billon, A. and Giappiconi, T. (1997) L'évaluation dans les bibliothèques publiques françaises: une situation contrastée. *Bulletin des Bibliothèques de France*, **43**(1), 78–84.

Goble, D.S. (1997) Managing in a change environment: from coping to comfort. *Library Administration and Management*, **11**(3), 151–156.

Gohlke, A. (1997) Benchmark for strategic performance improvement. *Information Outlook*, **1**(8), 22–24.

Graham, T. (1996) Funding arrangements for UK universities and their libraries. *New Review of Academic Librarianship*, **2**, 27–40.

Griebel, R. (1996) University library budgets – model and reality. *New Review of Academic Librarianship*, **2**, 59–67.

Haka, C.H. (1996) Organizational design: is there AN answer? *Library Administration and Management*, **10**(2), 74–76.

Häkli, E. (1996) Auf dem Weg zum Globalhaushalt. *Zeitschrift für Bibliothekswesen und Bibliographie*, **43**(2), 103–109.

Hamilton, F. (1998) The Internet as an information tool. In: Prytherch, R. (1998a) (ed.), pp. 214–230.

Hannah, K.C. (1997) Alternative funding for libraries: a plan for success. *Bottom Line*, **10**(4), 169–175.

Hardesty, L. (1997) College library directors mentor program: 'passing it on': a personal reflection. *Journal of Academic Lbrarianship*, **23**(4), 281–290.

Harnesk, J. (1998) The ISO standard on Library Performance Indicators (ISO 11620). In: *Proceedings* (1998), pp. 61–66.

Hart, E. (1997) Operating costs. In: Baker, D. (1997) (ed.), pp. 175–188.

Hayes, R.M. (1993) *Strategic management for academic libraries: a handbook*. Westport, CT: Greenwood Press.

Hayes, R.M. and Walter, V.A. (1997) *Strategic management for public libraries: a handbook*. Westport, CT: Greenwood Press.

Heimann, J. (1997) Drei Jahre Ausleihegebühren in der Stadtbücherei Heidelberg: ein Erfahrungsbericht. *Bibliotheksdienst*, **31**(5), 814–828.

Helfer, D.S. (1997) Insourced or outsourced: a tale of two libraries. *Searcher*, **5**(8), 68–70.

Hernon, P. and Altman, E. (1996) *Service quality in academic libraries*. Norwood, NJ: Ablex Publishing Corporation.

Hernon, P. and Altman, E. (1998) *Assessing service quality: satisfying the expectations of library customers*. Chicago: American Library Association.

Hernon, P. and Calvert, P.J. (1996) Methods for measuring service quality in university libraries in New Zealand. *Journal of Academic Librarianship*, **22**(5), 387–391.

Hersberger, R. (1997) Leadership and management of technological innovation in academic libraries. *Library Administration and Management*, **11**(1), 26–29.

Hewitt, J.A. (1997) What's wrong with library organization? Factors leading to restructuring in research libraries. *North Carolina Libraries*, **55**(1), 3–6.

Hill, C. (1998) Insourcing the outsourced library: the Sun story. *Library Journal*, **123**(4), 46–48.

Hill, D.W. (1998) To outsource or not: University of Alabama Libraries engage in pilot project with OCLC's TechPro. *Cataloging and Classification Quarterly*, **26**(1), 63–73.

Hipsman, J.L. (1996) Strategic planning for academic libraries. *Technical Services Quarterly*, **13**(3/4), 85–104.

Hirshon, A. and Winters, B. (1996) *Outsourcing library technical services: a how-to-do-it manual for librarians*. New York: Neal-Schuman Publishers. [How-To-Do-It Manuals for Librarians 69.]

Holt, G. (1998) Private management of a public library LSSI at Riverside, CA. *Bottom Line*, **11**(1), 31–33.

Honea, S.M. (1997) Transforming administration in academic libraries. *Journal of Academic Librarianship*, **23**(3), 183–190.

Hout, T.M. (1999) Are managers obsolete? *Harvard Business Review*, **77**(2), 161–168.

Hutchins, J. (1997) Costing of materials, operations and services. In: Baker, D. (1997) (ed.), pp. 98–109.

Izquierdo Alonso, M. *et al.* (1996) Un modelo de gestión de calidad total para las bibliotecas públicas. *Scire*, **2**(1), 63–92.

Jain, S.L. and Gupta, D.K. (1996) TQM in library and information science. *Annals of Library Science and Documentation*, **43**(2), 41–47.

Janke, E. (1997) Reengineering und Chaos-Management in Informationseinrichtungen. *Nachrichten für Dokumentation*, **48**(1), 3–7.

Johannsen, C.G. (1996a) Strategic issues in quality management: 1. Theoretical considerations. *Journal of Information Science*, **22**(3), 155–164.

Johannsen, C.G. (1996b) Strategic issues in quality management: 2. Survey analysis. *Journal of Information Science*, **22**(4), 231–245.

Kirkland, J.J. (1997) The missing women library directors: deprivation vs. mentoring. *College and Research Libraries*, **58**(4), 376–384.

Klut, B. (1996) Sponsoring – Allheilmittel für öffentliche Bibliotheken? *BuchMobil*, **10**(2), 13–17.

Kyrillidou, M. (1996) *Developing indicators for academic library performance: ratios from the ARL statistics 1993–1994 and 1994–1995*. Washington, DC: Association of Research Libraries.

Lamont, S.W. and Robu, I. (1997) Self-financing services in libraries: a method of increasing limited library budgets in post-communist Romania? *Inspel*, **31**(2), 95–102.

Lapsley, A. (1996) Keys to a fundraiser's success. *Bottom Line*, **9**(3), 39–42.

Larsen, S. (1998) Contract management in research libraries: the Danish case. The contract of the State and University Library and the Royal Library with the Ministry of Culture. *Liber Quarterly*, **8**(3), 351–363.

Latimer, K. (1997) Free to fee. *Art Libraries Journal*, **22**(1), 24–28.

Lee, S. and Clack, M.E. (1996) Continued organizational transformation: the Harvard College Library's experience. *Library Administration and Management*, **10**(2), 98–104.

Leiserson, A.B. and Montgomery, J.G. (1997) Outsourcing revisited: what are recent events telling us? *Trends*, **8**(5), 5–8.

Lewis, D.W. (1984) Bringing the market to libraries. *Journal of Academic Librarianship*, **10**(2), 73–76.

Lewis, D.W. (1986) An organizational paradigm for effective academic libraries. *College and Research Libraries*, **47**(4), 337–353.

Lewis, D.W. (1994) Making academic reference services work. *College and Research Libraries*, **55**(5), 445–456.

Libby, K.A. and Caudle, D.M. (1997) A survey of outsourcing of cataloging in academic libraries. *College and Research Libraries*, **58**(6), 550–560.

Lichtenstein, A.A. (1997) A field guide to library managers: giving field marks of species found in the Northeastern United States. *Arkansas Libraries*, **54**(3), 5–7.

Line, M.B. (1996) Managing change in libraries. *Journal of Information, Communication and Library Science* [Taiwan], **2**(3), 3–11.

Littlejohn, N. and Wales, B. (1998) Measuring unit effectiveness: a pragmatic approach to quality assessment in academic libraries. *College and Undergraduate Libraries*, **5**(1), 103–121.

Lovecy, I. (1997) Information technology. In: Baker, D. (1997) (ed.), pp. 158–174.

Lubans, J. (1998) How can something that sounds so good make me feel so bad? The Dilbertian dilemma. *Library Administration and Management*, **12**(1), 7–14.

McBeth, R. (1997) Managing in the information age: new rules for a new reality. *Advances in Library Administration and Organization*, **15**, 165–185.

McDonald, A. (1997) Space planning and management. In: Baker, D. (1997) (ed), pp. 189–206.

McGregor, F.M. (1997) Quality assessment – combating complacency. *Australian Library Journal*, **46**(1), 82–92.

Mackenzie, C. (1997) From forward plan to business plan: strategic planning in public libraries. *Australasian Public Libraries and Information Services*, **10**(4), 191–200.

Malinconico, S.M. (1997) Librarians and innovation. *Program*, **31**(1) 47–58.

Marcum, J.W. (1996) Can the college library become a learning organization? *Advances in Library Administration and Organization*, **16**, 39–62.

Marcum, J.W. (1998) Outsourcing in libraries: tactic, strategy, or 'meta-strategy'? *Library Administration and Management*, **12**(1), 15–25.

Marino, N.R. and Cooney, M. (1996) Winning corporate support: keys to a successful grant proposal and presentation. *Journal of Business and Finance Librarianship*, **2**(1), 15–27.

Martin, L.A. (1996) *Organizational structure in libraries*, rev. edn. Lanham, MD: Scarecrow Press. [Library Administration Series 5.]

Martin, M.S. and Wolf, M.T. (1998) *Budgeting for information access*. Chicago: American Library Association.

Martin, S.K. (1998) The changing role of the library director: fund-raising and the academic library. *Journal of Academic Librarianship*, **24**(1), 3–10.

Mayère, A. and Muet, F. (1997) Le démarche qualité appliquée aux bibliothèques et services d'information. *Bulletin des Bibliothèques de France*, **43**(1), 10–18.

Miles, K. (1996) Outsourcing in private law libraries since the Baker and McKenzie action. *Bottom Line*, **9**(2), 10–13.

Milner, E. *et al.* (1997) Quality management and public library services – the right approach? In: Brockman, J. (1997) (ed.), pp. 121–262.

Mintzberg, H. (1994) *The rise and fall of strategic planning*. New York: Prentice Hall.

Moeske, U. (1997) Kosten-Leistungsrechnung und Bibliotheksstruktur. *Bibliothek*, **21**(3), 301–306.

Morris, B. (1996) *First steps in management*. London: Library Association Publishing. [The Successful LIS Professional Series.]

Mulye, R. and Deshpande, N.J. (1998) A review of quality systems and its applications to libraries. *Library Science with a Slant to Documentation and Information Studies*, **35**(1), 3–20.

Nitecki, D.A. (1998) Assessment of service quality in academic libraries: focus on the applicability of the SERVQUAL. In: *Proceedings* (1998), pp. 181–196.

O'Connor, S. *et al.* (1997) Scenario planning for a library future. *Australian Library Journal*, **46**(2), 186–194.

O'Keeffe, J. (1998) Small college library directors: getting in the door and surviving on the job. *College and Research Libraries*, **59**(2), 140–153.

Olaisen, J. *et al.* (1996) Pathological processes in library systems. *Libri*, **46**(3), 121–140.

Osborne, R. (1996) Evaluation of leadership in Ontario public libraries. *Canadian Journal of Information and Library Science*, **21**(3/4), 20–34.

Pardo, J.V. (1997) El control en la gestión bibliotecaria. *Boletín de la Asociación Andaluza de Bibliotecarios*, **13**(46), 9–27.

Pastine, M. (1996) Academic libraries and campus computing costs. *Bottom Line*, **9**(3), 20–32.

Pilia, E. (1997) La misurazione dei servizi delle biblioteche delle universita. *Bolletino AIB* **37**(3), 281–326.

Pinto, L.G. (1998) Measuring the performance of Portuguese public libraries. In: *Proceedings* (1998), pp. 357–362.

Pitkin, G.M. (1997) Empowerment through strategic planning, financial redistribution, and structural reorganization. *Colorado Libraries*, **23**(2), 24–29.

Pluse, J. (1998) Human resource management. In: Prytherch, R. (1998a) (ed.), pp. 231–248.

Poll, R. (1996) Possibilities of income generation in German academic libraries. *New Review of Academic Librarianship*, **2**, 73–81.

Poll, R. (1998) The house that Jack built: the consequences of measuring. In: *Proceedings* (1998), pp. 39–46.

Poll, R. and Boekhorst, P. te (1996) *Measuring quality: international guidelines for performance measurement in academic libraries*. [Prepared by IFLA Section of University Libraries & Other General Research Libraries.] München: K.G. Saur. [IFLA Publications 76.]

Prins, H. and Geer, W. de (1995) *The image of the library and information profession: how we see ourselves – an investigation*. München: K.G. Saur. [IFLA Publications 71.]

Proceedings (1998) *of the 2nd Northumbria International Conference on performance measurement in library and information services*. Ed. P. Wressel and Associates. Newcastle upon Tyne Information North.

Prytherch, R. (1998a) (ed.) *Gower handbook of library and information management.* Aldershot: Gower.

Prytherch, R. (1998b) Strategic management. In: Prytherch, R. (1998a) (ed.), pp. 195–213.

Prytherch, R. (1998c) Strategic planning: the key to managing change. In: Prytherch, R. (1998a) (ed.), pp. 76–92.

Quinn, B. (1997) Adapting service quality concepts to academic libraries. *Journal of Academic Librarianship,* **23**(5), 359–369.

Quinn, B. and Coffman, S. (1996) Library-to-library outsourcing: interview with Steve Coffman. *Searcher,* **4**(8), 24–31.

Ray, P.M. (1996) Information economics and libraries in the digital age. *Bottom Line,* **9**(2), 29–34.

Renaud, R. (1997) Learning to compete: competition, outsourcing, and academic libraries. *Journal of Academic Librarianship,* **23**(2), 85–90.

Revill, D. (1997) Self-assessment of an academic library. *New Review of Academic Librarianship,* **3**, 151–168.

Riggs, D.E. (1997) What's in store for academic libraries? Leadership and management issues. *Journal of Academic Librarianship,* **23**(1), 3–8.

Roberts, S.A. (1998) *Financial and cost management for libraries and information services,* 2nd edn. East Grinstead: Bowker-Saur.

Robertson, M. and Trahn, I. (1997) Benchmarking academic libraries: an Australian case study. *Australian Academic and Research Libraries,* **28**(2), 126–141.

Rosenberg, D. (1998) The financing of university libraries in Africa. *Information Development,* **14**(2), 73–79.

Rossoll, E (1997) Situation und Entwicklungstendenzen bei den Gebühren in öffentlichen Bibliotheken. *Bibliotheksdienst,* **31**(1), 15–23.

Rowley, J. (1997) The library as a learning organization. *Library Management,* **18**(2), 88–91.

Ruth, H. (1998) The use of performance indicators in Helsinki public libraries. In: *Proceedings* (1998), pp. 363–368.

St. Clair, G. (1997a) Benchmarking and restructuring at Penn State Libraries. In: C.A. Schwartz (ed.) *Restructuring academic libraries: organizational development in the wake of technological change.* Chicago: Association of College and Research Libraries, pp. 206–212.

St. Clair, G. (1997b) *Total quality management in information services.* London: Bowker-Saur.

Savenije, B. (1998) Developing a strategic plan for the University Library of St. Petersburg: a project within the EU's Tempus Tacis Program. *Liber Quarterly,* **8**(4), 373–388.

Schneider, K.G. (1998) The McLibrary syndrome. *American Libraries,* **29**(1), 66–70.

Shaughnessy, T.W. (1996a) *Perspectives on quality in libraries.* Urbana, IL: Graduate School of Library and Information Science.

Shaughnessy, T.W. (1996b) The library director as change agent. *Journal of Library Administration,* **22**(2/3), 43–56.

Shoham, S. (1998) Fees in public libraries. *Public Library Quarterly,* **17**(1), 39–48.

Simpson, J. (1997) Strategic planning in a learning organization. *Nebraska Library Association Quarterly,* **27**(4), 15–18.

Sinitsyna, O.V. (1997) Paid services at the Library for Foreign Literature: new objectives, experience, perspectives. *Inspel,* **31**(2), 88–94.

Smith, M. (1998) The use of service level agreements in the British Library. In: *Proceedings* (1998), pp. 31–38.

Snyder, H. (1997) Protecting our assets: internal control principles in libraries. *Library Administration and Management*, **11**(1), 42–46.

Snyder, H. (1998) When fund-raising is too innovative. *Library Administration and Management*, **12**(1), 26–38.

Snyder, H. and Davenport, E. (1997) *Costing and pricing in the digital age: a practical guide for information services*. London: Library Association Publishing.

Solimine, G. (1997a) Carta dei servizi, obietto da non mancare. *Biblioteche Oggi*, **15**(10), 6–12.

Solimine, G. (1997b) Efficienza vs efficacia. *Biblioteche Oggi*, **15**(5), 30–35.

Spiller, D. (1998) Benchmarking in practice. In: *Proceedings* (1998), pp. 431–440.

Steward, J. (1997) Service level agreements and performance indicators. In: Baker, D. (1997) (ed.), pp. 85–97.

Stoffle, C.J. *et al.* (1996) Choosing our futures. *College and Research Libraries*, **57**(3), 213–225.

Sutter, E. (1997) La démarche qualité en bibliothèques: questions-réponses. *Bulletin des Bibliothèques de France*, **43**(1), 20–23.

Swanepoel, A.J. (1996) What is expected of library managers in a new democracy? *IATUL Proceedings*, **5**, 176–180.

Sweeney, R. (1997) Leadership skills in the reengineered library: empowerment and value added trend implications for library leaders. *Library Administration and Management*, **11**(1), 30–41.

Tammaro, A.M. (1997) La biblioteca universitaria quantificabile. *Biblioteche Oggi*, **15**(2), 66–77.

Trzan-Herman, N. and Kiauta, D. (1996) The organizational map: an important aspect of achieving total quality management in a pharmaceutical and medical library: a Slovenian case. *Libri*, **46**(2), 113–119.

Usherwood, B. (1996) *Rediscovering public library management*. London: Library Association Publishing.

Viljoen, J.H. and Underwood, P.G. (1997) Total quality management in libraries: fad or fact? *South African Journal of Library and Information Science*, **65**(1), 46–52.

Wätjen, H.-J. (1996) Financing higher education libraries in Germany. *New Review of Academic Librarianship*, **2**, 11–25.

What (1996) business are you in? Eliminate confusion with a good library mission statement. *The One-Person Library*, **13**(2), 5–7.

White, G. and Mack, D.C. (1996) ISO 9000 quality standards: new directions in quality control. *Journal of Business and Finance Librarianship*, **2**(1), 3–14.

White, H. (1998) Library director/provost relationships and faculty attitudes toward changes in libraries: addressing the specifics. *Library Issues*, **18**(3), 2–4.

White, H.S. (1997) Should leaders want to be managers and give up all that freedom? *Library Journal*, **122**(5), 48, 50.

White, M.D. (1997) Measuring service quality in libraries. *Advances in Library Administration and Organization*, **15**, 1–35.

Wilkinson, J. (1996) External funding sources: income generation in UK academic libraries. *New Review of Academic Librarianship*, **2**, 69–72.

Wilson, K.A. and Colver, M. (1997) (eds) *Outsourcing library technical services operations: practices in academic, public and special libraries.* Chicago: American Library Association, pp. 124–148.

Wood, L. (1998) Performance measurement and evaluation. In: Prytherch, R. (1998a) (ed.), pp. 124–148.

Copyright

10

Graham Cornish

Introduction

By their very nature, libraries, and to some extent archives and museums, rely on copyright material for their existence (Cornish, 1998d). Copyright protects whatever creators choose to create, whether journal articles, books, photographs, pictures or three-dimensional objects, and these are the items that libraries collect and disseminate to their users. Therefore the issue of copyright law is central to all library and information services. This is demonstrated by the number of guides to copyright law written specifically for those working in the library and information world (Pedley, 1998; Wall, 1998b; Cornish, 1999).

The context of copyright

The context of copyright as a whole is explored by Oakley (1998), who concentrates on the problems of images in libraries but extends this to copyright principles in general. However, when copyright law is discussed, the role and function of information intermediaries are rarely on the agenda. When they are raised, it is often as minor issues in comparison with the major reforms being proposed either nationally or internationally. A further complication is that developments in areas of copyright law totally unrelated to libraries often have a direct effect on the services they offer because of the interpretations put on the law in different contexts. Matters are further complicated in this area in that much of the reform proposed for copyright legislation comes from the leisure and entertainment industry, in which literally billions of pounds are involved on investment and potential revenue. Since the work done in the library and information field is relatively small, it is dragged along by reforms proposed by much bigger sectors. Effectively a journal article published in a local history society magazine may well be protected in the same way as the multitude of rights in a feature film representing an investment of several million pounds.

The international dimension

Neither libraries nor copyright exist in a vacuum and the international context of both is explored in detail by Liedes (1998), who outlines the major treaties in this area and their implications for the library and information world generally. As Marter (1998) points out, different cultures and traditions have a major impact on libraries, including library cooperation across frontiers. Also, Revelli (1998) reminds us that such concepts as 'fair dealing' and 'fair use' are not universal. The many changes that are proposed to international treaties will be reflected in due course in national laws, many of which will need careful study by librarians. The ramifications of the new World Intellectual Property Organization (WIPO) Treaty on Copyright are still being worked through in many legislatures. So far it has not been accessioned by a sufficient number of states to become effective, but this is likely to change in the near future. Nevertheless, as Giavarra (1998) points out, accession is a driving force behind European Union reforms. The impact on the electronic environment for libraries will be particularly serious unless strong representations are made. The WIPO Treaty is also behind changes being enacted in the USA (Grantham, 1999). It is already causing anxiety for librarians in Japan, where the impact on digital and electronic library services is still being worked out (Murakami, 1998). As Kemper (1998) notes, there is a long way to go, as in most major industrialized countries there are rapid moves to implement the treaty, whereas many developing countries see little point in doing so, since it strengthens considerably the bargaining power of the owners against the needs of the users. In short, many developing countries simply do not have the money to finance this sort of legislation.

The importance of copyright, as well as other issues on an international scale, has been recognized by IFLA, which has set up a Committee (1999) on copyright and other legal matters (CLM). This committee has already provided representation to WIPO at some of its major hearings and is in the process of setting up a series of sub-groups to deal with specific issues, not all of which are directly related to copyright. At the same time, the work of the European Copyright User Platform (ECUP) is being extended by a similar project in central and eastern Europe called CECUP, backed by the Finnish Library Association.

The European Union

In the European Union there has been a huge amount of activity as a result of the introduction of a draft directive on copyright (CEC, 1997). Wall (1998a) states that as proposed this would severely limit the rights of individuals to make copies for themselves. This view is reflected by Crosby (1998b), who thinks that the role of the library as an information provider is under serious threat in the digital world. As Cornish (1998j) reports, despite claiming to be harmonizing law, the draft would in fact continue to create disparity in the legislation of the member states as the privileges granted to users would be entirely optional. Hielmcrome (1998) also points out that the proposed legislation would limit the possibilities of importing books and journals into Europe as well as limiting access to online services, with the result that the legislation would limit access at the very time when imports too are being limited. Copying by institutions would be limited to establishments that are accessible to the public. While this would clearly include public libraries as normally understood (i.e. those serving the general public in towns and villages), whether or not an academic institution would be considered accessible to the public, or even a national library, could be a matter of considerable debate. The European Commission proposed that there should be no exceptions to the rights enjoyed by owners in the electronic environment. Despite heavy pressure and much lobbying by a number of organizations, the Commission has been unwilling to yield. In fact, the member of the European Parliament steering this legislation through its procedures actually said 'if you go to the cinema you pay, if you go to a concert you pay, so why not pay for other forms of information as well?' He took the view that the public sector should put more money into libraries so that they could recycle this to the copyright owner (R. Barzanti, oral communication, Rome, November 1998).

Music libraries are also worried about the proposed changes. Jewitt (oral communication, 1999) made representations for continued special library treatment in the discussion at the 'Music, copyright and the customer' seminar in Vienna, organized by the EC's Harmonica Project.

In an attempt to improve this legislative nightmare, the European Bureau for Library Information and Documentation Associations (EBLIDA) has carried out an enormous amount of lobbying (Cornish, 1998f). This continues and progress is notified through the EBLIDA website. This stand is supported by French librarians (Danset, 1998), who feel strongly that some privileges should be given for digitization. In the light of the expensive programme of digitization embarked upon by the Bibliothèque nationale de France, this is not surprising. Strong opposition to the proposals is expressed by FOBID (Federation of Library and Information Associations in the Netherlands) (Heuff, 1998b), which has drawn attention to the far-reaching consequences of the proposed legislation. EBLIDA has also been instrumental in helping to set up European Fair Practice in Copyright

Campaign (EFPICC), which brings together libraries, archives, organizations serving the blind and visually impaired, consumer associations and the microelectronics industry (*European*, 1998). An enormous number of articles have been written and a huge amount of website space taken up by the debates on this subject. A press release from the UK Library Association (1998) puts the case for fair practice very clearly and was widely circulated. While some governments are sympathetic, many owners are adamant that the privileges (exceptions) are no longer required and can be managed in quite a different way.

Library privileges and requirements

Library privileges

The privileges enjoyed by libraries have to be seen in the context of those also enjoyed by individuals and are by no means universal in nature (Hugenholtz, 1998). He outlines the different types of privilege enjoyed by users of copyright materials and likens them to a zoo in which some animals are harmless (paper copying) and others may present various kinds of threat (electronic networking). As the emphasis in copyright law shifts from 'making copies' to 'making use', the requirements of the individual user become more and more constrained by legislation. Therefore the emphasis on privileges both of individuals and libraries needs to be increased to counterbalance these moves by the owners. Whether or not such privileges will survive and whether they can be overruled by contracts which libraries may sign with copyright owners is a matter of much debate in legal circles (Hugenholtz, 1997) and will not easily be determined except by court cases. It also has to be re-emphasized that such privileges are not worldwide; they exist primarily in the so-called Anglo-Saxon legal tradition and are also found in Scandinavia. They are alien to many aspects of Roman, European and continental law, although they are found in the legal traditions of many former socialist countries. In Canada draft legislation proposes that some library privileges be retained (Canada, 1999), but this is still under debate – the proposals have been around since 1996, when the first part of Bill C-32 was first introduced into parliament. The implications for some of this legislation for libraries and librarians are discussed by Larivière (1998) in a paper which is unusually attentive to library problems for a legal journal. Crosby (1998a) feels that Canada may benefit from the debates in Europe and the USA, since legislators should learn something from the points put forward and avoid some of the pitfalls.

Fair practice

This heading is intended to encompass a basic concept that is found in the UK, the USA and a number of Commonwealth countries but that bears different names, all indicating some degree of 'fairness' to both owners and users. Cornette (1998) expresses some anxiety about libraries, especially in the USA, which may be held responsible for infringements carried out by those using library materials. Librarians might be held responsible because they knew, or ought to have known, that such actions were taking place. At the same time, J.Y. Davis (1998) expresses frustration that while the discussions of the Conference on Fair Use (CONFU) have produced one or two guidelines, so far they have produced nothing applicable in the digital context, especially for libraries. Further criticism of the CONFU process comes from Linke (1998), who looks at the problem as an opportunity for librarians and other information workers to re-educate themselves on the whole question of copyright. Nevertheless, a great deal of debate has taken place about the exceptions to copyright that are required for individuals for legal and judicial purposes, for parliamentary work and for the needs of those with various handicaps in using print. The work of projects such as IMPRIMATUR is significant in this area. Initially such projects started with the concept that all exceptions were unnecessary, but the Amsterdam conference (*IMPRIMATUR*, 1998) held in late 1997 was a turning point in the formation of attitudes. The divergent views expressed by the many major players in the copyright field at this important event are usefully summarized by Pearson (1998).

Electronic Rights Management Systems (ERMS)

The whole question of rights management and payment for copyright use is a matter of continuing debate. Owners claim that libraries are at liberty to access any material in an electronic form, providing that they pay. Libraries defend their traditional role of offering a service which is free at the point of use. In one possible scenario, everybody pays except those in particular socioeconomic groups, people with various kinds of handicap and those who have specific needs for legal or other reasons. In this situation the library is seen as developing a new role: it becomes an intermediary between the owner and the user with its role expanded to that of a rights management organization. As Cornish (1998h) points out, although some people have viewed the library as a sort of information supermarket, this model is hotly disputed by others. The supermarket offers a range of products dictated by economic considerations only. Opponents argue that the library does not, and should not, take such an approach to the information it provides.

Licences

The reaction by rights owners to any type of electronic cooperation between libraries was initially negative, but during 1998 major changes in licensing mechanisms and attitudes took place, as exemplified by Academic Press (Articles, 1998) in their IDEAL collection. Several initiatives have been set up to facilitate library cooperation on a campus-wide or company-wide basis (Häkli, 1997). In describing the work done by the Joint Information Systems Committee (JISC), Oppenheim (1998d) demonstrates just how much attitudes have changed and how common ground has been identified between owners and users. As the NESLI (National Electronic Site Licensing Initiative) in the UK shows, the attitude is changing from paying for every transaction to paying a negotiated licence fee so that both sides can be relaxed about exact volumes of use (White, 1997). Friedgood (1998) emphasizes the value of a managing agent (or trusted third party) in such schemes. Similar initiatives in other European countries, such as the Netherlands, are described by Niggemann and Reinhardt (1998). The development of a Copyright Permissions Pages Website is seen by Hu (1998) as an important step forward for both libraries and educational institutions. However, as Knowles (1998) points out, licensing has its downside. Providing data to a number of licensing agencies simultaneously can be a traumatic experience. The CLA is anxious to extend its licensing schemes and has already done so to higher education by licensing course packs (Barrow, 1998).

Rosenblatt (1998) argues that in the digital world library privileges are unnecessary. She believes that the real issue is authenticity and integrity rather than minor exceptions to copyright control. She argues that the three-step test under the Berne Convention cannot be met in a digital environment, a sentiment largely echoed by the European Commission itself. However, MacDonald (1997) believes that there is a danger of the world falling into two distinct halves: commercial licensing and academic/scholarly use where mutual benefit outweighs financial reward. Morton (1997) reports on the need to define the user community as well as clarifying what is meant by a 'site' in licensing negotiations. T.L. Davis (1998) sets out the possible areas of difficulty very clearly, and the National Federation of Abstracting and Indexing Services (NFAIS) suggests that the scholarly community needs guidelines such as those it has set out in a white paper (NFAIS, 1998). Publishers still take a different view of some issues. The area of library short loan collections is explored by Muir (1998) as part of the ACORN project. The librarians' view is put by Woodward (1998) as part of the same project, and Gadd (1998b) also builds on ACORN to discuss the issue of clearing permissions with publishers. The project also provides some experience of discussions on electronic copyright management systems (ECMS) through CLEAR (Copyright Licensed Electronic Access to Readings) (Gadd, 1998a). In ELINOR, another related project, attention is paid to the problems of obtaining permission for using high-use academic texts (Zhao, 1998) and the difficulties of arriving at a single, straightforward licence rather than a multiplicity of different ones is explored by Ramsden (1998).

Special materials and services

Databases

In 1998 European Union legislation on databases was introduced in the UK, with all its problems of interpretation, which Oppenheim (1998a, 1998b) describes in stark clarity. Wall (1998c) in turn demonstrates that various, often disturbing, interpretations can be put on the new legislation and librarians need to be on their guard to ensure that the law carries the meaning they want. Although Norway is not a member of the European Union, it is a member of the European Economic Area (EEA) and it too has anxieties about implementing the legislation to which it is bound. It is doubtful that it can adhere to the rules by the required dates (Nilssen, 1998b). The UK government is certainly aware of the difficulties about the new database legislation and is to set up a Database Marketing Strategy Group to monitor the arrangements for protecting databases and making them accessible to the public. In the USA this legislation was seen as so alien that a meeting was planned with the Standing Conference of National and University Libraries (SCONUL) in the UK to discuss the implementation of the law in Europe and its consequences for the USA (Bainton, 1998).

Initially the legislation was seen as a way of locking up data so that it was monopolized by one owner, but careful inspection shows that this is not the case. The law was needed because databases are not seen as copyright works in many parts of the EU, on the grounds that they do not represent sufficient intellectual activity. Therefore a database would be protected in the UK or Ireland but not in France (Institut national) or Germany (Deutsches Patent). The new law introduces very specific rights in databases for a period of fifteen years and the database is defined as a separate type of work. This has many implications for libraries beyond their original expectations. First, it provides protection for works such as library catalogues, lists and bibliographies. It also severely limits what can be done with such databases for the benefit of the user, whether as an individual or a library customer (Nilssen, 1998a). The way that a database is defined in both European and UK law makes it clear that it is not merely an electronic document that can be included. Material on paper or in any other format is covered, provided that it is arranged in a systematic and methodical way and each item can be separately accessed by the user. This very broad definition means that items outside the normal concept of a database are included.

Perhaps the most complex problem is created by maps. As Wall (1998d) points out, although a map in paper form would almost certainly not qualify as a database, this is far from certain in the case of a digital map, where each item is capable of being accessed separately. The legislation also has wide implications for the archive and museums community (Cornish, 1998g). There is the problem of images of items in collections that are subsequently organized into a systematic presentation on a website or in a 'coffee table' type of application.

Similar legislation is being proposed in the USA (Oppenheim, 1998c), where it is meeting considerable resistance, mainly because it is seen as a way of locking up data for a monopoly exploitation. Jaszi (1998) discusses US resistance to database legislation, dubbing it 'pseudocopyright' as it is a sort of *sui generis* right enjoyed only by database owners. In the same paper he also presents the concept of 'paracopyright' to indicate those extra levels of protection that owners of electronic materials want in addition to traditional copyright protection. These extra layers are usually embedded in some kind of ERMS rather than being provided for by legislation as such. Bachilo (1997) discusses an interesting issue in the context of databases: in Russian law it is not clear who owns a database compiled by a library or other institution. The author urges caution to ensure that the rights in works created by researchers of all kinds are properly protected. A similar approach to intellectual property created by staff in higher education is adopted by Wagner (1998), who emphasizes that higher education is one of the primary producers of intellectual property, especially copyright.

Official publications

In the UK (1998) proposals have been made for the reform of Crown copyright. Most European governments do not protect material produced in the public sector in the way practised in Britain; this is also completely contrary to normal practice in the USA. The draft proposals suggested a number of possibilities for reforming government control, ranging from total abolition through to retention of copyright with general waivers for uses in specific circumstances. An update on these developments can be found at the Stationery Office website (United Kingdom). Crown copyright generates a considerable amount of income, especially in the case of the Ordnance Survey (UK mapping agency). This organization grudgingly allows libraries to copy some of its materials under very restricted circumstances.

Whether or not some US government material is in the public domain at all is discussed by Ardito (1998a), especially in the context of databases. The content of these may belong wholly to government or partially to the private sector or even individuals. Highly complex copyright issues are also faced by the National Technical Information Service which 'publishes' some three million documents altogether (Guthrie, 1998). The USA is one of the best documented countries for copyright legislation, both actual and proposed; up-to-date information can be found at the Library of Congress website.

Pictures and other media

The increasing importance of images in the information chain is emphasized by Tottrup (1998) who points out the different legal situations in the Nordic countries, UK, USA, Russia, Japan and China, which make the management of image collections complicated when international cooperation takes place. An alarming case was heard in the USA, in which the judge declined to allow copyright protection of a photograph of a painting (Copyright, 1999). His argument was that merely taking a photograph of a painting did not create a new work, a view much disputed by those working in the museum and archive communities. Soderdahl (1998) underlines the complex problems of multimedia caused by the embedding of so many different rights in any one work. He emphasizes that the practical issues of obtaining permissions needs more attention than the philosophical basis of exceptions. The use of some images can cause problems because they have been registered as trade marks rather than merely being protected by copyright (Rich, 1998).

Andersen (1998) advises librarians in Denmark to examine the law carefully and look at each different type of medium they handle to see what differences there are in the regulations. Librarians need to know what 'use only on the premises' means, for example, and to look carefully at licences which accompany any such material.

Cultural materials

The copyright issue is important in the archive and museum field. This leads into the question of cultural materials generally. Whereas in the European Union, and to some degree the USA, a protective attitude is being taken, in Australia (Australian Copyright Council) the approach of government has been quite the reverse. Fairly liberal rules and regulations have been introduced there, extending the concept of fair practice to the electronic and digital world for cultural and heritage purposes generally (Alston, 1998a, 1998b). The work of the Australian Copyright Law Review Committee as it relates to libraries is discussed by Woodberry (1997), who sees signs for hope, rather than despair.

The Internet

The implications of the famous *Shetland Times* versus *Shetland News* case continue. As Cornish (1998e) points out, although initially it had to do with one paper using the resources of another to aid its reporting of the news, it has spilled over into all sorts of areas which impact on library information services. Attention now has to be given to making clear which source of information a user is accessing when passing from one website to another through a hypertext link. The positioning of these links so as to lead to home pages rather than into the body of another website is thus of increasing importance. Latham (1998) and Lingle (1998) emphasize the importance of considering copyright as well as many other legal issues before building a website or even designing a webpage.

The Internet, because of its relative ease of access and use, gives an illusion that anything put on a website is there for free use and makes it easy to forget copyright restrictions. Mann (1998) says that copyright restrictions as to who can use material and what they can use are quite impossible to enforce within non-localized cyberspace. By using the word 'non-localized' he gives the clue to his solution: this is to limit copyright by where an item can be used, whether this is a literal geographical area or a location such as the library. Nevertheless, it is not always easy to determine what is licensed either by agreement or implicitly, and Kaye (1999) emphasizes the fuzzy nature of the boundaries when dealing with the Web.

News reporting

Libraries which offer news services also need to pay attention to whether or not they can use websites for reporting current events in the traditionally understood sense. As Benjamin (1999) reports, in the UK the whole idea of what constitutes news and a current event has recently been considerably clarified by the action taken by the Newspaper Licensing Agency against the retail store Marks and Spencer. There is also the action, described by Pike (1999), which was taken unsuccessfully by Mohamed Al-Fayed, the proprietor of Harrods, on the use of a video which belonged to him for reporting an event which might or might not be considered current. Libraries offering current awareness services need to be aware themselves of what these terms actually mean in different legislative situations. There is still an unresolved issue as to whether a website is a broadcast or not. This will depend on highly technical issues requiring interpretation by the courts (Cornish, 1998c). In the Netherlands publishers won a court action (Heuff, 1998a) to obtain compensation for use of material from daily and weekly newspapers in a news-based CD-ROM. The Netherlands Centre for Libraries and Reading (NBLC) takes the view that this will lead to CD-ROM material having to be paid for by users on a per-use basis.

Lending and interlending

The lending of non-print materials through libraries is still a matter of controversy and is restricted under European legislation. As Norman (1999) points out, public libraries in the UK may lend sound recordings and videos only with the consent of the owners as a body. A new problem has arisen in that the performers, who have separate rights in these works, are now seeking separate payments in addition to those made to the owners of the rights. At the moment sound recordings are licensed for free, but the performers are unwilling to accept this and want an arrangement similar to Public Lending Right, in which the government funds payments to authors for the lending of their books through public libraries.

As lending and rental also become embedded in copyright protection, the role of the library both in lending and interlibrary loan is likely to need revision. Much interlibrary activity depends on copying as well as lending, and both activities may soon need to be monitored for the management of library services. Norman (1998a) outlines in some detail the problems faced by 'interlending', which is often document delivery by another name. She also points out the problems of international document delivery when laws from different countries contradict one another. In Germany there have been one or two cases on the legality of document delivery (Mengels, 1998). Cornish (1998a) identifies copyright as a major barrier to the development of interlibrary cooperation both in the electronic context and between libraries in developed and developing countries. In some situations document delivery services are working with copyright owners to develop royalty payment systems (Eiblum, 1998). As Cornish (1998b) demonstrates, the problems facing electronic document delivery are many faceted and include not only protection to prevent networking and unauthorized use, but also protection of the integrity and paternity of the document. He questions whether technical solutions really are the answer.

For those taking refuge in the law to defend their document delivery activities, there is little comfort in the recent case against CARL, which operates the UnCover document delivery service in the USA. As Kozlowski (1998) explains, the case is about the reproduction by a document delivery service of articles in a format other than that for which they were initially contracted, without the authors' permission. The argument turned on the right of publishers to allow this. A further issue was that UnCover's claim not to store digital copies of the works was shown to be untrue. Hackemann (1997) describes an experimental document delivery service (AutoDoc) in Germany which checks the accuracy of orders before passing them on to a large library for supply, in the context of German copyright law.

Other issues

Preservation and conservation

The problems facing preservation in the copyright area are twofold: the conversion of existing materials to digital form to preserve the content, and the preservation of materials that are originally in digital format. Cornish (1998h) suggests that work needs to be done to ensure that unnecessary legal barriers to preservation for non-commercial purposes should be removed. He suggests that cooperation with producers should be the way forward for original digital materials. Groeneveld (1998) laments the fact that in the Netherlands legislation is not as generous as in the UK and USA and the making of copies of outdated software by libraries for preservation purposes is not permitted. Encouragingly, the new US (1998) Digital Millennium Copyright Act gives libraries of a non-profit nature the right to make digital copies for preservation purposes (US, 1999). Jennings (1998) provides a useful and easily digestible summary of all these proposals.

Legal deposit

In most countries that have signed up to the Berne Convention legal deposit is not a prerequisite for obtaining copyright protection. The important distinction between having no formalities because of the Berne Convention and the ability to retain them for other formats is emphasized in a paper by Dacosta (1998) in which the link between legal deposit and sound recordings in Uruguay is described. This link may still legitimately exist in other countries if they wish, despite the normal practices under the Berne Convention.

Copyright management systems

There have been extensive debates on electronic management systems. The proposed legislation from the European Commission states that Electronic Rights Management Systems (ERMS) should be protected under law and that it would be an infringement to attempt to circumvent such systems. The argument from the library and information community is that this gives owners power over whether or not to allow the privileges provided for particular groups of people under the law. Norman (1998b) sees this as a real threat to the concept of fair dealing/use/practice and wants libraries to have simple clearance mechanisms instead. Such systems will in future be linked to various types of metadata and identification systems such as the Digital Object Identifier (DOI) described by Lupovici (1998), which can be used to track usage and even link to systems of remuneration for users. Bakken (1998) gives a clear outline of how DOI might work in the context of copyright management but does not draw any alarmist conclusions from its use. However, Ardito (1998b) is uneasy because DOIs can be used by publishers to track the use of documents in the document delivery process. The argument is that such systems should be capable of circumvention if they do not respect the privileges given under the law. Legalization has now been introduced in the USA by the Registrar of Copyrights, who is also charged with producing a report on how this particularly complex situation can be resolved or managed.

The needs of specific groups

There are many different groups in society that have particular needs, the satisfying of which may well be impeded by copyright considerations. There is, for instance, the desperate need of countries with limited financial resources and even more limited hard currency to provide the necessary academic materials for their researchers. As Ogunrombi and Bello (1999) point out, attempts to enforce copyright respect often meet with at best indifference and at worst derision. Their findings demonstrate that the principal reason for making copies is the sheer lack of books and the funds to buy them in libraries. This attitude problem is not limited to developing countries. In developed industrial communities the relevance of copyright is seen as marginal and an attitude 'It is not doing any harm if I copy this' is prevalent. The needs of certain social groups such as the unemployed, low income families, the elderly or those with handicaps all need careful consideration. As Cornish (1998i) says, libraries traditionally do not favour any one group of users but attempt to serve everyone within their remit. If this attitude is maintained, a change in approaches to funding may be needed as copyright owners increase their demands for payment and libraries face continuing budget cuts. Just who will pay is a continuing issue. Cornish (1998k) sees a 'smart' future in much of this. A smartcard could be used for purposes ranging from access to swimming baths, use of public transport and payment of housing benefit right through to allowing access to electronic information sources. The implications of this are that the state will somehow pay for such access. The alternative is having to make some hard decisions on who can and cannot access information.

Those with various kinds of handicap in using print, especially but not exclusively the visually impaired, have particular concerns about copyright. Although in many countries there is specific legislation to enable copies in formats such as audio and braille to be made for them, modern digital technology permits output in almost any suitable form. In the UK, for example, there is currently no legislation to allow such copies to be made, unless the copyright owner gives permission. This seriously hampers the work of traditional libraries serving visually impaired people. It also prevents public and academic libraries from offering a full range of services to readers in this group. Furber (1998) underlines the injustice of this and welcomes the initiative by the CLA (Copyright Licensing Agency) to introduce a licence to overcome this legal problem.

Conclusion

Finally, it is worth remembering that librarians may occasionally find themselves involved in court cases on copyright matters. Sakagawa (1998) describes how the Japan Library Association was accused of distributing videos without the owners' permission by the Japanese journal *Shinbunka*. The accusations were firmly refuted, as they were based on a misunderstanding of both the law and the circumstances surrounding the distribution of videos.

References

Alston, R. (1998a) *Copyright reform and the information economy.*
   http://www.dca.gov.au/nsapi-text/?Mlval=dca_dispdoc&ID)=2223
Alston, R. (1998b) *Cultural sector boosted by progressive copyright reform.*
   http://www.dca.gov.au/nsapi-text/?Mlval=dca_dispdoc&ID=2229
Andersen, J. (1998) Ophavsretten i praksis. *DF Revy*, **21**(1), 15–16.
Ardito, S.C. (1998a) Feds in a Web world: public domain vs. copyright. *Searcher*, **6**(3), 35–40, 42–45.
Ardito, S.C. (1998b) Inevitability: death, taxes and copyright. *Online*, **22**(1), 81–82, 84–85.
Articles (1998) from IDEAL collection now available on ECO. *Advanced Technology Libraries*, **27**(5), 4.
Australian Copyright Council [website]. http://www.copyright.org.au
Bachilo, I.L. (1997) Pravovye voprosy formirovaniya gosudarstvennykh nauchnykh, nauchno-teknicheskikh i informatsionnykh resursov. [Legal aspects of developing state scientific, technical and information resources]. *Nauchno-Teknicheskaya Informatsiya.* **1**(10), 15–18.
Bainton, T. (1998) United States Government seeks SCONUL's advice. *SCONUL Newsletter*, (13), 30–31.
Bakken, F. (1998) ECMS – Electronic copyright management systems. In: *Nordisk Forum för bibliotekskafer.* Espoo: NORDINFO, pp. 74–77. [NORDINFO Publikation 40.]
Barrow, E. (1998) New directions for CLA. *Serials*, **11**(3), 242–245.
Benjamin, J. (1999) Fair dealing with copying newspaper articles for internal company distribution. *European Intellectual Property Review*, (4), N64–N67.
Canada (1999) *Bill C-32: an Act to amend the Copyright Act, January 1999.*
   http://www.pch.gc.ca/wn-qdn/c32/12472bE.html
CEC (1997) *Proposal for a European Parliament and Council Directive on the harmonization of certain aspects of copyright and related rights in the Information Society.* Brussels: The Commission. [COM(97)628 final – 97/0359(COD).]
CLA [website on copyright and visual impairment].
   http://www.cla.co.uk
Committee (1999) on Copyright and Other Legal Matters (CLM). *IFLA Journal*, **25**(1), 55.
Copyright Permissions Pages [website]. http://www.law.wfu.edu/library/copyright

Copyright (1999) United States. *International Media Law*, **17**(2), 15.

Cornette, L. (1998) A different type of challenge: the dilemma of copyright. Are you a 'contributory infringer'? *Ohio Media Spectrum*, **50**(1), 11–13.

Cornish, G.P. (1998a) The book stops here: barriers to international interlending and document supply. In: *Interlending and document supply: resource sharing possibilities and barriers. Proceedings of the 5th Interlending and document supply international conference, Århus, Denmark, 24–28 August 1997*. Eds S. Gould and D. Johnson. Boston Spa: IFLA UAP Programme, pp. 89–97.

Cornish, G.P. (1998b) Copyright and document supply in an electronic environment. *Interlending and Document Supply*, **26**(3), 123–129.

Cornish, G.P. (1998c) Copyright and intellectual property rights. In: *Beyond the beginning: the global digital library; an international conference organized by UKOLN, London, June 1997*. http://www.ukoln.ac.uk/services/papers/bl/blri078/content/repor33.htm

Cornish, G.P. (1998d) Copyright and related issues. In: R. Prytherch (ed.) *Handbook of library and information management*. Aldershot: Gower, pp. 168–189.

Cornish, G.P. (1998e) Copyright and the Internet. In: *Theatre and the Internet: proceedings of a conference held at the University of Glasgow, May 1997*. London: Theatre Information Group, pp. 24–28.

Cornish, G.P. (1998f) EBLIDA meeting on the Draft Directive on Reproduction and Related Rights, Copenhagen, February 1998. *Information Management Report*, (May), 18–19.

Cornish, G.P. (1998g) Electronic rights and multimedia – what's it all about? *Museum Shop and Publishing News*, (9), 12–13.

Cornish, G.P. (1998h) Legal problems of digitisation and some possible solutions. In: G. Dupoirier (ed.) *Les bibliothèques numériques. Document numérique 2(3/4)*. Paris: Hermes, pp. 161–167.

Cornish, G.P. (1998i) *Looking both ways: the challenge to the intermediary in an electronic age*. [Unpublished paper presented to the DELOS Workshop within the 2nd European conference on research and advanced technology for digital libraries, Heraklion, Crete.]

Cornish, G.P. (1998j) Opinion: libraries and the harmonisation of copyright. *European Intellectual Property Review*, **20**(7), 241–243.

Cornish, G.P. (1998k) Universal availability of publications and its importance to human development, regeneration and growth. In: *Libraries as leaders in community economic development: conference proceedings, Victoria (BC), June 1998*. London, Ontario: ASM Associates. [Disk A, file 6.]

Cornish, G.P. (1999) *Copyright: interpreting the law for libraries, archives and information services*, 3rd edn. London: Library Association.

Crosby, J. (1998a) Canadian libraries should benefit from European, US copyright debates. *Information Outlook*, **2**(5), 37.

Crosby, J. (1998b) European copyright directive lacks adequate protection for libraries. *Information Outlook*, **2**(4), 43–44.

Dacosta, G. (1998) Copyright and legal deposit in Uruguay. *IASA Journal*, (June), 51–55.

Danset, F. (1998) L'accès aux documents numerisés dans les bibliothèques. *Bulletin d'Informations de l'Association des Bibliothécaires Français*, **178**(1), 58–63.

Davis, J.Y. (1998) Fair use after CONFU. *College and Research Libraries*, **59**(3), 209–211.

Davis, T.L. (1998) Understanding license agreements for electronic products. *Serials Librarian*, **34**(1/2) 247–260.

Deutsches Patent-und Markenamt [German website on database protection].
   http://www.dpma.de/
EBLIDA [website on European copyright legislation]. http://www.eblida.org
ECUP [website on European Copyright User Platform].
   http://www.eblida.org/ecup
Eiblum, P. (1998) Royalty fees part II: copyright and clearinghouses. *Online*, **22**(3), 51–52, 54, 56.
European (1998) *Fair Practice in Copyright Campaign*. Brussels: EFPICC. [Press release 15 May.]
Friedgood, B. (1998) The UK National Electronic Site Licensing Initiative. *Serials*, **11**(1), 37–39.
Furber, D. (1998) Are disabled users getting a fair deal from copyright? *SCONUL Newsletter*, (13), 29.
Gadd, E. (1998a) CLEAR design: developing an electronic management system for Project ACORN. *Electronic Library*, **16**(4), 253–259.
Gadd, E. (1998b) Copyright in the digital library. *Bibliothek: Forschung und Praxis*, **22**(2), 229–234.
Giavarra, E. (1998) Copyright in Europe. In: *Nordisk Forum for bibliotekschafer*. Espoo: NORDINFO, pp. 41–53. [NORDINFO Publikation 40.]
Grantham, B. (1999) Legislative changes to the copyright law of the United States. *International Media Law*, **17**(1), 1–6.
Groeneveld, C. (1998) Auteursrecht versus behoud van elektronische publicaties. *Informatie Professional*, **2**(10), 42–43.
Guthrie, L. (1998) Copyright issues at NTIS. *Information Outlook*, **2**(1), 33.
Hackemann, M. (1997) Urheberrechtliche Probleme der Volltext-Versorgung am Beispiel des Auromatischen Volltextservice des FIZ Karlsruhe. *Bibliotheksdienst*, **31**(12), 2348–2354.
Häkli, E. (1997) Diskussionen om licenser till elektroniska tidskrifter kommer i gang i Europa. *Nordinfo Nytt*, (3-4), 3–9.
Heuff, I. (1998a) Bibliotheken en hun nachtmerrie: NBLC zet zich schrap tegen dreigende commercialisering van de informatievoorziening. *BibliotheekBlad*, **2**(22), 6–7.
Heuff, I. (1998b) Wel eerlijke prijs, geen uitbreiding van rechten: FOBID Juridische Commissie ageert tegen Europese richtlijn auteursrecht. *BibliotheekBlad*, **2**(22), 6–7.
Hielmcrome, H.V. (1998) Harmonising af ophavsretten i EU: informationsfriheden i informationssamfundet. *Nordinfo Nytt*, (1–2), 7–10.
Hu, H. (1998) Introducing the Copyright Permission Pages Website. *Information Outlook*, **2**(7), 42.
Hugenholtz, B. (1997) *Contracts and copyright exemption*. Amsterdam: Institute for Information Law.
Hugenholtz, B. (1998) Rights, limitations and exceptions: striking a proper balance. In: *IMPRIMATUR Consensus Forum, 30–31 October 1997: Forum report*. London: IMPRIMATUR Project, pp. 11–20.
IMPRIMATUR (1998) *Consensus Forum, 30–31 October 1997: Forum report*. London: IMPRIMATUR Project.
Institut National de la Propriété Intellectuelle [French website on database protection].
   http://www.inpi.fr
Jaszi, P. (1998) Is this the end of copyright as we know it? In: *Nordisk Forum for bibliotekschafer*. Espoo: NORDINFO, pp. 58–67. [NORDINFO Publikation 40.]

Jennings, A.F. (1998) The state of copyright. *Against the Grain*, **10**(1), 60–61, 63.

Kaye, L. (1999) Owning and licensing content: key legal issues in the electronic environment. *Journal of Information Science*, **25**(1), 7–14.

Kemper, K. (1998) A response for the World Intellectual Property Organization. In: *IMPRIMATUR Consensus Forum, 30–31 October 1997: Forum report*. London: IMPRIMATUR Project, pp. 53–55.

Knowles, C. (1998) Copyright surveys: one college's experience of the CLA and ERA methods. *Learning Resources Journal*, **14**(1), 22–24.

Kozlowski, M.J. (1998) Initial ruling favours freelance writers in copyright suit. *Law Journal Extra*, (20 October), 1–2.

Larivière, J. (1998) Les bibliothèques et la nouvelle loi canadienne sur le droit d'auteur: un commentaire. *Cahiers de Propriété Intellectuelle*, **10**(2), 351–358.

Latham, J. (1998) Copyright resources on the Web. *Information Outlook*, **2**(7), 39.

Library Association (1998) *The case for fair practice*. London: Library Association. [Press release, January 1998.]

Library of Congress [website on copyright legislation]. http://www.loc.gov/copyright/

Liedes, J. (1998) International evolution of the copyright system. In: *Nordisk Forum for bibliotekschafer*. Espoo: NORDINFO, pp. 16–40. [NORDINFO Publikation 40.]

Lingle, V.A. (1998) Policy aspects of Web page development. *Internet Reference Service Quarterly*, **3**(2), 33–48.

Linke, E. (1998) On beyond copyright. *Serials Librarian*, **33**(1/2), 71–81.

Lupovici, C. (1998) Le digital object identifier: le système du DOI. *Bulletin des Bibliothèques de France*, **43**(3), 49–54.

MacDonald, A.H. (1997) A tale of two futures. *Feliciter*, **43**(11/12), 30–31.

Mann, T. (1998) Reference service, human nature, copyright and offsite service - in a 'digital age'? *Reference and User Services Quarterly*, **38**(1), 55–67.

Marter, A. (1998) Propriété intellectuelle et bibliothèques françaises. *Bulletin des Bibliothèques de France*, **43**(3), 12–16.

Mengels, U. (1998) Urheberrecht und Bibliotheken: Uberblick über neue Entwicklungen. *ABI Technik*, **18**(1), 2–14.

Morton, E. (1997) License or perish? *Feliciter*, **43**(11/12), 33–34, 39.

Muir, A. (1998) Publishers' views of electronic short-loan collections and copyright clearance issues. *Journal of Information Science*, **24**(4), 215–229.

Murakami, Y. (1998) Digital libraries and copyright in Japan post-WIPO Copyright Treaty. *Toshokan-Kai* [Library World], **50**(2), 100–106. [In Japanese.]

NFAIS (1998) The rights and responsibilities of content creators, providers, and users: a white paper. *Online Libraries and Microcomputers*, **16**(1), 1–7. Also published in *Australian Library Journal*, **47**(2), 177–182.

Niggemann, E. and Reinhardt, W. (1998) 1000 Zeitschriften in Volltext elektronisch verfugbar. NRW-Bibliotheken uns Elsevier: ein Konsortialvertrag. *Bibliotheksdienst*, **31**(11), 2147–2150.

Nilssen, K.O. (1998a) E-post og postlister: noen opphavsrettslige aspekter. *Synopsis*, **29**(5), 283–286.

Nilssen, K.O. (1998b) Nasjonale implikasjoner av EU's databasedirektiv: EBLIDA Workshop 7 November 1997. *Synopsis*, **29**(1), 25–27.

Norman, S. (1998a) Copyright issues in document supply. In: S. Gould and D. Johnson (eds) *Interlending and document supply: resource sharing possibilities and barriers. Proceedings of the 5th Interlending and document supply international conference held in Århus, Denmark, 24–28 August 1997.* Boston Spa: IFLA UAP Programme, pp. 77–87.

Norman, S. (1998b) Information provision in the electronic age: copyright protection. *Refer*, **14**(1), 3–4, 6–9.

Norman, S. (1999) *Copyright in public libraries.* London: Library Association.

NTIS [website for US National Technical Information Service]. http://www.ntis.gov

Oakley, R.L. (1998) The copyright context. *Collection Management*, **22**(3/4), 177–184.

Ogunrombi, S.A. and Bello, M.A. (1999) Photocopying and the awareness of copyright in tertiary institutions in Bauchi State, Nigeria. *African Journal of Library, Archives and Information Science*, **9**(1), 49–58.

Oppenheim, C. (1998a) LISLEX. *Journal of Information Science*, **24**(1), 39–55.

Oppenheim, C. (1998b) LISLEX. *Journal of Information Science*, **24**(3), 186–191.

Oppenheim, C. (1998c) LISLEX. *Journal of Information Science*, **24**(4), 267–270.

Oppenheim, C. (1998d) LISLEX. *Journal of Information Science*, **24**(6), 437–441.

Pearson, S. (1998) Rights, limitations and exceptions: striking a proper balance: IFLA/ IMPRIMATUR Conference, 30-31 October 1997, Amsterdam. *Audiovisual Librarian*, **24**(1), 51–53.

Pedley, P. (1998) *Copyright for library and information service professionals.* London: Aslib.

Pike, J. (1999) *Copyright and the public interest.* London: Farrer. [Leaflet.]

Ramsden, A. (1998) Copyright, rights clearance, and licensing texts. In: *ELINOR: electronic library project.* London: Bowker-Saur, pp. 29–39. [BLRIC Report 22.]

Revelli, C. (1998) Discussioni sul copyright. *Biblioteche Oggi*, **15**(10), 46–54.

Rich, L.L. (1998) Protection of graphic characters. *Against the Grain*, **10**(2), 44–46.

Rosenblatt, H. (1998) Copyright protection in the digital environment: riding the waves in stormy seas. *Law Librarian*, **29**(4), 204–210.

Sakagawa, R. (1998) Strong protest against the libel of the Japan Library Association: regarding the report in *Shinbunka. Toshokan Zasshi* [Library Journal] **92**(9), 800–801. [In Japanese.]

Soderdahl, P.A. (1998) Multimedia and fair use: the practical side of a philosophical debate. *Library Issues: Briefings for Faculty and Administrators*, **18**(4), 1–4.

Tottrup, M. (1998) Internet and copyright of pictures: an international overview. *Inspel*, **32**(1), 1–7.

UK (1998) *Crown copyright in the information age: a consultation document on access to public sector information.* London: Stationery Office. [Cm 3819.] http://www.hmso.gov.uk/document/cfuture.html

UK. Stationery Office [website on Crown copyright reform]. http://www.hmso.gov.uk/

US (1998) *Digital millennium copyright act. Public law 105-304, 112 Stat 2861.*

US (1999) copyright law. *International Media Law*, **17**, 5–6.

Wagner, K.I. (1998) Intellectual property: copyright implications for higher education. *Journal of Academic Librarianship*, **24**(1), 11–19.

Wall, R. (1998a) Copyright crisis: Aslib responds to new EC proposal. *Managing Information*, **5**(4), 14–17.

Wall, R. (1998b) *Copyright made easier.* London: Aslib.

Wall, R. (1998c) Database right or wrong? *Managing Information*, **5**(9), 41–43.

Wall, R. (1998d) Mapping it out. *Managing Information*, **5**(8), 31–33.

White, M. (1997) From PSLI to NESLI: site licensing for electronic journals in UK academic institutions. *New Review of Academic Librarianship*, **3**, 139–150.

WIPO [website for World Intellectual Property Organization]. http://www.wipo.int

Woodberry, E. (1997) Copyright at the crossroads. *Australian Academic and Research Libraries*, **28**(4), 297–301.

Woodward, H. (1998) At what cost? Access to digitized journal articles. *Inspel*, **32**(2), 83–87.

Zhao, D. (1998) Copyright, monitoring and usage reports. In: *ELINOR: electronic library project*. East Grinstead: Bowker-Saur, pp. 41–56. [BLRIC Report 22.]

Contents of previous volumes, 1991–1999

1991

1992

1993

1. The context of library and information work worldwide: global realizations
2. Academic libraries and change
3. The public sector
4. National libraries
5. Collections
6. Services
7. Management
8. Performance indicators
9. Trends in library and information provision in business and commerce
10. Trends in patterns of publishing
11. Access to information, networking and cooperation
12. Epilogue

1994

1. The context of library and information work: the role of information and information technology in libraries and publishing
2. Public libraries
3. Academic libraries
4. Information management
5. The virtual library
6. The service-oriented library
7. Management of change
8. Libraries and information in the Third World
9. Collections
10. Preservation
11. Education and training
    Epilogue

1995

1. Library and information services in context
2. National libraries
3. Public libraries
4. Academic libraries
5. Parliamentary libraries
6. Bibliographic control and access

1996/97

1997/98

1999

Subject index

Note: Entries appear under separate countries and regions, with the exception of the United Kingdom and the United States of America, for both of which the references are too numerous for page numbers to be useful.

Author index